KHE SANH

ERIC HAMMEL

KHE SANH

Siege in the Clouds

· An Oral History ·

CROWN PUBLISHERS, INC., NEW YORK

Published by Crown Publishers, Inc.,
225 Park Avenue South, New York, New York 10003
CROWN is a trademark of Crown Publishers, Inc.

Manufactured in the United States of America

Library of Congress Cataloging-in-Publication Data

Hammel, Eric M.
    Khe Sanh : siege in the clouds : an oral history / Eric Hammel.
    Includes index.
    1. Khe Sanh, Battle of, 1968.   2. Vietnamese Conflict, 1961–1975—
Personal narratives, American.   1. Title.
DS557.8.K5H36   1989
959.704′34—dc19   88-39767
ISBN 0-517-57268-0
Book design by Shari deMiskey
10 9 8 7 6 5 4 3 2 1
First Edition

THIS BOOK IS DEDICATED TO
THE MEN WHO ENDURED THE SIEGE OF KHE SANH,
TO THEIR SURVIVORS AND LOVED ONES, TO THOSE WHO
SUCCORED THEM,
AND—MOST OF ALL—TO THOSE
WHO DIED AS A RESULT OF THE SIEGE.

Guide to Terms and Abbreviations

A-1	Douglas Skyraider propeller-driven attack bomber
A-4	Douglas Skyhawk jet attack bomber
A-6	Grumman Intruder jet attack bomber
AK-47	Soviet-pattern 7.62mm assault rifle
AN/TPQ-10	Ground-based aircraft radar guidance system
Arclight	B-52 high-altitude bombing program
ARVN	Army of Republic of Vietnam
ASP	Ammunition Supply Point
ASRT	Air Support Radar Team
B-52	Boeing Stratofortress jet heavy bomber
BGen	Brigadier General
C-123	Fairchild Provider medium cargo transport
C-130	Lockheed Hercules medium cargo transport
C4	Plastic explosive
Capt	Captain
CH-46	Boeing Sea Knight medium cargo helicopter
CH-53	Sikorsky Sea Stallion heavy cargo helicopter
Chicom	Chinese Communist (used for NVA hand grenade)
CIA	Central Intelligence Agency
CIDG	Civilian Irregular Defense Group
Claymore	U.S. directional antipersonnel mine
CN	Teargas
CO	Commanding Officer
COFRAM	Controlled Fragmentation Munitions (Firecracker)
Col	Colonel
Comm	Communications

CP	Command Post
CS	Teargas
DMZ	Demilitarized Zone
Duster	U.S. Army tracked 40mm gun carrier
EC-121	Lockheed Super Constellation electronics warfare aircraft
EOD	Explosive Ordnance Disposal
Exec	Executive Officer
F-4B	McDonnell Phantom jet fighter-bomber
1stLt	First Lieutenant
FOB	Forward Operating Base (Special Forces)
Gravel	Pressure-detonated explosive device
GySgt	Gunnery Sergeant
H-34	Sikorsky Sea Horse medium transport helicopter
H&I	Harassment-and-Interdiction
H&S	Headquarters-and-Service
HM3	Hospital Corpsman 3rd Class
HMC	Chief Hospital Corpsman
HN	Hospitalman
Hooch	Living quarters
HST	Helicopter Support Team
Huey	Bell UH-1E light attack/transport helicopter
KC-130	C-130 fuel tanker variant
KIA	Killed In Action
KSCB	Khe Sanh Combat Base
LAAW	U.S. light antitank assault weapon
LAPES	Low Altitude Proximity Extraction System
LBJ	President Lyndon B. Johnson
LCpl	Lance Corporal
Lt	Lieutenant
LtCol	Lieutenant Colonel
LtGen	Lieutenant General
LZ	Landing Zone
M-16	U.S. 5.52mm rifle
M-60	U.S. 7.62mm machine gun
M-79	U.S. 40mm grenade launcher

MACV	Military Assistance Command, Vietnam
Maj	Major
MCHD	Marine Corps Historical Division
Med	Medical (e.g., 3rd Medical Battalion)
MGen	Major General
MGySgt	Master Gunnery Sergeant
MIA	Missing In Action
NOD	Night Observation Device
NVA	North Vietnamese Army
Ontos	U.S. tracked 106mm recoilless rifle carrier
PAVN	People's Army of Vietnam (NVA)
Pfc	Private First Class
PT-76	Soviet tracked amphibious reconnaissance vehicle
Puff	Minigun-armed C-47 airplane
Pvt	Private
R&R	Rest and Rehabilitation (i.e., leave)
RPG	Soviet-pattern 40mm rocket-propelled grenade
S-3	Operations Officer
2ndLt	Second Lieutenant
SFC	Sergeant First Class
Sgt	Sergeant
SgtMaj	Sergeant Major
SKS	Soviet-pattern 7.62mm bolt-action carbine
SSgt	Staff Sergeant
TOT	Time On Target (artillery technique)
UH-1E	Bell Huey light attack/transport helicopter
USA	U.S. Army
USAF	U.S. Air Force
USAID	U.S. Agency for International Development
USMC	U.S. Marine Corps
USN	U.S. Navy
USS	United States Ship
VC	Viet Cong
VT	Variable Time (artillery airburst fuse)
WIA	Wounded In Action
Willy-Peter	WP (i.e., waterproof)

Phonetic Alphabet

Alpha	November
Bravo	Oscar
Charlie	Papa
Delta	Quebec
Echo	Romeo
Foxtrot	Sierra
Golf	Tango
Hotel	Uniform
India	Victor
Juliet	Whiskey
Kilo	X-Ray
Lima	Yankee
Mike	Zulu

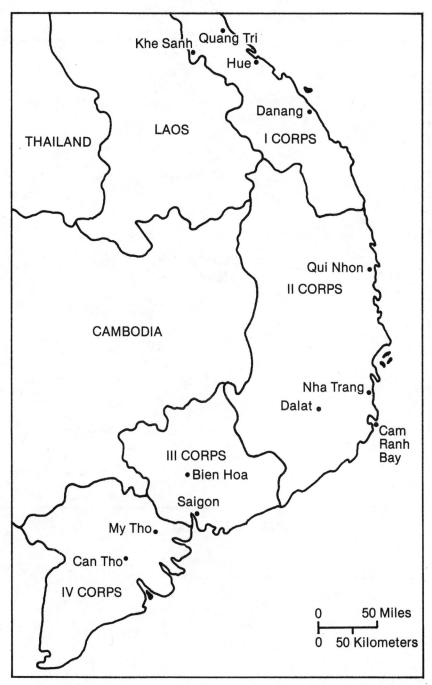

Khe Sanh •   Quang Tri •

Hue •

THAILAND

LAOS

Danang •

I CORPS

Qui Nhon •

II CORPS

CAMBODIA

Nha Trang •

Dalat •

Cam
Ranh
Bay •

III CORPS

• Bien Hoa

Saigon •

My Tho •

Can Tho •

IV CORPS

| 0 | 50 Miles |
| 0 | 50 Kilometers |

© F. F. Parry (used with permission)

I CORPS TACTICAL ZONE

K.W.White

NORTHERN QUANG TRI PROVINCE

E. L. WILSON

KHE SANH VALLEY

KW White

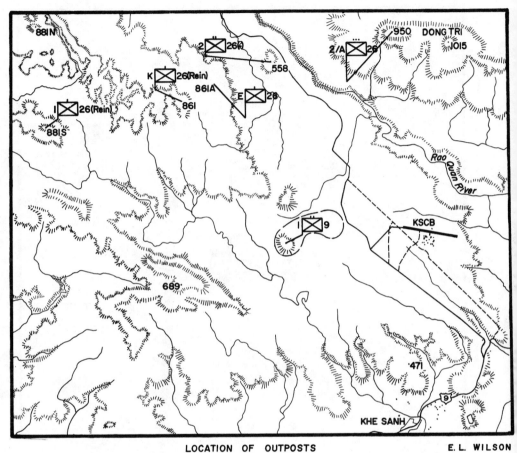

LOCATION OF OUTPOSTS

E.L. WILSON

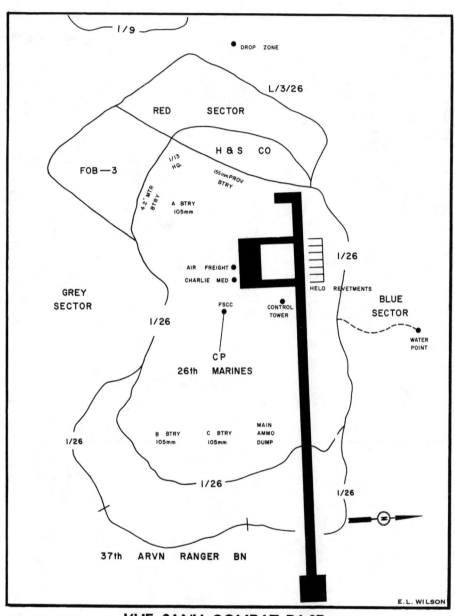

KHE SANH COMBAT BASE

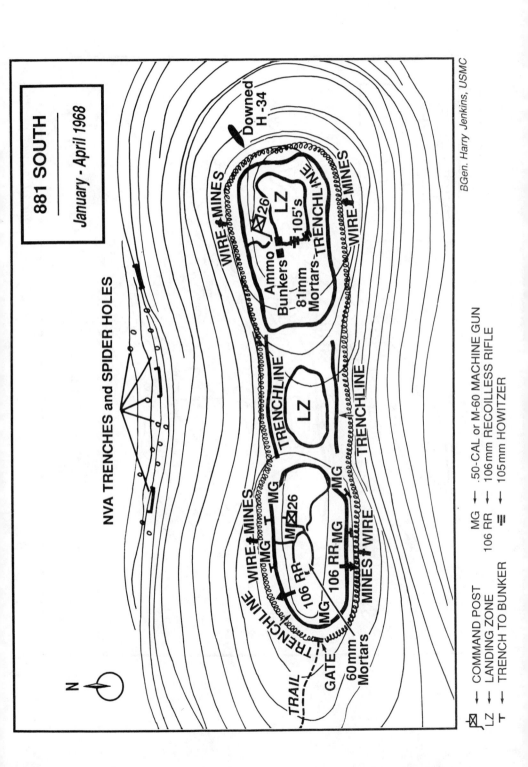

881 SOUTH

January - April 1968

NVA TRENCHES and SPIDER HOLES

BGen. Harry Jenkins, USMC

- 🗲 — COMMAND POST
- LZ — LANDING ZONE
- ⊤ — TRENCH TO BUNKER

- MG — .50-CAL or M-60 MACHINE GUN
- 106 RR — 106 mm RECOILLESS RIFLE
- ≣ — 105mm HOWITZER

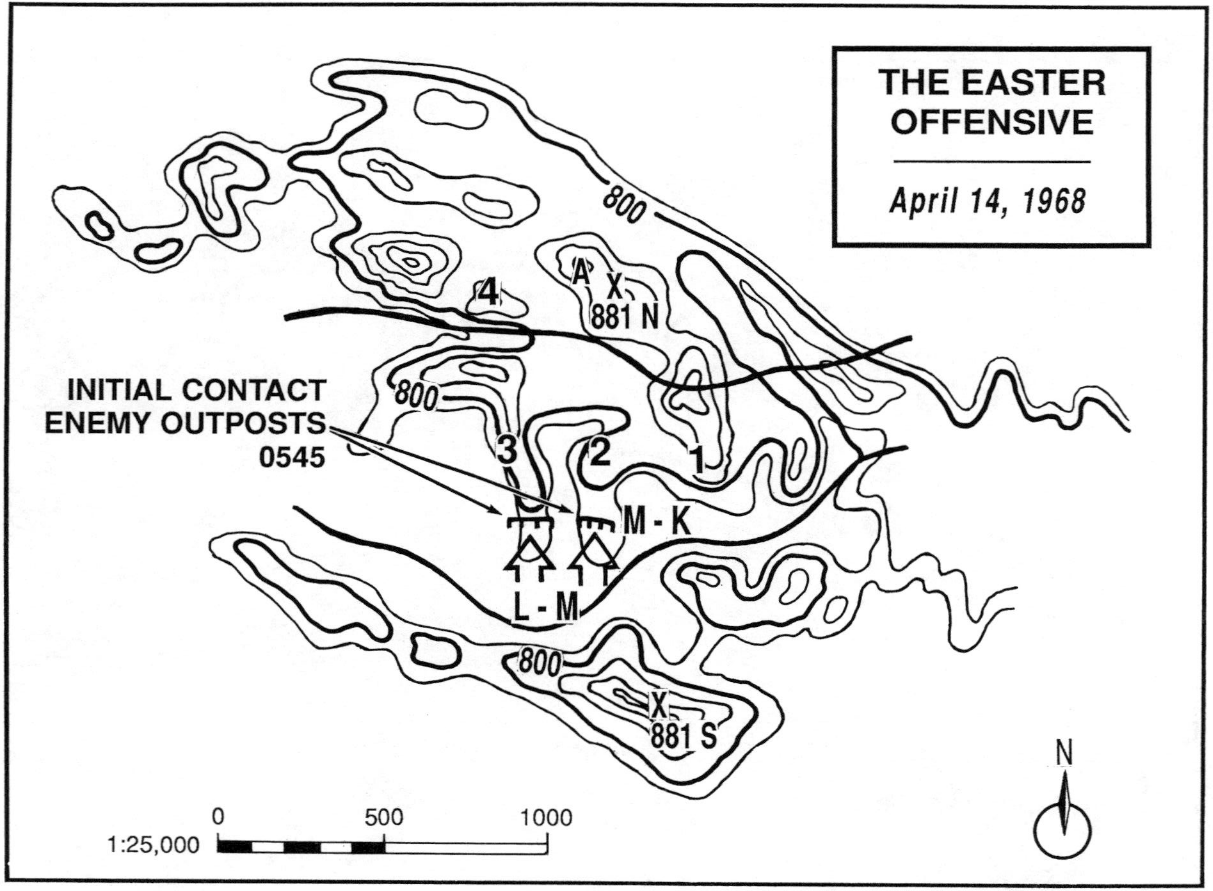

THE EASTER OFFENSIVE

April 14, 1968

INITIAL CONTACT
ENEMY OUTPOSTS
0545

881 N

881 S

M - K

L - M

800

800

800

1:25,000

0   500   1000

N

Marine Corps Gazette (used with permission)

"They have us just where we want them."

LtCol Lewis "Chesty" Puller, USMC, to his men when surrounded by a superior Japanese force on Guadalcanal in 1942

PART ONE

BEFORE
*January 1–19,
1968*

Prologue

It is generally held that the importance of the Khe Sanh Combat Base lay in its position astride a major North Vietnamese infiltration route, via Laos, around the Demilitarized Zone (DMZ). Located in western Quang Tri Province, nearly at the corner of South Vietnam, bordered to the west by Laos and to the north by the DMZ and North Vietnam, the Khe Sanh Plateau is a smuggler's dream of hilly trails obscured from aerial observation by high, dense, triple-canopy foliage and from ground patrols by rugged, piedmont-type hills covered by dense bamboo thickets and sight-obscuring high stands of elephant grass. Americans who served on the Khe Sanh Plateau found it ruggedly beautiful—a Shangri-la for the eye—and pleasantly cool during seasons when the Vietnamese lowlands were virtually too hot to live in. Sparsely settled, the region is vast, high, and impenetrable, and it can suck up many thousands of precious troops if it is to be effectively interdicted.

The United States military became involved in at least patrolling the Khe Sanh Plateau in 1962, when a U.S. Army Special Forces contingent set up a base camp and recruited local Bru montagnard villagers into a Vietnamese Civilian Irregular Defense Group (CIDG) they established there. In April 1966, fully thirteen months after the first U.S. Marine infantry battalions arrived in coastal northern South Vietnam, a battalion of the 1st Marine Regiment (1st Marines) passed through the Khe Sanh Plateau during a large-scale sweep. Shortly thereafter, U.S. Navy

Seabees hard-surfaced the small dirt runway that had been serving the Special Forces encampment since 1962. In October 1966, another Marine infantry battalion, plus an artillery battery, moved into the Special Forces camp, and the Special Forces detachment and its force of Vietnamese irregulars established a new camp at nearby Lang Vei village.

The Marine battalion remained at Khe Sanh until February 1967, when, having made no significant contacts with enemy forces, it was replaced by a single Marine rifle company. That company became involved in a significant fight in March 1967, and a second Marine company was sent to support it. At the conclusion of the fight, one company withdrew and the other remained. Around the same time, a Marine combined action company and a South Vietnamese Regional Forces company took up residence at Khe Sanh village, home of the Huong Hoa District Headquarters, the local "county seat."

At some undetermined point, at least one of the high hills overlooking the Khe Sanh base was turned into an electronic intelligence listening post devoted to eavesdropping on radio traffic in North Vietnam. The records in this regard, where any are available, are understandably evasive, but the rumors are so persistent that the existence of such an installation—or installations—can be taken as virtual certainty.

Aside from the electronic eavesdroppers, the combined South Vietnamese and American military establishment on the Khe Sanh Plateau was devoted totally to denying the North Vietnamese a strategic invasion route through Laos into the heart of Quang Tri Province. Emphasis was on patrolling. If anything turned up, air and artillery support could be provided from all over the region, and reinforcements could be airlifted into the area aboard helicopters or by means of the hard-surfaced runway at the Marine base atop the plateau.

The North Vietnamese apparently decided to overrun Khe Sanh in early May 1967, but their plans came a cropper when a Marine patrol operating out of the base became heavily engaged with a large North Vietnamese Army (NVA) force on April 24.

In a continuing action since dubbed the Hill Fights, the Marine plan to come to the aid of the Khe Sanh base was put into action. A full infantry battalion of the 3rd Marines was sent up on April 25, and another followed on April 26. On April 27, a second artillery battery was dispatched.

Beginning on April 28, 1967, the two-battalion Marine force drove out of the base and moved to wrest from enemy hands three hill masses—Hill 861 (names of hills are their heights in meters), Hill 881 North (881N), and Hill 881 South (881S)—that dominated the combat base. Support was provided by the howitzers and heavy mortars inside the base, by a U.S. Army 175mm artillery battery located at Camp Carroll, and by Marine tactical aviation units based mainly at Danang.

The two Marine battalions engaged in the Hill Fights ground forward against all three objectives until, on May 3, the North Vietnamese defenders spent themselves in an abortive counterattack and apparently withdrew.

Beginning on May 11, 1967, the 1st Battalion, 26th Marines (1/26) relieved the two battalions of the 3rd Marines, which left the area. Hills 881S and 861 were outposted, each by one company of 1/26. On May 13, the skeleton headquarters of the recently activated 26th Marine Regiment arrived at Khe Sanh to establish a permanent presence.

Within months of the Hill Fights, the major focus of action in the I Corps region of South Vietnam shifted to Con Thien, far to the east of Khe Sanh and directly overlooking the DMZ. The North Vietnamese Army laid siege to the tiny, Marine-held Con Thien Combat Base, and supporting and maintaining the action took virtually all the assets either side was willing to contribute to a formal, protracted, set-piece battle.

Meanwhile, around Khe Sanh, a rather endless spate of small-unit sparring ebbed and flowed well into the summer. In due course, on June 13, the 3rd Battalion, 26th Marines (3/26), was committed to the Khe Sanh Plateau. However, in August, 3/26 was drawn off to help in a distant operation south of Con Thien.

Through the last quarter of 1967, 1/26 took steps to build up the Khe Sanh Combat Base, maintain its hill outposts, and conduct aggressive patrolling throughout the plateau. Also, the U.S. Army Special Forces established its Forward Operating Base 3 (FOB-3) at the Marine combat base and began running deep patrols from there—undoubtedly including forays into Laos—using Bru montagnard tribesmen recruited from local villages and formed into a new CIDG company. During the same period, the hard-surfaced runway was lengthened, to 3,900 feet, and upgraded to all-weather status. To accomplish the mission, the

Seabees quarried their own rock from a hill to the west of the base perimeter, laid it over the runway and its extension, and covered it over with aluminum matting to make it absolutely weathertight. Soon, for the first time in the base's history, new building materials, armaments, troops, tracked weapons, and supplies were being lifted in aboard rather large Marine and Air Force C-130 Hercules transports.

Beginning in early December 1967, reconnaissance patrols conducted by a resident Marine recon company—Bravo Company, 3rd Reconnaissance Battalion—picked up increasing signs of escalating North Vietnamese activity in the area. It soon became a matter of faith among intelligence analysts that the NVA was planning a major sweep through the Khe Sanh Plateau and, very likely, on to Dong Ha and Quang Tri city. The number and size of North Vietnamese units spotted by Marine patrols centered on Khe Sanh rose to the point where, on December 13, the entire 3rd Battalion, 26th Marines, was returned to the combat base.

On December 21, Col David Lownds, the 26th Marines commander, sent 3/26 on a sweep starting at Hill 881S, running five kilometers west toward Hill 981, and returning to the combat base from the southwest via Hill 689. The five-day sweep turned up no hard contacts with the large North Vietnamese forces identified by recon patrols, but it did turn up numerous signs of the reported enemy presence—bunkers, fresh fighting holes, well-used trails, and arms and supply caches. There was no doubt by Christmas 1967 that a large—if elusive—NVA force was settling in around the Khe Sanh Plateau.

Chapter I

The area of operations, consisting of some 403 square miles, is located in northwestern Quang Tri Province. Bordered on the north by the DMZ and west by the Laotian border, the area of operations generally encompasses all of Huong Hoa District.

The area is thinly populated, rugged, and mountainous. Heights over 500 meters are common throughout the area. Terrain is severely dissected and thickly vegetated with dense undergrowth, broad-leaf evergreen forests, and bamboo thickets. Trail networks are plentiful, but trafficability to vehicles is almost uniformly restricted to National Route 9. Excellent cover and concealment exist throughout most of the area of operations and provide both friendly and enemy forces numerous covered approaches to attack positions and protection from enemy fire.

The heavy vegetation throughout the area of operations consists of a 60-foot-high jungle canopy, elephant grass, and dense areas of bamboo and vine thickets, which, combined with the steep slopes, create an effective natural obstacle to cross-country movement and greatly reduce long-range observation. In general, cross-country movement is restricted to existing trails and streams. Periods of steady heavy rainfall also make many of the streams in the area of operations difficult to impossible to cross.

There are five avenues of approach into the area of operations. Two avenues of approach enter from the north-west. One crosses the Laos/Vietnam border and moves southeast along streams and valley that join the Rivere De Rao Quan and continues southeast until it joins Route 9. The second approach from the northwest crosses the Laos/Vietnam border and continues southeast along the ridgeline to Hills 881S. Route 9 provides a major east-west avenue of approach across the area of operations. The approach from the southeast is the Da Krong Valley, which enters the area of operations and moves northwest until it reaches Route 9. An approach from the northwest enters the area of operations just south of Hill 1123 and runs southwest along the Khe Xa Bai River to a point just north of Hill 558.

Dong Tri Mountain, the highest peak (1,015 meters) in the area of operations dominates the Khe Sanh Valley. Hill 861 controls the approaches from the north and northwest. Hills 881S and 881N and Hill 918 dominate the approaches from the west. The [hill masses] south of Route 9 are important as they dominate the eastern approaches of Route 9 into the area of operations.

The area is lightly populated. The population center of the area is Khe Sanh Village, located on Route 9 approximately 5,000 meters from the combat base, where approximately 1,250 Vietnamese reside. This is also the Huong Hoa District Headquarters. The natives of the area are predominantly from the Bru montagnard tribe of the Mon Khymer ethno-linguistic group. The Bru tribal area extends throughout northeast Laos, southern North Vietnam, and the local area. The Bru, numbering approximately 10,000, primarily reside in a dozen small villages and resettlement areas located within 5 kilometers of Khe Sanh Village. There are also three French families who own coffee plantations, two French Catholic priests, two nuns (one French, one Vietnamese), and one American missionary family in the immediate area.

26th Marines After Action Report _____

The mission of the 26th Marine Regiment was to conduct reconnaissance and combat patrols in the assigned [area] to detect and destroy enemy personnel infiltrating into and through the Khe Sanh Tactical Area of Responsibility; provide security for the airfield and ancillary facilities at Khe Sanh and other vital installations in the area; open and secure lines; maintain active ground surveillance within the tactical area of responsibility; provide artillery support for [the] combined action company [at Khe Sanh village]; and be prepared to conduct operation in relief of or reinforcement of the CIDG Camp at Lang Vei.

The concept of operations [is to]:

a. Establish and maintain defensive positions on prominent terrain features within the area of operations for surveillance and control purposes. Utilize reconnaissance elements in the area of responsibility within artillery range to maintain surveillance over the area, and exploit sightings primarily with artillery and aircraft.

b. Conduct search-and-destroy operations with all available forces throughout the area of operations, taking advantage of intelligence provided and generated.

c. Maintain the defense of the KSCB [Khe Sanh Combat Base] and ancillary facilities.

BOB BREWER
Quang Tri Province Senior Adviser

My main emphasis was on the *chieu hoi*—defector—program. I directed that, each morning before the regular 0700 staff meeting, the picture and biographical data of each defector coming in within the last twenty-four hours would be on my desk for review. In early September 1967, there appeared a five-inch-by-eight-inch card on an individual who I felt needed more questioning. His hair was too long for his alleged rank and his listed education, versus age, didn't sound right. I asked our Special Branch (Vietnamese FBI) adviser to zero in on this guy. Within a few days, this defector was unmasked as a Moscow-trained long-range penetration agent. We "doubled" him immediately, and the take was astounding.

For example, he brought us "Resolution 13." The intelligence community had been looking forward to it for years. (Ho Chi Minh had issued Resolution 1 in 1918, and only eleven others had been promulgated in the intervening fifty years.) Resolution 13 was the master plan for the Tet Offensive, including the elimination of Khe Sanh.

Our double agent, whom we tabbed "X-1," was not to be totally trusted, but I drew up a long list of indicators which, if they surfaced between September 1967 and January 1968, would validate our double agent's Resolution 13. In November 1967, he brought out an updated version of Resolution 13. It was much more specific as to targets and timetables, and it was not written in the usual Communist argot.

Throughout December 1967 and January 1968, the enemy tripped one indicator after another. . . . I called a meeting of the principal American and Government of Vietnam advisers in Quang Tri. I told them that the attack was coming, aimed primarily at the seats of government, and that it would be launched at 0100 hours, January 31. I stressed that our U.S. bases—such as Khe Sanh, Con Thien, and Gio Linh—would be engaged by the enemy so as to diminish U.S. military support to the Government of Vietnam power seats and the civilian population in our prime pacification areas.

Chapter 2

JANUARY 2

Capt DICK CAMP
Lima Company, 3/26

As we did every night, Lima Company got ready for its night defense. In the fifteen or twenty minutes before dusk, we had our usual stand-to. Everyone got all his gear laid out in case we got hit during the night. I had dug my own foxhole, which was where I slept alone. It was four feet wide and about six feet long, a little cramped for me. As was my custom, I spoke briefly with the radio operators and everyone else in the command group before I hit the sack.

Somewhere around 2030, I woke up on sheer intuition just as one of the radio operators crawled over to me and whispered, "Skipper! Skipper! Get up. The 1st Platoon listening post hears something." It was standard operating procedure in Lima Company that when a listening post made contact or heard something, the situation immediately belonged to the company commander.

A listening post was a fire team—four riflemen—which was sent out by each platoon to monitor a likely avenue of approach on our lines. We usually had three or four listening posts out on any given night, depending on how many avenues of approach we had to cover.

The alert had come in from the 1st Platoon listening post,

which was screening the company right flank. One of the members of the fire team had heard something and had immediately alerted the company radio operators, who immediately alerted me.

The radio operators were all in a big hole near my hole. Their hole had a tarpaulin stretched over the top of it in such a way as to make it absolutely lightproof. As I crawled to the radio bunker, I whispered a call for Corporal Brady, my mortar section leader. As soon as Brady crawled up beside me, I whispered, "Brady, get your ammo humpers up and have them stand by." The 60mm ammo party was my reaction force, the group of Marines to which the company commander had immediate access in case something happened. I could use them to stop a break-through or reinforce a listening post—whatever—without having to steal men from the rifle platoons.

Next, I rolled beneath the radio bunker tarp and dropped into the hole. As soon as I got there, one of the radiomen gave me a handset and I called up the 1st Platoon listening post, which was "Lima 1-1"—1st Squad of 1st Platoon of Lima Company. My call sign was Lima 6.

"Lima 1-1. Lima 6." I waited, but there was no response. "Lima 1-1. Lima 6." No response again. I tried it two or three more times, but the listening post was not answering—or could not.

I was sorting out options when we heard two clicks from the radio. Someone in the listening post had keyed his own handset twice to tell us he was alive but did not want to talk. I came right back up on the radio and said, "Lima 1-1. Lima 6. If you hear this transmission, key your handset twice."

"*Click. Click.*"

I knew the fire team could not talk but that they were listening to me.

"Lima 1-1. Lima 6. When you can talk, let me know what's going on."

And then we waited. The adrenaline went straight through me. I had four Marines out there who thought they saw or heard something. It was darker than pitch. I had no idea what was coming in on them, and maybe they didn't either. I worked up a lot of empathy for those four Marines, but there was not a thing I could do until I heard from them or until something happened.

I was listening so hard I almost missed the faint whisper coming in over my handset: "We see something. Out."

That was enough for me. I was galvanized to action. "Brady," I yelled, "Brady, get your people up and get them ready to go." At the same time, I called the 1st Platoon commander, 1stLt Nile Buffington: "Lima 1. Lima 6. Are you monitoring this transmission?"

"Lima 6. Lima 1. Roger that."

"Lima 1. Lima 6. Did you personally put them out?"

He replied that he had put them out and that he knew precisely where they were.

There was a small draw that came out of a valley seventy or eighty meters from our main line. There was a tree there we called the Hanging Tree because it had an odd-shaped, bent-up limb. When Buffington told me that the listening post was out near the Hanging Tree, I knew right where it was.

"Lima 1. Lima 6. Stand by. I'm going to send a reaction force down to you. You take it over. We might go out and reinforce the listening post, depending on what they've got out there."

Typically, a listening post was like a grape. If we did not get them in on time, they stood a good chance of being swallowed up as the enemy moved right up to our main line to launch an assault. On the other hand, if we pulled a listening post in too early, we would not know what the hell was going on right in front of our line. Timing was everything.

My solution to this age-old quandary was to try to reinforce a listening post that had detected a movement on its front. Doing so would offset the possibility of its being overrun if it stayed out too long. It also might be given more time to report everything it could hear and see. In the best of all worlds, a reinforced listening post just might provide us with a sizable force in the enemy's path or even in his rear.

This was an extremely delicate operation. We had practiced it several times in the past, but this was the first chance to do it live.

As soon as I made my decision, Corporal Brady sent his ammo humpers—eight Marines in all—down to the 1st Platoon command post.

There was one little flaw in the plan. The eight men in the reaction force were all mortarmen—not riflemen. Moreover, they were all very junior in rank, all privates first class and lance corporals, if that. All of a sudden, they were faced with the very real prospect of having to advance beyond our prepared defenses in the dead of night. Once they were in the open, they would have to locate a well-camouflaged friendly position they had never seen. If they got that far, there was a good chance that they would have to duke it out with who knew how many NVA Regulars. I knew that the ammo humpers were pretty excited about what they faced, but they were all I had. Short of defending a key sector during an all-out attack, there was no way I was going to thin out my platoons manning the main line.

The adrenaline was coursing through everybody at this stage.

After Brady sent out the reaction force, I finally got back in touch with the listening post. During the course of five or ten minutes—time was going fast *and* slow—I spoke with the fire team twice more. During the first transmission, the fire team leader out there was whispering so low that I could not make out what he was saying. But the last transmission was, "We see something. Six of them just walked by us." Then there was a pause and the fire team leader asked, "You want me to tell you what they are armed with?" I knew that he wanted to make sure that I knew that he wasn't bullshitting out there.

"No. Hold your position. We're gonna reinforce you."

Next, Lieutenant Buffington came up on the net to tell me that he was with the reaction force. I said, "Lima 1. Lima 6. Take them out. Be careful."

I now had a four-man Marine listening post standing by near the Hanging Tree. One officer and the eight ammo humpers were going to work their way out to the listening post. I had an unknown number of NVA out there, too—at least six. The situation was extremely dangerous.

LCpl CHARLIE THORNTON
Lima Company, 3/26 _____

As we moved up to and through our concertina wire it was so dark I literally could not see my hand in front of my face.

Capt DICK CAMP
Lima Company, 3/26 _____

While I was waiting to hear back from Buffington, I had the radio operators contact Battalion and let them know what we had.

When my radiomen got through, I told them at Battalion, "We have some friendlies out in front of the wire. Alert the line at Khe Sanh so they don't start shooting at our people out there." Battalion verified that they had heard and understood my transmission, which is not the same as assuring me that my Marines would not be endangered by other units if they were heard or seen.

I was tense from waiting, so I told Corporal Brady to break out his 60mm mortar illumination rounds and prepare to fire them immediately on my command. I had no sooner said that than, all of a sudden, Lieutenant Buffington came up on the net: "Lima 6. Lima 1. We made contact with the listening post." So that part was over with. Lima Company now had a dozen Marines and a lieutenant out in front of our lines.

Brady reported back that he had the illume broken out. I told him, "Have them standing by to fire."

We had three 60mm mortars in the company position, all under my direct control. Brady actually had a round "hanging" in each tube—that is, a gunner was holding a round at the mouth of each tube, ready to drop on command. There is no faster way to get the first rounds up.

As soon as I knew Brady's mortars were set, I told Buffington to get all his people on line, that as soon as we started the illumination he was to sweep through the area where the listening post fire team thought they saw the North Vietnamese. We were all set to go. Buffington was then about seventy or eighty meters in front of the 1st Platoon line, about a hundred meters in front of the company command post.

There was another wait. Then Buffington came up on the net: "Lima 6. Lima 1. I'm ready to go."

I turned to my mortar squad leader. "Brady, start the illumination."

LCpl CHARLIE THORNTON
Lima Company, 3/26

From behind the wire, our mortars began popping flares overhead. The night was illuminated in a very strange manner as the flares slowly drifted through the cloud cover, swinging back and forth suspended on their parachutes. There were intervals of darkness and light between the rounds fired.

Capt DICK CAMP
Lima Company, 3/26 _____

I was staring as hard as I could, dead ahead into the harsh white magnesium light of the illume, but I could not see anything. I hopped out of the radio bunker for a better look, and all my radio operators stood up around me. I was waiting for something to happen, but it was dead quiet out there. The only thing I heard was the *thung* of the second illumination round being fired as the first one started to wane.

LCpl CHARLIE THORNTON
Lima Company, 3/26 _____

The lieutenant had us get on line, spread out, and begin moving into the darkness ahead. As we walked on line, hunched over and listening only to the sounds of the night, my heart pounded in my chest with anticipation. I heard the lieutenant, who was just off to my right, shouting at someone to identify himself. He finally said, "Identify yourself or we will fire." Just at that moment, all hell broke loose. There were weapons firing from all around, and tracer sounds from automatic weapons cutting through the darkness. We returned fire in the direction from which the first shots began.

Capt DICK CAMP
Lima Company, 3/26 _____

All of a sudden, there was a burst of fire, ten or fifteen rounds. This was followed a half-beat later by a terrific volume of automatic-weapons fire. It all sounded like one continuous roar, and I do not think it lasted for more than a few seconds. Then there was nothing, absolutely nothing—dead silence. The next thing anyone heard was me yelling into the handset, "What the hell's going on? What the hell's going on out there? Tell me what's happening out there! What's happening, Nile? What's going on?"

Suddenly, I heard Buffington's voice break into my stream of questions. He was yelling at the top of his voice. I heard him on the handset and through the air. We did not need the radio.

"We have contact. We can't figure out what's going on."

I tried to sound calm. "Tell me what the hell's happening!"

Before Buffington could answer, an Army duster [a dual 40mm automatic antiaircraft gun mount on a tracked armored chassis] opened fire from our right flank. I could not hear anything except the 40mm guns and I was afraid that the Army people were blowing away our people. The only thing I could do was call Battalion and scream at them to get the Army to knock off the fire, that we were trying to find out what was going on with Buffington and his crew.

The duster kept putting out rounds, but somehow I managed to hear Buffington's next radio call: "We're down; we can't see anything."

The Army duster was still throwing rounds out there, so I yelled into the handset, "What've you got?" But Buffington said he had no idea. "Well," I asked, "is anybody hurt?"

"No, not that I can tell."

"Okay, then, bring them on in, bring them on in." I was not sure he could hear me over the continuous roar of the Army duster. "I said bring them all in, bring them all in before somebody gets hurt."

I did not get acknowledgment that I could understand, but I passed the word all up and down our line to watch for friendlies trying to reenter the company position.

LCpl CHARLIE THORNTON
Lima Company, 3/26

As the fighting subsided, we again got on line and swept through the area where we thought the firing had originated. It was very dark, and after finding nothing or encountering any additional resistance, we returned to the company perimeter. I was scared, but I also felt the rush of excitement my first fire fight had generated.

Capt DICK CAMP
Lima Company, 3/26

About ten minutes later, someone told me that Lieutenant Buffington was back inside our wire. He had come back in through his own platoon's lines because they knew him and knew where he was. I sent word for him to come straight to the company command post, and he and the ammo humpers and the original fire team got to me all at once within a minute.

I was going to ask what happened, but the whole bunch of them started talking a mile a minute before I opened my mouth. They were all incredibly hyper, and they all wanted to talk. I could see the adrenaline pouring through them. They were all bunched up in front of me, jabbering away, talking with their hands. They looked like a bunch of escapees from the asylum.

There was no way they were going to wind down on their own anytime soon, so I yelled, "Shut up, goddammit! Sit down!" That snapped all of them out of their high. They all sat down—fell down, really—and I said as calmly as I was able, "Okay, Lieutenant Buffington, tell me what happened."

Buffington told me that he had gotten all twelve Marines formed up in a single line and started moving them forward to sweep out in front of the listening post. All of a sudden, almost as soon as the first illumination round popped overhead, the Marine in the middle of the line, right in front of Buffington, stopped in his tracks. Instantly, the entire line stopped with him. Then the kid said, "Who's there?"

Nothing happened and the kid kept staring at something straight ahead, so Buffington closed up on the kid, looked ahead over the kid's shoulder, and said, "You fuckers better say something."

And that is what they did; one of them fired about fifteen rounds right over Buffington's head. Fortunately, there is a tendency to fire high at night. Buffington said he felt the rounds missing his head.

Every one of the Marines had set his weapon on full automatic, and each man had eighteen rounds in the magazine. That is thirteen Marines with eighteen rounds apiece. Every one of them instantly opened fire on full automatic. Naturally, every one of them ran out of ammunition at exactly the same moment. That was when I heard it get quiet all of a sudden.

As soon as everyone had emptied his first magazine, all hands dropped onto the ground to present less of a silhouette. Then everyone started fumbling around on the ground trying to find a fresh magazine, and trying to put the fresh magazines into their M-16s. Of course, when they all fell down, some of them were pointing their weapons one way and others were pointing their weapons the other way. The result was that they were as likely to blow away one another as any North Vietnamese. Buffington was yelling at them, trying to get them squared away: "Where the hell is everybody?" and calm questions like that. Everyone was crawling around out there, thoroughly confused, thoroughly scared.

Buffington finished telling the story and I patted everybody on the back while exclaiming, "Way to go, Marines!" and "Well done!" and "Good job! Whatever's out there, I know you just scared the shit out of them. They know you alerted the lines. Well done." I made a special effort to pat the listening post Marines on their backs; they had done good.

Nile Buffington and I trekked down to Battalion to give them a brief. I was stunned to see that no one at the battalion command post appeared particularly interested in our story. Noting all the bored expressions, we gave a quick brief and headed home.

By the time we got back to my command post, it was probably 0400. I told Buffington to send out another listening post, but not in that same vicinity. Then I jumped into my hole and crashed.

After a few hours sleep, I called Buffington and told him that we had to search around the Hanging Tree to try to find out what had happened in the night.

As I was getting set to go down to 1st Platoon, two of the ammo humpers who had been in the fire fight came over and asked if they could help search for bodies. I told them they sure could, and they accompanied me to the 1st Platoon command post. I guess they had become bored with the easy life of the rear echelon.

I was just rubbernecking while Buffington's people and the ammo humpers were kicking around out in front of the lines. I had even less of a sense of what to look for than they did. I doubted we would find anything; it was always extremely difficult to find any results from a fight because the North Vietnamese were always very good about dragging their bodies off. I happened to be watching the two ammo humpers, who were about seventy meters from where I was standing. No sooner did I take my eyes off them than I heard them both yell, "Skipper! Hey, Skipper!" When I lifted my eyes, they were jumping up and down and yelling, "Come out here quick. Come on out here. See what we got!"

I grabbed a bunch of other onlookers and we ran out there at high port. The ammo humpers had found five dead NVA officers, all stretched right out on the ground. All of them had been hit literally from the top of their brain housing groups to their toenails, and it looked like somebody had raked the ground around them. That was the result of all that automatic fire that the listening post fire team and the reaction force had put out. They put out over 230 rounds, and all of them were right on target. My Marines had really hit the mark.

The dead men were all wearing black pajamas and Ho Chi Minh sandals. And all of them were really big men, a lot bigger than most Vietnamese are. One of them had pulled a hand grenade halfway out of his pouch, and another one was gripping a pistol with his arm outstretched. Rigor mortis had set in, so they were all frozen in the positions in which they had died, like wax statues.

After staring at the bodies for a few moments, I noticed that all their shoulder straps had been cut. The listening post had told us early on that there were six of them. That explained the cut shoulder straps. One of them had survived and had apparently had the presence of mind to cut away their dispatch cases before he took off out of the area. That is fantastic discipline, particularly if he had been wounded, which was a good bet.

For once, we had the proof of our success. I turned to Lieutenant Buffington and the others. "Let's bring the whole company out here by squads to see the results."

First, I brought out all the ammo humpers who had been on the reaction force; it was important for them to see what they had accomplished.

While the squads were rubbernecking, I told my exec to contact the 17th ITT—Interrogation-Translation Team—to get them out to view the remains and take whatever they needed for intelligence purposes. The dead North Vietnamese were definitely big fish; every one of them was wearing a gold or silver belt buckle, not the standard aluminum type. Dispatch cases, pistols, expensive belt buckles—it was obvious to me that these people were special.

GySgt MAX FRIEDLANDER
17th Interrogation-Translation Team

Early in the morning, I received a call from Regiment asking me to go out and check the bodies that were lying in front of the lines. I did so, and I found that there was very little information—

papers, documents, maps—to be gathered from the bodies themselves. There was a bit of evidence, though, that there had been another member of the group. There were five bodies and a sixth had probably been wounded and dragged himself off. It was our guess that he had collected the documents that may have been valuable to us and took them with him.

One of the NVA was still holding a hand grenade. One of the Explosive Ordnance Disposal [EOD] people had to be called to get the hand grenade out of his hand. All of the other weapons, if they were carrying any, were missing.

There were a few things that were rather unusual about these five bodies. One of them was extremely tall for a North Vietnamese. A lieutenant colonel who was out there and I sent word back to Colonel Lownds about this because there was a possibility he was Chinese.

While we were waiting around, I started following what I thought was the route the escaped NVA had taken. I started walking in that direction, which led me toward a wooded area. I didn't see anything and I lost the trail, so I walked a little bit further. By then, I was about sixty yards from the bodies. I saw a large log on the right, where the treeline was, and for some reason I stopped, looked around, and walked back up to where everybody was standing around. I later learned that an NVA company was in the treeline, ready to open fire on me and the Marines around the bodies if I took even one more step.

By the time I got back to the bodies, word had come back from Regiment. Colonel Lownds asked us to take the body down to one of the empty tents in back of Charlie-Med and have him examined by both the medical officer and the dental officer to see if there was any way to determine if he was, in fact, Chinese.

I accompanied the tall NVA soldier to the tent. The doctor was checking him over, and the dental officer came in and tried to make some sort of a determination on his teeth. There was nothing definite that could be determined. They could not come to a definite conclusion that he was Chinese. However, since there was a possibility he was, Colonel Lownds had radioed the news down to 3rd Marine Division headquarters, at Phu Bai. I heard it threw a scare into people. If the Chinese were involved and were sending high-ranking officers, it could have turned into quite a big thing. However, it was all forgotten shortly thereafter.

I did get some information off several of the NVA bodies—a

pay card from one, one or two watches, some photos of a family. We were able to determine their units and ranks.

Capt DICK CAMP
Lima Company, 3/26 ⎯⎯⎯⎯⎯⎯⎯⎯⎯⎯⎯⎯⎯⎯⎯⎯⎯⎯⎯⎯

What it all added up to is that we had killed the commander of an NVA regiment and his staff. This was incredibly lucky for Lima Company. The only thing officers as senior as that could have been doing out there was reconnoitering our lines in preparation for a major ground assault.

The only casualty we suffered came to my attention when one of the kids in the listening post fire team showed me an ugly bruise over the orbit bone of his right eye, which, he told me, had been inflicted when a bullet glanced off his face. I had the first sergeant write him up for a Purple Heart, and I made sure everyone in the fire team and all the ammo humpers got souvenirs, the gold and silver belt buckles, the officers' pistols, whatever.

1stLt NICK ROMANETZ
Charlie Company, 1/26 ⎯⎯⎯⎯⎯⎯⎯⎯⎯⎯⎯⎯⎯⎯⎯⎯⎯⎯

The bodies of the NVA officers were the first dead bad guys any of us had seen in a long time. They drew a lot of attention.

CHAPTER 3

JANUARY 5

At 0655, Charlie Company, 1/26 (reinforced), departed the Khe Sanh Combat Base with the assigned mission of conducting a two-day combat patrol/search-and-destroy operation northwest of the combat base, and with the additional mission of inserting a reconnaissance team. At 1615, while the reconnaissance team was being inserted, it observed three NVA. Small arms were exchanged and the reconnaissance team withdrew to the Charlie Company position. Charlie Company continued its assigned mission without incident, returning to the Khe Sanh Combat Base on January 6 at 1215.

At 0730, Alpha Company, 1/26 (minus) (reinforced), departed the Khe Sanh Combat Base to conduct a two-day combat patrol/search-and-destroy operation southeast of the combat base. The patrol proceeded without incident and Alpha Company returned to the Khe Sanh Combat Base on January 6 at 1530.

26th Marines Command Chronology

At 1600, Recon team 2B1 made contact with three NVA. The team received automatic weapons fire and observed 10 NVA wearing green utility uniforms and carrying AK-47s trying to outflank them from the northeast. The team broke contact.

At 2031, Recon team 3B3 observed 7 red lights. An artillery mission was fired and the lights went out.

1/26 Command Chronology _____

At 2245, Alpha Company, 1/26, listening posts heard movement and received one incoming grenade resulting in one friendly WIA (non-serious).

JANUARY 6

26th Marines Command Chronology _____

At 1055, Recon Team 1B3 exchanged small-arms fire with a small enemy unit resulting in 1 NVA KIA (confirmed).

JANUARY 8

1/26 Command Chronology _____

At 0230, Bravo Company, 1/26, listening posts observed two lights near the trash dump. The area was searched at first light, revealing three sets of footprints heading in a southwesterly direction. Patrol unable to follow due to thick vegetation.

At 0700, 1/26 (minus) commenced a battalion search-and-destroy operation for a period of six days. The assigned mission was to interdict likely enemy routes of infiltration southwest of the Khe Sanh Combat Base. There were no enemy contacts during this operation.

At 1010, the Alpha Company, 1/26, platoon on Hill 950 found fresh footprints. The footprints headed in a westerly direction for approximately 100 meters and disappeared.

At 1245, Bravo Company, 1/26, found a 10–15-man harbor site approximately a week old. Conducted search of trails leading from the area with negative results.

JANUARY 10

Lt RAY STUBBE
1/26 Battalion Chaplain _____

[DIARY ENTRY] At the regimental briefing, Colonel Lownds said the enemy has completed their recon and he expects an attack in the next ten days. "They're going to attack, and we're going to inflict a heavy loss on them."

JANUARY 11

26th Marines Command Chronology ———————————

At 1315, an aerial observer observed 12 NVA on a trail. The [helicopter] gunships on station took them under attack, resulting in 6 NVA KIA (confirmed).

JANUARY 12

26th Marines Command Chronology ———————————

At 1417, two Special Forces patrols observed NVA in their general vicinity. Artillery and small-arms fire resulted in 12 NVA KIA (confirmed). Special Forces had one friendly WIA and one friendly KIA.

JANUARY 13

Capt KEN PIPES
Bravo Company, 1/26 ———————————

During our sweep into the hills west of the combat base, one of my platoons ambushed an NVA recon unit that had been tracing all the avenues of approach into the combat base. Apparently, in the gear they left behind were maps showing the approach routes into the base and the hill outposts. The routes provided that long columns of troops could move off the trails if they were discovered and bombed by aircraft, so the troops wouldn't be exposed to the aircraft in long, easy-to-hit columns.

LtCol JIM WILKINSON
1/26 Commanding Officer ———————————

Bravo Company killed one member of the NVA recon team. Regiment was in such a state because we had killed an NVA that they ordered us to bring in the body. In fact, Colonel Lownds personally flew out in a helicopter to check the NVA. We were quite impressed. He was taller than the average NVA, well clothed, and well armed.

One of the maps we captured showed indications of where the major thrust was going to take place at Khe Sanh.

Capt KEN PIPES
Bravo Company, 1/26 _____

As soon as the information we sent in—along with one of the NVA bodies—had been checked by higher headquarters, the sweep operation was cut short and we were all ordered back to the combat base to assume defensive positions.

1stLt NICK ROMANETZ
Charlie Company, 1/26 _____

As we were coming into Khe Sanh following our battalion sweep, we could see the base from a couple of miles off. I was astounded at how many C-130s the Air Force and Marines were landing. Almost like cars going through a tollbooth, these things were coming down with material, ammo, food, and troops. Helicopters were coming in, too. Up until this time, we had not received much indication of hostile activity, so I was really astounded. I began thinking that something was really going to happen.

Lt RAY STUBBE
1/26 Battalion Chaplain _____

[DIARY ENTRY] Colonel Lownds announced the following at the regimental meeting:

> 1. All personnel will have fighting holes where they work and where they live.
>
> 2. These holes will be built so one can fight from them, and they will be covered with runway matting to be brought up from the south.
>
> 3. The holes will be supplied with rations. All water cans will be always filled since the water point will probably be hit.
>
> 4. Beginning Monday [January 15], all personnel will wear flak jackets and carry a weapon.
>
> 5. Wire will be laid for internal security all about the base.

Leaving the meeting, I asked [the 26th Marines regimental intelligence officer] if it was really as bad as all that. He said, "All indications are that we're going to be hit. How bad, I can't say."

IstLt NICK ROMANETZ
Charlie Company, 1/26

An order came down that every Marine was always to wear his helmet and flak jacket and carry his weapon and gas mask. Until this point, the only time we wore a flak jacket or helmet was when we went on patrols or work parties outside the wire, or when we were standing to or standing down. When this word came down, it really had a lot of guys chuckling. Everybody was saying, "Hey, who are these guys kidding? This is Khe Sanh. It's the quietest place." It really took a lot of getting used to to carry a weapon at all times and keep that flak jacket on. A lot of guys thought it was a real joke.

LCpl CHARLIE THORNTON
Lima Company, 3/26

We began to dig in deeper and prepare for the worst. We were told that we were surrounded and heavily outnumbered by thousands of NVA regulars.

JANUARY 14

Capt BILL DABNEY
India Company, 3/26 (Hill 881S)

The intelligence that filtered down to my level was minimal, virtually nonexistent. India Company had been on 881S since about December 20. Since I was not able to sit in on regiment or battalion briefings, I was not informed in specific detail of the probability of attack. . . . However, the potential was obvious to myself and my officers and I therefore patrolled actively as far as four kilometers from the hill to the north, south, and west. Hill 861 was to the east, so there wasn't any patrolling in that direction.

Until about January 13, the patrols turned up no evidence of recent NVA activity. On the fourteenth, I sent 2ndLt Tom

Brindley's 3rd Platoon to patrol Hill 881N. Accompanying it was an eight-man reconnaissance patrol which was to drop off clandestinely along the route of march on 881N. There was no contact and the recon patrol remained on 881N after the platoon left to patrol. The platoon set up a patrol base with one squad plus two 60mm mortars and sent the other two squads out—one about 1,000 meters along the ridgeline west from 881N and the other along the fingers extending southwest. There were no contacts or sightings. Then, on January 14, 2ndLt Mike Thomas's 2nd Platoon patrolled to the ridge about one kilometer or so south, then along the ridge, and then returned via the valley between the ridge and 881S. Again, there were no sightings, no contacts. However, at about 1400 on January 14, Battalion informed us that the recon team inserted by 3rd Platoon on the thirteenth had made contact with NVA on the north slope of 881N, had wounded, and required assistance. I said we'd provide same. Lieutenant Brindley volunteered to take his platoon to assist. Time was critical, both because the recon team could not carry its own casualties and because the platoon (Brindley's) would have about four kilometers to cover—two up and two back—to the north side of 881N. Since there were NVA in the area, the platoon had to be back on Hill 881S by dark since India Company's mission was to hold that hill; we couldn't leave large units out overnight.

Simultaneously, while I sent the 3rd Platoon north to recover the recon team, I ordered 2nd Platoon to return expeditiously from the southern patrol, which it did. Brindley's 3rd Platoon shucked its packs, flak jackets, and all except weapons, ammo, and water, and literally double-timed to 881N in three squad columns. We planned but did not register fires because, one, we didn't have time, and, two, we didn't know exactly where the recon team was. In that country it was risky tactics, but justified, Tom and I felt, by the situation and by the fact that the platoon knew the terrain intimately, having patrolled there several times before, both day and night, in the past month. In less than two hours, about 1600, the platoon found the recon team, set up a landing zone to evac the wounded, and returned to 881S, arriving about 1900 with the six uninjured recon team members in tow. There was no contact. Upon debriefing the recon team, we discovered that during the contact they had abandoned a radio and some [code] sheets. We so reported to Battalion.[1]

26th Marines Command Chronology _____

Enemy sightings and contacts increased slightly during the first two weeks of January, and emphasis was shifted from harassing and reconnaissance activities to probes. Reconnaissance teams consistently made sightings or saw indications of heavy enemy activity, and contact was made frequently. Each contact and sighting added to an evolving pattern which indicated that the enemy was increasingly interested in the defensive posture of Hills 950, 881S, 861, the Combined Action Company at Khe Sanh village, and the combat base itself.

During January 9–13, patrols from the CIDG camp at Lang Vei made five contacts. Similarly, a rash of sightings along the perimeter of the combat base culminated in the slaying of five of a party of six NVA near the wire on the night of January 2–3. Later in the month, the wire was reported cut and replaced by the NVA in such a manner as to escape detection.

1/26 Command Chronology _____

On January 14, increased emphasis was placed on the defense of the Khe Sanh Combat Base as a result of an overall intelligence build-up in the 26th Marines area of operations. An additional company was placed in the perimeter to meet the increased enemy threat.

JANUARY 15

26th Marines Command Chronology _____

At 1120, a patrol from India Company, 3/26 [near Hill 881S] found 50 old fighting holes which had been cleaned out and showed recent use. Also found were three canisters of 82mm ammunition with Chinese writing.

During the afternoon, a Special Forces patrol observed 30–35 NVA bathing in a stream and called in artillery fire from the Khe Sanh Combat Base. Artillery resulted in 10 NVA KIA (confirmed).

MGen TOMMY TOMPKINS
3rd Marine Division Commanding General _____

On January 15, I decided that Colonel Lownds didn't have enough people at Khe Sanh—he had a regiment less a battalion—so I sent a UNODIR—"Unless Otherwise Directed"—to LtGen Robert Cushman [III Marine Amphibious Force commander]. I told him I was going to send another battalion in. I waited sixty minutes, didn't hear from him, and so began loading [2/26] in.[2]

2/26 Command Chronology _____

> The 2nd Battalion, 26th Marines, was relieved of the Phu Bai Tactical Area of Responsibility on January 15 by the 5th Marines. An advance party [had] departed on January 14 to establish facilities in the Dong Ha Combat Base to receive the remainder of the battalion, which was to depart Phu Bai on January 16 and 18. However, on the afternoon of January 15, the destination of the battalion was changed from Dong Ha to Khe Sanh.

The arrival of 2/26 at Khe Sanh marked the first time since World War II that the 26th Marine Regiment was whole.

HM3 DAVID STEINBERG
3/26 Battalion Aid Station _____

> January 15, 1968
>
> My Dearest Sharon,
>
>   I was sitting on the airstrip at Dong Ha awaiting a flight to Khe Sanh. Would you believe I sat there twelve days, and slept there also? Back at the airstrip this morning, I was still sitting there on my thirteenth day, and it looked bad for me as far as getting out. Suddenly, out of the sky came, not a bird or a transport plane, as planned, but a lousy helicopter. Well, I drove my ambulance full of needed supplies

aboard, and off we flew for Khe Sanh, elevation 1,500 feet in the mountains. I started to say a prayer as we lifted off because, the day before, one of these copters crashed, killing 40 Marines.

Needless to say, I made it safely, as did my ambulance. I had a heck of a time backing it off the copter with a trailer on it, but I made it and am now joined again with my unit.

Khe Sanh is at the top of South Vietnam, on the Laotian border. It is in a jungle region where, unlike the rest of Nam, we have no rice paddies. Here, we have Montagnard Indians of the mountain tribes. Elephants are plentiful and have been sighted. I keep my weapon close at hand to shoot elephants with gym shoes out of trees. You can tell they're there by the peanuts on their breath.

Presently, it is 0115, January 15, and I am on watch. Actually, I am to lay awake in my rack for two hours and listen for sirens or incoming attacks. My watch ends in fifteen minutes and I can wake my relief and go off to sleepville. This candlelight may be romantic, but it sure makes letter writing hard.

JANUARY 16

2/26 Command Chronology ───────────────────────────

Commencing at 0800, 2/26 was flown by fixed-wing aircraft to the Khe Sanh Combat Base. Upon arrival at Khe Sanh, the battalion established an assembly area west of the combat base. All four companies closed the assembly area before darkness. Foxtrot Company moved from the assembly area to the northwest to occupy Hill 558 at 1400.

Capt EARLE BREEDING
Echo Company, 2/26 ───────────────────────────

I went to a meeting down in what looked to me like an underground dungeon—Colonel Lownds's command post. I had worked for Colonel Lownds years before, when he was a regimental intelligence officer and I was a slick-sleeve private acting as his chief scout. I didn't even know he was the 26th Marines regimental commander until I saw him in his command post bunker because 2/26 had never once worked directly for Regiment since it had been in-country. I didn't think he remembered me, but he did.

I was standing in the back, minding my own business, while

he delivered his pep talk. At one point he said, "We're going to hold," and, looking at me, "Aren't we, Captain Breeding?"

I was stunned, but, never being at a loss for words, I said, "Colonel, as long as Echo Company is here, Khe Sanh will hold."

You can imagine the look the brass gave me, but, in a way, that's how it worked out.

JANUARY 17

2/26 Command Chronology

> On January 17, the remainder of 2/26 conducted a tactical march to Hill 558 to form a battalion defensive position to block enemy movement through the Rao Quan Valley. After a reconnaissance of the area, the companies were deployed as follows: three companies formed a perimeter defense encompassing Hill 558 and one company [Echo] was chopped to 3/26 and occupied high ground west of Hill 558. Reinforced platoon-size patrols were conducted from the battalion's position to determine the enemy's location and disposition.

HM3 DAVID STEINBERG
3/26 Battalion Aid Station

January 17, 1968

My Dearest Darlin',

It is 0400 in the morning and I am on watch. I just sit here and think about you. What else can take my mind off war and put me into the future at a time very near, yet far, when I'll be home again. We have so much to look forward to and many memories to cultivate. I miss you so much, but thanks to all your pictures I can stare at you as though you were right before me.

I guess that Khe Sanh is getting to be an important place nowadays, and I even heard that the Stateside newspapers call it the hotspot of Nam. Things are quiet, although we have spent a week filling sandbags and building bunkers. Hanoi Hannah (the Tokyo Rose of this war) has told us on the radio that they would take this place. I thought it was all talk, but General Westmoreland was here today, and enemy troops are a day away.

We have to set up a clearing station for casualties, and I

have been working with the battalion surgeon, getting a treatment facility and a medevac landing zone set up here. While nothing may ever take place, we will be ready in case something breaks.

It is funny to walk in Khe Sanh because, being at 1,500 feet on top of a mountain, the clouds roll along the ground. It's like a fog except it rolls in small white patches. When there is a thick cloud cover, it's like being in heaven, and you're lucky to see two feet in front of you.

Well, I have to hold reveille on the troops, so I'll close. Sharon, you know that I truly love you and always have you on my mind. Well, Smokey Robinson is on the radio, so excuse me while I do the boogaloo.

JANUARY 18

26th Marines Command Chronology ─────────────────────

There was a sudden increase in enemy sightings, and heavy activity was noted on the extensive trail networks to the north and northwest of the combat base.

JANUARY 19

Cpl WILLIAM ROBERTSON
Logistics Support Unit ──────────────────────────────

Until mid-January, whenever we went to the trash dump, there would be at least a hundred montagnards out there. We didn't ever have to unload anything. We just backed the truck up and they would unload everything, going through and getting wood or anything else they felt they could use. Starting in mid-January, the number of montagnards at the trash dump started dwindling down. When I went to the dump on January 19, there probably weren't fifteen montagnards there. That was enough right there to let me know that things were bad. These people knew what was going on. They had their intelligence sources. They were clearing the area, moving out.

Pfc ELWIN BACON
Kilo Company, 3/26 (Hill 861) ────────────────────────

My first time as point was when we took off on a routine patrol on January 19. We took a route that had been taken many times before by our platoon as well as others. We headed northwest up a little smaller ridge between us and Hill 881S. When we got to the summit of the hill, the area was pretty well open except for the tall elephant grass that is typical of the region. However, the trail was well walked on in the past so there was no reason at first to see fresh footprints on it. But it didn't take but a few steps to realize they were a lot different than the prints our boots would make.

I stopped and motioned to the guy behind me, who I think was one of the snipers. I didn't like the look in his eyes when he looked back at me. The squad leader was called up immediately and a discussion took place, but I was completely left out.

About this time we could hear the clanging of heavy metal in the valley just below us. This was accompanied by the distinct voices of Vietnamese, and they weren't trying to talk that loud either. The squad leader went back and talked on our radio. The word came down to be alert. We had support fire from our 4.2-inch mortars coming into the valley.

As pointman, I was looking down the trail, not knowing what I would do if something moved up the trail toward me, but I stayed in a crouched position until the 200 mortar rounds were delivered into the valley below.

Smoke and the sounds of screaming people were all that came out of that hollow. At this same time we could hear small-arms fire coming from the direction of Hill 881S. We stayed there for a few minutes, then my squad leader came up and told us that we had orders to go down into the valley and report on the results.

I was told to lead out at a slow pace, and that was just what I did. The bridal step is about the speed we were going, knowing from the sound that there were many mad bastards still making noise down there. I knew that they knew someone was watching them and that they would be looking for us also.

God was with us. Well, at least the battalion commander was, because we only got about fifty or so feet when I was told to stop. We had direct orders from the Khe Sanh base to get back to our hill. I guess it took us about an hour and a half to get to that position, but it took us only about ten minutes to get back to our base on Hill 861.

1stLt JOHN KAHENY
1/26 Combat Operations Center _____

The commander of the battalion 106mm Recoilless Rifle Platoon, 1stLt Paul McGrath, came in to tell me about a "neat stunt" he had pulled. He told me that he and his platoon sergeant had taken a starlight scope—a piece of highly classified equipment—and had gone out and tracked "a platoon of Charlie Company" as it was making a night patrol. Since I worked in the operations center, I knew that the Charlie Company patrol was not operating anywhere near the position Paul described. It must have been a reinforced platoon of NVA. I did not want to ruin Paul's career by telling the story, but I did have to do something. I went to the battalion commander, LtCol James Wilkinson, and told him the story, but added that I could not reveal the source. Lieutenant Colonel Wilkinson did not press me to tell him.

HM3 DAVID STEINBERG
3/26 Battalion Aid Station _____

January 19, 1968

My Dearest Sharon,

Well, they're at it again with no mail for a week. Bullets, bandages, and bombs have priority over mail, so we have plenty of everything except mail.

We have been on alert for three days now and the tension is easing up because the NVA said they would attack yesterday, and they didn't. I even slept in a six-foot-deep foxhole last night.

The month of January is about over, and time is really moving now. I can hardly wait to get home so we can be together. I can't tell you how much I miss you, Sharon. I'll just have to be content with your picture and, of course, your letters and cards, which are great, just like you.

Nothing too much new because the Nam is the same from day to day. Your letters are all that make a difference, and thoughts of you make me feel closer to home.

On January 18, India Company, 3/26, on Hill 881S, was directed to dispatch a patrol to recover a radio and codes that had been left behind in the wake of the January 14 ambush of a recon team on Hill 881N.

Capt BILL DABNEY
India Company, 3/26 (Hill 881S) ⸻⸻⸻⸻⸻⸻

2ndLt Richard Fromme's 1st Platoon—reinforced with a section of M-60 machine guns, a section of 60mm mortars, and the 81mm forward observer—jumped off about dawn on January 19. Since there were no friendlies to the north, we both preplanned and registered 81s along the route. First Platoon maneuvered carefully, and, about noon and about 500 meters short of the crest of 881—that's the south side of the hill—made point-to-point contact with an NVA unit which Fromme estimated to be about platoon size. It was maneuvering south along the same finger. There was brief fire fighting, during which 1st Platoon's pointman killed the NVA pointman. In accordance with my instructions, Lieutenant Fromme immediately withdrew 300 meters and called in 81s to his front. There was no further contact and the radio and [code] sheets were not recovered. We never got to where we thought they might be.

I also sent squad-sized patrols around 881S to check out the valleys on either side while Fromme was going north. No contacts, no sighting, but it was obvious to me that something was about to happen.[3]

Lt RAY STUBBE
1/26 Battalion Chaplain ⸻⸻⸻⸻⸻⸻⸻

[DIARY ENTRY] It's almost hard to keep track of the casualties. Lieutenant Yeary and Corporal Healy, from Recon, [killed] on Sunday [January 14]. One was one of the worst casualties here; he received an RPG round, and his whole body from the diaphragm down was missing. Then Wednesday [January 17], the Air Force plane [crashed] with the pilot and FOB [Forward Operating Base] man killed. Both were charred. In fact, the bodies were still simmering. Then more casualties the same day—two dead, four wounded.

Now the men from India Company, 3/26, at Triage. One was the 3/26 chaplain's clerk who wanted to go back to the field. He was hit in the groin. Then a man with a back wound; they put a tube in his chest to drain off the internal bleeding. Then two heat-exhaustion cases.

Then a dead [India Company] Marine, hit in the right eye socket. I helped carry him to Graves Registration. The others left. All there was was myself and an empty tent, a stretcher over the corpse. The sun was shining on the toes of two combat jungle boots.

Now, six more casualties. Then two Bru *children* were brought in with shrapnel wounds. One girl had her femur broken, crying in almost a chant, and had to go to the hospital in Danang. The other, a boy, had minor wounds.

26th Marines Command Chronology _____

> Intelligence reports . . . [are] showing a tremendous move-ment south from the DMZ and east from Laos, of large numbers of personnel and several trucks. On one occasion, tanks were reported just across the Laotian border on National Route 9. As a result of this information, the regiment began conducting heavy H&I [harassment-and-interdiction] fires on known and suspected enemy lo-cations. . . . Planning commenced for the interdiction of enemy avenues of approach by CS [tear gas] chemicals and special [delay-fuse and cluster] bombs to be placed in position in early February.

BOB BREWER
Quang Tri Province Senior Adviser _____

The enemy we faced was quite human. They had the same physical discomforts, bad habits, morale problems, etc., etc., as we did. It was important, then, to read each piece of intelligence in that light. They made mistakes, and often repeated them. In looking for those indicators of the coming attack, I constantly encountered these little human foibles that helped sort things out. For instance, I knew that getting food to the assembly areas would be an enemy problem. Solution: Look for Communist midnight requisitions in the nearby pacified areas. When not much happened in that vein, I suspected that the hostiles might try a forced march from the DMZ around Cam Lo District timed to arrive just before the battle. In comes the Marine intelligence officer from Khe Sanh with a question, "Why are the villagers around Ca Lu being ordered to make hundreds of paper cones?" Elementary! So the NVA can put them on their flashlights as diffusers when they go for their forced march!

Capt HARRY BAIG
26th Marines Target Information Officer _____

When Khe Sanh was invested by the 304th and 325C Divisions of the People's Army of Vietnam (PAVN), a 3rd Marine Division Intelligence augmentation team was flown to the combat base for the purpose of assisting in the development of intelligence and target information. It consisted of myself and Maj Robert Coolidge. A third member, Maj Jerry Hudson, had arrived earlier and had been appointed intelligence officer of the regiment. Major Coolidge became the 3rd Marine Division intelligence representative and Special Intelligence Officer and I became the regimental Target Intelligence and Information Officer. Together we developed the intelligence and target information, which helped deny the ambitions of General Giap and destroy the best part of two enemy divisions.

I went to Khe Sanh with four assumptions in mind:

a. That the enemy would conduct the investment of the base in accordance with a master plan, prepared and promulgated by a headquarters other than that of the field force conducting a siege.

b. That, because of this, the North Vietnamese commander in the field could not and would not alter the battle plan to any significant degree, regardless of facts bearing on the subsequent situation on account of doctrinal requirements— other than to retire from the field.

c. That the modus operandi was predictable and the general concept determinable once the opening moves had occurred (or were revealed—as in fact happened).

d. That the plan encompassed classic siege tactics as practiced and studied by General Giap during and after the siege of Dienbienphu and as modified by experiences at Con Thien in September 1967.[4]

Maj JIM STANTON
26th Marines Fire Support Coordination Center _____

The activities reported around to the north, west, and south were very heavy. As an artillery aerial observer, I flew mission after mission and saw literally hundreds of North Vietnamese soldiers in their bright green, easy-to-see uniforms. They were in large numbers, they were bivouacking in the open, they were doing things that made it very difficult for Marines to patrol. I could go out and recon areas by fire and *always* get North Vietnamese to scatter. I knew where to shoot artillery and get immediate reaction by their troops on the ground and in the open.

Capt DICK CAMP
Lima Company, 3/26 _____

I could smell them.

PART TWO

ASSAULT
January 20–21, 1968

CHAPTER 4

JANUARY 20

ATTACK ON HILL 881N

Capt BILL DABNEY
India Company 3/26

[Following the patrol contact on Hill 881N on January 19], I requested from Battalion permission to have a reconnaissance-in-force to 881N with India Company, reinforced, the next day and to man the perimeter of 881S, with Charlie Battery, 1/13, Radio Relay, our 106mm recoilless rifle section, and other non-infantry personnel. I asked them to send up a platoon from Mike Company, 3/26, which was then at the Khe Sanh Combat Base perimeter, to help man the 881S line while we were gone.[1]

HM3 MIKE RAY
India Company, 3/26

The morning of January 20 started early. First call went out at 0530, with 1stSgt Willis Happlo, affectionately known as "Happy," sticking his head into each bunker to wake us. Little did we know that this day would take us into a fiery hell and back. Many would never receive another first call.

When I emerged from my bunker a few minutes later, the

43

sun was up. The day was clear from our vantage point on Hill 881S. But, as I looked over the valleys and mountain slopes around the outpost, I could see that all but it and the highest peaks were enveloped in fog.

There was small talk among some of the boys in the 3rd Platoon, mostly about how short a time each had and how good it would be to get home. Some had only a couple of months, others a little longer. Me? Well, I had only been in-country a little over two months, so I didn't get too excited with the conversation.

When I finished my meal, I headed for my bunker to inventory my aid bag. I wanted to make sure I had the necessary items—battle dressings, tourniquets, and morphine. I didn't want to be caught short in case the shit hit the fan. I then took a few minutes to write a short note to my wife and son. I left it with my personal gear so it would be found and delivered if I didn't return. This was a ritual before each patrol into the bush. I feared that I would get blown away and my family would have no last word from me. I didn't dwell on death, but I thought endlessly about the sadness I would bring into the lives of those I loved in the event of my death. This made me fear my death.

The word was finally passed around at 0800 to saddle up and get into platoon formation. The order of march would be the 3rd Platoon, then the 1st Platoon. The 2nd Platoon was to be held in reserve. By 0830, the 3rd Platoon departed the outpost. This patrol was to be a company-size move, but not in mass. Each platoon was to act independently. Once we left the hill, we didn't see the rest of the company again.

We moved silently away from the hill, keeping our intervals as we slipped through the waist-to-head-high elephant grass. We followed the trail down from our vantage point into the valleys and sloughs and then edged along the ridges of the lower hills. We came down through the fog cover. As we went deeper, the bright sun turned into a faint glow. Then, in time, we were in a gray, overcast world. The fog must have been at least several hundred feet thick! Moving as slowly and cautiously as we did, it took quite some time to get completely through that fog.

The morning grew long, but eventually we reached the base of what I later found was our objective, Hill 881N. The platoon paused there for a short time and then started our long climb to the top, entering the fog a short time later. Time seemed endless while we moved only short distances at a time without being able to see the sun.

The fog was still pretty thick, even though the platoon had started through. The word came down the line to take a short break. The word was usually to take fifteen minutes, but we expected ten, and most of the time we only got five. This time, though, it seemed like we got the entire fifteen minutes. I sat on that well-worn trail in the fog, in silence and alone with my thoughts. I don't remember all that went through my mind, but I do remember wondering why we had stopped. Our intelligence had been telling us that the enemy's presence was here in force. This was hard to believe because there had been very little contact, and none of it had been by our battalion. We had gone out a couple of times to rescue some recon elements that had gotten into trouble, but both times all we found were dead bodies.

My thoughts rambled through that and the two small fire fights I had been involved in since I had been in-country. I did not want to be involved in any more, but found that desire unlikely since I had been in-country only a short time. I drifted in and out of reality, looking into the long, sober faces of those men closest to me, both in front and behind me. I could see in their faces the fear of the unknown that I felt inside. I wondered if my eyes revealed the same about me. I felt a sense of responsibility to them for two reasons. First, I was older than the average trooper in the platoon. Second, they called me "Doc." They expected me to be there if they went down. I represented to them the link to life, the small thread to which they could cling when there was no hope left. They expected me to save them from death, and at the age of twenty-two, that was a heavy burden to bear. I had already found that it didn't always work that way.

Soon the signal to move came silently down the trail. As each man passed the signal to another, he rose to his feet almost instantaneously. The column started to move as slowly as ever, but it was with the hope that we could reach our objective and return without incident.

The platoon had only moved a few meters when that gut-wrenching sound rang across the silence of my mind. The first shot was fired. The sudden rush of adrenaline made me want to instantly vomit. Before I could blink an eye, there were more shots fired. These had the distinctive pop of an AK-47, and I knew that I would be dead before long. From then on, events took place so rapidly that they are difficult to remember. The whine of bullets could be heard all around. The fire fight intensified. The platoon finally recovered from the shock of being taken by surprise and started returning fire. The initial sickness remained even though we were minutes into the fire fight. It seemed the enemy was on both sides. They were so close that their grenades rained in on us from everywhere.

Capt BILL DABNEY
India Company, 3/26

The right platoon [1st], under 2ndLt Richard Fromme, held fast on good ground. . . . Lieutenant Thomas Brindley's [3rd] platoon, on the left, found itself pinned down on exposed ground about two hundred meters short of a commanding knoll from which the North Vietnamese were firing with telling effect.[2]

Capt DICK CAMP
Lima Company, 3/26

I was in my rack, resting and sort of listening in on the chatter over the battalion tactical radio net, when the India Company platoon commander announced that he was under attack. Shit, I thought, this is it. I was so sure the whole battalion would counterattack that I ordered Lima Company to saddle up and get ready to fly to Hill 881S. But the call never came.

HM3 MIKE RAY
India Company, 3/26

The cry "Doc, up!" rang above the noise of the fire fight. I wanted this to end. My God, what was I doing here? I had been in fire fights before, but nothing like this. I tried to move forward in response to the call for "Doc." The fire was so intense that I felt I couldn't move, but I did, slowly, holding the earth close to my breast. Fear gripped every fiber of my being. As I moved forward, I began finding the wounded. My squad leader was a sergeant from Kentucky, a hill boy. He would play his guitar and sing at night when the situation permitted. He wouldn't sing again for a long time. His chin had been shot off from the corners of his mouth to about three-fourths of the way back to his throat. He asked me, "Doc, how bad is it?" I didn't have the heart to tell him. He asked me for morphine, but I refused, telling him I didn't want him to be a litter case while he could still walk. I gave him a large battle dressing and told him to hold it to the area where his mouth would have been. I sent him back down the trail, promising him, when things quieted and when it came time for his evacuation, that I would give him the coveted morphine.

There was another call, "Doc, up!" This boy had gotten a piece of sharp metal from a grenade. It had entered to the right and below his left eye, gone through the roof of his mouth, and exited under his chin. This left a small but gaping hole that bled profusely. I administered first aid and sent him back.

I moved forward, for the first time looking at my hands. They were caked with mud, but the liquid agent, I realized, was blood. What a putrid smell! I will never forget that smell; it was an indescribable smell. I rolled from my belly to my back and tried to wipe my hands off on my utility pants. Some of the debris crumbled from my hands, but it was under my fingernails too. I realized that I was too busy to worry about something like that. As I resumed my prone position, I saw a grenade bounce onto the trail not more than twelve feet in front of me. It was like staring a rattlesnake in the eye, on his level. I hollered, "Grenade!" and buried my face in the dirt and waited for it to go off. It never did, thank God. Who knows what damage it would have done.

I moved forward. By the time I reached the point where the grenade had been, it had been disposed of. Someone had thrown it back from where it came. By this time, relief had come. We had gotten our pointmen out and we were to fall back. There are no words available to describe this scene. It was panic—pure bedlam. The retreat was anything but orderly. Men got up and ran in a low crouch, dropping magazines full of ammunition and grenades. They kicked these items as they ran. I'm surprised they didn't leave their weapons where they stood. The platoon leader, 2ndLt Thomas Brindley, was screaming for people to pick these items up as they went. Few listened. As the lead men in the platoon came by me, I could see the terror in their faces. This was the first time I had looked into their faces. I followed, finding myself at a plateau about halfway between the top and bottom of the hill. The pointman was delivered to me seconds later. The other platoon corpsman was beside me. We looked into the face of the dead trooper at our knees. We looked at each other and a nonverbal message transmitted between us: there was no doubt in either of our minds that he was dead. We made the attempt to save his life—CPR, mouth-to-mouth, and starting an IV solution of serum albumin, a blood-volume expander. The IV could not be started because there was no blood pressure to expand his veins. There was no pulse and no breathing, but still we tried. His flesh was cold to the touch, his lips were blue, and his eyes were half open and lifeless. There was no one in there. He was dead.

This was the man for whom the first call "Doc, up!" had gone out. Could I have saved him? I don't know; he was shot bad. If I had taken more of a chance with my own life—the ultimate gift of risking my life for his—would he be at home with a family now? How could I have altered time and history? Someday I may know, but for now I can only wonder. I suffered with the burden of that man's death for years. I considered myself cowardly and tried desperately to block it out of my mind. I will never forget. I can see his face as clearly now as I did that day. I was responsible; maybe I even let him down when he depended on me for life. He was dead. Not the first I had seen, but each time the horror of the violence sends every sense reeling. The touch, smell, sight, and taste of war leaves its mark on those who remain. Sometimes I think those who died were the lucky ones.

For the first time in over an hour and a half I had the opportunity to sense what was going on around me. Now that I wasn't so busy trying to stay alive and care for the wounded, I had a wider perspective of what was going on around me. I realized the fog was gone. The sun was shining brightly and the cool, muggy morning had turned into a sweltering furnace.

Capt BILL DABNEY
India Company, 3/26 ⸺⸺⸺⸺⸺⸺⸺⸺⸺⸺⸺⸺⸺⸺⸺

A squad of the 2nd Platoon was assigned to provide security for a medevac landing zone immediately behind the heavily engaged 1st Platoon. As the medevac aircraft [a CH-46 helicopter] approached the zone, it was hit by a burst from an antiaircraft weapon and immediately caught fire. The pilot, apparently realizing the consequences of crash-landing a burning aircraft in a landing zone where several severely wounded men were staged, sheered off into a gully and made a controlled crash about 200 meters west of the zone, close to where the antiaircraft fire had come from. The members of the landing-zone security force immediately and spontaneously, without waiting for orders, rose from their positions and charged down the side of the hill at high port toward the burning aircraft. The suddenness and speed of their rush probably ensured its success and the quick extrication of all Marines from the aircraft before it was engulfed in flame. About five NVA soldiers, who, unknown to the Marines, were between them and the crash site were so surprised by the mad dash that they turned tail and ran off to the west.[3]

HM3 MIKE RAY
India Company, 3/26

We had pulled what the Marines called a retrograde. I called it a retreat. Whatever. We were no longer engaging the enemy. We medevacked our wounded and dead. The platoon leader called for fire support and we got 106mm recoilless fire from our outpost on 881S. The fire continued for fifteen or twenty minutes. During that time, we talked about what had just happened—more like joked, trying to cover the fear we all felt. We believed, with all the fire being leveled on the top of the hill, that there could be nothing left. The fire subsided and we all wondered what was going to happen. We didn't have long to wait before the word came down: "Take the hill and hold it."

Capt BILL DABNEY
India Company, 3/26

[Lieutenant] Brindley, a man who was by nature not inclined to retreat, realized he could not hold his present position without support, and so he directed several barrages of artillery on the [NVA-held] knoll. Moving his Marines into position under cover of the shell fire, he then launched a classic infantry assault and stormed the hill.[4]

HM3 MIKE RAY
India Company, 3/26

My gut turned flip-flops and I became instantly sick. Who was the nut who gave that order? Didn't he know we could be killed?

That was an insane order. Our platoon suffered ten casualties—nine wounded and one dead—from our first contact with the enemy. One of our two M-60 machine guns was out of action, and the remaining one only had 500 rounds of ammunition left. For an M-60, that's nothing. The troops had divided their grenades and ammunition equally. Then the clincher came. Not only were we to capture the hill from the entrenched enemy, we were to do it in a certain manner. We were to form skirmish lines, fix bayonets, and take the hill.

At that very moment the rush of adrenaline was sufficient to make me feel as if hot lead had been poured through my veins. My heart started pounding in my ears, my mouth became dry, and I again became sick to my stomach. I took a drink from my canteen and realized I didn't have a choice; someone else had made the decision for me. The line formed as the troops affixed their bayonets to their weapons. I thought it was stupid enough to go back up there, but to expect hand-to-hand combat—I couldn't imagine it. To get into a fire fight when taken by surprise or ambushed is one thing, but to go in knowing the enemy is probably going to be there to greet you is another.

Nonetheless, the 3rd Platoon moved forward with me to the rear of the skirmish line. I found myself hoping the enemy had gone, had run away, but it was not to be. As we climbed closer to the summit, we started drawing fire. I found myself on a trail, which I left quickly for the cover of the elephant grass. I looked around and quickly found I was alone. My God, what would I do? I was lost! I feared two things the most. One was being killed by a sniper and the second being taken prisoner. That's exactly what ran through my mind at the time—"I'm going to be taken prisoner."

The fight had intensified in its fury, and I could hear the bullets ripple through the elephant grass above my head. For the first time, I drew my weapon and cocked it. I wished my head could turn 360 degrees continuously. I shook with fear, still trying to decide what to do. Finally, with gun in hand, I jumped back to the trail, hoping that from there I would be able to at least see other troopers. Just as I landed firmly on the trail, so did a young Marine. He had been in the elephant grass only a few feet in front of me. We were both relieved to see each other. I reholstered my weapon as we talked about what we should do.

I never carried a bigger weapon than my .45-caliber auto-

matic pistol. I always felt that if the situation dictated that I
become offensive there would be plenty of other weapons lying
around. I found that a long weapon was too cumbersome and
only got in my way while I was doing my job.

The fire fight was very intense by this time. We could hear the
wounded screaming for help, and it seemed as though one lay
only a short distance in front of us. The Marine said, "Let's go
help him, Doc." I replied, "Lead the way. I'll follow." We crawled
forward, following the call for help. We had gone about half the
distance when, out of nowhere, the Marine in front of me was
shot. The bullet entered his upper thigh just below his hip,
traveled along the bone, and exited just above his knee. It whizzed
past my left ear. This stopped us short in our quest, and we
decided that we should remain where we were. I ripped his pants
leg open and checked his wound. It was a neat entrance and exit
wound with little bleeding, so there was not much I could do for
him at the time.

Lost, with no help, battle raging around us, and now a
wounded trooper for me to take care of. The rest of the platoon
must be close, but where? Which way to go? I thought east, then
west. Then I thought the worst thought of all: *Prisoner of war.* A
vision flashed across my mind of what I thought being a prisoner
would be like. I didn't like it, so for lack of direction, we stayed
where we were. Where was the sucker who shot the Marine? Was
he toying with us? Were we in his sight now? Was he squeezing the
trigger this instant? Yet we stayed there, not knowing what to do.
For fear of doing something wrong, we did nothing.

Suddenly, my senses returned to reality and I could hear the
screaming of the wounded. The cry for help rang above the
intensity of the battle. I saw the elephant grass to my left move,
and all my fears were once again manifest in my head. I drew my
weapon and nudged the Marine, pointing in that direction. We
both turned to face the oncoming doom. Once again, my heart
beat like a drum in my ears. My whole body shook. We readied
ourselves, I with the thought of now dying. We raised our
weapons. I took the slack out of the trigger and waited. We didn't
have to wait long. A gun barrel appeared. Then a head. Thank
God, it was a friendly face! He smiled and said, "I came to get you
guys. The platoon is right over here." The tension left my body,
and if I could have, I would have collapsed. I was sick again. My
"savior" turned, and I followed without question. I didn't care

how he knew we were there. Maybe it was just luck, but I didn't want to know. I just followed. With the wounded Marine between us, we moved off through the elephant grass. Just a stone's throw from where we had been, we joined what was left of the platoon. They were in a tight 360-degree defensive position, firing just enough to keep the enemy from pouring over us. We were hurt; we had no momentum left. I only hoped the enemy could not make an offensive move. We would have been eliminated in the twinkling of an eye.

Capt BILL DABNEY
India Company, 3/26

[Lieutenant Brindley] was killed as he reached the crest [of the NVA-held knoll], and with numerous other casualties, the [3rd] platoon found itself holding the piece of high ground with depleted ammunition stocks and . . . a lance corporal in command.

An enemy skirmish line then charged up the rear slope to retake the hill but was annihilated by a napalm drop so close to the Marines that several had their eyebrows singed.[5]

HM3 MIKE RAY
India Company, 3/26

We finally got close air support. I was impressed. Never before had I been in such a position that it was needed. Jets started coming in. They were so close, they almost gave me the impression I could reach out and touch them. I watched plane after plane come in. One pilot turned his head our way, and if his visor hadn't been down, I believe I could have seen his face. Those big bombs came slipping from underneath the planes. They looked like they drifted effortlessly to the ground. Once they made contact, the results would lift us off the ground. The napalm was neat. I enjoyed watching it tumble end over end and then seeing a huge fireball rise high into the air.

Capt BILL DABNEY
India Company, 3/26

The situation, however, was still desperate, and, with Fromme [1st Platoon] holding on the right, I took [2ndLt Michael] Thomas's reserve [2nd] platoon across the intervening gully to relieve the Marines on the knoll and move the wounded back for medevac.[6]

HM3 MIKE RAY
India Company, 3/26 _____

The 2nd Platoon moved up to enlarge our perimeter. The 2nd Platoon leader brought his platoon forward, distributing his men to the north of us. He laid down about six feet in front of me. The cries of our wounded still rang out. The lieutenant turned and said, "I want four volunteers and you, Doc. We're going to get our boys." I thought, "Why me? I didn't volunteer." The lieutenant got up in a low crouch in preparation to move forward, but instantly got back down into a prone position. Then he said, "Okay. We're ready to go." He got up, but fell to the ground. This time he had a bullet wound to the gut and another to the head. He was dead by the time he hit the ground. The clincher is that the bullet that ripped through his guts also sliced through my shoulder and lodged in another Marine's ankle. Three with one shot! Not bad! One dead and two wounded.

I had been lying down with my head across my left shoulder, because the weight of my helmet had been difficult to bear. When the lieutenant had said, "Let's move," I had looked up. The bullet that had gone through his guts whipped past my face. I saw the bullet; not many wounded can boast of that. When it exited his canteen, my perception was that a solid stream of water connected me to the lieutenant. The water spiraled, and so did the bullet. The water spread out as the bullet moved along. It sounded like the first drops of an impending rainstorm. The bullet came so close to my face, I first thought it had smashed through my chin. I heard a loud slap—much like hitting a bare butt with an open hand—as the bullet violated my flesh. I moved back a foot or two in an attempt to get away from what had already happened.

The bullet carried water from the canteen the lieutenant was carrying in the small of his back. The bullet was so close that the water it brought with it from the canteen stung my face. I thought the water was blood. I grabbed my face in terror. I rubbed the liquid between my fingers and looked at it. No blood! I quickly repeated the action. Only this time, the wetness had dried. Still no blood! Even though my face still stung, there was no blood. By then, however, the pain in my face had been replaced by a larger one, the one in my shoulder. As I realized I was not hit in the face, I grabbed my shoulder. Luckily—if you could say anything of that nature is lucky—the wound was minor. The bullet missed my shoulder socket and left my bones intact.

The other platoon corpsman had worked his way around the platoon and found me. He dressed my wound and gave me some words of encouragement, then he moved on to tend other wounded men. Next, the company senior corpsman [HM3 Robert Wickliffe] appeared and told me to gather the wounded and prepare them for evacuation. He also said he would need my help taking them down to the medevac point. We got a couple of Marines to help us with litter patients. There were five of us wounded, plus two other Marines and the company corpsman. We moved down and away from the battle. The company corpsman took the lead and I took the rear. We moved quickly. I had my .45 in hand to protect our rear.

We reached the evac point and a chopper came in. We loaded all the wounded and then the company corpsman turned to me. Yelling to make himself heard above the chopper, he said as he slapped me on the back, "You can go or you can stay. The choice is up to you." I couldn't believe it! I hesitated. I didn't want to run out on my friends. The pilot of the chopper motioned for clearance to leave; he wanted to get out of there. I turned and hopped into the doorway of the chopper, sitting down with my feet and lower legs hanging out the door. The company corpsman smiled at me, gave the pilot the "clear" sign, and, as the chopper lifted off, waved good-bye. That was the last time I saw him. He was killed on 881S. He was a good man; he impressed me with the way he lived and with his ideas. He would have contributed so much to life. I miss him.

Capt BILL DABNEY
India Company, 3/26

Contact began about noon, and by 1500 it was obvious that whatever we found was more than we could handle. The rest of the afternoon was spent evacuating the wounded and dead, recovering the helicopter crew, and breaking contact. The Mike Company headquarters, plus a second Mike Company platoon, was sent to 881S, and the new platoon moved forward to cover our withdrawal.[7]

Sgt FRANK JONES
26th Marines Scout-Sniper Platoon

I spent two days down at the airstrip because we could see the fight in the hills from there. I kept trying to get on a chopper and go out there so I could be with my snipers, but I ended up carrying wounded Marines off the medevac choppers. I couldn't believe the wounds those guys had. They were missing big chunks of their skin, their faces, their legs, their private parts. They were crying and screaming.

26th Marines Command Chronology

> It is estimated that India Company had made contact with an NVA battalion. Results of this day's action were four friendly KIA, 39 WIA (medevacked), and 1 WIA (minor) with 103 NVA KIA (confirmed).

Capt BILL DABNEY
India Company, 3/26

The mission was still to hold 881S, so withdrawal was essential—not that there was much notice, since the prospects of success if we continued north were dim. There were a bunch of those guys up there, and they had come prepared to fight. During and after this scrape, we hosed down 881N and the ground between it and 881S until dark with air, 81mm mortars, 60mm mortars, and all the artillery we could get. For once, we knew where they were. We were not assaulted that night.[8]

Chapter 5

CHIEU HOI

Capt KEN PIPES
Bravo Company, 1/26 _____

Early in the afternoon of January 20, Bravo Company's 2nd Platoon reported the presence of a possible NVA waving a white flag on the northeastern side of the runway. At the same time, an Ontos with a Marine lieutenant acting as safety officer was at that location, preparing to fire on the "range" out toward Hill 1015. I happened to be in the area with my radio operator, walking the lines. With the Ontos on the range covering us, a fire team from the 2nd Platoon, the Ontos officer, and I moved some 500 meters outside the wire. The NVA soldier initially disappeared, so I shouted "Marine *dai-uy* [captain]" several times as we proceeded. The NVA soldier reappeared and surrendered. He was a lieutenant.

GySgt MAX FRIEDLANDER
17th Interrogation-Translation Team _____

We got a call on the radio in my bunker for me to go down to the east end of the runway to pick up a North Vietnamese lieutenant who had just surrendered. I got in my jeep and zoomed down there. I found several Marines holding the man, and they turned him over to me. When I first met him, he seemed very complacent, not a bit scared. It didn't appear to me that I had to worry about him running away. I put him in my jeep and drove him back to the bunker.

When we got to the bunker, the first thing I did was offer him a cigarette and ask him if he was hungry. He said he definitely was, so I got him something to eat. He devoured it very quickly.

He identified himself as Lt La Thanh Tonc, and he seemed to be kind of anxious to start telling me why he had surrendered and a lot of other information. While he was eating, he talked about his family. He was married and had several children. He was very disillusioned, especially with politics. For example, his superiors were telling him things he knew were not true. He obviously didn't believe in the cause he had been fighting for anymore. He had seen too many of his own people being slaughtered. He didn't like the way many officers had treated him. He was disgruntled because he had been passed over for promotion.

I liked the guy. I was sorry for what his family had been going through and what they were going to go through. He had not even been able to get a letter off to them for two years, which was not unusual for the NVA. Before he finished eating, he asked me if I could get a radio music channel from up north. I did, and he thoroughly enjoyed it. It was the first time he had heard music in a long, long time.

After a while, we got into the actual interrogation. At this point, without my having to goad him or lead him, he started telling me what was going to take place that night. My interrogation notes read as follows:

Hill 881N is presently surrounded. There is a company of sappers presently deployed in general area of 881N. This sapper company will be the company used against Hill 861.

Once Hill 861 has fallen, the general attack against the Khe Sanh Combat Base will begin. This will consist of a reinforced regimental-size force from direction of Lang Hoan Tap by way of Hill 861, where they will link up with the occupying force there. Once linked up, Khe Sanh Combat Base will begin receiving heavy artillery fire and rockets from unknown positions, but from northwesterly direction. When this occurs, the first regiment will move to assault positions under cover of fire. One mortar platoon on northeast side of Hill 1015 will cover the Marine heavy weapons on

Hill 950. One mortar platoon will begin 82mm mortar barrage on parked helicopters and airstrip. Each of the mortar platoons has one 12.7mm antiaircraft gun platoon in their adjacent areas to cover them from counter air attack. If the first and second regiments are forced to withdraw, they will link up with the third regiment (position unknown) and commence another attack on Khe Sanh Combat Base. This will occur before Tet.

At this point, I broke the interrogation off. The other ITT man who was in on the interrogation stayed with him while I literally ran down to the regimental combat operations center with this information. Colonel Lownds sent me straight down to Lang Vei by chopper to tell them what the lieutenant had said. Then I came right back. All the other information was sent down to 3rd Marine Division headquarters, at Phu Bai, and General Westmoreland's headquarters, in Saigon. Also, at the same time, alerts were put out to all the units in and around the combat base, out along Highway 9, and in the town of Khe Sanh.

I continued the interrogation when I got back to the ITT bunker. The lieutenant was at ease. Once he saw how it was going to go—once I explained that he was going to be sent to a prisoner-of-war camp and how he would be treated there—he opened up even more. I got a lot of detail about various units that were going to be involved in the attacks on the hills and the base. I also got a lot of information on routes they were using, types and numbers of vehicles—the information I got was just endless.

MGen TOMMY TOMPKINS
3rd Marine Division Commander

Lieutenant Tonc revealed to our interrogator not only the dispositions of the two assault regiments of the 325C Division (the 95th and 101st Regiments), but also the general plan of attack, which was to take place very early the next morning. I decided that we would accept Tonc's information as valid since we had nothing to lose and much to gain.

Capt HARRY BAIG
26th Marines Target Information Officer

The battle plan for Khe Sanh, as revealed by Lieutenant Tonc, had a complementary plan, which was to take effect in the Eastern

DMZ, Cua Viet, Dong Ha, and Quang Tri at the same time and on the same night as the commencement of the overture to Hills 881S and 861. Until that time, I was the 3rd Marine Division Intelligence coordinator for military intelligence agencies in the division tactical area of responsibility. The 15th Marine Counterintelligence Team and U.S. Army intelligence units had established collection nets far across the Ben Hai River [in North Vietnam]. These nets had penetrated several NVA headquarters and other organizations. One of the tasks of the net was to report movements of the 4th Battalion, Van An Rocket Artillery Regiment, and of the Vinh Linh Rocket Battery, together with those of their escorting infantry. These units had caused much damage to the Dong Ha and Cua Viet bases earlier, during the summer and autumn of 1967. On the night of January 19–20, 1968, the rocket units moved south once more. Reported and traced along their route by the agents of the 15th Counterintelligence Team, the batteries and their escort were caught and trapped against a bend in the Cua Viet River. Prisoners taken reported that their mission was to rocket the airstrips at Dong Ha and Quang Tri on the early morning of January 21 to prevent helicopters from flying in support of Hills 881S and 861.[1]

lstLt NICK ROMANETZ
Charlie Company, 1/26 ——————————————————

Right away, word went out for everyone to wear helmets and flak jackets. Not only that, we were ordered to sleep in our fighting positions and stay at 50-percent alert on the lines.

ATTACK ON HILL 861

Cpl DENNIS MANNION
Charlie Battery, 1/13 ——————————————————

On the morning of January 20, I was sitting in my bunker, on the north side of Hill 861, next to a 2,000-pound-bomb crater. We were listening to the artillery requests and jumping the radio frequencies, listening to India Company's fight on Hill 881N. We weren't in any position to help.

Sometime around noontime, someone on the western side of

the hill spotted five or six North Vietnamese soldiers on the top of the ridge 500 yards away from us. They weren't visible for more than a couple of seconds, but Capt Norman Jasper, the Kilo Company commander, asked me if I could fire some artillery at that spot. We fired thirty or forty 105mm rounds from the combat base. We had registered targets over the two previous days, so most of them impacted pretty well right up on that hill.

Captain Jasper wanted to send out a platoon to see if it could find anything as a result of the shelling. As the only artillery forward observer attached to Kilo Company since we had arrived on Hill 861 in very late December, I had been on every single patrol off the hill. I volunteered to go with the Kilo platoon on January 20. I didn't have to go on this one because it was only going 500 yards and would be within sight of the hill the whole way. I was so casual about it that I wore my low black Converse sneakers.

We went out the north gate, crossed over through a deep, wooded ravine, and on up to the ridgeline west of Hill 861. Just as we got up into the area where we could see the impact of the rounds and smell the cordite, we got a call on the radio to come back in. The patrol leader replied that we were right at the spot where the shells had landed and asked permission to drop down over the western side of the ridge, just to see if there were any blood trails or bodies. Captain Jasper personally came up on the radio and told us to come back—immediately, without even taking another look around. So we did. We were back on Hill 861 by 1700 at the latest.

As soon as the patrol was back, I was called with all the platoon commanders and platoon sergeants to a command meeting at Captain Jasper's command-post bunker. The captain told us that we were supposedly going to get attacked that night by a fair-sized number of North Vietnamese soldiers. He told us we would be on 100 percent alert. His concern was with the platoons, but he spoke with me about the targets we had pre-registered with the 105s at Khe Sanh.

During the late afternoon, we registered 175mm guns located nineteen miles away at Camp Carroll. They were programmed and targeted to strike into the area just north of the hill, which is a hell of a shot from nineteen miles out. We had to clear people out of the trenches on the north side of the hill while we were firing the 175s to mark the target.

We settled in to wait. Everybody cleaned their weapons and

we ate our C-rations for dinner. Eventually, it got dark. It wasn't a real clear night, but it wasn't the worst fog we had seen up there. It was very dark.

Pfc ELWIN BACON
Kilo Company, 3/26

January 20 was just another normal day—routine military life on a godforsaken hill. Nothing unusual was happening, but there were lots of rumors going around the hill that there was an NVA buildup in the area and that we could expect trouble. Everyone took it for granted that the CO would keep us on our toes.

It got extremely foggy that night. There was no visibility. I couldn't see outside my foxhole. I had to focus my ears for the perimeter watch, not my eyes. Hopefully, if anyone was out there, he would set off a tripflare.

Cpl DENNIS MANNION
Charlie Battery, 1/13

At about 2030, after it got really dark, word came up from one of the platoons that they could hear the North Vietnamese outside the wire, down in the ravine off the northwest corner of the hilltop. That was the only place we couldn't put artillery. It was obviously the place they were going to attack from.

I made four or five trips with my radioman, from my bunker through the trenchline, to the 3rd Platoon command post. From there I could hear the NVA outside the wire. They were talking and giving commands. I could hear the wire being cut, could hear the tinny sound when the wire sprang back in both directions. We threw grenades and popped flares, but we never fired a shot. Captain Jasper had specifically ordered us not to because he didn't want us giving away our positions. The North Vietnamese took it—with laughter and an occasional scream. They kept right on cutting. It was almost as if they were out there on a high school field day.

Sgt MIKE STAHL
4.2-inch Mortar Battery, 1/13

We had been running 100-percent alerts for quite a while. We'd all get out of our hooches, man the lines, wait until it was called off, and go back to our hooches. The night of January 20 was just like that. We had received a 100-percent-alert order from Regiment that, unknown to me at that time, was based largely on the information obtained from the North Vietnamese lieutenant who had surrendered that afternoon.

We went down and got into the trenches. Then, around 2300, the alert was secured and we went back to our hooches.

Pfc ELWIN BACON
Kilo Company, 3/26

We—the 2nd Platoon—started hearing noises on a ridge to the west of us. We had patrolled it on January 19. Now it was swarming with gooks, and they were not being all that quiet about it. Between us and the ridge was a steep-sided ravine. We didn't understand what was going on.

It started by sounding like a party. They were making noises with pans and blowing horns. They were also calling at us with warnings of "Death tonight." Some of them had had an English lesson or two in the Bronx, I think. We were right in among the clouds, so the visibility was bad and I was about ready to shit my trousers.

Cpl DENNIS MANNION
Charlie Battery, 1/13

I was back in my bunker a little before midnight when Captain Jasper called on the land line to tell me that someone at the southern end of the hill had spotted some North Vietnamese near the landing zone. He wanted me to go down there in case artillery was needed. I grabbed my rifle on the way out the door, but my radioman, Pfc Dave Kron, took only his .45-caliber pistol and our radio.

Dave and I crossed over the top of the hill, heading south, and made our way across the landing zone to find the platoon commander in charge of that sector of the hill. He told us that whoever had been out there had not been seen since the original sighting, that they had been seen only momentarily in the light of a flare when the fog lifted.

We were about to use the platoon radio to call back up to the company command-post bunker, to see what they wanted us to do, when, at that very moment, everything started up.

HM3 Malcolmb Mole was an all-around decent guy. He wasn't the biggest guy around, but he did his job on all the patrols I was ever on with him. He wanted to be a radio deejay when he got out of the Navy. He was always going around practicing his deejay voice and using radio sayings.

Just before Dave and I were ordered south to the landing zone, Malcolmb had come up from the 3rd Platoon trenchline to use the fairly elaborate shitter that was just to the right of our bunker. Dave and I had seen him come out of the mist, and we had tensed. But he had identified himself with that radio deejay voice, and we had laughed out loud at that. We spoke for a few minutes, and then Captain Jasper called.

Apparently the NVA opened up as Malcolmb was walking back down to the northern trenchline after using the shitter. He was caught out in the clear. There wasn't much left to identify him.

Sgt MIKE STAHL
4.2-inch Mortar Battery, 1/13

At about 2300, word came around to go on 100-percent alert again. I woke up again, put on my gear, and went back down to the trenchline held by Kilo Company's 2nd Platoon. This was the trenchline nearest the 4.2-inch mortars. I went there because, as the 4.2-inch platoon sergeant, I was useless when the crews were running their guns. When I got there, one of the new guys asked me, "Gee, Sarge, do you think we're really going to get it tonight?" Months earlier, I had worked with the Special Forces out around Lang Vei and I knew what we had out there; I knew it would be impossible to mass a meaningful assault on Khe Sanh without someone in Saigon knowing all about it. So, being the sage war veteran I had become, I told him, "There isn't a North Vietnamese within a hundred miles of here." Just as I said that, the first RPG slammed into the hill.

Pfc ELWIN BACON
Kilo Company, 3/26

As the assault started, the first thing I knew was that the top of the hill was being completely saturated with mortars and RPGs. I could hear rounds from the NVA .51-caliber machine guns on the next ridge pounding into the hill. They had at least three .51-calibers over there.

Sgt MIKE STAHL
4.2-inch Mortar Battery, 1/13

I went down the trenchline to find the 2nd Platoon commander, 2ndLt Benjamin Fordham. By the time I found him, 2nd Platoon had already begun taking casualties from the incoming. Almost immediately, I saw green tracer and heard the distinctive sound of AK-47s. We fought back, but it wasn't easy. The rolling fog was extremely thick, which obscured the North Vietnamese attacking up the slope toward us. Also, there was a lot of growth in front of us, and we had not effectively covered the dead space with indirect-fire weapons. We couldn't see them until they got to within fifteen or twenty meters of the trenchline. We fired into the fog, mainly at muzzle flashes and the sources of the green tracer.

Pfc ELWIN BACON
Kilo Company, 3/26

The NVA were coming through their own storm of fire. I'm sure that better than half the casualties they were sustaining were due to their own supporting fire. It was obvious to me that they were drugged up. Some were not fully equipped with weapons; they were picking them up from the dead. They were coming through the wire and running around from one hole to another, trying to find places to hide, to jump out of. There was a tremendous amount of noise, a tremendous amount of firepower being directed against the hill.

Sgt MIKE STAHL
4.2-inch Mortar Battery, 1/13

They penetrated several concertina barriers and evaded fougasse traps, neither of which was very effective. They had apparently reconned the hill very effectively, leaving behind bamboo stakes they later set their RPGs and other weapons on so they could hit our key positions and crew-served weapons. Fairly quickly, they took out the company command post, both of the 106mm recoilless rifles, and, eventually, the 81mm mortar positions at the top of the hill.

Cpl DENNIS MANNION
Charlie Battery, I/I3 _____

As soon as the RPGs and mortars started hitting the hill, my radioman, Pfc Dave Kron, and I headed back over the top of the hill, on our way from the landing zone to the northwest corner, where the attack was coming in. When we reached the Kilo Company command post, we found GySgt Melvin Rimel dead on the ground right outside. It was too dangerous to look for Captain Jasper or the first sergeant; rounds were hitting and bullets were going by overhead. Dave and I went right back down the hill, heading south, and then veered off toward the west side of the hill, toward the 2nd Platoon area.

When we got to the trenchline, without checking in with anybody, I started calling in target numbers for the ridgeline 500 yards to the west, the one we had hit with artillery and briefly scouted during the day. I pulled the rounds as close as I could get them to the northwest corner.

Communication by radio was extremely difficult because someone out there in the jungle was keying a radio handset, breaking up our voice transmissions and causing background noise over the open mike to interfere with conversation. For all that, the guns in the combat base were extremely good about putting in rounds. I couldn't necessarily see where they were going in, but I could hear them.

Sgt MIKE STAHL
4.2-inch Mortar Battery, I/I3 _____

Within ten or fifteen minutes, word began to spread from our right, from the 3rd Platoon area, that North Vietnamese were in the wire. Their sappers had gotten up close by using the dead space in front of the 3rd Platoon trenchline.

Cpl DENNIS MANNION
Charlie Battery, I/I3 _____

As I called artillery fire from the combat base, Pfc Dave Kron and I moved up the trenchline, northward, toward the northwest corner. Then, suddenly, there wasn't anybody there. The last Marine we encountered told us, "I don't think there's anybody to my right. I haven't heard anybody up there in a long time, and nobody's come down from that direction." Dave and I continued up the trench until we got to a machine-gun bunker. There was only one guy in the bunker, and he was firing periodically. As we approached the bunker—the entrance was in the back, right in from the trenchline—we yelled that we were coming. The gunner knew my name. As we got inside the bunker entrance, I said to the gunner, "Where's your team?" He said, "They're gone. I don't know where they are." I asked, "What happened to them?" and he said, "I think they ran."

I asked him if he was firing at people he could see, but he said, "No, I'm just reconning by fire." He told me that there were plenty of North Vietnamese around. I asked him how he knew, and he told me there were grenade holes right by the entrance. I shined my red-lensed flashlight to see them. Sure enough! He told me that the North Vietnamese who had thrown one of the grenades was out in the trenchline, that he had been hit by his own blast. As Dave helped the gunner break out a fresh can of ammunition, I shined my light out real quick and saw a North Vietnamese soldier lying on the ground in the trenchline. I could hear him groaning.

The North Vietnamese soldier in the trenchline presented a problem. We had to get farther up the trenchline if we were to gain any real sense of where our rounds were landing. I took Dave's .45, knelt in the doorway, and reached out with my left hand until I touched the man's head. As soon as my hand made contact with the top of his head, he raised his head up. I put the .45 underneath my left hand, took my left hand away, and pulled the trigger four or five times. When Dave and I moved out from the bunker, we had to step right on the dead North Vietnamese to get by him.

We only went another fifteen or twenty feet before we had to stop. There was small-arms fire back down the trench. There were no Marines, dead or alive, in the trenchline between the machine-gun bunker and where we stopped. Dave and I hugged the inside wall of the trench, but we couldn't go any farther because of the gunfire. We continued talking with the fire direction center down at the combat base—we had been in constant communication from the very start of the action.

Our position was tenuous. The lead wasn't flying in every direction, but we couldn't go any farther. As I continued to direct the artillery fire, an RPG struck the front of the machine-gun bunker and killed the gunner whose teammates had run out on him. Dave and I pulled back most of the way to the bunker and climbed into two fighting holes we found dug into the side of the trench. We directed fire missions from there for the rest of the night.

Sgt MIKE STAHL
4.2-inch Mortar Battery, 1/13

All of a sudden, the 2nd Platoon began taking fire from the rear, so I maneuvered up to a .50-caliber machine-gun position which was just above the 4.2-inch mortar position. The NVA had already wiped that position out, killing the gunner and his assistant. I moved another Marine in there to man the gun and went back down to tell Lieutenant Fordham that they were in behind us, that he should shift some of his people to protect the rear.

While I had been up the hill, at the .50-cal position, I had noticed that I had not heard a lot of firing coming from the 3rd Platoon position. I brought that to the lieutenant's attention, and he said, "Well, we're going to have to send someone over there to check on the 3rd Platoon." I said, "Yeah, that's a good idea. I recommend that you do that." And he said, "Sergeant, I don't have anyone to spare. Guess what!" And I said, "Okay, no problem. I'll do it."

As I started maneuvering up the trenchline, a couple of guys asked me where I was going, and then they followed along. The only one I knew was LCpl Dennis Mutz.

As we maneuvered up, there was a tremendous volume of fire from our front, from four or five North Vietnamese who were in the trenchline, advancing toward us from the 3rd Platoon sector. The fog was very thick there, and they didn't see us until about the time we saw them. There was a furious fight. I emptied one magazine, popped it, threw another magazine in, and went through that, too. I killed the first guy. The second guy killed the Marine right behind me. I took a round in back of my left hand as I was dropping the next NVA. The next NVA hit Mutz, but not badly, and Mutz killed him. It was just a frenzy of firing from very close range.

Next thing I knew, I was face-to-face with a North Vietnamese. I had run through my second magazine. I had no bullets left in my M-16. He had me. He fired, but nothing happened. In that instant, I cringed and tightened up. Quicker than I could react, he bayoneted me in the right chest. Then Mutz shot him. The point of the bayonet punctured me and ripped downward. It didn't penetrate very far, but it broke a rib and left a gash. Not bad. The bayonet damaged my M-16, so I grabbed one of the dead NVAs' AK-47s and a magazine pouch.

Mutz and I continued up the trenchline. The volume of firing around us was incredible. At one point, Mutz said, "Fuck this. I'm not going any farther." It was not the sort of thing you ordered someone to do, so I left him there and continued to work up the trenchline alone. I didn't blame Mutz at all.

I eventually ran into the first 3rd Platoon bunker, which was firing at me. We had built the bunkers across the trenchline. They had apertures on both sides and the front, but none in the back. To get into a bunker from the trenchline, you had to duck your head, get on all fours, and crawl inside.

I tried to throw a grenade in through the aperture on my side of the bunker, but it didn't go in. It rolled back and blew up, and I caught some shrapnel. The explosion knocked back the NVA inside the bunker, and they quit firing. I managed to roll up next to the bunker and drop another grenade in. That killed several NVA.

About this time, there was a big explosion on top of the hill, to my right front. It was either the 106mm or 81mm ammunition. A lot of AK-47s were firing to my right, well inside our perimeter. It wasn't impacting around me, so I tried to continue up the trenchline toward the next 3rd Platoon bunker. I was looking for 3rd Platoon Marines to link up with, but I couldn't find any. In the next bunker were more North Vietnamese. I took it out with a hand grenade and then sprayed it through the aperture with my AK-47.

As I moved on the third bunker, firing into it from a distance, I heard someone yell something that sounded like *"Chieu hoi!"* I stopped firing and yelled back, "Come on out, motherfucker!" And they did; the three North Vietnamese in there surrendered. I guess they must have seen me take out the second bunker, and I'm sure they thought there were more of us than me. When they came out, two had their hands up, but the third was an arrogant, defiant type of guy. When I motioned them back down the trenchline with my AK-47, the last one tried to grab my weapon. I broke his jaw with the AK's butt, which took the fight out of him. I herded the three down to where I had left Lance Corporal Mutz, and I told Mutz to take them back to Lieutenant Fordham.

I went back up the trenchline because I still hadn't made contact with anyone from the 3rd Platoon. While I was gone, no one had occupied the three bunkers I had retaken, and the fourth bunker was empty. I found Marines in the fifth bunker. The gap in the line had to be seventy-five meters, so I went back to tell Lieutenant Fordham that he needed to shift troops into the gap. I led them back up, placed them in the bunkers, and left them.

Pfc ELWIN BACON
Kilo Company, 3/26 _____

The word got passed down the line that every other man was to go over and support the other side of the hill, where the main assault was getting through. The hill was just a mess of people. I couldn't tell who was next to me, who was friend, who was foe. There was no way to count off every other man. It was mass hysteria.

I got the feeling that we were by ourselves, that there weren't going to be any supporting elements coming to help us out. We couldn't get any direct fire support from Khe Sanh that night. I think it was because we were so close to the enemy. They must have thought they would blow us up, too. The only thing we got was some illumination, which, mixed in with the NVA illumination, gave us some shadowy indication as to who was coming up the hill or down the hill. The hill was just a mass of people fighting, some hand-to-hand. Total chaos and fear filled everyone who was on that hill. Because of the heavy fog that mixed with the darkness, we had little chance to focus on who or what was coming toward us.

Capt BILL DABNEY
India Company, 3/26 (Hill 881S) _____

When Hill 861 was assaulted from the northwest on the night of January 20–21, the NVA attacked up a slope that was not within high-angle range of the Khe Sanh Combat Base artillery, and was masked by the hill itself from any other Khe Sanh supporting fires. Our two 81mm mortars fired several hundred rounds on that slope, well-controlled by the Kilo Company command post on 861.[2]

LCpl WALT WHITESIDES
3/26 Tactical Air Control Party (Hill 881S) _____

All the troops on Hill 881S were put on alert, and we went out to the trenchline. The 81mm and 60mm mortars were firing in support of Kilo Company, on Hill 861. The mortar tubes became so hot that the gunners poured water and fruit juice on them to cool them off. When the NVA fired illumination rounds to guide the attack, we also fired some. This was intended as a deceptive measure in case they were using the illume rounds to orient themselves. This probably just provided them with additional light, since they probably knew their attack positions very well. Everyone was apprehensive as to what was going on, and we were all wondering when *we* were going to be attacked.

Pfc ELWIN BACON
Kilo Company, 3/26 _____

I was scared shitless, totally in fear. I wasn't quite paralyzed—I did what I was told to do—but I had no idea what to expect, what was going to come down the ridge at me. My mind was blank; I was totally caught up in trying to survive. The hill was totally out of control. Sometime during the night, teargas was set off. On the 3rd Platoon side of the hill, we had a box type arrangement that was full of CS canisters that could be shot out in all directions. I assume it was tripped. Maybe the NVA set it off. I don't remember anybody wearing a gas mask. I was so psyched up in the fight that the gas didn't affect me at all.

Sgt MIKE STAHL
4.2-inch Mortar Battery, 1/13 _____

After dropping off the 2nd Platoon Marines in the four unoccupied 3rd Platoon bunkers, I went up the side of the hill to a silent

.50-caliber machine-gun position. The Marines in the position were dead, so I started firing the machine gun in front of the 3rd Platoon bunkers that I had retaken. That was where most of the North Vietnamese were. As soon as I opened fire, they threw every goddamned weapon they could in against me. I got a shitload of RPGs and .51-cal, and I think I was even taking some mortar fire. It was a real pain in the butt because I didn't know how to fire a .50-cal real well; no one had ever explained the nuances of headspace and timing to me. I expected to be really working out with the machine gun, but I'd get off only two or three rounds before I had to recock it. I was taking so much fire myself that the position caved in around me and I had to keep repositioning the gun, lower and lower. I got hit a few more times with pieces of shrapnel, but nothing really major. It went on like that until the firing let up, hours later.

Sgt Mike Stahl was awarded a Navy Cross for his role in stopping the NVA attack on Hill 861.

Cpl DENNIS MANNION
Charlie Battery, 1/13 ⎯⎯⎯⎯⎯⎯⎯⎯⎯⎯⎯⎯⎯⎯⎯⎯⎯

I fired as many rounds as the 105s at the combat base could give us. At the same time, the 175mm guns at Camp Carroll were dropping some seriously big stuff down into the ravine, as close as they could get it. But the way the guns were lined up with the hill, there was no way they could get rounds right down into the dead space the North Vietnamese were using to get in up through our wire. They tried, but they couldn't do it. I know that there were at least five or six 105mm rounds that hit the southeast side of Hill 861. They were fired by the guns in the base, which were trying to skim the rounds right over the top of the hill.

Pfc ELWIN BACON
Kilo Company, 3/26 ⎯⎯⎯⎯⎯⎯⎯⎯⎯⎯⎯⎯⎯⎯⎯⎯⎯⎯

The first sign of it letting up was daylight. We were able to make out silhouettes, but the fog was still so thick that we couldn't really see much. The NVA withdrew, but some of them got caught and were unable to get outside the wire.

We found NVA bodies all the way up to the command-post

area. It was just saturated with bodies. There were dead bodies everywhere I looked. Many of them had towels over their faces or plastic bags over their heads—instead of gas masks.

Sgt MIKE STAHL
4.2-inch Mortar Battery, 1/13

When the sun came up, we began to police the hill. We took their dead down to a flat place and burned them to keep the rats off them. We got our badly wounded down to the landing zone and called in medevacs, but they couldn't get in because of the thick fog, which just didn't burn off.

We were hurt very badly, and about out of ammunition. If they had tried one last assault, they'd have had us. I was down to a .45-caliber magazine for my pistol, less than a magazine for my AK-47, just about bingo on my last can of .50-cal, and I had two grenades left. No one could have been much better off.

We had a lot of wounded, and our leadership was gone; the company gunny had been killed early in the battle, the first sergeant was holding the ends of his severed carotid artery together to keep from bleeding to death, the company commander had been very badly wounded, maybe more than once, and the company radioman, who remained at his post, had been blinded by powder burns from a bursting grenade. The Marine survivors were physically and mentally drained. Fortunately, so were the NVA survivors. We wound up punching ineffectually at one another, like punch-drunk fighters who were unable to muster a last blow or give up. Anytime they wanted to get back on line and take us, they could have.

Pfc ELWIN BACON
Kilo Company, 3/26

I was asked to guard one of the prisoners, of which there were only two. They did have three, but one tried to crawl away and was dispensed with. My prisoner was covered with a poncho, and the only thing that was showing was his wounded leg. Someone told me that he was only thirteen years of age while the other one, who they had on the landing zone, was sixteen years old. I was told that the older was an officer and the younger was some sort of noncommissioned officer.

Even though I was very emotional after the night's activities, I offered this guy a cigarette, but he motioned refusal by spitting at me. Boy, did I go through cigarettes that day!

Sgt MIKE STAHL
4.2-inch Mortar Battery, 1/13 _____

There were still NVA between the two outermost wire barriers. The Marines didn't have the strength to go out and get them, and they didn't have the strength to come in and get us—or, apparently, withdraw. It was a stalemate.

Kilo Company eventually received some replacements and was reinforced by a platoon from Alpha Company, 1/26. More important, the adjacent hill, dubbed 861A, was occupied on January 23 by Echo Company, 2/26, which was transferred to the operational control of 3/26.

CHAPTER 6

JANUARY 21
ARTILLERY ATTACK

2ndLt SKIP WELLS
Charlie Company, 1/26 _____

On January 20, Charlie Company had been moved from the
battalion reserve and assigned the northern part of the perimeter,
north of the airstrip and opposite the water point. My 3rd Platoon
had the center, 1st Platoon was on the left (west), and 2nd Platoon
was on the right (east). We had responsibility for the east end of
the airstrip; 2nd Platoon's lines extended just south of it and tied
in with Bravo Company.

When we got to the position, all the bunkers were entirely
above ground, there was no continuous trenchline, and in places
the existing trenchline was only about waist-deep. There was one
line of triple concertina, and the elephant grass came right to the
trenchline in spots. I think the main reason our position was so
poor was because it was on the north side and was not a very likely
spot for the NVA to attack; there wasn't enough room—800
meters—between the gorge and the perimeter. That's a poor
reason for being unprepared, but I think that's what happened.

Once we were assigned our sector, I further assigned the
squads. We did it by the book: I put out the listening post (the
company command post monitored it), set up both M-60s, and

began digging the trench. But it was much too late, so my platoon began the night mostly aboveground. We did no work on the bunkers. We worked until about midnight, and then went to 50-percent alert until about 0300. We were still working when the first rounds came in.

Cpl WILLIAM HUBBARD
Echo Company, 2/26 _____

January 20 was the day I was supposed to go home, but I didn't make it out. A whole planeload of boots showed up and they sent me and six or seven other short-timers down to the runway to pick them up. We got them all unloaded and then had to get them to set up tents. There were all kinds of Marines there—gunnery sergeants, lieutenants, guys just out of boot camp—and none of them knew up from down about being in Vietnam. We always said if they didn't have any time in-country, they didn't count, so we put a bunch to work digging trenches, burning shitters, setting up tents, carrying seabags in. It didn't matter if they were privates or officers, we ordered them around. It was up to the short-timers to help the new guys learn the ropes. *We* had the only rank that mattered—experience.

About ten of us—the guys who had been there a long time and a few new gunnery sergeants—slept in the company first sergeant's tent that night. We knew we were going down to the helo pad the next morning to catch a chopper out to Phu Bai and Danang so we could head back to The World. We knew there was a lot of activity around the base; we could see it in the hills that evening. But, mostly, our minds were on going back to the States.

About 0400, I bummed a cigarette off a friend of mine, Corporal Houska, from Hotel Company. He asked me if I knew what that morning was, and I said, "I sure do. We're next."

At just about the crack of dawn, all the guys in the first sergeant's tent got up. I started feeling sorry for the new guys in the next tent. I had been through it all, was getting out in one piece, but they had it all ahead of them. Lots of them were going to get hurt or killed.

I was thinking about that when I heard a rocket. It sounded just like a roman candle going off. Everybody in my tent reacted. I threw the tent flap back and yelled for all the boots to get their asses out. "Get in them holes!" At about the time I finished yelling,

I remembered I had left my rifle on the deck in the tent. Cardinal sin. As I turned around, about seventy-five of those boots ran right up over me and right into the trench. I got up cussin' and heard more rockets. Scared me! Half the Marines in the trench were out there without their rifles, and most of them didn't have their boots on. We had some boys there that were pretty salty, and they took care of the boots pretty quick; sent them back in to get their rifles, helmets, flak jackets, and boots.

Sgt FRANK JONES
26th Marines Scout-Sniper Platoon

The Sniper Platoon was assigned to provide security for the North Vietnamese lieutenant. I was given the swing shift, 1600 to 2400. After the assignments were made, a bunch of us were drinking some home brew with dehydrated orange juice when Sgt Terence Smith came up and asked me if I would trade shifts with him. He had been assigned the graveyard shift, from midnight to 0800, but he wasn't feeling well. I told him I'd be more than happy to do that for him.

Nothing happened during my original shift. I got up at midnight and went down to relieve Sergeant Smith. All I took was my .357 handgun—no cartridge belt, no rifle. The lieutenant was at the communications center, in an eight-foot-thick concrete bunker. To get in, I had to go through an eight-foot tunnel almost on my hands and knees. I told Sergeant Smith to go on and sleep in my rack. I had some ammo boxes laid out, a rubber air mattress blown up, and my poncho liner and mosquito net hung up.

The lieutenant was young—twenty-five or twenty-six years old—about five-nine or five-ten, and weighed about 150. He had on a khaki uniform. I heard he had advised us that we were being surrounded by several North Vietnamese divisions, and that they were well supplied with mortars, artillery, and rockets—that they could hit us with several hundred rounds of artillery and rocket fire a day until summer came. He had said they were going to overrun us and annihilate us, the way they did the French at Dienbienphu. I thought about how stupid it sounded. I had no opinion. I had been drinking, and I didn't really want to hear it at that time.

Sometime after 0500, January 21, he had to go to the bathroom. He was handcuffed to my partner and me, and we escorted him outside the bunker to one of the piss tubes. We thought nothing of it. As we were walking back, he stopped. The next thing I saw was what appeared to be gigantic orange beach balls—five or six of them—bounce in front of me, about fifty or sixty yards away. It was incoming rockets or artillery rounds exploding. I hadn't even heard them coming in.

They started getting closer. I was terrified. The rounds were hitting all around us. It seemed like the whole Earth had exploded. I wasn't hit, and neither was my partner, but we were so scared that we lay down next to the bunker with the NVA lieutenant handcuffed to us. There was an empty cardboard box that a case of Cokes had come in. I took the box and covered up with it. Finally, I scrambled to my feet, got my partner and the lieutenant, and scrambled back inside the bunker.

LtCol JIM WILKINSON
1/26 Commanding Officer _____

I was ready for it. As soon as the first rounds landed, I jumped off my cot, got on my helmet and flak vest, and raced from my living bunker over to the command post. By then, the mortars were really starting to fall in. I took a dive and slid in down the staircase.

Lt RAY STUBBE
1/26 Battalion Chaplain _____

[DIARY ENTRY] Woke up to the sounds of rockets whizzing and loud blasts! We were under rocket and mortar attack. Rockets and mortars were going off all over. Got dressed slowly, stunned, cautiously. I knew my bunker would protect me from flying shrapnel and perhaps a direct hit by a 60mm or 82mm mortar, but not by a 122mm rocket. I was all alone, so I knew I had to run to the Charlie-Med bunker. The whole area was lit up. The [supply dump] was on fire to the east, with the smell of burning sandbags and the tar drums, and gasoline from the [fuel] area was on fire to the west. Red flares lit up the sky all over, and there was a lot of whizzing, cracking, and exploding. They came in quite rapidly; there were brief pauses, a couple of seconds. I cautiously went to the door, wondering if I dared run the seventy or so feet to the Charlie-Med bunker. A round would come whizzing in and

exploded nearby. This went on for about fifteen minutes. I knew
that one must never run in an attack, but that it is much safer just
to lie flat on the ground. Finally, I just ran the short distance to
the trench bunker of Charlie-Med.

Cpl WILLIAM ROBERTSON
Logistics Support Unit

When I got to Khe Sanh in July 1967, the base Ammunition
Supply Point [ASP] was sitting on top of the ground. We were on
the edge of the perimeter. On two sides of us there was nothing,
on one side was a 105mm artillery battery, and back on the other
side was where the motor pool people stayed. We went through a
long quiet period, but we more or less knew it was only a matter
of time before we were going to get hit. The ammo dump was
volatile. Through pestering Colonel Lownds, we were finally able
to come up with a bulldozer. During the process of digging berms,
we got down deep enough and built up some protection around
what we had to leave on top of the ground. But the berms were
still only about fifty feet apart. This was not very safe due to the
amount of ammo we had there. We were trying to get another
location so we could spread the ammo out. When our staff
sergeant left in December, I was in charge.

When the rockets or artillery—whatever it was—came in, one
struck within probably thirty feet of my bunker. It hit one of the
motor pool sandbag bunkers, right at the edge. It knocked the
sandbags out. A rather large tree was in the center of the bunker,
holding up the steel stakes that were holding the sandbags and the
roof. The end of the tree fell down and crushed one of the men
who was sleeping in a cot. There was enough concussion to shake
me out of my cot.

We grabbed our clothes and headed out. By this time, quite
a few rounds had come in. The ASP was on fire. There was very
little we could even attempt to do. The only things we had to fight
fire with were two shovels and about twenty 55-gallon metal
drums full of water that were sitting around through the dump.
We had buckets sitting beside those. Once an illumination magazine caught, buckets of water and shovels of dirt couldn't do
anything. We just had to make everybody get out and get back to
the bunker.

LCpl DAN ANSLINGER
3rd Marine Division Air Section _____

I had been dumped at Khe Sanh on January 20 while "playing hooky" from my unit, which was at Dong Ha. I was aboard a helicopter that landed at the combat base as all hell was breaking loose in the hills. The chopper crew kicked the load off—including me—and left to fly some emergency mission. I was technically absent without leave.

I found my way to the fire support coordination center because I knew some guys working there. It was also one of the few decent-looking bunkers in the combat base.

On the morning of January 21, the fire support coordination center was crowded with people coming and going. Everyone seemed tense, calm, and cocky at the same time.

Right after the heavy incoming started, the dump blew up with the most godawful explosion I had ever experienced (including when the Dong Ha dump blew the previous September). The concussion knocked me around inside the bunker, and I thought that no one near the dump could have survived. I was surprised when I later learned how few people were killed.

1stLt NICK ROMANETZ
Charlie Company, 1/26 _____

We were on Red Alert because the NVA lieutenant had indicated that something was going to happen. We were sleeping with our helmets and gear. Unfortunately, some of the early rounds hit the ammo dump, which we were close to. The ammo dump started blowing up and it was just raining mortar rounds, artillery rounds, smoke grenades, and gas grenades all over our sector. We were really concerned that some of those rounds, which were hot, could have been very sensitive. We tried to locate them and get them out of our trench or wait until the Explosive Ordnance Disposal people came to remove them. Suddenly, a lot of people were thinking, Geez, this is what it's all about.

There was a lot of C4 plastic explosive stored near us. It took a round and started to burn. It sounded like a lightning bolt that cracks through the air and strikes the ground close to you.

2ndLt DONALD McGUIRE
Explosive Ordnance Disposal _____

Several rounds landed in Ammunition Supply Point No. 1, initiating secondary fires and detonations that continued for approximately forty-eight hours and resulted in total destruction of the ASP. Unexploded and hazardous ordnance was thrown to an approximate 2,000-foot radius in all directions from the ASP, contaminating the airstrip, the 26th Marines regimental command post, living areas and quarters, artillery and mortar positions, and the eastern defense perimeter.

LtCol JIM WILKINSON
1/26 Commanding Officer _____

The shock wave from the ammo-dump explosion cracked the timbers holding up the roof of the 1/26 command post. As the roof settled, several members of my staff were knocked to the floor. The battalion adjutant was injured but continued to function effectively. For a moment, I thought that the entire roof of my command post was going to collapse, but after it settled about a foot, the cracked timbers held. We quickly made jury-rig repairs and the command post was not affected.[1]

MGySgt JOHN DRIVER
Explosive Ordnance Disposal _____

The dump held about a dozen 55-gallon drums of CS teargas crystals. These were broken open and their contents were scattered throughout the dump.

LtCol JIM WILKINSON
1/26 Commanding Officer _____

We had been alerted to the possible use of gas, so I had ordered all the troops in 1/26 to be carrying gas masks. We were ready.

Cpl WILLIAM ROBERTSON
Logistics Support Unit _____

We had one person in the bunker who didn't have a gas mask, and we didn't have any for anyone except for the guys who lived there. We had to sit on him and hold him so we could put towels and water on his face. He wanted to go back out and attempt to find a gas mask. This would have been certain death, as close as we were to the ammo dump and as much stuff as there was flying around.

Lt RAY STUBBE
1/26 Battalion Chaplain

[DIARY ENTRY] All of a sudden, someone yelled, "Gas!" It was CS. Not everyone [in Charlie-Med] had a mask, so they used wet blankets over their faces. I put on my mask and immediately felt claustrophobic, but I knew I had to have it on, so I fought a tremendous battle in my mind and kept it on.

Cpl DENNIS SMITH
Bravo Company, 1/26

Teargas was being blown back and forth around the base by the breeze. I would say that about half the people at Khe Sanh had gas masks, and that only about half of them were serviceable. But that was all inconvenience. Rockets were another matter.

1stLt NICK ROMANETZ
Charlie Company, 1/26

We had to don our gas masks and man the lines. We kept looking out into the fog to see what was going on.

≋

Lt RAY STUBBE
1/26 Battalion Chaplain

[DIARY ENTRY] Practically everyone [in Charlie-Med] had to piss very badly, but no one would go out. We just held it in. Rounds kept falling and exploding. Flashes of light. A round landed near the triage tent.

They started bringing in casualties. One man, conscious and eyes and head moving about, had all his abdominal guts hanging out. The doctor later told me that the man would die. I was numb; I didn't even go over to comfort him.

HMC FRANK LILES
Base Preventive Medicine Chief _____

So there we were, getting shelled from outside and inside. During this time, several people were wounded and needed to be brought to the medical station, Charlie-Med. Marines and medical personnel alike were busy getting the wounded into the aid station to administer emergency treatment. There were several wounded Marines on stretchers and under treatment when an explosion rocked the top of the aid station and a shell came flying through and into the medical supplies. It was spewing dangerous white-phosphorus smoke. Here's where I got to be a John Wayne hero. I have no idea why I chose to get that shell out of the way. I mixed copper sulfate with intravenous solution in a couple of old towels, wrapped it around the shell, and ran it outside. On the way, the fire was still spewing and was burning my face and arms, and the smoke and fumes were searing the inside of my chest. I couldn't wait to get rid of that hot prick of a shell. Just as I got down into the mud ditch alongside the sickbay, the damned thing went haywire and began getting hotter and spewing more. I couldn't do anything more with it because they were bringing a wounded Marine through the bunker door at the same time, so I climbed that sucker with a flak jacket and field jacket until they got that young man by. This was just a matter of five or ten seconds, but it was enough to burn my face and cause a hell of a lot of respiratory distress.

I made it back into the aid station and went back to my room. To really make my day, those little fuckers had scored a direct hit on my room, getting my new tape deck. I was pissed, pissed, pissed. Next thing I remember was waking up in Danang hospital.

1stLt JOHN KAHENY
1/26 Combat Operations Center _____

I went to the battalion commander's living bunker—which served at the time as our alternate command post—with the operations chief, the battalion sergeant major, and a few other Marines. As we sat out the initial volleys, we had a young lance corporal out front guarding the door. Every once in a while, one of us went outside to see if he was okay since he had just a small hole with no overhead cover for protection. My turn to check the lance corporal's welfare finally arrived. As I got up and reached for the door of the bunker, a round hit right outside and blew the whole bunker door in, throwing all of us against the wall and covering us with a lot of dirt, debris, and shrapnel.

I received a long, thin piece of wood in my thumb. I pulled it out, turned to SgtMaj James Gaynor, and said, "Sergeant Major! Look! I've been wounded!"

"Well, Lieutenant," he replied, "you better run as fast as you can to the aid station to get your Purple Heart, because that thing's liable to heal before you get there."

Sgt FRANK JONES
26th Marines Scout-Sniper Platoon _____

All we could hear on the radios was word about the incoming rounds. The only thing we could hear was that there was heavy artillery coming in, that rounds were exploding, that the combined action company in Khe Sanh village was being overrun by the North Vietnamese.

There was no way to see out of the bunker, but I could hear all the explosions outside. I thought I was having a heart attack. I was hyperventilating and had chest pains. I was very scared. I was twenty-three years old, and I was scared almost to death. I thought we were being overrun, that they were in the wire, because I heard it on the radio from the combined action company, which was calling in fire and air strikes on his own position. I didn't know then that he was at Khe Sanh village, and not at the combat base.

They just kept pounding us. The dust and dirt was falling in. It seemed like everything became very pronounced—I could really smell the odor of the sandbags and the dust, the sounds were magnified, the colors were brighter. I sat with my back to a pillar, looking at the entryway tunnel into the bunker. I had my six-shot revolver and was thinking I would stack up anyone who came through the tunnel in front of me. We kept hearing the lieutenant in Khe Sanh village calling for artillery to be fired on top of his own position. It was like listening to a movie. I couldn't believe it was happening, that they were overrunning us, that they were going to take us down. I started thinking that we were all going to be killed. I kept having chest pains. I kept talking and laughing, trying to keep my partner calm and not let the NVA lieutenant know that we were scared.

LtCol JIM WILKINSON
1/26 Commanding Officer

I was mentally prepared to be hit by rockets; it took nothing for a few guys to hump in and set up a rocket, warhead, and launcher. But the artillery was something else. It was completely unexpected; we didn't have a clue it was out there. I was not prepared for it, and the implications of its being there worried me.

HN ROD DeMOSS
26th Marines Regimental Aid Station

We all made it to the bunker, but the regimental aid station was pretty much destroyed. Quite a bit of the damage was from our own ammo dump. We took care of the wounded the best we could, but the bunker wasn't big enough for the wounded who kept coming in. This was my first taste of treating combat wounds, but one guy really stood out in my mind. One of the Marines came in with a completely blue face. A blue smoke canister had gone off in his face and the pigment was pretty well embedded in his skin. It wasn't a funny situation for him, but the sight of it was comical to me.

Sgt FRANK JONES
26th Marines Scout-Sniper Platoon

It seemed like it went on all day. The artillery really only came in from about 0530 until 0800. Then it just got quiet. We heard people on the radio asking for casualty reports. I was too scared to go outside the communications bunker. I was afraid of what I'd see or what I'd find. I had to have been thinking that we were the only people left alive on the base. I crawled outside the bunker, laid flat, and looked around the corner. It looked like the moon. There were craters everywhere. There were bodies. There was no noise. There was a lot of dust settling. The smell of gunpowder— the smell of war—was in the air.

I was sure we were the only ones left, that they had overrun us, that everyone else was dead. I didn't see anybody moving, and nobody was around. I crawled out a little farther and heard a lot of small-arms fire, and a lot of what sounded like hand grenades going off, or mortars. I didn't know at the time that it was our ammo dump cooking off.

I got up on my feet and headed down for the sniper hooch. All the tents I could see were burning and leveled. There were vehicles blown up, and the runway had big holes in it. Nobody was moving. I crawled and ran to the sniper hooch, but it was empty. The whole east end of the combat base around the ammo dump—including what used to be my hooch—was leveled. There was no tent.

The first person I saw was Sergeant Dooley, another sniper. I asked him where everybody was. He said some of them were wounded, a couple were dead. He told me that Sgt Terence Smith was dead; the sergeant I had traded shifts with—the man who had been sleeping in my rack—was dead. I couldn't believe it. I went down into the bunker next to the tent and called for him to find out where he was. I felt around in the dark and grabbed an arm that was up in the air. When I pulled on the arm, the top half of a body came down. When I looked, I saw that it was Sergeant Smith. It scared me and I got out of the bunker. As I did, a close buddy who had been wounded came up to me. I just hugged him. I was relieved to know that anyone was alive after all that.

They took me over to a position on the perimeter. There was some whiskey there, and we drank it. We tried to get a damage assessment and a body count, tried to figure out who we had and who we had lost. It was chaotic, but we got the count. Then we were assigned out to different sections of the perimeter. I was sent to the south side of the base. All my gear, including my sniper rifle, had burned up in my tent. I picked up an M-16 I found lying around and started digging in. I talked with the Marines around me, about home and what we would do if they hit us again. At this point, we had a determined attitude. We knew that they had waxed our ass, that if they had hit us right then they'd have had us. But they didn't.

There were a lot of air strikes going on that afternoon, a lot of close air support from Navy and Marine Corps fighters. It looked like a war movie.

Maj JIM STANTON
26th Marines Fire Support Coordination Center _____

On the next aerial-observer mission I flew off the Khe Sanh airstrip after the shelling, I found what I suspected to be an NVA regiment in the open. We stacked up about eight flights of airplanes. I had Air Force, Marines, and Navy. Everybody wanted to get in on the act. Unfortunately, these were all aircraft that had been out in the Khe Sanh area planting time-delay bombs along the NVA routes of approach. These were acetone-fused bombs that were simply planted in the ground to go off hours and hours later. So I had aircraft making runs on this NVA unit that had no live ordnance at all on them! Hopefully, those NVA thought the bombs were duds and stuck around four or five hours until they went off.

Capt KEN PIPES
Bravo Company, 1/26 _____

Bravo Company was in a very exposed position, covering the northeast, east, and southeast perimeter line around the combat base.

One of the first casualties resulting from the ammo-dump explosion was my company radio operator. He had forgotten his gas mask when the incoming started. There were several 55-gallon drums of CS blown right into our company area, so we immediately got gas into our low-lying command-post bunker. As we were trying to get organized, he ran back to his living bunker to get his mask. A 122mm rocket explosion caught him as he was scrambling back down into the command-post bunker. When we missed him, I went up to look for him. I found him lying inside the entrance to the bunker, just outside the canvas tarp we used for a door. He was very badly hurt.

A steady stream of unexploded 105mm rounds were hurled through our command-post bunker's entrance by the continuous explosions in the adjacent ammo dump. Many of them were smoking when they landed. One of my Marines, a corporal, cradled each one in his arms and ran outside with it. Many of those rounds exploded after he left them in the open. We soon had to move south, away from the main dump. The new position eventually caved in, and we finally moved into an unoccupied French concrete bunker.

This was the day the combat base was at its most vulnerable. If the NVA forces in the area had attacked down the long axis of the runway, from east to west, they probably could have punched through. Doctrine told us to keep our heads up, looking and watching, because that was the best time for them to hit us. That was true, but when you're getting hit like that—by the incoming and from the dump—you just don't get up and mess around in the open a whole lot.

The incoming eventually stopped, but we were plagued by the secondary detonations for many hours after that. The dump blowing up caused us an awful lot of problems. Wire communications to the mortar pits—to everywhere—were out. I had to move my company command post several times during the five or six hours that things were really hot, and that disrupted my control over the company. In the 2nd Platoon area, the trenches were almost filled. Bunkers, which were supported with the flimsy, rotten local wood, were caving in. Flechettes from blown-up beehive artillery rounds were on the ground and in the trenches, all over the place. Some of the troops emerged with the flechettes stuck in their flak jackets and clothing. The 2nd Platoon trenches were filled with exploded and unexploded ordnance. Throughout the ordeal, men were hit in the legs, body, and head with unexploded 155mm, 105mm, 106mm, 81mm, and 3.5-inch rounds. There was so much CS gas that gas masks were only marginally effective. It was just a complete mess and chaos. The troops continued to man the positions, but, with the bunkers caved in and trenches filled, it was a prime time for the NVA to attack.

As soon as it was halfway safe, the platoon commanders and I moved out into the trenches. We had to see the troops, talk with them, let them know we were still organized.

Cpl DENNIS SMITH
Bravo Company, 1/26 _____

I hate to think what might have happened if General Giap had sent an infantry attack against us right after the first rockets came in.

2ndLt SKIP WELLS
Charlie Company, 1/26 _____

We did not suffer many casualties, as most of the rounds seemed to be directed at the airstrip and center of the perimeter, around the artillery battery. However, we were pretty well confused and shocked, and any serious ground attack would have really made our lives difficult. We did not do much except take whatever cover was available until things quieted down. Then we really got to work. There's nothing like a little motivation!

LtCol JIM WILKINSON
1/26 Commanding Officer _____

That was our weakest moment. The ammo dump was still blowing up and I'm not sure we had complete command and control over the units manning the perimeter. Worst-case scenario: If the NVA had rounded up all the local civilians, put them in front of them, and launched an all-out attack with rockets, mortars, and artillery, they might have been able to penetrate the perimeter that morning. We would have been able to contain it, but it would have been a very costly fight. They could not have controlled the base. They could *not* have. There would have been pockets of Marines all over the place, fighting them every step of the way. We had a tremendous amount of firepower in the trenches—automatic weapons, 106s, Claymores, LAAWs, fougasse traps, tanks, Ontos, Army dusters, air. . . . At no time did I feel worried about losing the perimeter.

Sgt MIKE STAHL
4.2-inch Mortar Battery, 1/13 (Hill 861) _____

I took the wounded Kilo Company commander and first sergeant aboard the first chopper that got to Hill 861, at about 1400. I also took one other wounded Marine and the three NVA I had captured during the night. When the chopper set down, I was sure it would be full of reinforcements, but none—not one fresh Marine—was sent to Hill 861 that day.

When we landed at Khe Sanh, I told the regimental intelligence officer everything I knew as I was being carried on a stretcher to a medical bunker. I got my many wounds treated and stitched up. When they were done, I was put in a wooden hooch, above the ground. Khe Sanh was just getting blown to shit, so I just left. I wanted to get back to Hill 861, so I went down to the Ammunition Supply Point to get some ammo for Kilo Company, but the ASP was gone. Since I had been on Hill 861 for about six months, I knew a lot of the infantry officers and noncoms whose companies had cycled through there. I scrounged a case of bullets here and a case of grenades there, until I had a fair amount. I got it all out to the helo pad and commandeered a chopper to get it and me back to 861.

Lt RAY STUBBE
1/26 Battalion Chaplain

[DIARY ENTRY] Returned to my hooch [from Charlie-Med]. There was a large part of an 82mm mortar round just by the entrance. Inside, everything was knocked down.

Rounds kept exploding on the east side of the base, where the ASP is located. I walked in that direction, stunned, carrying a brass cross and a metal ammo box with a large wine bottle for communion. It was Sunday, time for church services—that couldn't be held.

The [dump] continued to smolder. Unexploded rounds, dozens of them, were all over. The regimental mess was all burned out. The post office and post exchange were collapsed. Rounds kept exploding nearby, but I wanted to check to see that all the men were okay, so I kept walking. I just kept going, as though in a trance. Our 1/26 command-post mess was smoking; it had been hit by three direct hits.

After that, I continued over the whole base. Got a whiff of teargas. I didn't bother to put on my gas mask, but just let the tears come out until I could no longer see as I aimlessly walked up the road toward Regiment. I finally put the mask on and stopped briefly at the regimental bunker, where I got some water and washed out my eyes.

Returned to the Charlie-Med area and talked with all the newly brought-in casualties. We were all congregated around the triage when a round exploded just by the air terminal on the road. Everyone scrambled. My helmet fell off. Casualties were on stretchers all over, in the open, and couldn't help themselves. I was blown down by a round!

Eight wounded men were brought into my bunker. One was the CO of Kilo Company, 3/26, from Hill 861. One man had white-phosphorus wounds, and his whole face was covered with copper sulfate. His hands were all bandaged, but I helped him eat. I gave them the chocolate cookies I had received from home, and a can of cashews. One man had a leg wound and almost passed out. The captain lay down on the floor; he had shrapnel in his leg.

2ndLt SKIP WELLS
Charlie Company, 1/26 _____

The worst part of the whole time at Khe Sanh for me was that afternoon from 1700 to 1800. At 1700, the NVA hit us with one hour of nonstop rockets and mortars. I don't have any idea how many, but there weren't any lulls. It caught me by surprise, checking the positions that we had been digging nonstop since first light. For the first ten or fifteen minutes I was more scared than I ever had been—or ever would be during two tours in Vietnam. Then it stopped at 1800—with no ground attack, probe, or anything else.

MGySgt JOHN DRIVER
Explosive Ordnance Disposal _____

The ammo dump was a mess. Only a small part of the ammo was destroyed in the explosion. Ammunition involved in an explosion, if it is not destroyed, becomes sensitized. Safety devices are often removed and sensitive detonators exposed. White phosphorus is a special hazard. It would burn and then crust over. The burning might cause the fuse and burster to detonate, or it might cause a fire in other ammunition. If one moved the round and broke the crust, it would spontaneously ignite upon exposure to air. Added to all this was the enemy fire, which slowed things up and caused new fires. Clearance operations disturbed the dust and caused the CS teargas crystals to float in the air, where it irritated skin, eyes, and respiratory systems.

PART III

THE RING CLOSES

January 22–February 8, 1968

Chapter 7

LCpl DAN ANSLINGER
3rd Marine Division Air Section _____

Almost everyone walking around the combat base had little scabs all over their faces and hands from being peppered with tiny bits of shrapnel from the ammo-dump explosion.

HN ROD DeMOSS
26th Marines Regimental Aid Station _____

On morning of January 22, it seemed like everybody was out walking around, assessing the damage and picking up supplies, or whatever. All of a sudden, in the background, I could hear *boomp* . . . *boomp* . . . *boomp*. Then someone cried out, "Incoming! Incoming!" I was scared shitless. I frantically searched for cover and dived into a foxhole with another guy. Rounds hit pretty close—close enough. From then on, this became a daily routine. If I was outside, I listened for the *boomp*. This meant that a mortar or rocket or artillery round was about halfway there. I took cover and waited for the round to hit, praying that it didn't have my name on it.

Lt RAY STUBBE
1/26 Battalion Chaplain

[DIARY ENTRY] In the middle of our 1/26 briefing, an incoming mortar round exploded and everyone dispersed throughout the old French bunker. The battalion CO, LtCol James Wilkinson, continued the briefing just where everyone was—all scattered. He said he wanted no groupings of more than ten. Therefore, no regular worship services. 1stLt Andy Sibley, our battalion intelligence officer, reported that we are encircled by two NVA divisions.

1stLt NICK ROMANETZ
Charlie Company, 1/26

January 22 was my twenty-third birthday.

At this time, the combat base in my sector was in quite a bit of confusion. The messhall had been blown up, the ammo dump had been blown up, we didn't know the status of our ammunition. My sector was very, very vulnerable to ground attack. We did not have real good defensive positions; we did not have good, deep trenchlines; we did not have enough barbed wire or minefields or interlocking fields of fire; we did not have covered fighting positions for all of our men. If the enemy had decided to attack the combat base in force with a ground attack during those first few days, there is no doubt in my mind that they would have penetrated our defenses and caused quite a bit of havoc. I think they missed a good opportunity to get their feet in the front door.

Around 1100, there was suddenly a lot of commotion at the water point. A lot of guys were standing there—we always had someone down there checking on the pumps or drawing water, so it was not unusual to have a bunch of guys walking up and down that road. An NVA soldier had surrendered to 2ndLt Skip Wells's platoon, which covered the road that led to the water point.

NEW ARRIVALS

1stLt ERNIE SPENCER
Delta Company, 1/26 _____

Khe Sanh is hit on my last day of R&R. I felt like a chickenshit for not being there with my company. That's how I return—pissed at myself for not being there.

A CH-46 helicopter takes me back to the base. No trouble getting connections to Khe Sanh now. All hell has broken loose. Khe Sanh is now the hottest show in Nam. Tents are still up, I notice during the approach, but everything has changed since I left. There is an ominousness, a harshness everywhere. Next to the landing pad, full fuel bladders lie scattered like large pillows. Almost like a Charlie Chaplin movie, people are moving in a quick, jerky fashion. . . . Incoming rockets and artillery had changed things.

We take incoming within fifteen minutes of when I land. I come in wearing a soft cap, and it feels good to put my piss pot on again. I'd missed my piss pot when I was on R&R. The thing fit real comfortable; it rode me just right. After wearing one for a while, you rock your head differently when you walk. I also put on my flak jacket, which I never wore before. Flak jacket would not stop a rifle shot, just shrapnel. But life is about adjusting. Khe Sanh meant rockets and artillery, and rockets and artillery are all about shrapnel. Everyone looks fat in a flak jacket. They have square nylon plates sewn in individual packets and overlaid on each other. Like scales, they form another layer of skin for you. You begin to understand other beings when you wear a flak jacket for any length of time. Like turtles. Flak jackets aren't comfortable, but any fool knows they are more comfortable than the alternatives.[1]

Capt JIM LESLIE
26th Marines Assistant Communicator _____

On January 22, my commanding officer called me into his office. The good news was I had been promoted to captain. The bad news was I was going to a place called Khe Sanh, which needed a captain communications officer. I packed my seabag and caught a chopper to Khe Sanh.

We tried to land at the airstrip at Khe Sanh, but each time we tried to touch down the airstrip got mortared. On the fourth attempt, we touched down for a few seconds. My seabag and I went tumbling out the door and the chopper took off.

I didn't see anyone around, and for good reasons. Khe Sanh was in the midst of a barrage of artillery and mortar fire. "Welcome to the Big Leagues," I thought. I found a ditch between the runway and a red dusty road. I saw a few cruddy-looking Marines in there, so I jumped in. I lay there for twenty or thirty minutes as the incoming continued. Eventually the noise stopped and the other Marines got up and casually started walking on their way. I asked one of them how to find the communications bunker. He directed me to a pile of sandbags about halfway down the runway and about fifty meters to the right.

Like a lost sheep, I moseyed down the dusty trail, seabag on my back and .45-caliber automatic on my belt.

I found the comm bunker, opened the plywood door, and said in typical Marine Corps fashion, "I'm Captain Leslie reporting to the 26th Marine Comm Section."

MGen TOMMY TOMPKINS
3rd Marine Division Commanding General

On January 21, Colonel Lownds sent me a dispatch and asked for another battalion. I had given him three, and at that point the division reserve was the 1st Battalion, 1st Marines, at Quang Tri. I notified General Cushman [III Marine Amphibious Force commander] that I was committing the division reserve, 1/1, from Quang Tri and sending them to Khe Sanh, and that I would reconstitute a division reserve from cooks and bakers, or some bloody thing.

Cushman sent me a dispatch and said that instead of sending 1/1, which was to chop back to 1st Marine Division, to send 1/9 from Camp Evans, that he would cover Camp Evans with 2/4, which was the afloat battalion landing team.[2]

LtCol JOHN MITCHELL
1/9 Commanding Officer

At this time (1100, January 22), no mission [order] was given to [me] by higher authority other than "Destination Khe Sanh." In view of the lack of further information on the current situation at

Khe Sanh, and not knowing whether this would be a tactical or administrative assault, I directed all company commanders to prepare for helo assault, with only two days ration of food and ammo to be taken, and only the barest personal necessities.[3]

Cpl BERT MULLINS
H&S Company, 1/9 _____

We were notified shortly after noon that we would be going to a place called Khe Sanh. None of us had ever heard of the place. It didn't mean anything much to us. We were told we would be there about three days and not to take much gear with us, that we were all going to travel light.

I was assigned that day to be the battalion commander's radioman, so I got my radio gear together. But this was going to be my first time in the field, so I didn't know what to take with me. I was bright enough to take my poncho because I had noticed it was monsoon season, but I didn't take much else.

HM3 BILL GESSNER
Delta Company, 1/9 _____

Delta Company was in a fire fight with a small group of Viet Cong when Battalion told us to break contact and move to a pickup zone. We were picked up by CH-53s and brought back to Camp Evans.

The entire battalion—including the headquarters—was staging on the airfield. Ammunition and C-rations were being distributed. Medical supplies were available in great quantities, so I gave each man in my platoon two battle dressings, and each squad leader got a bottle of plasma to carry. The chaplain was holding religious services, and we had our choice of steak or chicken for a hot meal. It was easy to see that we were going to be going somewhere terrible. The officers were at a briefing, and rumors flashed through the unit every few minutes. What amazes me is how accurate a picture we had if we knew what rumors to hold on to. I don't remember the bad rumors, but I remember "Khe Sanh," "helicopters not trucks" (a real novelty for moving a battalion at that time), "big attack by the NVA," and "we're getting screwed again." All the rumors scared us. The chow, church, and medical supplies made it worse.

Cpl BERT MULLINS
H&S Company, 1/9 _____

They told us we were going to go right away. Then they told us we wouldn't be leaving soon. Then choppers started coming in waves to the landing zone at Camp Evans. As they offloaded what looked to me like Vietnamese civilians, our troops loaded on and the choppers took off. As soon as the CO, LtCol John Mitchell, was ready to go, the command group went over to the landing zone and we took off in a CH-46. By then, it was fairly late in the afternoon.

As we flew into Khe Sanh, the weather changed on us. It had been clear and sunny at Camp Evans—a break in the monsoon—but it was overcast when we got to Khe Sanh. As we approached the base, the door gunners opened fire with their machine guns. I turned around and looked out the porthole at the ground and I saw muzzle flashes. They were NVA 12.7mm machine guns firing at us. That was my first experience getting shot from the ground. My father had been a B-17 tail gunner in World War II, and he had told me about the flak and how you could fool yourself that the metal skin was going to protect you. All I could think of was a round coming through the floor of the chopper and hitting me.

HM3 BILL GESSNER
Delta Company, 1/9 _____

The entire 2nd Platoon loaded onto one CH-53. The lieutenant got into the helicopter just before it took off and briefed the squad leaders. About the only thing I found out was that the landing zone probably was not hot. The helicopter ride lasted a long time, and our anxiety built during the ride. People were convinced we were going into Laos or North Vietnam. We could see the hills as we prepared to land. I was freezing. We had flown very high to avoid small-arms fire.

The helicopter landed on the airfield, which was strewn with artillery ammunition. At first, we didn't know why—were these duds?—but later we realized the ammunition dump had been hit. I was very nervous about all of those rounds lying around.

We hesitated only long enough to organize for movement, and then we moved through the base. It was in pretty good shape then. The hooches were still up, and we were envious of the relative comfort the Marines on Khe Sanh base seemed to have.

Cpl BERT MULLINS
H&S Company, 1/9

We landed without getting hit and the battalion command group immediately proceeded to the regimental command post, which was easily identified by all the radio antenna masts. The colonel and other officers went in, but I stayed outside with the other radiomen. After a while it got dark. Someone came outside and told us we didn't have to wait around any longer. He told us they had been taking incoming all day and that the ammo dump had been hit. Somebody took us to one of the old French bunkers that was being used as the artillery battalion fire-direction center. They gave us a place to sleep that night, on a concrete floor. We spent a rather uneasy night listening to the stories these guys had to tell about the massive amounts of incoming they'd been taking.

LCpl PHIL MINEER
Bravo Battery, 1/13

Bravo Battery [a six-gun 105mm howitzer unit] got a close-station march order on January 22. We were packed and out of Dong Ha, just like that. They brought in CH-46 helicopters which set down two at a time near the battery area. Gun-3 was ready to go; all it needed was the hook. The gun section got on the CH-46, the CH-46 hovered over the top of the gun, hooked it up, pulled it up in the air, and flew the section right into Khe Sanh.

LCpl RAY NICOL
Bravo Battery, 1/13

Our particular gun, Gun-6, fell after the cables broke. It had to be returned to our former position for test firing.

LCpl PHIL MINEER
Bravo Battery, 1/13

Coming into Khe Sanh, everyone was looking for ground fire. I was so damned scared, I don't know if we took fire or not. We came in very low and set down on the runway. That's when I knew it was serious. There were pieces of choppers lying all over the runway, and craters in the runway. I looked over the compound, where guys used to live aboveground. There wasn't much left of any tents. Parapets were blown to hell. I had never seen anything like it.

Shortly after we set down, a few mortars started coming in on the runway. We beat it off there. When we got over to what I believe was the regimental headquarters, they told us where we were going to billet.

LCpl RAY NICOL
Bravo Battery, 1/13 _____

From the air on the way into Khe Sanh, we could see an increasing number of shell holes and bomb craters. We knew from that and the increasing amount of ground fire on the way it was going to be hot when we landed. We had to hover over the landing pad to enable the ground crew to unhook the cable from the howitzer our CH-46 was carrying. As we hovered there, we could see the damage done by the preceding day's incoming artillery and mortars. The base ammo dump had been hit and was still burning. Very little stood aboveground that hadn't been hit. When the chopper touched down and the ramp opened, we were told to haul ass to the bunkers along the edge of the landing pad. Rounds began impacting all over the base, so we had to wait for a break in the incoming to get to our position.

LCpl PHIL MINEER
Bravo Battery, 1/13 _____

Charlie Battery, 1/13, had been there for a little while, and Alpha Battery was up at the other end of the compound. Because of Charlie Battery being short—they had three guns out on 881S— they put Bravo and Charlie together. As a joke, we called it "Barley Battery." We had six guns and Charlie had three—nine guns altogether.

Our position inside Khe Sanh Combat Base was down at the end of the runway, where the planes lifted off. They nestled us right in beside the ammo dump, which was brilliant. (The whole thing was brilliant. Everything they did was against the principles I had been taught.) We moved into the battery position, laid the guns, got all the aiming stakes out, started breaking out rounds— had to lay them right on the parapet—and then fired.

Cpl WILLIAM ROBERTSON
Logistics Support Unit _____

Everything in ASP-1 was gone, except for about 1,500 rounds of 155mm ammunition. I also had a large supply of 40mm antiaircraft rounds for the Army dusters. Also, by this time, Colonel Lownds had given us a small place toward the other end of the base, which we called ASP-2. I had about 800 rounds of 105mm ammunition there, and about 600 powder charges for the 155s.

   That was all we had left.

LCpl RAY NICOL
Bravo Battery, 1/13 _____

Since our gun would not be in until the next morning, Private Aguilar and I were sent on ammo detail. We dodged incoming half the night, bringing ammo from a temporary dump in a truck. We were very nervous loading ammo into the truck with several thousand tons of explosives piled around us. About 0200, we finally had enough ammo for the battery. We went back to our gun position, so tired we never bothered to dig a hole to sleep in. We just flopped on the ground and were asleep in seconds.

Capt BILL DABNEY
India Company, 3/26 (Hill 881S) _____

The hill had been socked in for about three days or so. Heavy fog—really clouds, because 881S was pretty close to 3,000 feet. We hadn't been able to see a damned thing, couldn't see two feet in the daytime, this stuff was so thick. So we had been on 100-percent alert for a while and were getting pretty tired. Finally it was starting to lighten up a little bit. We were standing down to 50 percent and some kids were getting some sleep. One kid from Charlie Battery took the opportunity to go into the gun parapet and swab out the bore on one of the 105s, which was sitting up there without its sight aboard. (We always dismounted the sights when we didn't have fire missions because there were so many mortar rounds. The guns were pretty tough; mortars didn't hurt them much, except for the tires, but the sights were always getting hit. We couldn't fire a gun very well without the sight, so we always dismounted the sights and took them down into the bunker hole when we finished our fire mission.) The gun happened to be oriented toward the southeast, toward Hill 784, a ridge a thousand or so meters toward the south. About the time the gunner finished swabbing the bore out, this valley opened in the clouds and he looked down this rift, as it were, and going up the face of the opposite ridge a thousand meters or so toward our south was what he described as about twenty guys with what looked like a couple of tubes of some sort on their shoulders, two or three tubes. It was obviously the enemy. We had a free-fire zone all around us. Without direction from anybody, he just hollered out, "Hey, got some NVA on that goddamned hill down there." He went to the tube and sighted right through the bore, and then ran over to the ready box and grabbed a round, fused it for point detonation—left every damned charge in it—and fired direct fire with that 105, without sights. According to the machine gunner up front with him—he was immediately awakened by the muzzle blast going off 50 feet behind him—the first round hit right amongst them. This guy fired off four or five more rounds. By this time, the rest of the artillerymen were scuttling out of the bunker, wondering what the hell was going on. About the time everybody else got out there, the machine gunner opened up— that hill was directly in front of him. What he could see was more or less the same thing that the artillery gunner had described. The clouds then closed up, and that was it. Dead silence; we couldn't see a damned thing anymore for another day or so.

We reported it just the way it happened. The rest of the evening and well into the night, we kept getting calls, "Give us some sort of feel for how many you got . . . any idea." We couldn't see *anything*. By the time we got our stuff together enough so that we could even look, there wasn't anything to see. It was just clouds. But they kept bugging and bugging. Finally my exec, 1stLt Rich Foley, got on the radio and said, "Look, if it's any help to you, from what the gunner described, it sounded like it could conceivably have been an 82mm mortar section. Our Order of Battle book says that the NVA 82mm mortar section has 21 men in it," and he hung up. Rich said that just to get them off our backs.[4]

26th Marines Command Chronology ─────────────────────

  21 NVA KIA (confirmed).

Capt BILL DABNEY
India Company, 3/26 (Hill 881S) _____

Now, we didn't say that.[5]

Pfc JIM PAYNE
Charlie Battery, 1/13 (Hill 881S) _____

Around midmorning, NVA 120mm mortar fire was hitting the hill. Up next to the landing zone, LCpl Ronald Pierce and myself were flattened out in the Gun-1 parapet floor with our arms wrapped octopus-like, up, over, and around our helmeted heads. Our comm wires to the artillery exec pit were out of action and in between incoming rounds, Pierce and I were both yelling, "Wireman on One! Wireman on One!"

During the incoming, approaching medevac choppers could be heard in the distance. Marine stretcher bearers were running back and forth across the landing zone. At that point, another round detonated near the trenchline just beyond Captain Dabney's bunker. I heard shouts of "Corpsman, up! Corpsman, up!"

As Pierce and I looked over a sandbagged wall, an officer with forward-observer glasses rounded the corner of Dabney's bunker and ran toward us shouting, "Arty up! Arty up!" Snarling and pointing toward 881N, he jammed the forward-observer glasses in my face, screaming, "Look down my fuckin' arm! That's a fuckin' gook mortar tube out there in that fuckin' crater! Git the motherfuckers!"

While this officer was screaming directions at me and pointing toward 881N, I looked through the glasses, scanning the bomb craters on the southeast slope of 881N, about a thousand yards distant. At the edge of one crater, I saw several dark figures moving around right on the lip facing us. I repeated back to the officer what I was seeing and he yanked the glasses from me, took a quick look through them, and said, "That's them! Git the motherfuckers!" Then he headed back down toward the trench, taking the glasses with him. Now that I knew where to look, I could see those figures out there with my naked eye.

Our 105 was already laid close to the action, so Pierce and I only had to shift the trails a couple of feet. Pierce ran to the ready bunker and assembled a projectile while I opened the breech block and cranked the handwheels. The tube came down and I looked right down the lands and grooves to center the figures in the crater just low of center bore. Pierce ran to the gun with a white-phosphorus round and rammed it home. I closed the breech block and fired.

Our round hit the far end of the bomb crater and the grunts in the north trench started hollering, "Ya-hoo! Git 'em, arty!" and stuff like that. After the shot, our 105 jumped back slightly off the action, but the trails were digging in. Pierce loaded up the second time with a point-detonating, high-explosive round, and we just kept firing straight into the white smoke billowing out of that crater.

After Pierce and I ceased fire, we just sort of stood there, staring at that smoking crater out there on 881N. The officer with the glasses trotted back into our parapet and shortly thereafter, so did 1stLt Tom Biondo, the 1/13 arty officer.

Pierce and I sat down on the ground next to each other with our backs to the parapet wall. We just sat there staring at the ground, puffing on C-ration cigarettes, with all our hands shaking.

HM3 DAVID STEINBERG
3/26 Battalion Aid Station

They told me to go up to some hill I had never heard of, so I caught a chopper, a Huey gunship. I had never flown on one of them before. I was half in and half out the same door some fanatical predator was shouting out of. I was hugging the guy next to me as tight as I could; if it hadn't been for him, I would have fallen out. Next thing I knew, the chopper went into a hot landing zone and I was shoved to the ground. There was mass confusion. The incoming had been hitting the top of Hill 881S all day.

I no sooner got out of the chopper than someone dragged me to the ground and the incoming hit. It was just chaos. People were running all over the place.

I had been a corpsman for a year, but the first time I ever got to really use the skills I had developed was right then, as soon as I landed on 881S. The first patient I ever treated in a combat situation, all by myself, far from any doctors, was a sucking chest wound. Sure enough, I pulled out my pack of cigarettes, pulled off the cellophane wrapper, slapped it over the wound, put on a battle dressing, and restored his breathing. We got him medevacked, but my life turned to chaos. It was "Corpsman, up! Corpsman, up! Corpsman, up!" without letup. I finally asked, "Where are the other corpsmen?" They told me that, out of eight corpsmen who had originally been on the hill a few days earlier, there were just two of us. They told us that replacements would be sent, but it never happened.

Chapter 8

KHE SANH VILLAGE OVERRUN

BOB BREWER
Quang Tri Province Senior Adviser

Political victories were the prime objective of the enemy's offensive. To capture the KSCB and all the troops there would have been a big political victory, but the capture of the Huong Hoa District Headquarters in Khe Sanh City was to them a bigger prize, and none of our brass have realized it to this day.

I had a detachment of advisers there. The team consisted of U.S. Army Capt Bruce Clarke and his staff of four, a Marine combined action company headquarters of about twelve working with the Bru militia, and a couple of U.S. Special Forces noncommissioned officers. The total strength, including the Bru militia, must have been about 175 men. The district chief was the pride and joy of the Vietnamese military because he was the first montagnard to graduate from the Vietnamese military academy at Dalat. The compound was not good from a defensive point of view. I had an agreement with Colonel Lownds that, should our advisory team at Huong Hoa District Headquarters wind up in extremis, a Marine relief force would come to their aid.

Bruce Clarke had done a lot of scrounging and digging, and his people had their confidence sky-high. I was never convinced, however. On my 1968 New Year's visit, I told Bruce that I would try to reinforce him, if the time ever came, by way of the coffee plantation just south of his perimeter. The trees there were only six or seven feet tall, and I felt they could easily be leveled in advance by fighter-bombers so we could put in one heliborne air assault.

Things happened just as I feared they might. Bruce reported on the night of January 19–20 that he was being invested by a well-armed force of North Vietnamese, estimated to be a rein- forced battalion in strength. (Later estimates, based on the number of heavy weapons captured, placed the strength of the attack in the regimental class.)

Bruce and I both called for the promised assistance from the Khe Sanh Combat Base. A Marine company sallied forth on January 20, but, only a few kilometers out, they found their going too rough and they turned back.

Maj JERRY HUDSON
26th Marines Intelligence Officer _____

A highlight of the battle for Khe Sanh village was the calling in of VT [variable-time] fire on the friendly positions and surrounding defensive wire. The district chief approved and called for more and more such fires. Well over 1,000 rounds of VT were expended in this effort and were probably a [great] factor in breaking up the attack on the village. . . . Bru villagers and other returnees frequently spoke of large groups of enemy dead in the area surrounding the Khe Sanh village during the days following the battle there.[1]

BOB BREWER
Quang Tri Province Senior Adviser _____

The District Headquarters did get good supporting artillery fire from the combat base, but by then some miscreants had already penetrated to the compound and had taken over the dispensary.

Bruce Clark and I talked that night, and he said he needed ammunition in the worst way, that he could maybe hold out for another day if he had ammo. I set it up to free-fall ammo into his compound the next day from low-flying choppers. This was a hairy and only partially successful operation.

On the second night, January 20–21, Bruce thought he

might be overcome on the morrow. So, at my initiative and with the approval of the 1st ARVN Division's BGen Ngo Quang Truong, I organized the reinforcement plan for Huong Hoa. The only force at my disposal at that point was a first-class company of Regional Forces troops belonging to the Province Chief, Col Nguyen Am, and a U.S. Army Huey helicopter unit out of Danang.

The council of war consisted of Col Nguyen Am, myself, LtCol Joseph Seymoe (my deputy province adviser), James Bullington (Department of State), Major Tuyen (chief of the tactical operations center), U.S. Army Major Sanders (tactical operations center adviser), U.S. Army Maj John Oliver (Chief Regional Forces/Popular Forces adviser), U.S. Air Force Capt Warren Milberg (intelligence adviser), and John Uhler (my USAID special assistant). We decided to call in the Army Hueys to airlift the Regional Forces troops into the area just south of the Huong Hoa District Headquarters defense perimeter. Lieutenant Colonel Seymoe volunteered to lead the expedition. I had some misgivings, but because of the shortage of time to brief the pilots, sending an authority who knew the plan seemed to have some merit.

Seymoe graduated from West Point in 1949. He went into the Air Force and won a Distinguished Flying Cross for his exploits in the Korean War. His hearing became impaired, so he transferred to the infantry. He was new to the province and Vietnam; none of us knew him well.

A good case can be made for bad communications being the root cause for the loss of many a battle: Waterloo and General Grauchy, Gettysburg and Jeb Stuart, and Pearl Harbor and Col Rufus Bratton. At Huong Hoa, it happened this way:

Colonel Seymoe, leading a dozen Hueys loaded with 120 Regional Forces troops, airlifted out of the provincial airstrip at Quang Tri at about 1100 hours on January 21. In the van was the U.S. Air Force forward air controller assigned to my staff, a Captain Cooper. He was to direct and coordinate the four flights of fighter-bombers we had specifically requested for the destruction of the coffee orchard just south of Captain Clarke's perimeter.

Problems began to surface when Captain Cooper arrived in the area with the four flights of heavily armed bombers orbiting above. There was an unexpected Marine forward air controller in the area in a spotter plane—very small, but a hazard to the jets in a precision-bombing run. Captain Cooper tried and tried to get the Marine on the horn, but he got nothing. Meanwhile, the heavily loaded choppers were bearing down on Cooper, and the jets were running out of fuel. Cooper was trying to chase down the errant Marine and, at the same time, telling Seymoe to hold off, that "the planned air strike can't be pulled off yet."

Apparently, Seymoe didn't hear the "yet," so he decided—directly counter to my orders—that he would put the Regional Forces company on the old French fort, then only a grassy piece of high ground about a mile east of the Huong Hoa District Headquarters compound.

Problem was, the old French fort was an NVA stronghold. It was crawling with the bastards. Colonel Seymoe landed his troops out of the first chopper, but as the Huey lifted off, a high-explosive round, either a mortar or a rocket, hit the front and propelled it sideways over the hill and down about seventy-five meters. When the machine came to rest, it was upside down and burning a little. One door gunner was crushed and killed, but the pilot and copilot crawled out through the broken windshield. Colonel Seymoe was alive but unconscious, pinned by an aluminum bar usually used to secure stretchers.

The pilots told me that they and the other gunner tried to free Seymoe, but they could not release him. While they worked, they could see and feel the fire spreading, about to explode on them. At that instant, the NVA soldiers began to descend on them. With pistols, the door gunner got two and the copilot got another. Then the bird went *WHOMPFF*.

The pilots and gunner ran around the chopper and, in the ensuing confusion, escaped into the jungled canyon below the French fort. They eventually made it to the Khe Sanh Combat Base. (In the spring, I recovered Seymoe's body from beneath the burned-out chopper.)

Bruce Clarke knew without being told that the screw-up had occurred. We talked on the radio that night, and it was agreed that he would try to fight his way out to the Khe Sanh Combat Base the next day.

Who should go with Clarke became a hot question. General Truong, of the 1st ARVN Division and thus the strongest Government of Vietnam official in the area with whom I had to deal, was totally opposed to this course of action. His point of view was that this would be the first Government of Vietnam political seat to be lost to the Communists, and that it shouldn't happen without a fight. My point was that the Marines were not prepared to fight for the place,. and I was not prepared to lose my team in an unsupported outpost. I sat with General Truong in the Quang Tri Tactical Operations Center for thirty minutes without either of us saying anything while radios chattered in the background. The ball was in Truong's court. Finally, he said, "All right. Try to get them out." Thanks to Bruce Clarke's leadership, we tried and *did,* with almost no help from the Khe Sanh Combat Base. Surprisingly, about seventy-five men from the Regional Forces company made it to KSCB, some with Bruce and some later. They closed ranks, re-formed, and were made a viable force again by the beginning of April. Bruce reported that the bodies of about 250 hostiles were counted on the wire around the perimeter, and many NVA crew-served weapons were temporarily captured.

The Communists were ecstatic about capturing their *first* political headquarters. They went bananas over this, and my Government of Vietnam counterparts could not understand why the American military was so unconcerned. What we should have done was go right back in immediately and retake Huong Hoa District Headquarters. But, by then, our military leaders had embraced the idea of the "set-piece" battle, which they expected to win.

Lt RAY STUBBE
1/26 Battalion Chaplain

[DIARY ENTRY] About 1,500 people were at our main gate, including Bru montagnards. About 150 were brought into the base at a time and flown out to Danang, but only the Vietnamese. The I Corps commander, General Lam, forbade the montagnards to leave! It was an example of selfishness to watch the Vietnamese. The older folks would run across the street, leaving their children to run themselves, if they could keep up. The man in charge would ask, for example, for three more, and papa-san and mama-san and another older person would cross, leaving all the baby-sans behind. The children would cry.

26th Marines After Action Report _____

All the Vietnamese who so desired were resettled after the
initial hostilities. During this period, the majority of local Bru
(approximately 6,000) assembled in the vicinity of Lang
Chen, just outside KSCB. However, for their protection, they
were advised to relocate to a safe area as they were vulnerable
to fire from both sides.

Chapter 9

LCpl DAN ANSLINGER
3rd Marine Division Air Section

I finally got out of Khe Sanh, to rejoin my section at Dong Ha, on January 23. I had to run to scramble up the ramp of a C-123 and hang on while the airplane seemed to take off straight up. I heard a loud metallic bang and, after the plane leveled off, the crew chief pointed out the holes in the deck that the antiaircraft rounds had made. It was horrible, and at the same time, it was wonderful. We were a bunch of kids who knew we were the best in the world and that the NVA was going to find out the hard way.

1stLt PAUL ELKAN
Bravo Battery, 1/13

I arrived at Khe Sanh a day after the rest of Bravo Battery. As the battery exec, I had had to stay at Phu Bai to test-fire the 105mm howitzer that had been incorrectly slung beneath a CH-46 helicopter the day before. The howitzer's muzzle had struck the ground and about six inches of hard, compact dirt had been forced into it.

As we landed at Khe Sanh, we were mortared on the strip. I ran from the chopper to the trench beside the airstrip and dived facedown into the trench. There, I found myself face-to-face with my Basic School roommate. The lucky son of a bitch was leaving as I was coming in, and he sure let me know what a picnic the battery had in store for it.

LCpl RAY NICOL
Bravo Battery, 1/13

On the morning of January 23, Bravo Battery moved to our permanent position at the east end of the base. While we were moving, we could see civilians from Khe Sanh village converging on the gate. All of them were trying to be evacuated out of the way of the fight. I felt sorry for them because their village had been blown away by the NVA artillery fire, and then by ours. They had no homes to go home to.

1stLt PAUL ELKAN
Bravo Battery, 1/13

Our battery position was located on the southern end of the perimeter, right next to the ammo dump for the entire base, which was between us and the airstrip. I remember thinking on the way about what a mess it was. The entire area looked like a photo of Berlin after the Russians had shelled it in 1945. There was wreckage thrown everywhere. Vehicles were smashed— windshields shattered, blown tires—tents were shredded, pieces of gear, a shredded airplane, airstrip matting, and torn sandbags were everywhere. The place had been beaten to shit by artillery fire. What had been a combat base looked like rubble.

As we got into the battery area and set the guns up, we noticed that there was a lot of shit lying around—unexpended shells which were steaming as they were being picked up. There was still a lot of smoke rising from hot metal, burning canvas, and burning wood. One of the problems was that we had COFRAM ammo all over the place. This type of round is shot through artillery; it consists of a "baseball" surrounded by vanes. The thing is led out of the shell by a parachute when it's in the air. It descends to the ground on the vanes, and when it hits the ground it springs up on a spring in the bottom and explodes at about one meter in height. There are thirty little bomblets per shell. Well, these bomblets were all over the area, so we had to be careful not to step on them for fear of blowing ourselves up. EOD came in the next day and started picking them up. They put plaster of paris around each bomblet, let it harden for a half hour, picked them up, and put them in a basket like they were eggs. Pretty neat.

2ndLt DONALD McGUIRE
Explosive Ordnance Disposal _____

When the ASP was hit, my EOD team was operating out of Phu Bai. When the combat-base commander saw the seriousness of the situation, he asked for EOD assistance. My team was dispatched to Khe Sanh and, on arrival, we were briefed on what areas had priority for decontamination. We went to work immediately. The Khe Sanh airstrip, which passed within fifteen meters of the ASP, came first so that the base could be resupplied and the wounded could be evacuated. The ASP was still burning and having secondary detonations. And, as if this wasn't bad enough, the NVA was still harassing the base with mortar, artillery, and rocket fire. That slowed us down some, but not completely.

As we got the airstrip cleared of unexploded ordnance, fragments, and other hazards, we moved to other areas with lesser priorities. During the time this was taking place, we started receiving additional duties in the form of being called to different areas to handle duds. We were constantly on the move. As time passed and things started cooling down, we received working parties to assist in the clearance of non-hazardous items, but they were always under the supervision of an EOD tech. The cleanup of the ASP lasted for several weeks.

1stLt JOHN KAHENY
1/26 Combat Operations Center _____

At about 1600, Dr. Ed Feldman, our acting battalion surgeon, 1stLt Andy Sibley, our battalion intelligence officer, and I were standing outside the battalion command post when we noticed that an A-4 pilot had punched out directly over the base. His parachute was drifting out to the east, past our lines, and on into enemy territory. We immediately jumped into the ambulance. I was so excited that I tried to climb in on the shotgun side, but there's no door on that side of a military ambulance. Also, we had two rifles and all of about four rounds of ammunition.

I was hanging on to the outside of the ambulance as Dr. Feldman drove through the ammo dump and out across the airfield—it was still covered with shrapnel, which I thought was going to burst the tires. Meantime, the A-4 pilot kept drifting closer and closer to the cliff on the east side of the base, but he fell in about fifty yards from the treeline. Fortunately for all of us, a squad from Bravo Company had seen him coming down, and they ran across the field and covered the treeline for us while we went over to see if the pilot was okay.

Capt KEN PIPES
Bravo Company, 1/26 _____

The pilot, Maj William Loftus, was saved from going over into a deep ravine beyond our reach when his parachute shrouds became entangled in our wire. He told the Bravo Company 2nd Platoon commander, 2ndLt John Dillon, "If you weren't so damned ugly, I'd kiss you."[1]

Cpl WILLIAM ROBERTSON
Logistics Support Unit _____

All day long, January 23, the first day planes were able to come into Khe Sanh, we received 155mm rounds, but no primers, no fuses, and no powder kegs. However, the gunners needed four pieces to be able to fire them: a primer, powder bags, the actual round, and the fuse. The gunners had to put the fuse on the round, then the round in the barrel, then the powder behind the round, then the primer behind the powder. Without any one of those four articles, the gunners had nothing to fire, they got no bang. We got planeload after planeload of 155mm rounds. That night, I called Danang and talked to some captain there. Except for the circumstances of what was going on at Khe Sanh, I probably would have been put *under* the jail because I was not too pleased with him. I asked, "What the hell are we supposed to do with these rounds? Bowl? There's nothing else to do with 'em. We don't have any fuses. We don't have any powder. We don't have any primers." In fact, we only had a few 155mm guns, and we had two full batteries of 105s. Everybody up there had a rifle. We had mortars. We had 106mm recoilless rifles. But they didn't send anything except 155mm rounds. I told the captain, "You must have a bloomin' idiot down there, deciding what's going to be sent out to us." Well, apparently he got the message. Starting the next day, we got diversified ammunition loads in. And Colonel Lownds was gracious enough to give us three places to put it. I guess he finally realized what we had been trying to get through to him—that apparently we knew a little something about what we were doing.

Pfc ELWIN BACON
Kilo Company, 3/26 (Hill 861)

For four days and nights following the January 21 attack on Hill 861, Kilo Company was on 100-percent alert. That's a very long time to be without sleep. If a second attack had come, we would have been in no shape to ward it off. The CO must have been terrified of what could have happened, but I don't think his judgment was correct on that point.

On the second night after the attack—January 23—three of us were told to go out in front of the lines and act as a listening post. The senior man was led out by the company gunny to an old stump which was all charred from fire. We were told that we should stay there until daybreak. Why the team leader disobeyed that command and moved us a little closer to the line and bunkers, I don't know, but we weren't there but an hour when a machine gun from our lines opened up on that stump. We would all have been dead for sure.

Our platoon exchanged positions with that of the one that had taken the brunt of the attack. The smell from in front of my new position was enough to make a hog vomit. As far as I could see into the little valley between our hill and that next ridge was nothing but bodies. As the days went by, the odor grew worse and unbearable. Nothing could be done about the bodies because the sniper activity continued.

Sgt MIKE STAHL
4.2-inch Mortar Battery, 1/13 (Hill 861) _____

Following their attempt to overrun Hill 861 on the night of January 20–21, the NVA evidently left many of their dead in the ravine fronting Hill 861. Over a period of days, we gathered up as many as we could safely reach and burned them.

We also had our own dead to contend with. The fog was so thick, and they were so slow getting choppers in, that we had wounded Marines on the landing zone, waiting for a ride out, for several days. Some of them died waiting on the landing zone. Our dead went out last, after the wounded. During that time we got few if any replacements and very little ammunition or other supplies.

Pfc JIM PAYNE
Charlie Battery, 1/13 (Hill 881S) _____

Incoming again, and choppers were medevacking from the hill. All these guys were getting hit and corpsmen were running all over the hill. When NVA 120mm mortars detonated on the hill, they left an acrid-smelling, soot-like cloud that hung there momentarily before drifting across the landing zone. On this day, Pfc Ronald Pierce and I were flattened out in the gun pit again. Corporal Blucher, who was new in-country, was lying alongside us. Our wires were back in action and Pierce had the gun team headset on.

While taking a quick look-see between incoming rounds, I spotted this big rat about five feet away. The rat was burrowing butt-first in between two sandbags on the parapet wall, leaving its head barely visible. Then I heard a round coming right into the landing zone and ducked back into my helmet. After the round detonated, I took a quick look at the rat. His head had been blown completely off and the headless body was crawling out of the little enclave like nothing was wrong with it. It hesitated, then dropped straight down to the parapet floor right next to me and stiffened to death. I stared at that rat, wondering how I was going to keep my five-foot-eight-inch, 140-pound body alive until noon.

A couple rounds later, Corporal Blucher leaped to his feet, saying, "I'll be right back." I never saw or heard of him again.

Shortly after that, Pierce and I got a fire mission. Pierce was leveling the bubbles and getting on the aiming stakes while I ran to the ready bunker to break out a round. Just as I turned back toward the gun with a projectile, an incoming round slammed into the landing zone and down went Pierce with an awful hole in his chest. I later heard that Pierce was convalescing back in The World, but I still don't know what happened to Blucher.

THE ROCK QUARRY

Cpl BERT MULLINS
H&S Company, 1/9 _____

The battalion—less Charlie Company and part of H&S Company, which had been delayed—left the combat base at about 0800, January 23.

HM3 BILL GESSNER
Delta Company, 1/9 _____

We left the perimeter and went down into the low ground. The elephant grass was very high. I had never experienced it before. I expected to be hit at any time, and I wondered how the lieutenant could know where he was going. It was hot down in the valley.

Cpl BERT MULLINS
H&S Company, 1/9 _____

We had been assigned to one of the hills outside the perimeter from which we could block the western approach route to the base. Our hill was called the Rock Quarry.

The Rock Quarry position consisted of one hill—not high, but large at the top—and a lower area from which the rock had been quarried. From the top of the hill, we could look down into Khe Sanh ville and the combat base. Bravo and Delta companies formed a perimeter at the top of the hill. Outside that perimeter, at the base of the hill, was a stream. The road from the combat base came out toward the hill, hooked back to the left, and went up the hill to the quarry. Alpha Company (and, later, Charlie Company) formed another perimeter along the road, and it met up with the Bravo-Delta perimeter. Hill 64 was north of our position. It was outposted by a platoon of Alpha Company.

LtCol JOHN MITCHELL
1/9 Commanding Officer

The first order of the day was to dig in and clear fields of fire. Starting from scratch, a storybook defensive perimeter was gradually, painstakingly molded. Except for the northern sector, no field of fire existed because of three-to-seven-foot grass surrounding the 1/9 positions.[2]

HM3 BILL GESSNER
Delta Company, 1/9

I was walking down toward the 2nd Platoon area when a couple of mortar rounds hit. I hugged the ground, cursing myself for being caught in the open. I waited to see if any more rounds would fall. When they didn't, I headed back toward my position. Just as I got close to my foxhole, I heard more incoming rounds, and I jumped right into the foxhole. I felt something round and soft under my feet. I knew that was wrong so I jumped out while the mortar rounds were still falling, and I hugged the ground until the incoming stopped. My foxhole buddy had seen what I had done, and he ran over to ask me if I was crazy. I said, "There's something in there." We looked in, and there was a cobra in the hole. We called the lieutenant over and then we threw a grenade in the hole to kill it. I must have landed on its head, otherwise I would have been bitten.

Cpl BERT MULLINS
H&S Company, 1/9

We spent the first night at Rock Quarry pretty much in the open. We had no wire or tripflares in front of us because we had gotten organized too late to put them in. Virtually every man along the line was awake.

The three of us in a fighting hole by the stream saw movement during the night, and we elected to throw a grenade out. One of the fellows, excitable and with less time in-country than me, wanted to throw the grenade. I was senior man, so I pointed out exactly where I wanted it thrown—just to the right of a tree in front of our fighting hole. I thought we had all seen the movement, and that he knew which tree I was talking about. It was one of only two trees, and it was the one farthest from the fighting hole. The Marine threw the grenade just to the right of the nearer tree, which was way too close. I knew what was going to happen as soon as he threw it. After the standard three or four seconds, we had shrapnel and dirt all over us. We spent the rest of the night awake. Next morning, we went out in front of our position and found a fiber canister similar to what 105mm rounds came packed in. It had a length of detonating cord attached. We did not touch the canister, and I don't know what was in it.

JANUARY 24

Lt RAY STUBBE
1/26 Battalion Chaplain

[DIARY ENTRY] I'm writing this at 2125.

We had another attack today, shorter in duration than the first one, but it was more devastating. One landed right on top of the recon bunker. Painter walked in, in complete shock, shrapnel wounds all over his back and face—little holes all over, with small burn marks and blood dripping out of a few of them. I talked with him, but he couldn't reply. Then more came in—Velardi, Noyes, others. We went into my bunker for safety. Then an Air Force lieutenant colonel who had minor shrapnel wounds in his lower buttocks came in. He took off his flak jacket, and there was a piece of shrapnel just below the collar, in the middle, where it would have hit his spinal cord and probably killed him. Then a shell-shocked postal clerk came in. These seven, in addition to Dr. King, Corpsman Heath, and myself. No one talked; everyone just sat there, silent.

[After the shelling stopped] the Air Force lieutenant colonel left. The rest of us slept in my hooch, in which perhaps two could comfortably live. There were four men sitting on my rack; they couldn't lie down. Wounded but unable to depart because the choppers aren't flying tonight, they just fell asleep in sitting positions, blood all over. I curled up on top of a field desk, about three feet by three feet. The surgeon was lying on the floor, as was Noyes and the shell-shock victim. Incoming kept coming in all night, a few rounds every now and then.

Capt BILL DABNEY
India Company, 3/26 (Hill 881S) _____

We had two NVA run up the nose on the east end of the hill—we had an observation post out there in the daytime—with their hands in the air, wearing nothing but skivvies, and it seems to me one of them was waving a *chieu hoi* letter or some piece of white paper; we couldn't tell what it was. They came to the edge of the wire. As the two of them stood there, one of them got shot from somewhere behind him. The other one started just tearing the wire, coming on through. He was unarmed, not dangerous. A couple of guys from the observation post went out and got him and brought him through the lanes and up on the hill. My exec, 1stLt Rich Foley, spoke Vietnamese. The NVA kid—a big, strapping, muscular, well-fed-looking guy who looked in good physical shape—looked like he wasn't hurt. Just after he came into the trenchline, we had a jet fly very fast over the top of the hill. They used to fly past because they bombed for us so much anyway—kind of saying hello. This NVA guy was standing in the trenchline, and as soon as that jet sound hit his ears, he defecated while standing there. About twenty minutes into our initial interrogation of him, some artillery cut loose from down Khe Sanh on some target near us. As soon as those tubes popped, he fell into the bottom of the hole. The guy was literally psychologically destroyed. You could clap your hands and he'd go spastic.

He said his whole unit was in that kind of shape. "Many, many sick; many, many go away"—that sort of thing.[3]

HM3 DAVID STEINBERG
India Company, 3/26 (Hill 881S) _____

January 24, 1968

My Dearest Darlin',
    I am sitting here on top of Hill 881S, sitting in a trenchline where I live 25 hours a day. I am now a corpsman attached to India Company, 3/26, the 3rd Platoon. The NVA

would love to have this hill, and we stay on watch all night and sleep in shifts by day. Two days ago, we received heavy mortar fire and lost a few men and had many wounded. I was running in every direction, treating one man and then hearing "Corpsman, up!" and off again. The other corpsman in my platoon was hit and medevacked, but, luckily, today I got a replacement for him.

Today, we had an NVA soldier surrender at the wire, and I had to treat him. I told him, "Me *bac si* (doctor)," and he grabbed my feet and then pointed at his wounds. I gave my .45-caliber pistol to the guard and put some Band-Aids and iodine on his cuts. In exchange, we got information.

The jets have been pounding the hills around this mountain, and we have about 3,000 confirmed kills, but there are many more of them out there. They want Khe Sanh and these mountains bad for a moral victory.

Mail is messed up again. In fact, we get rationed a half-canteen of water a day and three C-ration meals. I haven't showered or shaved in three weeks now and feel kind of scroungy.

JANUARY 25

1stLt JOHN KAHENY
1/26 Combat Operations Center

Our battalion commander, LtCol Jim Wilkinson, understood how serious the siege was and realized we were going to be in pretty bad straits for a while. The first thing he did was condemn our entire beer supply, which was staged in the enlisted and officers' clubs. He had it moved to a secured area, put a guard on it, and had it issued out at the rate of one can per man every other day. It lasted at least until mid-February.

This contrasts sharply with what the Air Force contingent had been doing. Just before the siege began, they had been caught by Colonel Lownds selling hard liquor to Marines for $65 per bottle—equal to our combat pay.

One morning, I was making my rounds, checking on the welfare of everyone in the command-post area, when a rocket came in. The nearest place to hide was in one of the Air Force bunkers—which far exceeded in strength anything the Marines had. When I got inside, I found that all the Air Force people were gone. They had left. I went back and reported this to Lieutenant

Colonel Wilkinson, and eventually the bunkers were taken over for use as an additional battalion medical facility.

Lt RAY STUBBE
1/26 Battalion Chaplain

[DIARY ENTRY] There were six dead bodies, four from the collapsed recon bunker last afternoon. I went from body bag to body bag, looking at the tags, praying my prayers. The first man was Rosa. The second tag—I didn't believe it—was Popowitz. I had just talked with him yesterday. I was with a group and asked, "Where's Popowitz?" "Here," he cheerfully said. He was standing right in front of me. I examined his head after partly unzipping the bag. There was a small hole in his cheek, about a half-inch in diameter.

Cpl ERNESTO GOMEZ
Marine Medium Helicopter Squadron 262

[NAVY CROSS CITATION] For extraordinary heroism while serving with Marine Medium Helicopter Squadron 262, in connection with operations against the enemy in the Republic of Vietnam. On 25 January 1968, Corporal Gomez was the Crew Chief aboard a CH-46 transport helicopter assigned an emergency medical evacuation mission on Hill 881 near the Khe Sanh Combat Base. The pilot proceeded to the designated area and landed in the zone as two Marines began leading a casualty, whose head and eyes were covered with bandages, toward the helicopter. When the entire landing zone was subjected to intense enemy fire, the two men were forced to drop to the ground. Observing the blindfolded casualty attempting to reach the aircraft unassisted, Corporal Gomez unhesitatingly left the helicopter and rushed across the 25 meters of fire-swept terrain to the side of the injured man. Quickly pulling the Marine to the ground, he selflessly used his own body to shield his comrade from the hostile fire impacting around them, and as the enemy fire continued, he took cover with the casualty in a nearby rocket crater. Corporal Gomez remained in this exposed area until another crew member rushed to his assistance. Then the two Marines, protecting their wounded comrade from further injury, carried him to the helicopter. The pilot was quickly informed that the injured Marine was aboard, and the aircraft lifted from the hazardous area for the medical facility at Khe Sanh. Corporal Gomez's heroic actions were instrumental in saving his companion's life and inspired all who observed him. By his courage, selfless concern for the safety of his fellow Marine, and unswerving devotion to duty at great personal risk, he upheld the highest traditions of the Marine Corps and the United States Naval Service.

"NO HEAVY ARTILLERY OUT THERE"

Capt BILL DABNEY
India Company, 3/26 (Hill 881S) _____

During an indirect fire attack [on the combat base], GySgt Robert DeArmond was standing in the trench with me, watching one of the rocket salvos. "Skipper," he said, "I just heard something I haven't heard in a bunch of years." I said, "What do you mean?" He said, "Somebody is firing heavy artillery, and the way my ears are working, it ain't us." I had never had heavy artillery fired at me, so I didn't really know what to keep listening for, but Gunny DeArmond had been at the Chosin Reservoir and in big fights in Korea, so he had some experience with it. I listened more carefully, and after a while, during the rocket salvos—more or less coincidental with them, if I listened closely—I could hear, way, way out west, a kind of *pop, boom,* that sort of thing. That's all I ever heard, but if I listened fifteen or twenty seconds later, over the hill I would hear this sound like a squirrel running through dry leaves. The rounds would impact on the base more or less at the same time as the salvo of rockets would impact. But the gunny was telling me those weren't rockets.

We reported it down to Khe Sanh by radio. The response we got back initially was, "Oh, they don't have any heavy artillery out there." We were trying to get somebody to go up with [a spotter plane] and go looking out there, but we got no response at all at first.[4]

Lt RAY STUBBE
1/26 Battalion Chaplain

[DIARY ENTRY] Chaplain William Hampton reported in. He was in my bunker for some time, having run in from the incoming. He later stated that I must have been under some shock, for I looked at him blankly and simply said, "Oh, you're here." We walked to the 3/26 command post. On the way, as we approached the 1/26 battalion aid station, on either side of the road, just missing the battalion aid station by no more than ten feet, were two large artillery craters from today's incoming. A man could stand in them and his head would still be below the surface of the ground! We all looked at the ominous holes and, although no one said a word, everyone who saw knew, "What protection is there against something like that?" Not even the regimental combat operations center could take one of these rounds.

Capt BILL DABNEY
India Company, 3/26 (Hill 881S)

After a few days, they started firing that kind of fire without coordinating with the rocket fire. They were still thinking in Khe Sanh that this was 122mm rockets. And we were telling them, "No, that was not 122mm rockets. That is artillery, it's coming from a long way out. We don't know what the caliber is, but we can tell you it's artillery." Well, eventually we kept a Marine (without his helmet, so he could hear) in a good tight hole on top of the hill with a radio for the specific purpose of listening for that little *pop* way out west, and the dry-leaf sound. And, as soon as he heard it, he would key his handset and call down to Khe Sanh ("Dunbar County" was the call sign of the battalion with which we had radio contact), and he would say, "Dunbar, this is India. Arty 305!" That is, a 305-degree azimuth from us was where we were getting the sound. And they'd say, "Roger, out." It got to be a joke after a while. He would give them, "Arty, 305, shot, over," and when he saw the stuff impact at Khe Sanh, he'd say, "Dunbar, India. Splash, over." They'd laugh and say, "Roger, splash, out!" Of course, it hit right on top of them. They had some sort of klaxon system down there. From the time those rounds passed over the hill to the time they hit at Khe Sanh was eight, ten seconds or so, which was plenty of time if you had some sort of warning for a guy to jump in a hole.[5]

Sgt MIKE STAHL
4.2-inch Mortar Battery, 1/13 (Hill 861) _____

My heavy-mortar platoon had an artillery spotting scope and, using it, I could see the NVA rocket trucks displace around the combat base. The trucks would move into covered positions north or northwest of Hill 861, fire off a sheaf of 122mm rockets, and then move back out of artillery range. Usually, we didn't find them until they fired, until we could focus on the smoke from the rockets. By the time we tried to get artillery or our heavy mortars on them, they were gone.

JANUARY 26

SSgt HARVE SAAL, USA
FOB-3 _____

My recon team set up a linear ambush along a "high-speed" trail on January 26. At about 0530, one NVA soldier was observed by my Bru scouts as he approached our kill-zone area. It was noted that his AK-47 was slung across his back and that he wasn't ready for a confrontation with the enemy—us. He was captured instead of being killed. On a quick interrogation, we learned that he was a scout and was looking for routes for *armor* to follow. We secured the man and escorted him to FOB-3 Intelligence for further interrogation. We were told there to take him to the Marine camp and allow their intelligence staff to take the first crack at him.

When I inquired about the NVA prisoner later in the day, I was told, "The Vietnamese person you brought in was waiting in a 'classified and secure' area, so he was asked to leave the bunker." He did. He roamed around the Marine camp for another two days trying to surrender to any Marine who would stop and listen to him. Finally, one Marine got suspicious and took him into custody. That's when FOB-3 was informed that the Marine security people had an unknown Vietnamese in their custody. They wanted to know if he belonged to us. We got him back under our control and were able to learn more about the tanks he was scouting for.

JANUARY 27

1stLt NICK ROMANETZ
Charlie Company, 1/26 ⎯⎯⎯⎯⎯⎯⎯⎯⎯⎯⎯⎯⎯⎯⎯⎯

On January 27, the 37th ARVN Ranger Battalion came aboard and took over the unoccupied outer eastern sector of the base, out in front of the ammo dump. About a hundred yards back were our Marines, in the older fighting positions.

Capt KEN PIPES
Bravo Company, 1/26 ⎯⎯⎯⎯⎯⎯⎯⎯⎯⎯⎯⎯⎯⎯⎯⎯

The 37th ARVN Ranger Battalion was a good unit—a good, scrappy bunch. When they came in, they were set in front of my 2nd Platoon, on the east flank of the perimeter, covering one of the main routes of advance into the base. If the NVA could have busted through the line there, they could have had the base. So, when the ARVNs set in, we left 2nd Platoon in place to back them up. After we met with the ARVN battalion commander, Capt Hoang Pho, it was agreed that my company's artillery forward observer, 1stLt Hank Norman, would go out with the ARVNs when they needed artillery called.

    We quickly built up a mutual trust with the ARVNs. They'd come over and steal stuff, but, hell, they didn't have a hell of a lot to begin with. I wasn't aware of any big problems.

1stLt NICK ROMANETZ
Charlie Company, 1/26 ⎯⎯⎯⎯⎯⎯⎯⎯⎯⎯⎯⎯⎯⎯⎯⎯

By the end of the first week of the siege, we had gotten into our daily routine: take more incoming, dig more foxholes, put in more covered positions. Eventually, minefields were put out and barbed wire was improved. On a routine day, we would have reveille around 0500 or 0530, make a head call, shave, stand to, go to meetings, check the wire, set up work parties, improve our fighting positions, clean weapons, brief the troops on what was happening, eat, wait, prepare the positions, just keep going. Once we had it in, we always had to check the barbed wire. There was a fear that the enemy would sneak in at night and cut the wire and put it back together so that, if the ground attacks ever came, they would be able to get through. Besides, the wire was always getting chopped up from the incoming. So, on a daily basis, we had to send a three- or four-man team out to check the wire. This was no big deal until we started to get snipers three or four hundred yards in front of the wire. As it turned out, we had to get up while there was still fog, and shimmy and shake the wire to see what was going on. Then, as the fog started to lift, we had to hope we could get back in. Eventually, a couple Marines did get shot by the snipers.

HM3 DAVID STEINBERG
India Company, 3/26 (Hill 881S)

January 27, 1968

My Dearest Darlin',
    We are still maintaining our position at the top of this hill. It has been three weeks since receiving mail and two and a half weeks since anybody here on the hill has shaved. We get only a half-canteen of water a day and all our ammo is dropped from helicopters, which don't land here anymore because too many have been shot down.
    We have left our sandbag huts on the hilltop and now we live in trenches just off the skyline, like World War I. We each dug a bunnyhole at the bottom of the trench that is big enough to curl up and sleep in. We stand 100-percent watch at night and sleep all day. It is safer because we usually get rockets and mortars during the day. I just stay in my little bunnyhole until dark. I don't come out for anything unless I hear "Corpsman, up," and then I crawl on my hands and knees.
    A little while ago, I dove into the trench and buried my head in the dirt and tensed for a mortar barrage, and that's how I fell asleep. I woke up an hour later in the same curled position at the bottom of the trench and realized that I had dreamed I was home. Yes, I was home with you again, which is my every wish. How shocking it is to wake up so far from you, only to brush dust off and grin and bear another day on Hill 881S.

Not having received mail in so long and not knowing
when we will, I can only hope that all is well with you and
your family. Here it is, almost February, and that much
closer to November.

All my clothes are buggy and my full beard and dirty
face make me look about like a person I don't know. Strange
how being like a caveman can change a person. It must be
the hill because I have treated four cases of battle fatigue in
the last two days. I had to befriend them and calm them, and
everybody reacts different, including pointing a loaded
weapon at you. It's like a novel of a strategic hill that must
be held and the men who crack up on it for two months.

Chapter 10

SWEEP

1stLt ERNIE SPENCER
Delta Company, 1/26 _____

Charlie has moved onto a small plateau near our water point, which lies just outside our wire. This northern part of the base is defended by Charlie Company from my battalion. We pump our water from an undefended pond beyond our wire. I always wait for someone else to drink first.

If I were Charlie, I'd fuck with our water. If I were given a shot at Charlie's water, I'd make every guy who had just been on R&R soak his dick in it. I'd poison the dinks if I had a chance. Give me this morality shit? It's being taken out that's the morality. How doesn't count a rat's-ass worth. I've seen guys die, die so hard, so bad, they would have taken a nuke if given a choice. So fuck the how. You're missing the point if you think that the morality is the how. It's irrelevant how you do it or get it done.

Regiment orders a platoon-sized search-and-destroy mission on the plateau. They choose Delta Company, and I pick 2nd Platoon. The entire plateau is only 600 meters long. I wait in my bunker, in radio contact with the lieutenant of 2nd Platoon [2ndLt D. S. McGravey].

Only minutes after starting, the platoon gets it. RPG—a

rocket-propelled grenade—a B-40. The lieutenant's first report is brief: The hissing of the open mike from the radio speaker ends, then, "Contact, point!" As usual, the assistant S-3 from battalion requests a report almost instantly. . . . I sit and say nothing.

The lieutenant of 2nd Platoon is new. A real cocky, macho, Boston kid. Right from the beginning he calls me Skip. He's fresh out of Basic School and hotter than a popcorn fart.

Again the lieutenant speaks. He's freaked. His voice is three octaves up. He wants a dustoff [medevac helicopter] right now. Got one guy done real fucking bad. I can hear the shooting.

I ask him, "You still taking?"

"We got something going with the one who hit us," he says. I hear grenades exploding and rifle fire over the radio as he speaks. "I need a dustoff, now!" More explosions. "Right now, goddamn it! You hear me?" He is screaming at me. "My guy's real, real bad."

As soon as the hiss of the open mikes comes on, I press the button on the side of the handset. Speaking deliberately and slowly, I say, "Okay . . . listen to me . . . listen to me. I don't care what else happens, you hang on. You hang on. You have got to hold it together. Hear me?"

A brief hiss from his open mike, then, "Roger, 6."

"Okay," I'm saying. "You carry him in. You're right outside the wire. It's faster than a chopper."

Behind me I hear the battalion radio net telling the hospital to send an ambulance to the wire at the water point. A short times passes. The lieutenant calls again. He's got a couple of others slightly wounded from that one rocket. They've killed two gooks, and the one who fired the RPG is critically wounded by a grenade. Pressing the green rubber-covered button again, I say, "Delta 2, this is 6. They want anyone who is alive to be brought in, copy?"

"The gook ain't going to make it, 6. He ate most of a grenade."

"If he's alive, you bring him in. You copy?"

"Roger, 6." For most of a minute the mike hisses like a tire going flat. Then, "Six, this is 2."

"This is 6, go ahead."

"We're coming in. The gook is a flunk. Over."

"Roger, 2. Six out," I answer softly.[1]

Meanwhile, Charlie Company, 1/26, had observed mortar flashes from their lines. The rounds landed near the patrol and reaction force. 1/26 called fires on the mortar site with excellent target coverage.

The NVA were believed to be a reconnaissance unit from an NVA infantry battalion. They were wearing cloth over their faces and heads which blended with the elephant grass. There were 3 NVA KIA (confirmed). The bodies were stripped of their clothing and documents, and the following weapons were picked up: 1 RPG-2, 1 SKS carbine, 2 Chicom grenades, 2 AK-47s, and assorted documents.

1stLt ERNIE SPENCER
Delta Company, 1/26 _____

After a man's been in a fire fight, his eyes light up, then they slowly darken and sink back into his head. By the time the lieutenant and I meet, he is fast sinking into his sockets. His jowls seem heavy as he speaks, his eyes are almost glazed and sleepy. With minimum details he recounts the ambush. Charlie was dug in and popped him first. His guys moved well, he says. No talking, just dumping. His guys really unloaded, just like in training. "I didn't even have to tell 'em," he said. "They just went at 'em." We stood alone near the entrance to my bunker.

As he is leaving, he says in a hushed tone, "Skip, I did the gook myself. I did him right between the eyes with my pistol. He never would have made it, Skip. I did the gook myself." The lieutenant's eyes are so sad. Good sign, I'm thinking, not the type to lay bad shit off on somebody else. Welcome to the war, macho man.

With that blank look of mine, I pause and say, "You did what you had to do, is all. You did what you had to do. You did real good. Real good."

I can teach guys how to play macho by now; I had become a teacher. If I had tried to comfort him, I would have ruined him, ruined him for war.

As I walk into J.B.'s [LtCol James Wilkinson, the 1/26 commanding officer] quarters, also the [operations] situation room, I can feel the sense of vengeance. Old-fashioned Marine Corps vengeance. J.B. is the first to speak.

"You want them?" His eyes are like those of a coach asking his player. He is looking at me.

"I can take them out, Colonel. I will take them out." We stand for a moment, staring into one another's eyes. "We're up. I'm up, ready."

After the briefing, the air officer walks over and says how great I had been on the radio. How cool, how I calmed the lieutenant right down. With the same blank look on my face, I say, "I was in my bunker. He was taking it. Talking in a bunker ain't shit."

Tomorrow I'll see whether I am just talking.[2]

JANUARY 28

1stLt **ERNIE SPENCER**
Delta Company, 1/26 _____

There is not much room for creativity. With the plateau my restricted area of operation, it would be like a bird shoot. Ol' boys in Regiment do like to fucking panic. To put an entire company of Marines on that small plateau is redundancy personified. It's a good thing we are understrength, or we would trip over one another. I hope to trick Charlie by having 2nd Platoon leave the base at the water point while 1st and 3rd platoons leave the wire at the other end of the runway. We will sweep outward across the plateau unless it is foggy in the morning. Fog will dictate.

I am ravenous that night. I eat two meals of Cs. I wait and check throughout the evening until the fog comes in, a nice thick fog. I sleep for several hours. Like a child on Christmas Eve, I go to sleep with hopes and dreams dancing in my head—my last remembrance is a wish for fog. I believe it will be close in the fog. I want to do it close. I want to see them. I hope the fog lasts tomorrow.

There is a nice deep, wet, still fog the next morning. After moving the men in small units to avoid arousing suspicion, I'm with 3rd Platoon. Second Platoon moves through the water point and fans out across the top end of the plateau—the place they'd started the day before. Most of the covering on the plateau is chest-to-head-high elephant grass. Numerous artillery and bomb hits scar it, leaving gaping wounds of bare earth like the acned face of one lightly bearded. Hidden from direct view from Khe Sanh, a second plateau lies hidden just below the one we will sweep. Beyond the plateaus a steep, deep valley dives almost straight down to the Rao Quan River. We slip quietly out through the openings in the wire. The fog hangs just beyond the trench-lines like a veil—full and white. There are unexploded artillery shells scattered about like toys tossed by a bored child. The shells are remnants of the ammo dump explosion. Charlie got a direct hit on the ammo dump one day, and the artillery shells started cooking off. Now I look down at them—sterile punches that never were.

With the fog holding and continuing to hide the plateau, I tell 1st Platoon to move out and over the east end of the runway and to move below the edge of the plateau. The plateau opens from that point like the tip of an arrowhead. Second Platoon radios that they are in the assigned blocking position. I stand just beyond the wire at the center of the sickle blade formed by 3rd and 1st Platoons. Sunlight scatters the fog. First in holes, quickly reclosed, and then in large gashes. The fog keeps retreating. It suddenly pulls back across the plateau, over the lip, and back down into the deep canyon.

Lying in front of me is a large cleared area, an area burned by napalm. The clearing is 60 yards across. Marines stand on either side of me, tense and restlessly waiting to go. We are at the edge. Right fucking there—not a doubt in any man's mind. I stand very still trying to show cool, but my heart is redlining like hell. I can hear it stroking in my ears. I feel every little bump and groove in my arterial system. That blood of mine is cascading through my veins like a river out of control.

We must wait for the tip of the sickle blade to show on the plateau to my right. When the lead squad of 1st Platoon shows on the plateau, we will have boxed Charlie in on three sides. The mountains out beyond the canyon jut above the fog. Clouds of fog rest against the mountains, forming a bridge over the canyon to us. The mountains are scarred by B-52 raids and show their earth, like frosting gouged out of a cake.

I see their heads now, the right tip of the blade. The lead squad and the rest of 1st Platoon step silently onto the plateau. I begin walking straight across the opening without saying a word. Marines begin fanning out around me, pointing their rifles from the hip. Some are moving tentatively, in a half crouch, ready to jump in any direction. They are moving too slowly. I want to get through the open space as quickly as possible. Quickening my pace and without a word, I begin waving my left arm, swinging it back to front like a farmer scattering seed in his fields. Walking straight ahead and not looking to either side I move quickly across the opening, waving my men on silently. I know my men will come. They will come with me. Almost rushing now, the men surge abreast of me. Like birds darting forward toward the seeds I've scattered, they now know what I want. I want into the brush as quickly as possible. It is still when we enter the grass, the only sound that of trousers scraping. No words.

This is the first time I'm using rock and roll prior to contact. My rifle is on full automatic and pointing straight out in front of me at hip level. Left hand on the forward handguard, right hand on the grip and just a finger pull away from making anything in front of the barrel trip the light fantastic. Each man points to an area in front of him. Marines on line. I now glance to my left and right as I walk. My eyes sweep in a wide arc around me. My rifle always in my arms as I walk and point out my kill zone, rocking left to right with the motion of my eyes, my rhythms.

I am watching the movement of the line. The lieutenants are up and slightly ahead of their men. I am tuned in to the picture, but an inner voice keeps reminding me over and over again, "If it goes off in front of you, pull the trigger! Before you move or shit yourself, pull the fucking trigger." I have no doubt we will hit that day. I have come to that point with myself: I know it is there, right there.

It goes off to my right, 50 yards away. To the distinctive pops of an M-16, my head and shoulders jerk to the right. I plant my left foot, my rifle instinctively rising to my shoulder. An M-16 sounds so much softer than an AK-47. We hit first. The line has gone down into firing position. More M-16 fire, grenades explode. Dropping to my knee, I yell to my company radio, "Ask 1st Platoon which is the best way to cover him."

"They're by the edge. Come straight across," he yells back a moment later.

Up, I'm yelling, "Let's go! Let's go straight across, come on!" Intermittent fire. Marines moving, grenades exploding. Everyone goes down when a grenade goes off. "Don't shoot unless you can see 'em," I'm yelling. "There are Marines in there. They're all in there. Don't shoot unless you can see 'em."

I hold my rifle down by my side so I can move quicker. I move into the site now and see a foxhole with a dead gook lying in it. A big machine gun sits next to him. A live gook is lying nearby. A Marine guards him and keeps himself under the sight lines of the gook's friends by lying next to him and pointing his rifle right into the gook's face. I move farther in.

"Grenade!" a Marine screams. I dive straight forward like I'm doing a starting dive into a pool. As soon as my elbows hit, I begin pulling in my hands toward my face. I feel the explosion come across me from behind and to my left. It rocks me, and I instantly feel a sting in the palm of my left hand. A sudden wet runs across my left buttock and hamstring. I'm hit. I can feel the blood. I pump my left leg twice. No pain. I do not want to look down. I rise to my knees and say to my radioman, "Am I hit?"

"You pissed yourself," he says. My canteen on my left hip had taken most of the hit, my flak jacket the rest. I thought the water from my canteen was blood—sure as shit felt that way. A loud ringing is in my left ear as we move on through the enemy position. I move to the edge of the plateau. Foxholes. They lie in a slight natural depression just out of sight of our trenchline at the base. NVA in the foxholes have clear fields of vision and—more important—a clear shot at the air approach to the runway. Shifting sights, I see that Marines to my left are firing down into the lower plateau.

I gaze down at the small treeline that lies hidden in the lower plateau, an ideal shelter. Just as I start to call to the 81mm mortar spotter to fire a mission, a voice behind me gasps, "Oh, shit! Your fucking head!"

My radio operator's eyes are riveted on me. Startled back so suddenly from my study, his words, my turn, his stare are all almost at the same moment of looking behind me over my right shoulder. "Skip, your fucking head!" He motions with one hand darting over his head.

I turn and run to a promontory to my right that gives a better view of the steep hillside. My radio operator runs behind me, chattering at me from a distance of twenty yards. Like a mother hen clucking to her chick, he says, "Went right over your head. Right over you. You didn't even see it. He almost took your head off. You were standing straight up." My radio operators are always giving me lessons that way, punchline at the end.

Reaching the promontory first, I shoulder my rifle. Semiautomatic on, selector straight up. Looking down the barrel at blurred visions, I pick up forms falling downward through the grasses that drop like a slide before me. While my right eye lines the front post in the center of the rear circle, my left follows the target. It's just like a camera mounted on a rifle. Both eyes are open, working independently. The rifle is jumping in its quick-shot jig. My left hand is firm but not fighting as it guides the jumping rifle to the images. My mouth is half open. It is as though I am merely recording this. Ten shots are fired before full realization of what I am doing comes to me. Up until then it felt like just a movie filmed over the barrel of my rifle. Fully in tune now, I finish my clip. The radiomen begin firing off to my right. Marines move over the promontory and down the steep hillside. Everyone is firing. I drop my first clip at my feet and insert another from my right pouch. After several more shots, it is pointless; they are gone from sight. I finish the clip anyway.

As I turn from the cliff, I see Marines at the base standing on top of the bunkers and along the trenchline cheering, screaming. I'm in a fucking game, I think. They're watching it live. They all wish they were down here getting some with us, but I'm just in a fucking game. I walk back to the two gooks.

One is lying down but up on one elbow. "Corpsman!" I call.

"You don't need the corpsman," says the scruffy Marine guarding him. "He's shot clean through his calf, is all."

The corpsman reports no casualties among us and starts bandaging the wounded NVA's leg, while several other Marines search the dead one. As they empty his pockets, the squad leader takes a Buck knife from his own pocket. In almost one motion he opens the blade, tilts the dead man's chin back, and slits his throat.

"Hey!" I yell.

"Just making sure he's dead's all. Don't want him getting some again," wild-eyed and grinning, the squad leader answers.

"Well, you don't take him apart, you hear me!"

Like a scolded dog he turns away and folds his knife. Quickly they unbutton the trousers of the dead man and pull his pants down to reveal his crotch. It's a habit we have, a recent tradition. The rumor is that NVA who are circumcised tend to be officers. Whenever we zap one and get our hands on him, one of our rituals is to drop his trousers and check his pecker. Part of our report is whether he is circumcised or not.

I have the dead man dragged from where he was killed. His buddies will come looking for him. Let 'em look. Let 'em look good. I am a low motherfucker. Charlie can fucking kiss my ass, too. When he's crawling around in the dark looking for his buddies and cussing, it's my payback for all the shit he's been dumping on me.

Even though we are just outside the wire, Regiment wants the wounded NVA flown back into the base. The pilot barely lifts off before he puts down again just outside the wire. I'm sure we impress the hell out of the gook, who gets his own helicopter for a ten-second ride.

As we resume the sweep toward 2nd Platoon, the heat of the day becomes relentless. The fear and exhaustion of the fire fight, its taste and smell are fresh upon me. The grass now seems taller and thicker. My senses are dull and drugged. Too much adrenaline has gone through me; I'm emotionally exhausted. Just before joining with 2nd Platoon, we move over the ambush site of yesterday.

One of the dead gooks is still here, unfound during his buddies' search the night before. In their haste the day before, 2nd Platoon had not searched this one, who was shot while running away. I know everyone up to LBJ will want to know everything they can about Charlie around Khe Sanh. I tell the chief of scouts to search the gook. The soldier had been so well lit up when the Marines shot him that it is like searching in a vat of worms—not too much solidly in place. The scout tosses me the man's personal possessions.

An energy hits me after we get back inside the wire. When I am sure that we have finished the sweep without casualties, new life surges into me. I have an arrogant feeling of power. I feel like a superstar walking down the gangway. Striding down Main Street, I walk oblivious to the possible rocket and artillery barrages. The eyes, the faces, the cheers, the shouts of the people who had fought the battle line my path into the colonel's quarters. Their fight has been watching a map on the wall or listening to radio transmissions from my company while dreaming their own battle. My presence now before them is the confirmation of their dream. The dream that all of us had been dreaming for so long: payback. Charlie has become so arrogant that he fucks with our airplanes, our lifelines, our umbilical cords. But the man who killed the shooters has arrived. I carry the NVA machine gun over my shoulder. It is the reality to those Marines' dreams. They now see that it is true. I stride down the stairs to the battalion headquarters bunker.

J.B.'s eyes hold his smile, his relief, his happiness, his joy. One of his men has done it: got Charlie and walked away. J.B. is very pleased that the men showed enough class to bring in a live prisoner to tell where the others might be. Everyone wants at Charlie.

J.B. pumps my hand while holding it with both of his. He breaks out his bottle of Jack Daniel's. Empty C-ration cookie cans serve as glasses. Toasts are offered to Delta Company by J.B. and the other staff officers. My toast is to my man who was killed the day before.

"What don't you know?" I ask. I know my battalion radio operator always gives an excellent running commentary to battalion during contact. He is as good as any play-by-play announcer. . . .

There are two facts that I omit reporting to Battalion. I don't tell them that the gook's machine gun had misfired. The guy who burned the gook gunner was saved by a misfire. I also don't tell them about thinking I am hit in the leg or about the shrapnel in my left hand. I'll be fucked if the only friendly wounded that day is me.[3]

Chapter 11

HM3 DAVID STEINBERG
India Company, 3/26 (Hill 881S) _____

January 29, 1968

My Dearest Sharon,
    This is your favorite caveman in the beautiful resort area on Hill 881S. There are great accommodations if you pick-and-shovel out a little hole to sleep in. The surrounding countryside is in full bloom, with assorted bomb craters and napalm-burnt hills to add to the beauty. Sunbathing while filling sandbags increases one's muscles while at the same time it tends to keep the waistline trim. C-rations are passed out three times a day, and a quarter-canteen per day keeps one's water intake to a minimum. Whenever a helicopter stops in with troops or supplies, the NVA give them a hearty welcome with three or four mortars or rockets. We in turn join the festival by shooting 2,000 rounds into the beautiful countryside from our automatic weapons. Hot during the day, freezing at night, with a fireworks display nightly all add to the great vacationing fun on the mountain called 881S.
    Well, dear, I'm still hanging in here despite the fun. I'm about due for R&R, but I'll wait until next month. I think I'll go to Taipei.
    Well, Sharon dear, I best get some sleep and maybe dream of you again. Don't worry or be mad if the letters don't

come as often, because I don't even know if mail is leaving
this damn hill.

I miss you very much and my love is mounting and my
impatience to be with you again is slowly coming to a boil.
I'm determined to make it home, and even if I have to spend
my next two months in a whole mess of mud and trenches,
ole Charlie won't keep me.

Gotta cut now and heat up a Meal, Combat, Individual,
Beef, Spiced With Sauce, Cookies, Cocoa, White Bread, Canned.
Love them C-rations! An assortment of twelve to choose from
for a whole year.

JANUARY 30

Sgt JESUS VASQUEZ
Explosive Ordnance Disposal

[NAVY CROSS CITATION] For extraordinary heroism while serv-
ing as an Explosive Ordnance Disposal Technician with the
Ammunition Company, Supply Battalion, First Force Service
Regiment/Force Logistic Command in connection with operations against the enemy in the Republic of Vietnam on 30
January 1968. During a mortar and rocket attack at the Khe
Sanh Combat Base, several rounds landed in the ammunition
supply point, igniting a stack of ammunition. Sergeant
Vasquez unhesitatingly rushed to the burning munitions and
assisted in fighting the fire. Observing an 81mm mortar
round burning and aware of the proximity of his comrades
and the possibility of detonation, he lifted the round in an
attempt to throw it into a deep crater where its lethal effects
would be absorbed should it detonate. In his attempt to
throw the round, it exploded, mortally wounding him. By his
bold initiative, gallant fighting spirit and loyal devotion to
duty, he was instrumental in saving his comrades from
further injury or possible death by absorbing most of the
impact with his own body. His great personal valor reflected
great credit upon himself and enhanced the finest traditions
of the Marine Corps and the United States Naval Service. He
gallantly gave his life for his country.

Maj TOM COOK
26th Marines Assistant Logistics Officer _____

I departed for Vietnam from Okinawa on January 23, my thirty-seventh birthday. Upon my arrival at Danang, I thought the first thing to do was go over and tell them I wanted a flight into Khe Sanh. It didn't work that way. After sitting around there for a day, I still didn't have a flight to Khe Sanh. I asked about it, and the man at the counter suggested I try flying to Dong Ha. So I hopped a flight to Dong Ha and sat around there for a day. Next morning, I inquired about how in the world I was supposed to get to Khe Sanh. The man suggested I try Quang Tri. So I got a hop to Quang Tri and sat around there for a day. Finally, I asked if they ever had anything going to Khe Sanh. They told me it wasn't likely, that I should try Danang. So I went back to Danang and sat there for days, until I finally found a C-130 that was going to Khe Sanh. I asked how to get on it and the man told me to just throw my duffel bag into a shovel on a front-end loader because it was going to Khe Sanh, that if I stayed with it I would get to Khe Sanh too. It worked. Me and the driver of the front-end loader took off for Khe Sanh on the morning of January 30.

When we landed at Khe Sanh, the crew chief started throwing stuff out the back of the C-130. Then the front-end loader started driving down the ramp. The plane hadn't even stopped yet! The crew chief yelled at me, "Get off!" So I ran down the ramp and got off. The plane just kept rolling. Before I could get off the runway, that C-130 was back up in the air.

Maj JIM STANTON
26th Marines Fire Support Coordination Center _____

Everybody wanted to try something out. For example, we got to test Controlled Fragmentation Munitions—COFRAM—which was just being introduced. This was artillery-delivered bomblets that were scattered when the air-burst artillery shell opened. A little vane stabilized each bomblet and caused it to flutter down to the ground, where a fuse extending out from the bottom caused it to bounce three feet into the air and detonate at the right level to take a man down. It arrived with new firing tables and fuse settings, different from the tables we used for standard-type rounds. The Army's Artillery Center at Fort Sill sent us a team led by a brigadier general to show us how to shoot this stuff! These guys—in clean, starched utilities—came down into the regimental Fire Support Coordination Center on January 30 with a movie projector and film—a film!—and we all crowded into the bunker to watch it. I cannot think of anything that could have been more incongruous.

On February 7, 1/13 fired the first COFRAM—or "firecracker"—rounds used operationally in the Vietnam War.

JANUARY 31

Cpl DENNIS MANNION
Charlie Battery, 1/13 (Hill 861)   _____

January 31, 1968

Joe—
    I guess we're in a pretty hot situation over here. The gooks are hellbent on trying to take over this area—and it isn't over by a long "shot" (pun!) yet. Sometimes it gets pretty hairy on this motherfucker—and I've come close a few times. Not close enough, though. Anyway, I want to say that I'm not afraid of dying. I'll just feel sorry for my folks, brothers, and sister. And you. There's no way I can describe what good friends we two are and how much your ugly presence means to me. I'll feel sorry about pulling out so early, Joe. Kinda like I let you down. Without being too, too clichéd, I'll say there's so much to say and do and no time or place to attempt it. If— if I should go, I'll have to say it's been a fantastic life, full of the best of everything. No regrets, a barrel of laughs, good times and bad, happy and sad, etc., etc. I wouldn't have wished it any other way. And I'll feel most shitty for you, man. So much we got planned. So much we're gonna do. Hell, I'm only taking it one day at a time now, leaving it up to the Big Referee in the Sky. He's the one who makes the rules and takes out players and sends in subs. Nothing else really counts.
    I feel shitty just writing this mess, but it's been on my mind *constantly* in the last twelve days and I had to let you know the score. Just in case. I think you know what I mean.

Now that's over and done with. Come October '68 I'm gonna stand in your driveway and watch you put a match to this piece of crap. And that's no lie.

I gotta hustle. Sun's almost gone. Another month shot to shit.

See ya pronto,
Dennis

P.S. What's this I hear about Anderson (#44) being off-side (but not detected) on the Dallas six-inch line? Why? Why? Why? Why!

DIGGING IN

Pfc JOE GIBNEY
Charlie Company, 1/26 _____

When Charlie Company first occupied the Blue Sector trench, there was only one strand of concertina wire in front of us. We put out concertina wire, a new type [German tape] with razor blades attached. There were three rows: two on the ground, next to each other, and a third row on top of the other two. Tall metal engineer stakes were driven into the ground so we could secure the wire. Right in front of the triple concertina we had 55-gallon drums cut in half and filled with fougasse—a sort of napalm mixture. Coming from the cans were Claymore mine igniters. Next, in front of the fougasse drums, was a wire apron— eight-foot engineer stakes with three rows of wire barrier pitched at an angle. A side view looked like the side of a tent or half of a house roof. Outside of the apron we had tanglefoot—wire stretched across two-foot-high spikes in one-foot squares— crisscross, up and down, across and over. In front of the tangle-foot was another wire apron. And, in front of that, was a wide minefield. There were also mines between the various rows of wire.

We dug night and day; twenty-four hours a day, we were digging. The NVA could hear us, and we could hear them digging. All that time, many of the black Marines were playing cassette tape players—Supremes, Temptations, all the soul music. We all loved the music, and I guess the gooks did, too. At night, the music was just blasting all over the place; there was no need to keep down the noise.

As we got heavier incoming, we dug the trenchline to shoulder height and moved underground. We stole aluminum matting blown up out on the runway and put it over our hooches. Eventually, they told us to dig down so the edge of the trenchline was over our heads. We had to build a step up to our fighting positions, which were in the wall of the trench. We built our living bunkers into the interior of the trenchline.

One day, just after I got off watch in the trenchline, a 152mm artillery round hit the fighting position I had just turned over to my relief. I was sure my relief had been killed—it was a direct hit—but I found him buried up to his neck. He was in shock and out of it. After we got him out, we squared off the shell crater, which was huge, and built a hooch bunker walled up with dirt-filled ammo boxes.

We had this constant battle between the Northerners and the Southerners in my platoon. It was constant trouble. One day, I had to tell a big Southern guy to stop leaving his trash in our living bunker because it was attracting rats. We got into an argument and then, after a while, into a fight. He was a real big guy and I was just a little shit, but I fought him. We were going at it head-to-head on top of the bunker, and incoming was coming in. Everybody—the officers, the sergeants—was screaming at us to stop. We couldn't hear them; we weren't paying any attention. We wanted to kill. I fought the big guy to a draw until, finally, other Marines came over and dragged us down into the bunker. The stress factor was really high.

All the heavy weapons that could be moved around were in Blue Sector, covered by Charlie Company. There weren't many tanks or Ontos in the combat base, so, during the day, they put them with us. At night, they moved to Gray Sector, on the south side of the base. Apparently, the commanders thought the NVA were going to attack from the south, over the flat ground in front of Gray Sector. To help fool the NVA, we built mock guns and vehicles from the canisters from the 81mm mortar rounds. We replaced the vehicles which were with us during the day with the dummies as soon as they left at night. The NVA observing the southern sector during the day saw no tanks or Ontos, so, if they had attacked Gray Sector at night, they would have run into them without realizing they were there.

I heard that the entire 101st Airborne Division was on constant alert, ready to come to our rescue if we were overrun. If that happened, we were to set off the fougasse drums in front of our position and call air and artillery strikes right in on our position. The 101st was supposed to parachute in a circle around our perimeter and attack toward the base, into the rear of the NVA.

One of the really weird aspects of the siege was the loudspeakers our people had set up to try to talk the North Vietnamese into surrendering. There we were, surrounded by two divisions of NVA, telling *them* to surrender. I thought that was a good example of reverse psychology.

When it all sank in, everybody was trying to get medevacked out. Some guys tried to put their butts in the air so they would get hit. Everyone was panicked. Communications were terrible. We never really knew what was going on. As far as I was concerned, the people running the show had their heads up their butts. They made a lot of bad decisions.

LCpl PHIL MINEER
Bravo Battery, I/I3

When we first got into Khe Sanh, one of my buddies and I dug a hole with an entrenching tool. We got very deep very quick, but it still wasn't enough. We were exposed, we had no overhead cover. We got hit all night that night. Didn't get much sleep until daybreak, when it let up.

Next morning, an engineer came in with a tractor to dig holes for everybody. When he got to us, where we left off with the entrenching tools, the hose on the side of the bucket broke and pink hydraulic oil splattered all over the place. So my buddy and I wound up digging our sleeping bunker by hand. I guess it was about eight feet by eight feet. We filled 105mm ammo boxes with dirt and stacked them on the inner wall like bricks. We looked for some kind of support to put up to hold all the sandbags we were going to put over the top. We went over to see the Seabees, who had stacks of big timber. We only wanted three timbers. Until then, the Seabees had always been cooperative when we needed stuff. This time, they told us, "You guys, we been telling you to dig in, telling you to dig in, offering to do it. But you been putting it off 'cause you macho Marines want to live aboveground. You need us now, but we don't need to give you this stuff." I couldn't believe it. I had just gotten there! I didn't give a shit about the sins of the guys before me. All I wanted to do was get some cover up. Anyway, we stole some runway matting and then snuck back over to the Seabees and stole one or two of their timbers. We got the top on our bunker, laid on sandbags about six deep, and built a baffled entrance to keep anything that blew up in front of the door from blowing in. We even built racks in there, and got a camouflaged parachute to drape from the ceiling and down the walls. We had a battery-operated record player, but the only record we had was "Sergeant Pepper's Lonely Hearts Club Band."

Word got around the battery about the trouble the Seabees had given us over use of "their" timbers. The feeling was that they deserved some payback. At the very end of January, we saw a chopper coming in with a 50,000-watt generator hanging off it. When they set it down on the runway, we saw it had a Seabee insignia on the side. When the skipper, 1stLt George Wood, heard, he allowed one of us to wear his cover with the silver bar on it and get a six-by truck. One guy even had a clipboard in his hand, to make us look official. We drove over to the runway and hooked the generator to the trailer hitch. As we were working, a guy on the runway asked us what we were doing, and the guy with the clipboard said, "If you get the manifest for this, we'll sign it. See the lieutenant." We were on the verge of bullshitting our way out when the NVA mortars started firing on the runway. There was a lot of confusion, and the kid checking us off the runway told us to "just get the hell outta here!" So we did. From the time I drove the truck into the battery area until that generator was in place was less than an hour. In that time, it was painted Marine green and marked in red with Marine insignia. We hooked it up and every hole and bunker in the Bravo and Charlie battery area had electricity. Even better, the Seabees went nuts trying to figure out what happened to their 50,000-watt generator. Believe it or not, in the middle of all the stuff going down at Khe Sanh, they started an official investigation, but it ended as abruptly as it started and we kept the generator.

1stLt JOHN KAHENY
1/26 Combat Operations Center _____

The Seabees were mad at the Marines because we used to rip them off all the time. If they weren't looking, we stole it. That was because we were at the end of the supply line, and the grunts were not getting the kind of support one would think they would be entitled to. For example, if they left a pallet of plywood out, it would be gone in the proverbial sixty seconds. Meantime, they lived in a very nice, secure bunker with all the amenities, such as a rather generous supply of Johnny Walker Black. There were thus some pretty hard feelings between the Marines and the Seabees.

When David Douglas Duncan interviewed the Seabees for his book *War Without Heroes,* they told him horror stories about how the Marines had not built the base up well enough during the summer and fall of 1967. I found this interesting because the Seabees weren't there during the summer; we had only the battalion of Marines—1/26—there, and the local timber was not useful for building bunkers or other structures. Other units, which arrived as the siege was getting under way, certainly could not be blamed for not digging in soon enough. And, in fact, 1/26 lost only one Marine killed during the bombardment on January 21, and not many altogether during any bombardments.

WEATHER REPORT

LCpl PHIL MINEER
Bravo Battery, 1/13 _____

They told me how hot Vietnam was going to be, but when there was cloud cover over Khe Sanh, the cold was bone-chilling. The temperature did not get to where it should have *seemed* cold, but it got me all the way to the marrow. It was a constant chill.

Cpl TERRY STEWART
Mike Company, 3/26 (Hill 881S) _____

A lot of folks believe that Vietnam is tropical and hot. That just isn't the case in the hill country in winter. The monsoons were wet, cold, and miserable. On many nights, we had to pry our nearly frozen hands from the pistol grips of our rifles after we came off watch. And when we were awakened to take our watch, it was necessary to have our partners help to get our fingers around the grip to hold our rifles and be instantly ready. We slept curled up in balls, leaning against the walls of our bunkers. It was wet, and the rain just washed right over us. It was as miserable a place and time as I have ever been or experienced. The damp chill seemed to knife directly to the very center of the body, then radiate out. Of course, the bones and joints were the places that we really felt it. Thank God we were young.

Cpl BERT MULLINS
H&S Company, 1/9 _____

I had to wear my rain suit as a windbreaker because we had brought no field jackets. When they did get us field jackets, there weren't enough, so the radio operators didn't get any. They all went to the riflemen because they had to stay outside.

The fog was really scary. Some days it didn't burn off at all, and visibility was only a hundred feet at the most. The NVA could have sneaked up on us very easily.

MORTALITY

1stLt PAUL ELKAN
Bravo Battery, 1/13 _____

I was laying the battery from a platform we had in the middle of the battery area, using an aiming circle. Some motherfucking sniper was actually trying to personally kill me. Bullets were zinging all around my ears. It was the last time we laid in the whole battery from the platform. After that, we did nothing but reciprocal lay—one gun would lay off another. Christ, there was nothing but gooks around us anyway, so it didn't make any difference where we shot.

We were surrounded. We knew we were cut off. We knew we were at what people said was another Dienbienphu. I wasn't really worried about it. The way I figured it, well, if I don't get hurt, that's good. If I get wounded, they'll ship me home. If I get killed, I won't care because I won't be here to think about it.

LCpl PHIL MINEER
Bravo Battery, 1/13 _____

Most of the missions that came down were shifting-zone missions. An order like "one round, shifting zone" worked out to nine rounds actually fired as we elevated and traversed the tube through a fixed routine. Of necessity, we had to keep a lot of rounds near each gun. We knew what that meant. If the ammo bunker on the gun took a direct hit, we'd get blown to hell.

In ten months in-country, I had never seen rounds come in like they did at Khe Sanh. It was relentless, constant. I used to lie in my rack with my face right up in the ceiling of the bunker, looking at our camouflage parachute. I thought, if I get a direct hit here, I'm already in the coffin.

Cpl WILLIAM ROBERTSON
Logistics Support Unit

On many occasions, when the incoming rounds started to come in, and they were getting close, and they just vibrated me in the bottom of a ditch, I thought, Go on, give me a direct hit and get it over with; it'll be a whole lot better. I was tired of putting up with it. Quite a few others felt the same way sometimes. It's one thing, I guess, when you can fight somebody, but this was coming from miles and miles away, and I had no defense against it.

Capt JIM LESLIE
26th Marines Assistant Communicator

During the first week or so at Khe Sanh, after seeing so many Marines killed or wounded near me, I gave up the hope of going back home alive. At that point, the war became tolerable. It was like back on the farm in Pennsylvania when it first started to rain. I would try to keep dry, but the harder it rained, the wetter I became until I got soaked. At the point when I could get no wetter, the rain became somewhat pleasant. So it was with the war. When I couldn't be more miserable, more hungry, more bored, more scared, or more lonely, then I got situated and the war became somewhat pleasant.

Chapter 12

THE SET-PIECE STRATEGY

26th Marines After Action Report

With the commencement of active hostilities on January 21, the enemy was generally disposed with the 95th Regiment [325C Division] to the north and west, occupying the high ground opposite the 881S/861 complex. The 4th Battalion was located with the regimental headquarters, the 6th Battalion was in the vicinity of Hill 881N, and the 5th Battalion was east of that position to, and south, along the Rao Quan River Valley. The 101st Regiment was believed to be headquartered with a battalion in the vicinity of Lang Hoan Tap. A second battalion was along the Dong Dang ridgeline. A third battalion was in the vicinity of Co Put and along Route 9 north of Lang Vei. One battalion from the 304th Division may have alternately held this site.

Following the Battle of Khe Sanh Village [January 20], the 66th Regiment, 304th Division, was identified from documents. Except for the position on Hill 471, which may have been alternately occupied with elements of the 101D Regiment, 325C Division, elements of [the 304th] Division generally remained south of Route 9. . . .

MGen TOMMY TOMPKINS
3rd Marine Division Commanding General _____

My whole plan for the defense of Khe Sanh was to make the enemy come to us.[1]

I was confident that, so long as our Marines held the key hill positions and we could keep them supplied by helicopter, the NVA would have a difficult time in attacking the base. It was clear to me that we could not allow ourselves to be bled to death by indulging in fruitless adventures that did not contribute to our assigned mission—"Hold on to Khe Sanh Combat Base; it must not fall into enemy hands."

The four infantry battalions at Khe Sanh averaged about 950 men each. The NVA infantry battalions—some eighteen in the two divisions opposing us—averaged about 550 men each. On the basis of infantrymen, the NVA had almost 10,000 against our 3,800. Or, to put it another way, the total ration strength at Khe Sanh was some 6,000 men against two NVA divisions totalling about 20,000 men.

In view of the manpower imbalance, we developed a "set-piece" type of defense against which the enemy would have to come to us.

The daily papers in the United States, I am glad to say, made much of the fact that we were "locked into our positions and did not engage in patrolling." I hoped that the enemy high command believed this rubbish because such was not the case. Patrolling outside the KSCB perimeter was constant, but I put a limit of 500 meters on them. This was to prevent a patrol from being "mousetrapped," with rescue forces, in turn, becoming entrapped.

Maj JIM STANTON
26th Marines Fire Support Coordination Center _____

General Tompkins, the division commander, and Colonel Lownds, the regimental commander, decreed that we would just defend the perimeter and not go out after them, that there were just too many of them. Effectively, we traded the offense for a defense in depth, which really meant that we expanded our perimeter through the use of fire. We ringed ourselves with fire. It became a battle of attrition. We couldn't patrol and they couldn't get close to us. On the strategic level, it became a hide-and-seek game. In this game, we tried to find them and shoot at them while we were trying to dodge the incoming.

ARCLIGHT

Maj JIM STANTON
26th Marines Fire Support Coordination Center _____

We had a massive grid that we applied to the entire Khe Sanh area. Every square kilometer was numbered with a discrete number so that if we wanted an Arclight in any three particular kilometer squares, we simply sent the Air Force a series of four-digit numbers. Sometimes we sent requests for double, triple, or quadruple Arclights. The typical Arclight was composed of three B-52s deployed in echelon, one behind and off the wing of the one ahead. We murdered them with the Arclights; if there was somebody there, he wasn't there when it was over, but each mission really only covered a very small portion of the combat area; 1,000 by 3,000 meters is not very much ground.

Capt HARRY BAIG
26th Marines Target Information Officer _____

A B-52 aircraft is an extremely accurate weapons system and is capable of being used with great finesse. I targeted these planes in the same manner as tactical aircraft or conventional artillery; and they were extremely responsive to all our requirements. Arclight missions were submitted to the Division Air Officer fifteen hours before drop time at the rate of eight strikes every twenty-four hours, each strike being made by six aircraft. At three hours' notice, I could divert a strike to a new, unscheduled target. This diversion capability enabled us to respond quickly to enemy buildup. On high-threat nights, indicated by the sensors or concluded by intelligence, these heavy bombers were diverted from their scheduled targets to a new target block, corresponding to the threat, which may be as close as 2,000 meters from the original target area. Close or far, it made no difference to the Air Force.

Our entire defense philosophy was to allow the enemy to surround us closely, to mass about us, to reveal his troop and logistic routes, to establish his dumps and assembly areas, his truck park and artillery positions, and to prepare his siege works as energetically as he desired. The result was an enormous quantity of targets, located in dispersed but common areas. Such complexes were ideal for heavy bombers. . . . Once the enemy had firmly embraced us, we had him fixed. His siege doctrine and battle plan (prepared at a headquarters other than Khe Sanh) forced him to stay; and the facts of military circumstances and logic bound him to perform foreseeable and determinable functions. He had to do certain things and to be in certain places because, given the situation, there was little choice open to him. Arclights were dropped on all the places where the enemy was known or estimated to be. Bombs were not cast into the jungle just for the sake of doing so. The vast number of secondary explosions and the considerable quantity of casualties reported by the Bru, which friendly forces discovered later, clearly indicated that our concepts were correct and the targeting accurate. The point to emphasize here is that the principles applied were those of normal Marine supporting-arms doctrine, which has guided us for three years. Ninety-five percent of all Arclight strikes were targeted and requested from Khe Sanh—*not* Saigon, as certain authorities would have us believe.[2]

Maj JIM STANTON
26th Marines Fire Support Coordination Center _____

When we began to get infrared photography of the combat zone, we could see little rings of fire. The NVA bivouac areas would always be characterized by small smudge fires—for boiling water—that would always be laid out in rings. The photos came to us the next day, so we only knew where they had been on the night before. But it was a tool we could use to help us target the enemy.

Pfc ROBERT HARRISON
Alpha Company, 1/26 (Hill 950) _____

A B-52 strike was truly awesome. There would be no hint of a strike arriving until the bombs exploded. The bombs fell in a staggered pattern. First one bomb, then another to the right and front of the first explosion, then another to the left and front of the second explosion, and so forth. The bombs created a long pattern of craters, churned up earth, and blasted trees. After the bombs had exploded, I would be able to hear the planes. They produced a weird, low moaning that lasted until they were out of range. I never saw the planes since they bombed from a great height.

Pfc MIKE DeLANEY
Echo Company, 2/26 (Hill 861A) _____

One day they told us, "Take cover! They're going to bomb the valley." My first reaction was, Run for your life! I thought fighters were going to do the bombing, but I couldn't see any in the sky. I was with my friend, one of the forward air controllers, and asked him what was going on. He just pointed to the sky and I saw several B-52s. They were just little dots in the sky. Little! They looked smaller than birds flying around. They started at the far north of the valley and walked their bombs toward the runway. I couldn't tell how close they got to the combat base from where I was, but it looked very close.

The bombs exploded in parallel lines. It started at one end and rippled like a chain reaction. Someone told me that the name "Arclight" was from the electricity the explosions threw in the air, a charge. It was a white light, bouncing back and forth across the valley in waves. The hill—861 meters up—was rumbling. The ground was shaking. Looking down into the valley, I could see that the explosions were devastating.

1stLt NICK ROMANETZ
Charlie Company, 1/26 _____

One day, at about 1630, we were told to get into the trenches and put our helmets and flak jackets on. There was going to be a B-52 Arclight on the ridgeline about a thousand meters in front of us. Everybody ran and got their cameras and stood up in the trenches to watch. It was still overcast at the appointed time, 1700, and we all looked up into the sky. Nothing. But three or four minutes later, we heard this eerie sound—a *bubba-bubba-bubba* sound, like when you put a balloon on your bicycle wheel so the spokes hit it.

Suddenly, the whole ridgeline exploded from one end to the other. There was a dark gray flash from dirt that started blowing up. Unfortunately, the wind was blowing right at the base, so this dark cloud of dirt and chemicals from the explosives drifted over the base. It was a sight to behold, a mountain blowing up right in front of us.

Sgt FRANK JONES
26th Marines Scout-Sniper Platoon

We had a prisoner, an NVA first sergeant, who had been moving south to join the siege when it seemed like the ground opened up and swallowed his entire battalion. He didn't even hear the bombs.

LCpl CHARLIE THORNTON
Lima Company, 3/26

The air power displayed was incredible. There were constant bombing runs by all kinds of fixed-wing aircraft. By far the most impressive were the B-52 bombing runs. The ground would actually rumble under our bodies as we lay in a bunker while the bombs erupted around our perimeter. I often wondered how the NVA withstood the constant pounding, but I guess their gear and determination was no different than ours. I am convinced that the bombing prevented a major troop confrontation at Khe Sanh and perhaps a major battle loss by the U.S.

1stLt ERNIE SPENCER
Delta Company, 1/26

If war is life, then bombs are religion. Bombs are religion because they can bring you right to the essence of existence. Any guy who gets caught in the depth or radius of an exploding bomb gets religion immediately. War religion.

I see what the bomb ceremony does to Charlie. I laugh my ass off when I hear about NVA officials mocking the effectiveness of American bombing. If our bombs aren't effective on Charlie, then there are a whole lot of dead motherfuckers from someplace else out there. I see them and smell them rotting. I am a witness for those big fucking Kahunas, the B-52s. Saturation religion. Baby, I believe![3]

Capt HARRY BAIG
26th Marines Target Information Officer _____

Without the Arclights, we would have been hard-pressed.[4]

Pfc MICHAEL LEE
Helicopter Support Team (Hill 881S) _____

We actually felt sorry for some of the NVA.

Sgt MIKE STAHL
4.2-inch Mortar Battery, 1/13 (Hill 861) _____

The tenacity of the North Vietnamese was awesome. If they had dropped an Arclight on me, I'd have *chieu hoi*-ed the next day.

FIRE SUPPORT

Maj JIM STANTON
26th Marines Fire Support Coordination Center _____

The best intelligence came from the guys who could see what was going on while it was going on, and who could assess the battle damage after we shot our missions. These were the aerial observers and forward observers, primarily, but also anyone else who could see the target and adjust fires real-time.

Capt HARRY BAIG
26th Marines Target Information Officer _____

The daylight hours were passed in a vulgar free-for-all, wherein air and artillery, under the local control of forward observers and tactical air controllers who attacked anything and everything that looked peculiar. Targets were taken under fire as they appeared. Repeated checkfires, caused by the presence of resupply aircraft and helicopters, prevented a systematic approach to target reduction. Arclights continued unabated in accordance with the regular schedule.

But the night was a different matter. As the siege progressed, more and more targets made themselves apparent. What is more, because of the enemy's rigid adherence to doctrine, it became possible, upon finding part of a target complex, to estimate the location of the remaining and unfound portions of that complex. Consequently, we had far more known and confirmed targets than we could possibly use. Eventually, we began to attack them en masse instead of individually. Radar-controlled artillery and radar-directed aircraft, as well as B-52s, were assigned overlapping portions of target complexes in a concentrated effort to destroy, damage, and slow down the construction of the enemy's siege works. Mortar and artillery positions, of which the former were not worth counting and the latter exceeded 160 separate sites, were bombed and shelled nightly in patterns of fire, corresponding to NVA doctrinal position-area engineering, to destroy the unseen battery ammunition dumps. Success was remarkable in pursuit of the latter intent.

In summary, at night Arclights, radar-guided aircraft, and artillery were employed together to obtain a single result. In the daytime, each type of supporting arms was employed separately to obtain multiple results.[5]

Maj JIM STANTON
26th Marines Fire Support Coordination Center _____

We were outgunned, totally outgunned. Their 130mm guns could sit out beyond our range and shoot us up something awful. We had nothing that could reach them, not even our two towed 155s. Their 130mm guns had a 27,000-meter maximum range and our 155mm guns had a 14,000-meter maximum range. Even their 100mm guns and 122mm rockets outshot us. They parked everything 1,000 meters outside of our artillery fan. We knew where they were, but we couldn't reach them from inside the combat base with our guns and howitzers. We needed Arclights and air strikes to get them.

When you're the target in an artillery barrage, it feels good to hear your own artillery shooting back. Artillery must never be silent during a rocket attack or artillery barrage. The artillerymen *must* get out of the bunkers and shoot back, even when they know they are outgunned. We had hip-pocket targets we could always reach out against, so we fired on them while their unreachable artillery and rockets were firing on us.

Capt HARRY BAIG
26th Marines Target Information Officer _____

Artillery response [was] . . . the least that [was] expected of artillery. We thought in terms of artillery attacks and bombardments—in the manner of the First World War. Separate or combined "time on targets" by massed batteries of Marine and Army guns; battery zones, shifts, or both; harassment-and-interdiction [H&I] fires by battery volley instead of single pieces; artillery boxes and rolling barrages: these and other types were the forms of fire adopted by the Fire Support Coordination Center. Our motto was "Be generous."[6]

Maj JIM STANTON
26th Marines Fire Support Coordination Center _____

The artillery time-on-target [TOT] mission was designed to bring rounds from all the guns involved to a particular piece of ground at precisely the same instant. Since there was no warning for the people being targeted, TOT shoots usually caught them in the open and did them serious damage.

Capt HARRY BAIG
26th Marines Target Information Officer _____

[At night] the artillery initiative was ours. . . . An average night's pattern of preplanned fires is as follows: combined TOTs from night batteries (4–6); separate battalion TOTs (Army 4–6, Marine 10–15); battery multiple-volley individual missions (40–50); battery H&Is (20–30). Normal, one-gun, one-round H&Is were not used; this type of fire is of little value. Marine and Army artillery were employed in target areas and at ranges to reduce to a minimum checkfires caused by the arrival of radar-guided and reconnaissance aircraft. Later, as we learned finesse, air was given the targets south of the base and west of the maximum range of the 175mm guns; one-third was given any target whose range required a maximum ordinate of less than 14,000 feet (altitude of a radar-guided aircraft run); and the 175mm guns were assigned targets to the north, northwest, and east of the base. Such were the preplanned fires.

There were targets of opportunity and missions created by

the constantly updated intelligence picture. Sensors accounted for at least twenty battery missions a night. Indications of high threat or imminent attack required the execution of area-clearance fires. For this, target blocks 500 meters by 500 meters were designed for multiple-volley, nine-battery TOTs; and when completed, the adjoining blocks would receive the same treatment. Intelligence later confirmed the correctness of this approach to disrupting enemy formations (prisoners, body count, surveillance, sensors, agent reports, etc.). In addition to these nonscheduled missions, there were the Mini- and Micro-Arclights, the artillery portion of which required multiple-volley TOTs also. Three or four Minis to six to eight Micros were executed on most nights. Frequently, TOTs were fired into a recent Arclight area ten to fifteen minutes after the bombers had passed to catch the survivors with a further issue of unpleasantness. Thus the scheduled and unscheduled missions accounted for a considerable volume of fire throughout the area of operations.[7]

Maj JIM STANTON
26th Marines Fire Support Coordination Center _____

The Mini-Arclight was a fire-support exercise par excellence. It consisted of a flight of two A-6s carrying a total of 56 500-pound bombs combined with every available artillery tube at the combat base plus the 175mm guns at Camp Carroll and the Rock Pile. We had an ASRT—Air Support Radar Team—manning an AN/TPQ-10, a relatively simple radar set with a computer. The ground controller would set the aircraft up on a heading and an airspeed and the computer would fly the *bombs* to the target. The A-6s were extremely flexible in that they could each drop their twenty-eight bombs one at a time or in pairs or in ripples or in strings of almost any size, interval, or frequency. The results were almost always awesome.

Capt HARRY BAIG
26th Marines Target Information Officer _____

The Mini-Arclights and Micro-Arclights were developed by Capt Kenneth Steen and myself. Captain Steen, the assistant fire-support coordinator, contributed the methodology and the mathematics; I contributed the initial concept and the subsequent targets. The regimental air liaison officer, Captain Fitzsimmons, contributed the names and the aircraft—and convinced the ASRT and Marine Air Support Squadron that this system of bombardment did not violate aircraft-safety procedures. Minis and Micros were employed nightly against close enemy siege works within a range, generally, of 500 to 1,500 meters. Often, secondary explosions were observed as [petroleum, oil, and lubricants] and ammunition dumps were hit. The troops on the line loved them because they could see this physical manifestation of the enemy's discomfiture. Successful strikes of this nature were often exploited further with nine-battery, multiple-volley TOTs.

The best and most intense Mini-Arclight was directed against a major headquarters shortly after the assault against Hill 861A. In the second week of February, Maj Jerry Hudson and Maj Robert Coolidge positively learned that a force-wide meeting of staffs and commanders would occur at a certain time in a schoolhouse located in a village near the Laos border. A special Mini was prepared to welcome the delegates. The target block was 500 meters by 300 meters—normally Minis are 1,000 meters by 500 meters—about the schoolhouse to take in the hangers-on and other idlers who usually congregate around large staffs. Twenty minutes after the meeting was scheduled to start, the Mini struck. Two A-6s and four F-4Bs dropped 152 500-pound bombs into the box in concert with the opening volleys from eight batteries firing a total of 350 rounds.

[Subsequent events tend] to lend credence to our hope that we did catch the senior commanders and their staffs in the schoolhouse with the special Mini; for, if anyone could have changed their attack master plan, in view of our determined opposition, these officers could. Since the plan was never changed, perhaps they died in that building.[8]

LtCol JOHNNY GREGERSON
Marine Air Support Squadron 3

A particular problem that was never solved to my satisfaction was caused by space limitations. The Direct Air Support Center could not be co-located with the Fire Support Coordination Center because of lack of space in the command bunker. This problem should not have existed and was caused by a lack of understanding and foresight on the part of personnel involved in the early layout of the Combat Operations Center complex. I pointed out the need for co-location of the Direct Air Support Center and the Fire Support Coordination Center to Colonel Lownds and LtCol Edward Castagna [26th Marines Operations Officer], but by the time they agreed to increase the size of the bunker, it was too late. Enemy incoming was zeroed in on the Combat Operations Center/Fire Support Coordination Center bunker, and it was impossible for working parties to function outside in that particular area. The Direct Air Support Center was set up in an Air Force bunker about seventy-five meters from the Combat Operation Center and remained there for the remainder of the operation. Problems occurred on coordination of the air effort in the overall fire-support plan because of lack of instantaneous communications and joint understanding of problems involved.[9]

Chapter 13

1stLt ERNIE SPENCER
Delta Company, 1/26 _____

In the first few weeks of the siege, company commanders and the battalion commander continue standing in the command bunker during a barrage. We are cool. Charles wasn't going to interrupt our morning briefing.

Nobody plays more macho than Marine Corps officers. Only cool, ice macho counts with us. Expressionless eyes. Passion is not a desirable trait in a Marine officer. Emotions kill.

But Khe Sanh is a bitch who does things her way with you. We go from meeting like that, standing, to where it is perfectly appropriate to sit your ass down any fucking place you want to. You can go down or under anything when a barrage starts.

After more time passes, we don't even bother with meetings.[1]

1stLt PAUL ELKAN
Bravo Battery, 1/13 _____

We walked around with our helmets off and our ears pointed to the north so we could hear their rounds going off. If it was 100mm, you could hear the *pop* about a second before it hit; about four seconds for a 152mm. You couldn't hear the mortars. I used a lot of Q-tips to keep my ears clean, so I could hear better. One time I heard a round popping off; I could tell by the sound it was a 152. Somehow, from the sound, I could tell whether a round was coming at me or not. I could tell with this one that I had about four seconds to find cover, that it was coming right for my ass. I dived down this chute stairway into the corpsman's bunker, and as I was diving, the plywood that formed the wall above the bunker was riddled with shrapnel.

Maj TOM COOK
26th Marines Assistant Logistics Officer

A young lady reporter from *The Christian Science Monitor* was at Khe Sanh for about a week. She was a brave girl, but she became a little shaken by the experience. When she was getting ready to get out of there, I told her I would walk her up to the airstrip in case something happened. We took off down the street, walking along, when I heard a distant *thump, thump, thump*—rockets leaving their tubes. My ear was tuned to the sound, but hers was not. I grabbed her and threw her into a ditch, and then I jumped on top of her. This kind of frightened her—why is this Marine throwing me down and jumping on me? She was squirming, fighting, trying to get out from under me. But then we heard large explosions. Suddenly she decided to lie there quietly until after the explosions stopped. I apologized to her for the rough treatment and she seemed to understand.

2ndLt SKIP WELLS
Charlie Company, 1/26

We had to run some air right in front of our lines, and I talked with the aerial observer in the spotter plane. We signed off and I watched the plane fly away to the east. I wanted to be in that plane so bad I had tears in my eyes. I was supposed to be one of the gung-ho ones. I still have this picture in my mind of that plane in the sky with the hooches and mountains in the background. I felt sad, lonely, and scared

1stLt FRED McGRATH
Bravo Battery, 1/13 _____

During January 1968, I was a member of Headquarters Battery, 4/12. We were at "Artillery Hill," north and west of Dong Ha. The battalion commander told me to pack my seabag and catch a hop to Khe Sanh. It seems that word came down that all units there were to beef up to 110 percent of authorized strength. Since I had been a forward observer with Bravo Battery, 1/13, for six months, I was the logical choice to go.

I flew from Dong Ha to Danang on a Marine helicopter. In Danang I boarded an Air Force C-123 for the flight to Khe Sanh. Prior to boarding, we were briefed that, since this plane was only delivering and not picking up, it would continue to taxi while on the strip and would not stop. We would debark from the rear, on the run. (Even though I knew Khe Sanh was heating up, this bizarre debarking procedure made the seriousness of the assignment sink in.)

It happened just the way we were briefed. On the strip, we were waved to a trenchline paralleling the runway as soon as we put our boots on the runway matting. After several rounds of incoming landed, we were given an all-clear. I asked for directions to Bravo Battery's position, thinking it could not be too far. The Marine at the terminal said he would call for transportation as it was quicker—and therefore safer.

I arrived at Bravo's position and checked in with 1stLt George Wood, the CO. I was greeted by the rest of the officers, whom I had not seen for two months. Fresh meat! They filled me in on life in the fast lane. They emphasized that bunkers and trenches were the way of life here, and movement in the open tempted fate. Each howitzer was dug in, and the crew of each had its own solidly constructed bunker. Very little interplay among gun crews was the order of the day. No troops were allowed to wander about. No business to conduct, no movement allowed. Simple.

I took a tour of the position, to get a feel for the relative placement of the guns. We ran from gun to gun—I'm a quick learner—and I talked with the men, who, if not physically on the gun, were either in their bunkers or hunkered down close by. I found them to be in good spirits. Most of them wished they could move about more freely, but all understood the jeopardy in doing so.

Pfc ROBERT HARRISON
Alpha Company, 1/26 (Hill 950) _____

Our normal conversation usually centered on getting back to The World and what we would do when we got back. Food was the central topic of a lot of conversations. Sex was not discussed as often as one would think, and I cannot ever recall discussing the politics of the war with anyone. All we cared about was doing our thirteen months and getting home in one piece. This is not to say that the people in the platoon did not care for one another, because we did. I believe one of the best things about the war was the camaraderie that existed among the people doing the actual fighting.

The 3rd Platoon, alone on Hill 950, consisted mainly of what you would call blue-collar kids. There was no racial tension within the platoon at all. I would say that the median age of the platoon was nineteen. Our day-to-day life on Hill 950 consisted of digging deeper trenches, improving existing bunkers, laying concertina and tanglefoot barbed wire, and playing a card game called Black Alley.

Action would usually pick up when we were being resupplied by helicopter. The NVA would open up with heavy-caliber machine-gun fire and mortar fire. We would usually be able to call in some close air support to suppress the enemy fire.

Each night we would be required to stand line watch on the perimeter or go out on the listening post. For me, the listening posts were the worst type of duty. They usually consisted of a four-man fire team. We would take a radio and leave the perimeter after nightfall. We were to listen for enemy movement and warn of an impending attack. The NVA would send in sappers at night to probe the perimeter and sometimes try to draw fire. If ever an attack occurred, the listening post would never make it back inside the perimeter. It seemed that when I was on listening post, all sounds were magnified. When leaving the perimeter, I would always get caught on the barbed wire and make a lot of noise getting untangled. Once we left the barbed wire, we tried to find a place to set in which offered some concealment and cover. Once we were set in, we informed the platoon command post by radio. The listening post checked in with the command post at least once each hour. Nighttime in the jungle has to be the darkest of dark; you cannot see your hand in front of your face.

My fire team was on a listening post one night in early February when, suddenly, we had movement in the wire. The sound was behind and to the left of our position. My hair literally stood up on the back of my neck. The barbed wire shook a little bit, as if someone was crawling through it. The next thing we knew, someone stood right next to us. We could have shot him, but we didn't want to give away our position. So we threw two or three frags (grenades) and hoped for the best. I don't know how he kept from getting hit, but he did. I could hear him running through the undergrowth toward the NVA position. The next morning, there was no blood or anything. It was like it never even happened.

1stLt NICK ROMANETZ
Charlie Company, 1/26

One day in February, a rocket hit dead center in the helo pad area. It buried itself and exploded several feet underground. Lo and behold, some yingyang up in intelligence decided we should send some Marines to dig up the fragments so they could find out what kind of round it was. Since it was in my sector, I had to take some guys out with picks and shovels and dig down several feet to try to find the fragments. This was the most asinine thing I was ever asked to do. There we were, exposing four or five Marines to possible harm, just so we could dig up that damn thing. We knew it was a rocket from the size of the entry hole. Who gave a damn if the thing was made in Czechoslovakia, Hungary, or Russia? Picking the unlucky guys to go out there was one of the hardest things I had to do during the siege. It would have been silly to lose someone if incoming got us or if a sniper shot one of us. I went out with them, and we dug the damn things up as quickly as we could, and got the hell out of there. The intelligence people got what they wanted and we were lucky, we didn't take any incoming or get sniped at.

Capt JIM LESLIE
26th Marines Assistant Communicator

After a day of running wire, patching antennas, and kicking the teletype machine, we would try to get our pinochle group together in the evenings, about dusk. I looked forward to that game with increasing anticipation every day. We would drink coffee, deal the cards, and discuss the day's events.

Sometimes the NVA would let us play cards in peace and sometimes they wouldn't. We had the routine pretty well analyzed by February. The NVA would start dropping in artillery rounds about dusk, but they would start at the far end of the runway and drop about twenty-five meters with each of their five-gun volleys in an attempt to cover our entire camp, volley after volley, day after day, night after night.

One evening the NVA started walking the artillery in on us. We knew from where they started—at the far end of the runway— that we had three or four minutes before they would start hitting around our bunkers. This was more than enough time to finish the cards we held in our hand before we dived into little rat holes that we had dug inside the bunker. Well, one of the NVA had his dope screwed up and dropped a round in our bunker about two and a half minutes early. Dust flew, our card table collapsed, and cards flew as all four of us lay on the floor waiting for the explosion to take us to the great card game in the sky.

We waited and waited, but the round didn't go off. We squirmed into our rat holes. The round still didn't go off. We waited twenty or thirty minutes. Still nothing. 1stLt Jack Blyze said, "It must be a dud. That was it, men. That was the one with our number on it, and the fucker didn't go off." After more than half an hour, we decided to see what had happened.

The artillery round had gone through the side of our bunker and into the ground. It left a hole about six inches in diameter just under our card table. Jack probed the hole with an eight-foot fence post to see how deep the round went. He could not touch it. We came back inside the bunker, set up our card table, picked up the cards, and just roared with laughter until the tears rolled down our faces.

"That was it," Jack said, "that was the one meant for us, and the little fucking gooks forgot how to make it go off." Just as he said that, the round went off. It blew our card table over, knocked sandbags down on us, and filled the bunker with dust, but no one was injured. I said a thank-you prayer as Jack and I made our way through the dark to our bunker, twenty meters away.

LCpl PHIL MINEER
Bravo Battery, 1/13 _____

There were times, when the cloud cover was real heavy, that we would take a few H&I rounds here and there. But when it was clear, they really laid it in on us. We didn't do too bad. Probably, for every round that came in, we gave them ten back. Every time it got bad, we'd be out on the guns, shooting back. A guy from 1/26 who was right in front of us, on the perimeter, told us, "You guys are crazy, out there in all that stuff." I reminded him that that was the artillery's job. There was always a little friction between the grunts and the artillery. They thought we rode everywhere we went. But the grunts who came into the base couldn't wait to get the hell out of there. A few grunts in from the hills came by and said, "Bet you wish you were out there with us. It sure is something in here!"

1stLt NICK ROMANETZ
Charlie Company, 1/26 _____

Life didn't stop because of the siege. We still had guys getting promoted when they deserved it. One day, during a lull, we had a promotion ceremony in our trench. There were seven Marines who were being promoted standing *in* the trenchline while the company commander and I were reading their promotion warrants while we stood *outside* the trench. I thought it would have been smarter if we had *all* stood in the trenchline. Apparently our NVA sniper was on a vacation that particular day, so nothing bad happened.

2ndLt SKIP WELLS
Charlie Company, 1/26 _____

Patrolling was difficult at first, because of the elephant grass. It was tough to move and impossible to see anything. On the first patrol, we made contact with a few NVA and never even saw them. We heard them firing at the perimeter off to our right (east) about a hundred yards away. We moved over that way, they heard us, and after an exchange of fire, they either left or stopped firing. We then moved through the area but didn't find anything.

Later, as the artillery and air strikes thinned the vegetation, we had another problem. Now we did not have any cover at all. We would leave the perimeter prior to daylight or under the cover of the fog, move to our objective, and then hold until we either got a reaction or had good support for our move back to the perimeter.

The north side of the perimeter was not good for the NVA. We never made contact with more than a platoon, and they never prepared any real positions—only separated bunkers and spider-holes. On the bad side, because of the low ridge opposite our perimeter and about 400 yards out, there were constant fire fights between our trenchline and their positions. We had quite a few wounded by small-arms fire during the first couple of weeks, before we learned that any movement outside the trenches in good visibility had to be rapid and covered by fire.

1stLt JOHN KAHENY
1/26 Combat Operations Center _____

One of my duties was to go out to Bravo Company or Charlie Company lines with Capt Neil Galloway, our battalion forward air controller. I would direct our artillery or 81mm mortars to mark the target for air strikes. The worst part of the assignment, of course, was when we would get spotted by the NVA. On one

Top
Khe Sanh Combat Base from the air looking north.

(Compliments of Richard Camp, Jr.)

Above
The five NVA officers killed by Lima Company, 3/26, on January 2, 1968.

(Compliments of Max Friedlander)

The Ammunition Supply Point shortly before the January 21 bombardment. Note the vulnerability of the explosives stored in the open.

(Compliments of William Robertson)

Khe Sanh Combat Base in early February. Nearly everything of value has been moved underground.   *(Compliments of James Stanton)*

Arclight near Hill 861A in February   *(Compliments of Earle Breeding)*

Sharpshooters from Bravo Company, 3rd Recon Battalion, trade shots with NVA soldiers facing the northern perimeter line in March. Note the fog at the edge of the plateau.

(Official U.S. Marine Corps photo)

An Air Force C-130 Hercules drops supplies outside the combat base wire. Note the nose-high attitude of the transport. It is very close to stalling.

(Official U.S. Marine Corps photo by Sgt T. H. Nairns)

This Air Force C-130 crashed and burned on the runway near the ammunition supply point while attempting to drop supplies.

(Compliments of William Robertson)

A pair of Marine Corps CH-46 helicopters bringing supplies and replacements to Hill 861A. Note the sling attached to one of the helicopters.

(Compliments of Earle Breeding)

This Marine Corps CH-53 was downed by an NVA recoilless rifle as it was lifting off. The pilot and copilot were killed when the rotor demolished the flight deck.

(Official U.S. Marine Corps photo by Cpl L. F. George)

Above

A wall of empty 105mm shell casings attests to the heavy involvement of the 1st Battalion, 13th Marines, in defending the combat base.

(Official U.S. Marine Corps photo by Sgt T. H. Nairns)

Above, right

An underground communications trench, heavily sandbagged and roofed over with aluminum pallets.

(Official U.S. Marine Corps photo)

Above, left

A Kilo Company, 3/26, corpsman attempts to revive a wounded Marine with mouth-to-mouth resuscitation following a mortar barrage on Hill 861.

Above, right   *(Compliments of Mykle Stahl)*

After the lifesaving attempts fail, the Kilo Company Marine's body awaits a flight off the hill while one of his buddies keeps him company and mourns.

(Compliments of Mykle Stahl)

A mid-February air strike against NVA soldiers moving in a newly discovered trench southeast of Charlie Battery's position, which is at the center of the photograph.

(Compliments of William Robertson)

Marines from Bravo Company, 1/9, man the trenchline around the Rock Quarry in mid-March.

(Compliments of Lawrence Seavy-Cioffi)

Left

South Vietnamese soldiers of the 37th ARVN Ranger Battalion man the outer trenchline on the east side of the combat base.

(Official U.S. Marine Corps photo)

Inset

Kilo Company, 3/26, Marines observe an air strike near Hill 861.

(Compliments of Mykle Stahl)

Life Goes On: Capt David Ernst and 1stLt Nick Romanetz promote six members of Romanetz's platoon of Charlie Company, 1/26, in February. The Charlie Company command post, blown up twice, is in the background.

(Compliments of Nicholas Romanetz)

National Route 9 was about the width of the average American driveway.

(Compliments of Nicholas Romanetz)

occasion we were spotted primarily because a CBS camera crew came out to ask us what we were doing. We kept telling them to get down in the trenches because the enemy could see us, but they kept asking us questions. The cameras were rolling, so I said some foul things—just before the snipers opened up and the mortars started coming in.

RATS

1stLt ERNIE SPENCER
Delta Company, 1/26 _____

There were always rats at Khe Sanh. Not your stereotypical Asian variety of chopstick-using rats. Khe Sanh rats are snarling gray suckers with big heads. Having evolved in a jungle environment, those rats are capable of fighting anything.

The garbage dump set off their population explosion. The dump is in a narrow gully just outside the south side of the base. Before the siege the rats had to stand in line to take their shot; a garbage dump in Vietnam is the trendiest restaurant around as far as the natives are concerned. How disgusting to watch the montagnards—a beautiful, gentle people—slogging around in our slop. With empty sandbags over their shoulders, they would diligently pick through the dump every day. They would swarm around and over any vehicle taking out a fresh load. Our garbage is the best we had to offer to those whom we are there to save.

The rats began exerting themselves several breeding cycles into the siege. A rat jumps on my chest one night. On my back on my cot, I slap the shit out of him with my left hand while I try to shield my face with my right. The fucker is grinning at me, I swear.

Rats love the sandbag walls. Since the walls are several layers thick, the rats have a lot of room for their quarters. You can hear them in there screaming, eating, fucking, and kicking each others' asses. Rats are nasty fuckers—they are always fighting.

Rats behave more logically during the siege than we do. They let their feelings out. You can hear them squeaking and going bullshit during a barrage. Us macho men just sit quietly and take it.[2]

1stLt PAUL ELKAN
Bravo Battery, 1/13 _____

I used to sleep with my pistol under my pillow. There were seven rounds: six for the gooks and one for me. The only thing I ever got close to shooting was a rat, a big motherfucking rat. I dreamed my hand was in a jet exhaust; I could feel the hot air on my hand. I woke up and a rat the size of a cat was breathing on my hand. By the time I got my pistol out, the rat had gotten out of there.

We had a big problem with rats. We used to feed them peanut butter mixed with C4, a plastique explosive. They were supposed to eat that shit and explode. Actually, they didn't explode. But they got really thirsty and drank themselves to death.

Pfc ROBERT HARRISON
Alpha Company, 1/26 (Hill 950) _____

Large jungle rats used to provide a form of entertainment. They lived in our bunkers and would come out at night to look for food. Each evening we would set out traps baited with peanut butter, then compare body counts the next morning. We could always hear them moving around when we were trying to sleep. No one was ever bitten, probably due to the fact that we were not able to bathe for about five months.

Cpl DENNIS MANNION
Charlie Battery, 1/13 (Hill 861) _____

We never went outside the trenchline to do anything about the North Vietnamese who had been killed on the night of January 20–21 within our three concentric rows of wire. Using heavy ship's binoculars that were flown in shortly after the attack, I was able to see clearly that the bodies turned to skeletons within three weeks. There was no flesh left on them, just skeletons wearing North Vietnamese uniforms, packs, and helmets.

1stLt PAUL ELKAN
Bravo Battery, 1/13 _____

I was walking around one of the guns to see if there was any trash lying around the back of the bunker. If there was, I would tell the guys to police it up. I had just turned the corner of the bunker when three mortar rounds landed in the gun pit. A couple of the guys were wounded. One of them, a lance corporal, was only lightly wounded and he was confined to his bunker to recuperate. He soon went batshit. He had an M-16 rifle, which he put on semiautomatic and started shooting at the rats inside his bunker. Unfortunately, his bunker mates were also inside with the rats. The shooting really pissed them off. We had the lance corporal flown out as a "head case" the next day.

Cpl DENNIS MANNION
Charlie Battery, 1/13 (Hill 861)

February 4, 1968

Joe—
    Yep. So today's the day. One year ago at this time I was doing 900 side-straddle hops because of the extra amount of mail I received. A whole mother year ago.
    I had a quiet day—only eight incoming mortar rounds hit the hill (1 WIA) and two rockets *missed*—not by much, but they missed. I spent the better part of the day digging a new hole and bunker. I had the feeling that our present one was getting to be too well known. Besides, a change is always good.
    Had my birthday dinner about ten minutes ago—beans and franks, bread with peanut butter and apricot jelly, and pound cake. All courtesy of Uncle Sam's Combat Meal, Individual. Not like some of the other birthday meals I've had—but I've had worse.
    Well, the USMC is fucking with us again (not unusual). Word has it that we (881S, 861, and Khe Sanh) are "bait" for a trap the generals hope to pull on the NVA. Plan is to let those bastards hit into us (supposed to be three divisions plus two regiments) and then, during the height of the attack, drop the entire 101st Airborne Division behind the NVA and close in. All well and good. I just don't fancy the idea of holding off so many NVA until the fucking doggies show up. I almost feel like Davy Crockett at the Alamo. This hill is tough, but it won't hold forever. And these NVA are run by some brass who kicked the fucking French to shit in

1954, mainly at the battle of Dienbienphu, the fight where they lugged 105s into the hills—and the French didn't think they could do it.

Anyway, that's the situation, and I don't really like it. Still, I'm confident, and no matter what happens we'll have their ass in a sling in the final quarter.

To be honest, I don't rate my chances of coming out unmarked too good. Sorry, man, that's the way I feel. However, I'm psyched for the best—and the worst—and I'm leaving it all up to the Good Lord. It's in his hands, just like it was on February 4, 1946. Somebody's got to come out of this mess A-OK—right?

Chapter 14

FEBRUARY 5
ATTACK ON HILL 861A

2/26 Command Chronology

On January 23, Echo Company, 2/26, was chopped to 3/26 and subsequently deployed on [Hill 861A], to the west of Hill 558, based on agreement between COs of 2/26 and 3/26. 3/26 assumed operational control because of the proximity of their forces on Hill 861.

Capt EARLE BREEDING
Echo Company, 2/26

The NVA couldn't take Khe Sanh Combat Base without first taking Hill 861 and, once we go there, Hill 861A. If the NVA had owned those two hills, they would have been looking down on the combat base and on 2/26, which was on Hill 558. It was very important to hold 861 and 861A.

Pfc MIKE DeLANEY
Echo Company, 2/26

After landing at Khe Sanh, Echo Company kept moving around. I don't know if they couldn't make up their minds or if we were supposed to be moving, but we kept going during the day and spent each night on high ground, then we moved again. It didn't feel like we had a purpose. We stopped moving around when we went up on Hill 861A.

There was nothing but double- and triple-canopy jungle on the hill when we got there. It was heavy, heavy growth, and we saw a lot of wildlife on the way up the hill. It was very pretty, very picturesque.

It was super hot. It was like a smothering heat. Very little wind. The vegetation held the heat close to the ground. It was also humid, constantly humid. The fog would roll up from the valley. Sometimes it was like looking down on the clouds. That was scary because we couldn't see anything below us.

Nobody had any idea what to expect. Until we got to Hill 861A, our unit had been running daytime patrols and nighttime ambushes, working out of villages and through rice paddies and small jungle areas. Then, all of a sudden, we're working in the middle of a huge jungle. There were no people, just other Marines.

We had very little communication about what was going on. The only events we knew about were those we could see—fighting on Hill 881S, for example. We knew something was going on around us. It didn't seem to be super heavy, but it was going on.

Tension was rising, the mood was changing, the people in charge of the company were getting very serious. When we first got to the hill, we just laid around. Then we started getting organized, digging in. The captain walked around, talked with the lieutenants, said, "I don't want a gun here, I want it there," getting ready for something. It was typical of the military; none of us seemed to know what we were doing. Captain Breeding seemed to know what he was doing. He was very squared away.

Pfc MIKE DeLANEY
Echo Company, 2/26 _____

January 28, 1968

Hi Mom & Dad,
    Well, I got your box of socks, magazines, and long johns. Boy, that stuff is great, but the radio doesn't play up here on

the hill. I might send it back to you. Tell Uncle Gene he can send some canned fruit and juice.

Mom, it is bad here, but I don't want you to worry. If you want to know, I'll tell you a little about how I've been living. For the last two days, we went without water and food. Then a chopper came in and we got a couple of meals and about a glass of water for two days. We don't wash or shave. I've got a full beard and no change of clothes. I sleep on the ground, and we get some of our water from the bamboo plants, and eat the roots. We try to catch rainwater and the dew with our ponchos. They try to make it better, but the NVA shoot down the choppers. We get bombarded every day, and at night we get sniper fire. The company on the hill next to us [Kilo, on Hill 861] loses a man or more a day. Our company has not lost anyone yet. I have lost about fifteen pounds. We work all day in the hot sun and get so little to eat and drink. But I'm in real good health. I'm fine and I watch everything I do, so don't worry.

We had been catching some hell by then. It wasn't a lot, but it was enough to catch our interest.

I wrote home again on January 30, which happened to be my nineteenth birthday:

January 30, 1968

Dear Mom and Dad,

Well, what's new in The World this morning? I don't feel any different today. Just hungry, and I need some water. Some ice-cold water would be fine.

Well, it's been a good day so far. I'm still alive, and I think that's enough to be happy about. People back in the States don't know how lucky they've got it. People take too much stuff for granted. A little letter to me makes me so happy. I can't wait to get back to the States.

Send me some V8 juice, orange juice, or canned pop. I want a bottle of pop or Pepsi so bad that I think I'm going to go crazy. I can't live on a glass of water a day, so please send a lot. Please. I just lie in the hole at night thinking of kinds of stuff to drink. I think I will go nuts if I don't get something to drink. Send me some Wash-'N-Drys and some cough drops. Mom, can you get a little mirror like the one you have that opens and closes? That way it won't break.

I will pay for all the liquid stuff you can send. Just tell me what it costs you.

I'm in good health. I need a bath and a shave, and I probably do smell. I sure would like to be home. There's no place like home. Take my word for it.

Thanks for everything you guys do. I couldn't ask for better parents.

February 1, 1968

Hello Mom and Dad,

What is my wonderful family doing?

Well, it's about 4:30 in the morning, and I've got gun watch (60mm mortars), and so I thought I would try to write a couple lines. I'm down in my hole in the ground. It's about six foot by six foot by five foot deep. That's my home over here. I've got a little candle, so I thought I would write. I can hardly see.

I just wrote Uncle Gene. I just got a box of goodies from him today. Boy, was I happy.

How is everyone at home? Great, I hope. Me? I guess I'm okay. I just want some water and food. Boy, I stink. I need a bath. No water to wash with—not much even to drink. People in the States don't know how lucky they are. At least a bum can drink all the water he wants and doesn't have to live in the ground like a rat. It's hot during the day and it's cool at night. We dig holes all day and build bunkers. They are really pushing us to dig more trenches. We're always working. No time to do anything, like writing. That's why I'm writing at night.

Did you get my letter about sending some pop and juice? I pray every night that you will send some, and hurry up. I must sound crazy to you, but I can't stop thinking about water and stuff to drink. I'm so dry.

Mom, you and Dad better not be worried about me. I'm watching myself pretty good over here. You take care of each other. I don't want anyone to worry about me.

On my birthday, I tried to hide, but they found me and put me to work. I told them I wanted a day off. They asked me, "Why, do you have a date?" How stupid!

My candle is just about gone, so I will be saying goodbye for now.

Capt EARLE BREEDING
Echo Company, 2/26 _____

I was not a commander who believed the troops should not shoot, so it was policy in Echo Company that anyone could fire his weapon anytime he wanted to unless he was on an ambush. But the troops knew that if a gun went bang, there had better be something dead at the other end of its trajectory. Some battalions had a policy that permission to *return* fire had to be granted by the operations officer.

One night, shortly after we got to Hill 861A, the troops on the west side of the company perimeter called the command post to tell me they had movement in the saddle between us and Hill 861. When I went out there, they told me they had heard movement and shouted a challenge. When the response came back in English, they assumed that Kilo Company was running a patrol down there. I knew that Kilo wouldn't run a patrol without telling us, but I called Kilo anyway. Sure enough, they didn't have any patrols out. As soon as I heard that, I got every weapon that could bear firing into that draw. I don't know if we got anyone, but I made sure I told my troops to shoot anything that moved outside our wire. They sure as hell weren't running a patrol of English-speakers for the hell of it. We were being targeted.

Pfc MIKE DeLANEY
Echo Company, 2/26 _____

February 4, 1968

Dear Mom and Dad,

What's happening back home? Well, things here are getting a lot better. We've been getting more food and water. I'm just fine. Nothing is wrong with me. Sometimes I feel like saying to hell with all this. But I think of coming home and I get to feeling better.

So many guys go nuts over here. There is so much stuff on your mind. I never thought stuff could be the way it is over here, and the Marines get the worst—but do the best of all of them. The Marines are the best and the hardest. To be a Marine is to be something else I can't put into words. You go through living hell, but when you're done you know you've really done something no one else could have done. You walk with your head up high and say, "I was a Marine and never had it easy. I did my part and am proud." They give the Marines the hardest and the roughest jobs over here because they know we can do it.

How is my family? Great, I hope. Mom, I wish and pray that you don't worry about me. I'm fine and I don't take any chances. My hair is getting longer now, and I can just about comb it. I think about being home all the time, watching TV, just you and me and Dad, and eating all the stuff in the house. It would be great to go on a vacation, just you and me and Dad, at least for two months or so when I get home.

I want Philip [brother] to go in the Air Force, like Dad told me to do. Philip could be a Marine, but I don't want him to go through what I go through. I want him to have it easy. No sense him being in this situation.

I'm writing this letter with a flashlight while I'm on gun watch. I've got to fire a round in a few minutes, so I better say good-bye for now.

After I wrote my letter and got off gun watch, I was lying in my sleeping hole, on my back. It was completely dark, pitch black. I couldn't see my hand in front of my face. As I was falling off to sleep, I had the sensation that my heart and lungs had stopped. It woke me up. I couldn't breathe. I thought, What the hell is happening? It was teargas!

MGen TOMMY TOMPKINS
3rd Marine Division Commanding General _____

Sometime around mid-January we received a message at 3rd Marine Division Headquarters, in Dong Ha, that set forth the format for "Spotlight" reports. We had no idea what this was all about, but within the next few days we were told that the sensor acoustical devices would be dropped by planes in the areas to the northwest of the Khe Sanh Combat Base and west along Route 9.[1]

Maj JERRY HUDSON
26th Marines Intelligence Officer _____

Approximately January 18, a team from MACV Headquarters, in Saigon, visited Khe Sanh and offered the use of some electric [sic] devices which would give indications of enemy presence. [These were later] called sensors. Within 48 hours we began receiving reports that the devices were being implanted in likely avenues of approach to the combat base. Approximately the same time, we also began receiving reports that the devices were indicating enemy activity. (Everything in the area was considered enemy.) These reports increased in volume to over 100 per day.[2]

Lt BARNEY WALSH, USN
Observation Squadron 67

We were stationed at Nakhon Phanom in northeast Thailand, a Navy outfit on an Air Force Air Commando base. We were committed to support the "electronic barrier" that Secretary of Defense Robert McNamara thought would keep the North Vietnamese from infiltrating down the Ho Chi Minh Trail. Our particular job was to use our old Navy antisubmarine warfare patrol planes, flying at 180 knots, to lay a string of sonobuoys along the trails to listen to troop and truck noises. Once the enemy was identified, air strikes would be called in on the trail adjacent to the listening devices.

We laid numerous strings of sonobuoys north and northwest of Khe Sanh. We dropped sonobuoys that hung in the trees and others that dug into the ground and transmitted seismic information. After we dropped, EC-121 aircraft were in constant orbit at altitude, relaying information back to Nakhon Phanom. Each sonobuoy had a unique frequency so the noise could be pinpointed and enemy progress through the area could be followed.

Around Khe Sanh, there weren't any trails that I could see, so I figured they just wanted a wall of buoys to give warning of infiltration. We had a sister Air Force squadron flying A-1 Skyraiders. They dropped "gravel" around the sonobuoys to protect them. The gravel was an explosive shaped like a Vietnamese leaf that was carried in a container along with a Freon solution. When released, it scattered over the ground like tree leaves, and when it warmed up, it could blow the tire off a jeep or the leg off a man. The A-1 squadron was trained to fly with us and drop the gravel around the buoys to discourage the enemy from picking them up. However, we didn't fly too many missions together because we were quite a gaggle, flying in big, slow aircraft at 180 or so knots with three or four A-1s on either wing—sitting ducks for antiaircraft.

Maj JERRY HUDSON
26th Marines Intelligence Officer _____

The information from the Infiltration Service Center (ISC) at Nakhon Phanom was passed direct to the intelligence officer of the 26th Marines over a dedicated clear-voice-radio circuit. A covered teletype circuit also existed. We talked to Nakhon Phanom many times a night attempting to "learn to swim."[3]

For the first days, the reports were received with some anxiety as their meaning was not clear. However, after exchange of numerous messages with various commands involved in implanting, read-out, and interpretation of the information, definite patterns could be detected and were targeted.

Prior to the advent of sensors, it was command doctrine to shoot numerous H&I artillery missions each night. These missions were usually based on map inspection, suspect areas, and yesterday's intelligence. The sensor provided [nearly] real-time information, and the words [harassment and interdiction] were virtually removed from the 3rd Marine Division vocabulary in favor of "Moving-Target Fire."[4]

MGen TOMMY TOMPKINS
3rd Marine Division Commanding General _____

For the first few weeks, we used the sensors as a targeting method, which was in accordance with instructions we were given by the MACV briefing officers. The results were better than H&I fires, but that is saying very little. We then began using the sensors as an intelligence-gathering medium. The trouble with using sensors as a targeting device was that we didn't know exactly where the sensors were located. The reports from [Nakhon Phanom] took some time to get to Khe Sanh Combat Base, and the sensors frequently reported our own fires.

Sensors as an intelligence-gathering medium were highly successful. At night and at times of low visibility, they were our only means of obtaining information on enemy movement and activity. When sensor reports could be checked by aerial observation, following an air/artillery strike, the system came into its highest development.[5]

Maj JERRY HUDSON
26th Marines Intelligence Officer _____

I believe that sensors played an important role in the defense of Khe Sanh. I know that they were relied upon heavily in determining my estimates of the enemy situation to Colonel Lownds.[6]

Capt HARRY BAIG
26th Marines Target Information Officer _____

During the nights of February 3–4 and 4–5, "Mussel Shoals" sensors had reported numerous heavy movements from the northwest of Hill 881S. At a distance of 4,000 meters, the movements turned south and later turned east. The intruders were last reported south of [Hill 881S]. Sensors to the southeast of the hill did not sound an alarm. The total count of enemy troops, reported by the sensors, added to a possible 1,500 to 2,000 men in the course of those two nights. During the first night [February 3–4], my interpretation lay in the direction of resupply convoys, and the Fire Support Coordination Center reacted by attacking each sensor target as it appeared. During the second night, I veered toward the thought of an enemy regiment and a probable attack. Majors Coolidge [Division Intelligence representative] and Hudson tended to agree.

We concluded that an attack in the thick mist was imminent. Enemy doctrine calls for an attacking force to move to its assault position in echelons, make a last-minute reconnaissance, and attack in waves. If this was indeed a regiment, then the force would probably be disposed in a regimental column, battalions in line one behind the other. As time passed without activation of the easterly sensors, we three became convinced. A target block, 1,000 by 3,000 meters, was described on the map south of Hill 881S at about a point where a large force, moving at two kilometers per hour (NVA rate of march in darkness and mist—more doctrine) would have reached in the time interval since the activation of the last sensor. At each end of the block, a gently curving 1,000-meter line was drawn, extending toward and about the southwestern and southeastern slope of Hill 881S.[7]

Maj JERRY HUDSON
26th Marines Intelligence Officer

[The enemy was getting ready to assault Hill 881S or Hill 861A, or both together.] A decision had to be made which one to interdict. The choice was in favor of 881S as the artillery there could be employed in support of 861A if required.[8]

Capt HARRY BAIG
26th Marines Target Information Officer

Colonel Lownds, having accepted the reasoning . . . gave permission to fire. For about thirty minutes, commencing approximately 0300, February 5, five batteries of 1/13 within KSCB and four batteries of [U.S. Army] 175mm guns from outside the base poured continuous fire into various places of the block and along the two circumscribing lines at each end. Later, [sensor monitors at] Nakhon Phanom Center told me that acoustic sensors in the area to the south of Hill 881S recorded the voices of hundreds of men running in panic, through the darkness and heavy fog, in a southerly direction. The seismic sensors went wild.[9]

Maj JERRY HUDSON
26th Marines Intelligence Officer

We felt we had preempted the attack on 881S.[10]

Capt HARRY BAIG
26th Marines Target Information Officer

It never occurred to me that night that the enemy's intent was, and always had been, to attack Hills 881S and 861 simultaneously. I had forgotten the NVA battle plan. There were no sensors near Hills 861 and 861A. So, when the latter was attacked two hours later, I, the Target Information Officer and alleged expert on NVA doctrine, was caught flatfooted.[11]

Capt EARLE BREEDING
Echo Company, 2/26

Marines on the point of the 1st Platoon sector passed the word, "They're coming through the wire." That news spread up the trenchline to the right and left. All the way along the trenchline and up the chain of command, Echo Company was hearing, "They're coming through the wire." Nobody said which part of the wire, and nobody could see anything. The average Marine thought the NVA were coming through the wire in front of him because he had heard it from the guy next to him. So, all of a sudden, within seconds of one another, I got the word from all three of my platoon commanders. It sounded to me like they were coming through the wire all around the hill. I thought I was getting hit from all sides at once. I had the troops throw gas grenades and I called for all the artillery support the combat base could give me.

The gas probably did us more harm than it did the NVA. It started filtering into the low-lying areas—our fighting holes and trenches.

Pfc MIKE DeLANEY
Echo Company, 2/26 _____

The gas—it must have been theirs—got everyone up and moving in the open, disoriented. When you're running around grabbing your chest and having the sensation that you can't breathe, you're not thinking about manning a weapon.

Then I started to hear gunfire. I could hear guns popping. It sounded like a little pop, followed by small-arms fire, and then another little pop. As I bolted out of my hole, it finally dawned on me that I was breathing gas. I got back down in my hole and ran my hand over everything, looking for my gas mask. I found it, climbed out of my hole, and started running around while I put it on and adjusted it.

Capt EARLE BREEDING
Echo Company, 2/26 _____

They had zeroed their mortars in on us the night before, but I hadn't realized what they had done. They had fired one round, not the normal group of three at maximum range. If it was us, we'd have fired round after round after round and adjusted the fire. They fired just one mortar round from fairly close in. They made their adjustment on that one round and held their fire until the attack started. When their 82mm mortars hit us, I believe they expected to catch our people fleeing toward and off the south side of the hill.

Pfc MIKE DeLANEY
Echo Company, 2/26 _____

The whole skyline to my left—the 1st Platoon area—was starting to light up. There was yellow and orange color coming off the horizon. There were things going off—the 60mm mortar over there, the Chicom grenades, machine guns—and I could hear people talking and yelling. People were screaming. People were running, scrambling. People were looking for their gas masks. All kinds of shit was hitting the fan. We were very disorganized at that point. Whatever the NVA had in mind, it worked. They definitely caught us by surprise.

Capt EARLE BREEDING
Echo Company, 2/26 _____

They came up the northern slope, the only approach they had. I knew they would; they weren't going to come around the other side of the hill in the face of direct artillery fire from the combat base and 106s from the 2/26 position on Hill 558. As it was, they had all the cover in the world between the dark of night and all that high elephant grass.

The company perimeter was much longer than it was wide, and there was a salient in the west side. We tried to round it off the best way we could on the northern point, which was held by 1stLt Don Shanley's 1st Platoon. That was a slight disadvantage for us because we could bring less fire to bear, but it was also a disadvantage to the NVA because they could not see how many troops I had set in on the rest of the hill. It is possible—reasonable—that they thought we were a platoon outpost from Kilo Company, which was on the adjacent hill. Without illumination, no one on the hill could see a white handkerchief in front of his face. It was absolutely pitch black.

Pfc MIKE DeLANEY
Echo Company, 2/26 _____

They hit the 1st Platoon because it was stretched across a finger that was lower than the rest of the hilltop, easier to get to. The

60mm mortar and M-60 machine gun with 1st Platoon got it right off the bat. The best anyone could figure out was that the NVA had watched us shoot H&I fire for days and had marked the gun positions. Since the crew-served weapons were dug in, we never moved them. The positions were permanent from the time the company lines were established. The NVA knew where all the crew-served weapons were before they started to attack.

Capt EARLE BREEDING
Echo Company, 2/26 _____

When the NVA broke through Shanley's 1st Platoon, they had nowhere to go. They were faced with a steep climb to the top of the hill. In fact, they didn't break through Shanley as much as they *absorbed* through him. There were 1st Platoon Marines down there manning their positions right through the fight.

Pfc MIKE DeLANEY
Echo Company, 2/26 _____

I had a stinging sensation down my nose and throat, but there was so much going on, so much adrenaline, that I overcame it. But my eyes were watering. It was night and I was trying to see through the gas-mask lenses with my eyes watering. It was a mess.

It was the first time ground forces had tried to enter our wire. We had been mortared before, but now they were in our wire. This was it! Everything I ever thought war could be was happening, right now. I wasn't scared like I had been when the mortars hit. There was so much going on that my mind couldn't comprehend it. We had the gas, there were people running, people screaming, stuff exploding. I knew I had a job to do, I had to go look for my 60mm mortar. It was only yards away from me—the whole squad was in bunkers we had built right around the gun pit.

The only members of my 60mm mortar squad in the pit were the gunner and the assistant gunner. Four of us, ammo humpers, were on the outside, opening crates of ammo and passing rounds in like a nurse would pass a scalpel for a doctor. When the round went out, *boomp,* one of us slapped another round into the assistant gunner's hand, whatever he called for—illume, high explosive, whatever. We tore off powder increments as we handed each round over, whatever charge the gunner called for.

When we started firing, the mortar was tilted slightly toward the north, toward the 1st Platoon sector. People were calling fire to us—"Bring it up the hill," or "Bring it down the point." They were calling the fire by screaming; no calls came in by radio. We were alternating illume and high explosives as fast as we could get rounds down the tube. It was obvious that the rounds were going too high, so we started firing the rounds with the base charge. When we got to the point where the NVA had crossed the 1st Platoon wire, most of our rounds were fired almost straight up because we really didn't want any distance on them. When the NVA penetrated the 1st Platoon bunkers and broke through, we fired straight up. We knew the consequence, but we had no choice. The only way to keep them off of us was to throw around as much shrapnel as possible. We had flak gear on, and we were laying in among the sandbags, passing rounds into the gun pit, so we thought we would be okay. The NVA were all in the open, running past us.

Capt EARLE BREEDING
Echo Company, 2/26 ⎯⎯⎯⎯⎯⎯⎯⎯⎯⎯⎯⎯⎯⎯⎯⎯⎯⎯⎯

I kept thinking, What am I going to do if they shoot off my radio antennas? When it was all over, I had no radio antennas up. They were all down. The only reason I was able to communicate with outside headquarters was because of our elevation.

My command post was about halfway back along the hill from the 1st Platoon area and a little to the east of the military crest. There was a big tree right at the top of the hill, and since I wanted to leave as much of the natural vegetation in place as possible, I tucked the command post in under its branches, mainly to protect the radiomen. Also, my company sickbay was in a huge bomb crater left over from the Hill Fights in mid-1967—also protected by the tree.

I had to keep the NVA away from the sickbay bomb crater, which was filled with men who couldn't fight back. Also, my command post was filling up with Marines who had been temporarily blinded by gas, flash burns, or grenades and mortar rounds going off at close range. So, as soon as things settled down enough for me to make sense of what was going on, I began feeding fire teams forward from the rear platoons in order to build up a line across the top of the hill. I truncated the company position with anybody I could get, more or less cutting off the 1st Platoon's nose and sealing off most of the NVA who had filtered through the 1st Platoon. The new line was made up mostly of 1st Platoon people, but anyone else who wanted to be part of it was welcome.

It sounds more organized in the telling than it really was. There was too much loud noise for me to shout direct orders; my desire seeped through the company, and individual Marines reacted on their own. I had to rely on training and instinct. But, from the time we got the new line built up, I wasn't concerned. I knew we were going to hold. Nevertheless, there was a moment in which I would have liked to get out of there, but I knew there was really no way. I wasn't about to retreat, and besides, there was no way to leave the hill. That was scary. There was no way to leave that hill at night, and certainly there was no way to do it without leaving our dead and wounded behind.

Pfc MIKE DeLANEY
Echo Company, 2/26

People were shooting with handguns. We were shooting at each other with handguns. We were throwing fragmentation grenades at point-blank range; I'd throw a frag, turn my back to it, and hunch up my neck and shoulders, hoping I wouldn't catch chunks large enough to take me out. We did whatever we thought would work.

While the 1st Platoon guys were fighting hand-to-hand—using entrenching tools, whatever—the NVA were running through the perimeter, doing as much damage as they could. They were throwing satchel charges and grenades at the crew-manned weapons. They were everywhere. They blew up the 60mm mortar near 1st Platoon, killing four of the Marines in and around the pit. It was such chaos from that point on that, whenever I brought up my M-16, I had to glance at whoever was going by to make sure he was an NVA, and not a Marine. We had illume, but it moved around overhead and made shifting shadows. They made it seem like *everything* was moving. It was just very scary.

Capt EARLE BREEDING
Echo Company, 2/26

It was uncontrolled pandemonium. I'd like to say that I was about to win this one fight, and the Marine I was fighting would like to say he was about to win, too. Luckily, a flare went off before we killed one another. .

Capt HARRY BAIG
26th Marines Target Information Officer _____

The artillery and air response to the enemy's assault may be divided into three phases, all of which occurred simultaneously. 1/13 loosed the protective fires on the slopes of Hill 861A with three batteries. A fourth battery concentrated in the area where the enemy movement was the thickest and then rolled down the slope to prevent the enemy from retiring or from being reinforced. This was the first phase.

The second phase began with the four batteries of [U.S. Army] 175mm guns from Camp Carroll and the Rock Pile delivering their ordnance along two arms of a broad V, which embraced the base of the hill from the northeast. The objective of the guns was to saturate the area wherein the enemy reserve battalion was estimated to be. Slowly, the V crept up the slopes until it reached a point 200 meters from the wire. Within this space, the fourth battery from KSCB rolled to and fro, covering the area from which the attackers had come and into which Captain Breeding was energetically heaving them. Meanwhile, the remaining batteries continued their protective missions or were adjusted in accordance with the garrison's desires.

The third phase involved the rapidly assembling aircraft. AN/TPQ-10 radar-directed air strikes, in the form of 200- and 300-meter ripples, were dropped outboard of, and parallel to, the V to avoid checkfires. Bombs fell on known mortar clusters, possible assembly areas, and throughout the area to the far rear of the assault battalion.[12]

Capt EARLE BREEDING
Echo Company, 2/26 _____

We were drawing fire support from five separate locations: our own 60mm mortars; the 81mm mortars and 105mm howitzers on Hill 881S; the 2/26 106mm recoilless rifles on Hill 558; the 105mm howitzers from the combat base, and the 175mm howitzers at the Rock Pile and Camp Carroll. But I couldn't adjust anyone's fire because I didn't know friendly from hostile incoming. Not only were our surviving mortars firing on the hill, we were under a constant NVA mortar barrage. In addition, I was later told, the friendly howitzers were dumping variable-time rounds on us—airbursts. Getting hit or not getting hit was a matter of luck, for us and the NVA.

Hill 881S was farther from Hill 861A than the maximum range of the 81mm mortar rounds they were firing. Firing the maximum charge at maximum range was barely enough, but the rounds reached us because we were 20 meters lower. They were barely accurate, but they did enough. The Marines on Hill 881S used up just about all their 81mm ammo to help us.

Capt EARLE BREEDING
Echo Company, 2/26 _____

The way the teargas didn't affect the NVA at all leads me to believe they were hopped up on drugs. The gas was an irritant, and they should have been bothered. *We* were bothered. During the first lull, I found one of them with his AK-47 slung over his shoulder. He and others were going through our living hooches, more interested in reading *Playboy* magazines than in fighting the war. That's when we counterattacked.

It would be nice to say that everybody stood there, did a dress right dress, and fixed bayonets while I shouted, "Port arms, forward march!" But it just didn't work out that way. It was a matter of individual Marines saying to their buddies, "Hey, come on. Let's go kick 'em outta here." All the troop leaders could do was lead the way or kick ass.

Capt HARRY BAIG
26th Marines Target Information Officer _____

Enemy attack doctrine frequently positions the reserve battalion directly behind the assault unit. At all costs, the Fire Support Coordination Center was determined to prevent their juncture. Hence the multiple bands of fire. The reserve battalion never materialized. The second attack, at 0610, was made by the survivors of the first assault. These unfortunate remnants could neither retire through the rolling barrage nor be reinforced by the reserve, which in turn had been caught between the 175mm artillery and the air strikes.[13]

Capt EARLE BREEDING
Echo Company, 2/26 ⎯⎯⎯⎯⎯⎯⎯⎯⎯⎯⎯⎯⎯⎯⎯⎯

I'm sure they were only out there to drag away the bodies of the NVA who were killed in front of our wire.

Pfc MIKE DeLANEY
Echo Company, 2/26 ⎯⎯⎯⎯⎯⎯⎯⎯⎯⎯⎯⎯⎯⎯⎯⎯

Finally it slowed up and they backed off. I looked around at all the powder increments I had ripped off 60mm rounds, at all the grenade canisters, LAAW rocket tubes, and piles of empty brass. Stuck in a sandbag only a foot or so from where I was handing rounds into the gun pit was an NVA rifle grenade that never went off.

When they first started to pull away, there was very heavy fog. It was clear when we started, but it was very thickly overcast when it petered off. I have no idea when the fog rolled in. It was just there.

There were bodies everywhere. Their bodies were in full uniform. That scared me. Until then, I thought we were fighting Viet Cong guerrillas. We had been fighting VC before we got to Khe Sanh; I didn't know they had NVA soldiers up there until I saw them dead on the ground inside our perimeter. It scared me; it really drove it home that we were fighting a uniformed army, not a bunch of people who were farmers by day and who ran around at night being VC. These people were well armed.

Captain Breeding grabbed me in the morning and ordered me to help get a body count. I went around to each position on the hill, asking Marines if they knew where any NVA bodies were, counting them up. After the count was completed, they were stacked up.

I had never seen young dead people. The only dead people I had ever seen were old. In my mind, old people are supposed to die, but not young people. I had sat around the day before smoking cigarettes and sharing C-rations with some of the dead young people on that hill. Their skin was gray and rubbery; they didn't look human anymore. Picking them up gave me a funny feeling. It never stopped bothering me, the feel of the bodies. I had never felt a dead body before. And now I was being asked to carry them around—and pick up body *parts*. That upset me, picking up an arm or a leg—from people I knew, from my own squad, from the 60mm mortar crew and the M-60 machine-gun crew that had been with the 1st Platoon.

Quite a few of the NVA we killed inside our wire were bandaged—that night. It was obvious that they had sent their wounded back up to fight the battle. That scared me to the point that I could not believe that people who had already been wounded and messed up still wanted to fight. I figured they had a lot more drive than I had. Those people were scary, like they were almost superhuman. We found drugs—syringes and chemicals.

Capt EARLE BREEDING
Echo Company, 2/26 _____

I don't think they would have gotten through us if we had had the gear we needed. We had been up there only a short while, and we had not had an opportunity to build our position up. We didn't have enough wire. We didn't even have sledgehammers to pound in the engineering stakes to secure the wire. It really came down to saving money over saving people's lives. It was just dollars.

After it was over, my top priorities were getting the wounded out and getting replacement people and crew-served weapons in. We were given top priority in all of I Corps. They gave us everything we needed—had needed before the attack.

LCpl WILLIAM MAVES
2/26 Tactical Air Control Party _____

After the second NVA effort toward morning failed to take Hill 861A, I started to take a count of casualties and move them into position near the landing zone for medevac.

At dawn, we were fogged in solid, which was common up there. It usually didn't burn off until 1000 or 1100. This forced upon me the biggest decision of my life. If Danang sent the fleet of choppers I had requested for thirty-five wounded and they couldn't get through the fog, it would be hours before they could come back again after refueling. What to do? I had emergency medevacs waiting in the landing zone who would not live another hour if I waited. If they couldn't get in, more would die with the longer wait.

I looked at the men lying there and told Danang to send the birds. When they got there, I stood in the middle of the landing zone with a red star cluster in my hand, staring up through the fog, listening to the rotors circling overhead. One pilot said he would circle lower and lower until I could get a visual. It seemed like forever until I finally saw the bottom of that bird go over in the fog. I shot the red star cluster up at him, and down he came through the fog, onto the landing zone.

The rest was easy. He left straight up and another bird was circling, ready to drop down in the spot the first one came out of. As it turned out, the fog didn't lift that day until about noon. Sunshine filled the valley and everything looked scenic again. I could only wonder if last night had been a bad dream.

Pfc MIKE DeLANEY
Echo Company, 2/26 _____

February 6, 1968—0230

Dear Mom and Dad,
Just in case you heard on the TV news or radio, last night they tried to overrun our hill, 861A, in mass-wave attacks.

0430—Well, I had to stop writing this letter for a couple hours. We just got hit again.

In two days we have lost eight men dead and about sixteen hurt, and about thirty-five WIAs, some in real bad shape. Four of my real good friends got killed on the night of February 5, Monday. No one died tonight, just three wounded. We had to use gas on them. We all had to wear our gas masks. Boy, is it hard to run around and work with one on.

I'm fine and only tired. I wanted you to know that I'm still alive and okay because I know this will be in the papers.

I don't want you to worry about me, so I thought I would let you know how it was. We won the fight. Everyone comes and thanks us for doing such a good job because, without our gun, I don't think we would have kept this hill. They call us the Dirty Half-Dozen because there are six of us and our gun is the best one they've got. There's only two. The other one was blown up the first night. That's when my buddies got killed. That morning, after the battle, I carried the dead and wounded to the choppers and counted the dead enemy.

Boy, Mom, it hurts to see people you know in little pieces. We just threw their arms and legs into rubber bags. It's really getting bad around here. We should be here for many months, on the hill.

I haven't got any mail for over a week now. If you send me any boxes or stuff, don't insure them because they won't get up here on the hill.

When they probed us on the morning of February 6, we threw a few grenades at them and they threw a few Chicoms at us. It was just enough contact to keep everybody up. It didn't last for more than an hour, and it wasn't continuous.

Chapter 15

FEBRUARY 7
LANG VEI

SSgt HARVE SAAL, USA
FOB-3

Just after midnight—February 7—the Special Forces camp at Lang Vei came under heavy attack from the west. Upon hearing heavy gunfire to the FOB's southwest, I turned on and monitored my recon team's radio, which was a radio frequency shared by the FOB and the Special Forces A Team in Lang Vei. At various times, I heard the following:

"They've got tanks out there." Moments later, I heard the FOB-3 [Khe Sanh] radio operator say, "We'll be down [off the air] for a short time." Then, within the next five minutes, the Lang Vei radio operator called the FOB, but got no answer. The Lang Vei operator called the FOB again and shouted, "There's tanks on our [radio bunker] roof." Then there was a rushing sound and the Lang Vei radio went silent.

1stLt FRED McGRATH
Bravo Battery, 1/13

I had the battery exec pit the night Lang Vei was overrun. We had Lang Vei on the radio and were providing fire support, based upon the Special Forces personnel adjusting the rounds. The last transmission was to the effect, "Oh, hell, they have tanks. They're right on top of us." We didn't hear anything else. We tried several other frequencies, but could not contact Lang Vei.

SSgt HARVE SAAL, USA
FOB-3

Since I felt that no one from the FOB radio team had monitored this last message, I notified the FOB sergeant major as to what I had heard. All attempts at communicating with the Special Forces camp at Lang Vei went unanswered. I told the FOB sergeant major that something had to be done for the Special Forces team in Lang Vei. He agreed.

The commander of the 26th Marines, Colonel Lownds, was notified and briefed on the Lang Vei situation. Since Lang Vei fell within his designated operational area of responsibility, nothing could take place in this area without his approval or knowledge. Colonel Lownds was asked to mount an immediate operation into Lang Vei in order to find and rescue all possible survivors. He refused the request and said that he would not sacrifice any *American* lives. He was reminded that the Special Forces survivors were, in fact, *Americans,* too! He just glared through us like an X-ray machine and dismissed our thoughts as so much bravado. He restated his refusal to mount a rescue attempt.

Maj JIM STANTON
26th Marines Fire Support Coordination Center

It is true that we had an agreement to go to the aid of Lang Vei in the event it was threatened with being overrun, but the situation at the combat base deteriorated so quickly and so completely that it should have been obvious to anyone that we could no longer guarantee their security. It was too long a march, particularly at night. Nevertheless, the night of the attack, there was serious talk about mounting a relief force. At the same time, the Special Forces headquarters in Saigon was saying that they would rescue their Special Forces people at Lang Vei. In the end, no one was sent. It was the right decision. If we had sent a company or even a battalion out there, they would have been murdered. We were sure that the attack on Lang Vei was a ploy to get the Marine relief force outside the combat base wire, that they had set an ambush for the relief column before they even began attacking the Special Forces camp. Our intelligence people were going crazy. We had no idea what they had out there, and Lang Vei was telling us they had "tanks in the wire."

LCpl ARMANDO GONZALES
Bravo Company, 1/9

I heard the sounds of tanks over our radio, and some Marines in the battalion claimed they could hear the tanks' engines themselves. Many of us wanted to go out to help the Lang Vei defenders, but there was no way that any unit large enough to help could have gone out at night through that terrain, with all those NVA out there, without getting ambushed. We knew it, we didn't like it, we felt bad and angry, but, realistically, we would have been wiped out easier than the base that was getting hit.

LtCol JIM WILKINSON
1/26 Commanding Officer

In November 1967, Colonel Lownds directed that I determine an overland route between KSCB and Lang Vei, with the time/space factor for moving a rifle company to Lang Vei on a tactical mission. Alpha Company, 1/26, moved through the jungle between KSCB and Lang Vei to determine possible routes to be used in the event Lang Vei was to be reinforced. It was determined that a rifle company, avoiding well-used trails to preclude ambush, could move by foot from KSCB to Lang Vei in approximately nineteen hours.[1]

1stLt JOHN KAHENY
1/26 Combat Operations Center

On the night Lang Vei was attacked, I heard their call sign, Spunky Hanson, on the regimental tactical net, asking that we go down there and rescue them. But we knew by then that it was impossible to get down Highway 9 without being ambushed.

The Army was really seriously upset because we did not send a convoy down to relieve the camp when it was under that armored attack. We did not know at the time that they were just

PT-76s, but, even given that, the chances of a successful break-through that night down Highway 9 were nonexistent.

SSgt HARVE SAAL, USA
FOB-3

We notified the pilots of several Marine Huey helicopters of our impending intentions to mount a rescue operation into Lang Vei. Then we rallied FOB Special Forces volunteers and Bru montagnards for the impending operation. Meanwhile, there was a degree of confusion concerning the basic rescue plan. I told the FOB sergeant major that all we needed was a search-and-security team, and he agreed.

The FOB Special Forces volunteers and montagnards were formed into search and security elements. I was placed in a search element because of my prior social visits to and knowledge of the Lang Vei Special Forces camp. I knew the layout at Lang Vei.

We were flying at a jerking-type pace to ensure that the NVA gunners weren't presented with good targets. As we bounced over the last treetops in choppers, we were able to see too-many-to-count smoldering embers on both sides of Highway 9 and basically concentrated inside the perimeter wire of the camp. Dense smoke, both gray and blackish, obscured the ground, so few details could be made out at a distance of approximately a half-mile.

I could see that some men from the lead chopper were jumping out into the camp at a height of about twenty feet. The forward speed of their chopper ranged from almost still to up to at least ten knots. At first I thought the chopper had been disabled by ground fire and that they were "unassing" the crashing chopper, but, as we came closer, it became obvious that there was a semblance of security. As they spread out toward the camp perimeter wire, it was evident that they were *not* firing their rifles. It therefore seemed that the NVA presence, so far, was not menacing. I hoped that they had not remained to secure and use the camp.

After I disembarked from the helicopter, and soon after it lifted off, I could smell burnt grass and burnt flesh. It was certain that the NVA had used flamethrowers in conquering this camp. I moved past a trenchline where burnt bodies were still smoldering. This was my first opportunity to see what effect flamethrowers had in the outcome of a pitched battle, and it was a devastating awakening for me.

A cursory look about the camp revealed some Russian tanks, which were disabled and motionless. I then recalled the radio message that morning in which the radio operator had reported, "There's a tank on the roof." I ran to the general area in which the A Team's underground bunkers were located. There it was. The tank was dead still, destroyed, over what I knew was the location of a bunker.

I paused briefly near the entrance of the bunker. A quick glance revealed a U.S. jeep with the body of a lifeless Special Forces soldier. He was slumped against the firing tube of a 106mm recoilless rifle. That tube was pointed directly at a destroyed Russian tank. It didn't take a genius to figure out that he had wiped out the tank at the same moment the tank gunner had shot and mortally wounded him. He was SFC Eugene Ashley, and he received a posthumous Medal of Honor.

I went to the bunker door and tried to open it from the outside. It was sealed tightly. I pounded on the metal door and yelled, "Is anybody in there?" Silence; no answer.

I tried again. This time, there was a faint reply from inside the bunker, a faint "Fuck you, asshole." I yelled, "Hey, motherfucker, open that fuckin' door so we can take you back to the FOB with us." The team sergeant, SFC Thomas Craig, reluctantly opened the door. Not much time was spent on thanks. I later learned that the NVA were yelling down the air shafts in English, trying to prod someone inside to open the bunker door so they, the NVA, could take the occupants prisoner. The NVA also used hand grenades, satchel charges, and CS teargas canisters against the defenders in the bunker. Fortunately, the survivors didn't give in so easily and still held hope that they would be rescued.

After we ate lunch at the main bunker, the surviving Special Forces soldiers were guided to and loaded on the Marine choppers. They were eventually flown out of Khe Sanh to Danang. Our original intentions were only to rescue the American survivors at Lang Vei, but, as it turned out, we managed to rescue a large portion of the CIDG force as well. Also, Laotian civilian refugees who were in the protection of the camp defensive perimeter began moving out of camp, east along Highway 9.

After the rescue, we could see that some of the Asian survivors were different in a peculiar sort of way. They didn't seem to fit in well with the others. They had short haircuts and appeared to be in better health than some of the other survivors. It developed, through interrogation, that a few of them were infiltrators. Their orders were to go to a refugee camp and gather intelligence. Some others were given the task of causing general havoc and distrust among the refugees.

I did not encounter any NVA troops while I searched through the camp for survivors. I really did not know until later, after the rescue, if there was any resistance from NVA troops still within the camp. To our delight, after we compared notes, it was thought by all involved that the NVA did not purposely leave any combat forces in the camp. After-operation intelligence estimates of enemy intentions during our rescue operation assumed that the North Vietnamese thought we were retaking the Lang Vei camp and that we would then prepare to hold it. With that in mind, they pulled back to regroup for another attack on Lang Vei.

We rescued sixteen out of twenty-three Americans that day and lost *no* lives as a result of our "lunacy." We were reported by Colonel Lownds to General William Westmoreland as being uncooperative and unprofessional. The general called our commander to Saigon for a tongue-lashing. He told him to be more responsive to the Marine commander. Then Westy congratulated him on a rescue job well done.

"TANKS IN THE WIRE"

Lt RAY STUBBE
1/26 Battalion Chaplain

[DIARY ENTRY] I saw casualties from Lang Vei, who began arriving. Captain Willoughby, their CO, told me the NVA pounded the camp with 152mm artillery and then brought in tanks. One tank stood directly on top of the command-post bunker. We, ourselves, are now more vulnerable—from Russian tanks! Everybody knows it!

The use of PT-76 amphibious tanks in the attack on Lang Vei Special Forces Camp made real the little-known NVA armor threat. The large, relatively safe area of Laos, the very thick vegetation common to much of that area of operations and neighboring portions of the country, and the flat or gently rolling terrain near the KSCB made the use of tanks against the base quite possible. The strongpoint defenses being used in the area of operations and the success at Lang Vei made the use of tanks likely because of their shock effect and their wire-breaching and bunker-busting capabilities.

Although the use of tanks against KSCB was quite possible, certain factors tended to reduce the likely effectiveness of such an enemy course of action. First, the abundance of antitank minefields and organic and attached antitank weapons would substantially reduce an attacking armor force. Second, the shock effect of the tanks had already been partially diminished by their initial use at Lang Vei. Also, it was believed unlikely that the shock effect would be as effective against American forces once [they were] alerted as it was on indigenous forces caught by surprise.

Maj JIM STANTON
26th Marines Fire Support Coordination Center _____

Our aerial observers found the camouflaged PT-76s that had attacked Lang Vei tied up to the bank of the Xe Pone River, in Laos. They apparently had run out of gas. We called in Marine A-4s. After a couple of strikes, we heard the aircraft had blown the camouflage away to reveal damaged and destroyed vehicles. As more bombs were dropped farther afield around the PT-76s, we got reports of secondary explosions, which indicated ammo dumps dug in along the river. This led to more strikes, more destruction, more serendipitous discoveries, and so forth.

Within ten days after the battle of Lang Vei on February 7, air reconnaissance showed that eight tanks and armored personnel carriers had been destroyed near Lang Vei and to the south along the Laotian border. Since only seven tanks had been used against Lang Vei and ten to twelve were [believed] to be the maximum likely enemy capability, it was felt that the most immediate threat had been substantially reduced. Reports of tank sightings in the DMZ and Laos continued to be received, and agent reports frequently made reference to major armor attacks in the northern Quang Tri area.

1stLt JOHN KAHENY
1/26 Combat Operations Center

We were as vulnerable to enemy armor as the Special Forces camp was. I had drafted the rough counter-mechanized plan for 1/26, and I knew that if the NVA ever deployed any armor against us, we would have a difficult time defending ourselves against it. This was mainly because we had only five M-48 tanks and ten Ontos in the area. Also, we didn't have an area in which we could operate our armor effectively. It would have been a very nasty scene if tanks had broken through. We basically said that, once we ran out of LAAWs, we could always tape thermite grenades onto the engine hoods. This was, on the face of it, a facetious way to allay our fears.

LCpl CHARLIE THORNTON
Lima Company, 3/26

Our commanders began to prepare for tank attacks by the NVA. Our weapons platoon was chosen as a "tank killer" group. We were trained how to stop a tank, crack it open with explosives, and finish it off with a flamethrower. It seemed like such a ridiculous idea during the days of modern weapon systems and explosives. I was chosen as the one to carry the flamethrower. As usual, the equipment was of World War II vintage. We prepared every day to defend against tanks.

LCpl ARMANDO GONZALES
Bravo Company, 1/9

After Lang Vei, we dug what we called "suicide holes" out in front of our lines. These were about six or seven feet deep and large enough for a good-sized Marine to jump into standing up. The idea was that volunteers carrying explosives would be in the holes, ready to attach the explosives to the bottom of a tank going by overhead. We knew that tanks never operated without infantry, so there was no guarantee that a Marine manning one of those holes wouldn't be found by the infantry.

Chapter 16

FEBRUARY 8
ALPHA-1

Pfc LAWRENCE SEAVY-CIOFFI
Alpha Company, 1/9

I was a forward artillery scout observer assigned from Delta Battery, 2/12, to Alpha Company, 1/9.

The 1st Platoon of Alpha Company, 1/9 (Alpha-1), manned a forward outpost slightly over a quarter-mile due west of 1/9's position [at the Rock Quarry]. Essentially, the platoon's observation post was a small, cleared hilltop [Hill 64], our farthest westward position in the valley. The perimeter was oval-shaped, with an area approximately 40 meters long by 20 meters wide. My artillery observation bunker was on the northernmost end of the hill, ten feet in from the hill's perimeter trenchline. I shared my bunker with my radio operator, LCpl D. A. Smith.

In the predawn hours of February 8, 2ndLt Terence Roach came to my bunker. He requested to borrow the penlight I used for night map reading; he said he needed it in order to check our lines. At the time, I did not think too much about loaning my penlight to him because late in the afternoon the day before I had been cleared for a registered on-call for close fire support directly onto our position.

My on-call artillery plan was given a target number by the Fire Support Coordination Center and personally cleared by

Lieutenant Roach. I had discussed this option with the lieutenant for several days. Numerous outposts were being assaulted along the rim of the valley, including Hills 881S and 861. These NVA attacks seemed to occur primarily at night, and the NVA were often in the barbed wire before artillery support calls were finally radioed out. Lieutenant Roach and I had discussed the option of a surprise attack at night, where the enemy might suddenly penetrate our perimeter by surprise. The low visibility, especially at night—low highland cloud ceiling of winter, patches of condensation, and wisps of fog that at times even prevented a full view of our hilltop from one end to the other at night and early morning—severely limited the use of artillery observation. Further, the slopes of our hill were too steep to predictably place artillery rounds at the exact bottom of our slopes. A shell may have been placed on the more gradual northern slope, but what if an attack was directed from another side? Therefore, Lieutenant Roach and I agreed, as a last resort, in the event of our being overrun and outnumbered, that I would call in the grid of our position for a fire mission of only one gun, one round at a time. In terms of howitzer ballistics and our outpost's topography, this translated into critically close artillery fire support but not necessarily a direct hit on top of our hill, because our position was less than one adjustment—forty meters by twenty meters. So my first shot would probably be a near miss, landing at the hill's base or on one of its slopes.

As a further safety precaution, Lieutenant Roach passed the word to all his staff noncommissioned officers that, in the event we were suddenly overrun, everyone was to remain in place, either in the trenches or preferably in their bunkers, with helmets and flak jackets on.

The attack against our outpost was launched in the absolute dark, at approximately 0415 on the morning of February 8.

The North Vietnamese laid down an accurate mortar barrage that hit within our perimeter and awakened me, Lance Corporal Smith, and everyone else, I'm sure. For a moment I fumbled in the darkness for my penlight. Then I remembered that Lieutenant Roach had needed it an hour earlier. We couldn't go outside, so we both listened to what developed into an all-out ground attack. After the three- or four-minute mortar barrage, there followed small-arms fire, screaming, and grenade bursts. Immediately after that, we could hear Vietnamese commands being shouted in the north trenchline, ten feet behind us. It happened incredibly fast. I quickly concluded that we were overrun, and then and there I decided to call in the registered artillery targeted directly onto our position.

Grenades were exploding outside our bunker, and I detected movement on our roof. Not only was I without my penlight, but my radio operator, in the dark, was unable to locate his pistol. We had only my rifle. Enemy grenades now were going off right outside our bunker. We could literally hear a conversation in Vietnamese being conducted just in front of our hole.

The on-call had been registered the afternoon before, but given the state of affairs and in total darkness, I was unable to remember its registration number. That was no problem, as I had it written down on my map. There was no penlight, so I had Smith hold my map while I struck a match. He blew it out and said not to light a match again. I can't blame him, as the poncho covering our entrance was partly open. No sooner had my match been blown out than several grenades were thrown down into our doorway. They were stopped by the poncho. We were blown back against the wall of our hole, hit in the legs. I struck another match and got the registration number, but Smith blew the match out and said they were right outside, not to light any more matches. We called in the registration number and gave the order to fire as more grenades were thrown. The reply from the Fire Support Coordination Center was "Checkfire."

Two more grenades rolled right inside with us. I kicked one of them into the doorway and Smith did something to the second one, or tried to, because both detonated in the doorway, which absorbed most of the shrapnel. At this point, nearly all I could hear was ringing. I was speaking at a very high volume and my radio operator was concerned about the enemy outside.

The reply on the radio said my fire mission had to be cleared by our commanding officer. I kept insisting that we had previous clearance, but to no avail. Then our outside radio was blown up and more grenades came in. We kicked them into the doorway. We had another radio inside. Smith was unable to reach Lieutenant Roach, there was a battle raging outside, and the checkfire by the Fire Support Coordination Center had us stymied. I told Smith that we had to locate Lieutenant Roach and confirm his clearance again for my close artillery fire support. The position of the Fire Support Coordination Center was that my fire mission had only been cleared to be registered and needed a second clearance to be fired. That was news to us.

Smith advised me against going outside because there was an NVA right outside. I told him we had to get out and find Lieutenant Roach, but he disagreed. I told him I was going out. He told me it was useless to go outside because there was an NVA right outside, less than three feet away. Smith took my rifle, went to the doorway, and commenced firing, killing the NVA.

I had no helmet, flak jacket, or weapon, and I was wounded in the thigh, but I was set upon finding Lieutenant Roach. This was my first time in close combat, things were not working as planned, and the confusion was the worst part of it. I thought, If only I can get to Lieutenant Roach, then he will know the solution. As Lance Corporal Smith fired, I attempted to run out across the top of the hill to Lieutenant Roach's command-post bunker. Except for my night vision and occasional explosions, visibility was close to nil. I sprinted painfully about five yards, but my leg slowed me up and I tripped on a prone body, stumbled, and fell right into the laps of three NVA. Before I could get up, I was being clubbed by their weapons. I spun around, still on the ground, so that their blows were falling on my legs. I thought they were breaking my knees, so I began kicking wildly. I was expecting to be shot at any moment. They didn't shoot, so I got to my feet. Two of the NVA literally jumped onto my back and weighted me down to my hands and knees. One of them pulled my right arm up behind my back. I was flailing my left arm wildly around so they couldn't get to it and pin it. At this point, I started thinking they weren't going to shoot me but were holding me as prisoner. At arm's reach, I could feel a metal object with a grip on it. Heavy, like a radio, I think it was an overturned jerrycan of water. When I got my grip on its handle, I suddenly dropped to my stomach so that the NVA straddling me and holding my right arm lost his balance. Still holding the jerrycan, I jumped up onto my feet and started spinning around like a top, holding the metal can straight out, whipping it horizontally like a propeller in the dark. It worked. I struck one of them squarely in the head, and, on the fourth or fifth spin, I also hit some steel and heard a weapon hitting the deck. I was becoming dizzy from spinning around and reckoned that one man was down and one weapon was down and that it was a good opportunity to try for Lieutenant Roach's bunker again. The only problem was, after wrestling in the dark, being clubbed, and spinning around like a helicopter's propeller, I had absolutely no idea which direction was toward the south end of our hill.

I stumbled and rolled down a depression that I assumed was angling toward the south side, but actually it was along the west side. In the dark, I was then running along this depression until I hit a sandbag and realized I was still on the northwest side of our hill. Right below me in the trench were two silhouettes talking in my direction, possibly to me, in Vietnamese. I picked up a trenchline sandbag and hit one of them over his helmet. Figuring I was now on the northwest side of the hill, I turned and tried running at an oblique angle toward the southeast or south. This time, I duck-walked because I still couldn't see well and didn't want to trip again. I heard objects clunking and rolling behind me. The NVA in the trench had thrown grenades after me. Oddly enough, at this point, almost all the fear had left me and I guess the adrenaline pumped me up so much that I was operating unconsciously or mechanically.

This time I crossed the hill, and as grenades were going off behind and around me, I was hit again in my lower left calf. More grenades were landing everywhere and suddenly I dropped safely below ground. I'd fallen into the east trenchline. A grenade detonated a second later, right over and behind my head, only inches from the trenchline's edge, just above the ground. I correctly assumed I was now somewhere on the east trenchline and, crouching, I started to slowly feel my way down the trench toward the south end.

There was a flash of illumination and small-arms fire up ahead, so I stopped. This was minor illumination, like a hand flare, so I assumed we must have had people up ahead who were still holding out. There was a little light to see by now, and I moved ten or fifteen feet at a time. After each staggered section of the zigzag trenchline, I looked around before proceeding. The trenchline was not in a straight line but slightly zigzag. There was still occasional shooting, explosions, and screaming, so I knew we were still holding out.

I worked my way down two or three sections of trenchline and noticed weapons and ammo scattered about. I spotted several rifles that were damaged and some others that seemed okay. I collected three rifles and I was proceeding down the next section of trench when I glimpsed two NVA advancing up the trench in my direction. I didn't know if they saw me. I knew there were still NVA behind me, as I could hear them calling out to each other from time to time, so I didn't want to go back to the north end. Now the passage to the south end was also blocked. I instantly stepped away around a zigzag, but now I had to completely check out at least one weapon to make sure it worked before trying to jump out and fire it. The NVA were walking and I had to move silently and slowly, so I crept up into a bunker to work. There were some Marine bodies, but no one was alive.

The first rifle's magazine was jammed. I put it down quietly and was trying to feel if the second one worked and if it had a round in its chamber when the two NVA stopped right outside the bunker I was in and talked to each other in low tones. I thought for sure they knew I was in there. I put the rifle down quietly and just listened. One of them walked away, but I knew there was one still outside.

I waited for what seemed like half an hour but probably was no more than a minute or two. I felt around for one of the rifles in the dark. My hand touched an entrenching tool. The spike on it was extended at a 90-degree angle, so I decided it was as good a defense as anything and a better club than a light, fiberglass M-16. I didn't want to shoot unless it was necessary. I still could hear him shuffling around outside the bunker. I was crouched with the entrenching tool inside the darkness of the bunker. With night vision, I could see his form squatting just outside my doorway. I had room laterally for a considerable stroke against the side of his head, like the swinging of a baseball bat, but I wanted to be absolutely sure he wasn't a Marine, though his form was small. I cocked my arms, studying him. There was a glimmer of light from a grenade explosion and I caught sight of his uniform and rifle silhouette. He was North Vietnamese. I swung furiously and with all my might.

I was about two feet away from his bare head. He jerked back and my sweaty grip slipped from the handle. He went falling back against the opposite trench wall, with the entrenching tool's spike embedded in his head. I looked up and down the trench and saw no one else. He rolled over and lay on the floor of the trench with the spike buried just above his ear. I didn't like looking, but he was making the most bizarre hissing sound that I ever heard another human being make. It sounded like an air hose, and it was nearly as loud. I hoped he was at least unconscious. I pulled the spike out and drove it in again, higher into the side of his head. He quieted, but in a few seconds he was gasping—not moving, just gasping for air. I didn't necessarily want to kill him; I really only wanted to quiet him. I wondered why he wasn't dead after two blows like that into his head. I had never killed a man before, and I couldn't pull out the spike to hit him again with that entrenching tool. It was an overwhelming thing for me to do for the third time. So I left it there, after the second blow, still implanted in the side of his head. I don't think I realized what I had just done.

He was still gasping, but not as much as before. Somehow, I had to quiet him. There was a Marine bayonet a few feet away and I picked it up quickly, trying to decide where to stab him. I was worried about stabbing him in the heart because I didn't know if he could still cry out. After deliberation, I decided on cutting his throat. I asked God to forgive me for what I was about to do to another human being, but then I figured, what the hell, and tried telling myself he was probably going to die anyway and that this was an act of mercy. Besides, he hadn't come onto my hill to discuss peace terms. So I tried cutting his throat. It was impossible. The damn bayonet was as dull as a butter knife. Weren't all bayonets sharp? Next, I tried stabbing and slashing at his throat to open it up. Blood was everywhere. I felt numb. At this point I was a wild man. I was somebody else and yet me. I clicked bone with the blade tip and realized I had torn down into his spinal column. Now he was no longer gasping, but he was gurgling. When was this man going to die? His chest was making wild, frantic heaves, and a haunting, gurgling rattle was desperately respirating out of the gap I had torn open in his throat. Oh God, I thought, please just quiet him down, let him die, for his sake as well as mine. I kept asking myself, Why isn't he dead yet? His gurgling was almost as loud as his gasping had been. It was too much. I had to get away from him. I started down the trench toward the south end of our hill again. Then, as an afterthought, I went back to the unconscious and dying NVA and covered his head with three sandbags, muffling his death rattle. I wondered, Why didn't I think of that sooner?

Private First Class Seavy-Cioffi found the Alpha-1 survivors holding the southern end of the hill and learned that Lieutenant Roach was missing and presumed dead. Seavy-Cioffi located the 1st Platoon co-commander, a newly arrived second lieutenant who, owing to his wounds, was restricted to a southern bunker and was thus unable to assume effective command. Taking command of the platoon, Seavy-Cioffi rallied the survivors, retrieved most of the immobile wounded, and began building up the outpost's interior defensive line.

Pfc LAWRENCE SEAVY-CIOFFI
Alpha Company, 1/9

We held a small crescent of trench on the southeast end of the hill with about a dozen able-bodied Marines, three or four rifles, maybe a dozen magazines, and half a dozen grenades. We had another dozen Marines on the southwest trenchline. The men reported to me that our northwest machine-gun bunker and its machine gun had been destroyed. Many bunkers had been blown up with men inside, and they represented the survivors who had pulled back. Altogether, there was less than one functional rifle for every three Marines. If the NVA had pressed their attack then, they might have wiped us out. But fortunately they paused and eventually several other live Marines were located.

At this point we had a total of about thirty Marines accounted for, and about ten of them were wounded, four of them seriously.

The NVA were now starting to lob grenades over to our south end of the hill, so I first ordered all our trenches on the south end cleared of wounded.

Had the NVA battalion realized our vulnerability at that time, when I first took command, they might have swept over and annihilated my platoon. But they hesitated. A lull now came after the first thirty to thirty-five minutes. I decided to take advantage of this lull in the action.

We were holding the south quarter of our hill, and I had the rifles, men, and ammo evenly distributed. I kept one extra rifle on our southeast end, and had Pfc Wayne Welchel and LCpl Arnold Alderete looking over the sides and out across the top of the hill. There was sporadic visibility now, as Khe Sanh was firing illumination.

I searched out the first three or four bunkers on the southeast trenchline. I made three or four trips with no complications. However, there was more ammo lying around than there were operable rifles.

In the first three or four trips, I brought back four or five bandoliers holding varying numbers of M-16 rifle magazines from the bunkers. I also brought back seven or eight rifles, but two or three of them were damaged beyond operation. We had about five good, additional M-16s and an improving supply of ammo. I had also passed up another five or six M-16s—pieces of M-16s—that I didn't even bother trying to salvage. Every now and then I might get a surprise and find things such as hand flares, some grenades, a first-aid kit, a canteen of water, etc. Generally, though, I first concentrated on ammo and weapons, and then finally on whatever else I could find that would be useful. The bunkers had no living occupants. Finally, I had picked the bunkers clean halfway up to the east side. We were much better off on ammo, but still every man was yet to be armed.

Desperate to obtain ammunition for the survivors' single M-60 machine gun, Seavy-Cioffi advanced northward to locate some that the gunner had been forced to leave behind. In a series of heart-stopping trips into overrun positions, Seavy-Cioffi retrieved the machine-gun ammunition and additional M-16s and M-16 magazines. In so doing, he armed most of the Marines still capable of putting up a fight. Despite Seavy-Cioffi's many absences, command of the defense fell into his lap, though he was outranked by many of the survivors and had only rudimentary training as an infantryman. In extreme combat situations, attitude and command presence often take precedence over rank.

Plagued by unexpected resistance and uncertain as to what they were facing, the NVA occupying the northern one-third of the outpost were reticent to press home an assault. The NVA had an ample supply of hand grenades, and these they used in ongoing efforts to dislodge the surviving defenders.

Pfc LAWRENCE SEAVY-CIOFFI
Alpha Company, 1/9

Grenades were still raining down, and people were taking cover in the bunkers. I told them not to do that or we'd lose ground. I told them to keep sandbags ready, and, if any grenades landed behind our walled-off barricades, to quickly cover the grenades with the sandbags, move back, let them explode, then move back up to the wall again and keep firing down the trench if anything moved—or we'd get pushed back into a tight bunch again and they would wipe us all out with their grenades.

Finally there was another lull on our east side and then the NVA started hitting our Marines on the other side, on the southwest side of our hill. I went over to them with my rifle and an extra rifle. It was a good thing, because two of their rifles were jammed up with dirt from grenade explosions and couldn't fire. I gave them two working rifles and took the jammed ones for Cpl Edward O'Connor to fix later. I went all the way up to the southwest trench wall, where the trench had also been barricaded with sandbags, checked to see if anyone was wounded, encouraged our men, and told them we were not only holding our position but also actually were gaining ground and that now everyone was armed and that we had just recovered the machine-gun ammo. Everyone's morale picked up with this news, and I gave our Marines on the southwest trenchline the same directions as those on the southeast side: that no matter how intense the hails of grenades or gunfire were, to keep firing from behind the sand-bagged wall, down the trench, when they saw movement, and to keep a lookout not only down the side of the hill but also out across the top of the hill, because we had no people we knew of in our hilltop's interior, so the enemy could be anywhere. Also, I directed, if grenades landed in the sections of trench behind their sand-bagged barricade, not to panic, but to calmly throw a sandbag or two over the grenade, temporarily pull back and let the grenade explode, then immediately push back up to the wall and commence firing up the trenchline so that no more ground would be lost.

I started back around again for the southeast side, where O'Connor, Alderete [the M-60 gunner], and Welchel were. I brought along the two jammed rifles for O'Connor. He was especially fast at unplugging jammed M-16s. He was something of an expert at it. Though he had been wounded several times, O'Connor provided the only ongoing maintenance for our M-16s and was thus instrumental in saving Marine lives on Alpha-1.

I went on around with the two jammed rifles to the southeast side, because now they were starting to get hit again over there. By the time I got over there, all hell was breaking loose. The NVA had advanced down to the bunker just outside our southeast barricade wall, about twenty feet away, and had showered the barricade with about thirty grenades, killing one Marine and wounding just about everyone else. Then they were storming our wall. The Marines had already thrown the last few grenades they had and fired their M-16s until their magazines were empty or jammed. When the NVA rushed, they had no other choice but to pull back. These were all men who were now wounded for the second or third time in this attack, ears ringing, some of them unable to hear, dazed, disoriented, and outnumbered. I stopped their withdrawal at the second bunker behind our wall, brought up some borrowed, unjammed rifles and magazines, and told them we had to rush the wall. We retook the wall, and then some more grenades hit, but I flung sandbags over them.

O'Connor came up—wounded again, but not too seriously—and I told him to go into the bunker behind us and unplug the two other jammed rifles. The trench wall had been kicked, knocked, or blown over. Welchel, Alderete, and I were starting to build it back up when the NVA rained another twenty or thirty grenades down on us once again, but they didn't follow it up with a charge. The grenades were bad enough. The NVA grenades were slowly thinning us out, but the fact that there were fewer of us made the grenade attacks less efficient.

The twenty-five survivors, many of them wounded, who were still able to fight, rebuilt and continued holding the perimeter trenchlines in the eerie light of virtually continuous overhead illumination within shifting eddies of fog.

Pfc LAWRENCE SEAVY-CIOFFI
Alpha Company, 1/9

Now that we were established in the southern third of our hilltop's trenchlines, I became increasingly concerned about our hilltop's interior. What if the enemy was crawling toward us over the interior? They might crawl up to a section of our southern third of trench and throw in grenades or try to launch a troop assault from within our hill's interior.

Because we could not see all the way across due to darkness, the shifting threads of fog, and the topographical rise in the center of our hilltop, I next decided we had to form a 360-degree defense and link up the two opposite barricades by positioning our Marines prone, out across the interior of the southern third of our hill. I went all along the trenchline, from east to west, and told our Marines that there would be someone checking out the interior, crawling about, so not to fire indiscriminately. I went back to the southeast barricade and had people keep an eye out across the top of the hill. I decided not to take a rifle along for this, but rather to concentrate on crawling quietly and trying to spot the enemy first. Shooting would only draw grenades anyway. I started out flat on my belly in a dead man's crawl. I would go ten or fifteen feet and then play dead. I observed only when the illumination was dimming. In full light, I lay still, as if I was dead. I maneuvered to different locations so that I could observe every square foot carefully and check out the one or two bunkers in our hill's southern interior. There were some bodies and debris in the interior, but, at the time, no living NVA.

I returned to the east barricade and positioned three of us in the hill's interior—myself in the center, one Marine between me and the southwest barricade, and Alderete, with his M-60 machine gun, on my right, between me and the southeast barricade, where Welchel and O'Connor were positioned with two other Marines. We now had a 360-degree defense line. It was just in time.

The NVA began probing our southern interior. We were always just one step ahead of them. They probed us first with hails of grenades. They began throwing twenty-five or thirty grenades at a time into our hill's interior. Fortunately, we only had the three of us out there or it would have been disastrous. Grenades were landing all around us. They often landed inches from us; one actually bounced off me. We would wildly flip back and roll away, yelling "Chicom!" to warn the others. That was good because the NVA knew the interior was occupied.

You had to be careful where you rolled. As one grenade blew up, I rolled right onto another one. I felt something like a brick under my chest, put my hand beneath me, and felt the grenade. I flipped my body away again. It blew up about three feet away, but a full C-ration case partially between me and the grenade saved me. The Marine to my left was not so lucky and was soon killed. We put another man out. For the next fifteen or twenty minutes, all the NVA did was throw twenty-five or thirty grenades every two or three minutes. It was unbelievable how many Chicom grenades they had.

At one point during this sustained hand-grenade barrage, just after we beat back an NVA charge on our east-side barricade, I

brought to the east-side trench some sandbags I had collected from our hill's southern interior. At that time, O'Connor was coming forward from the trenchline bunker we were using to stage ammo and gear and in which he had been servicing malfunctioning M-16s. Alderete was chucking sandbags to Welchel, making repairs on the trenchline barricade. I was in the trench with them just as more grenades hit all around us, all but one on our side of the barricade. Our having so many extra sandbags on hand was a blessing. As ten or so grenades landed in the trenchline, Welchel, O'Connor, Alderete, two other Marines, and I instantly covered seven or eight of them with sandbags and instantly pulled back. Other grenades that had missed the trenchline began blowing up aboveground all around us, and the concussion was deafening. After the NVA grenades stopped exploding, I had to dash to turn O'Connor around; he was calmly walking up the trenchline, through the partially blown barricade, right toward the NVA. I had become disoriented early in the fighting, so I understood his predicament.

Somebody reported to me that he had found an unopened box of our own grenades in a corner of one of our south-end bunkers. I had them move it up near to our southeast barricade, and then had Welchel and O'Connor pass grenades out to Alderete and then on out to me. Keeping count (fifty in a box), I decided to immediately throw twenty-five to make the enemy think we were better off than we really were. It was a gamble of sorts, but we had to answer these new grenade attacks or they might think they were weakening us. I wanted to make the enemy think it was more than just one man in one location, throwing the grenades—to appear stronger than we actually were. I threw the 25 grenades in every possible direction, most toward the north end, but a few over the east, west, and south slopes for good measure, one right after another. I really gave them a taste of their own medicine. I threw some with all my might, briefly standing up, so they detonated way out over the north side, at our hill's base. Others I threw way up into the air, letting the spoons spring first, so some fuse burned, so that they exploded just about when they hit the ground. Otherwise, they would all have rolled down the sides and exploded beyond our hill's base. I heard three screams—two of them from the north end, the other one from somewhere down the north slope or in the valley beyond. The NVA on the north slope only knew that the grenades were coming down on them from the hilltop.

I passed the remaining 25 grenades out among our men. I instructed them only to throw our remaining grenades at specific targets with extremely careful aim.

After observing NVA on the north slope throwing their hand grenades into areas he knew were held by other NVA, Seavy-Cioffi concluded that the attackers were still confused as to the number and location of the American defenders.

Pfc LAWRENCE SEAVY-CIOFFI
Alpha Company, 1/9 _____

I concluded three things: (1) the enemy apparently did not yet fully realize we were restricted to the southern end of the hill; (2) the enemy did not realize how great our losses had been in the first twenty to twenty-five minutes; (3) the enemy did not have coordinated, if any, communication between their men in our north trenchlines and their men spread out on our north slope.

I began to think of ways I could use this to our advantage and further confuse the enemy.

The NVA were still pelting us with grenades now and again, though not as intensely as earlier. However, every casualty we took, whether dead or wounded, was very serious as we were now down to fewer than twenty-five functioning Marines, not counting all the seriously wounded, who were unable to participate. So it was now less the question of our weapons and ammunition supply than the question of our troop strength. We had to get the NVA grenades off us. I began thinking again about the NVA on the north slope who had mistakenly thrown their grenades up onto the north end, killing their own men. If we could make the enemy think we were not where we actually were, we could get them to waste their own grenades. I called Alderete over and told him my plan, a decoy tactic.

There was an abandoned bunker in the north center of our hill, the highest point on our outpost. It was about ten or fifteen meters ahead of where I had lain out in the center of the southern third of our hill's interior. I told Alderete that if we waited until the illumination burned out, we could then crawl forward on our stomachs to the south side of this bunker, wait until the next illumination burst overhead, stand straight up, throw a grenade each, and shoot if we saw some NVA. During the last few seconds of illumination, we would lower our heads straight down and move back to the southern third of our hill's interior, attempting to draw their grenades onto the bunker.

Alderete and I crawled up. We decided I should throw only one grenade, as we were down to our last two dozen grenades. Besides, he had to handle his machine gun and its ammo can. The idea was that firing the machine gun would make them think we were in a permanent position. We got up to the bunker and, when the next overhead illumination burst, stood up. I could see a dozen or so NVA heads sticking up in our north-end trench. After Alderete commenced firing short bursts, I tossed my grenade in their direction. After it exploded, I sprayed about one-half of my rifle magazine at a few heads that popped back up again. No one fired back; they seemed surprised. Then the illumination dimmed and we lowered our heads straight down. We were beginning to crawl back when the NVA completely covered the decoy bunker with grenades. Of course, we were back on our hill's southern third by the time they exploded.

Each time we did this, the NVA threw at least fifteen to twenty grenades, all wasted because, by the time they exploded, we had pulled back. The first few times we stood up we let out fierce growls and guttural howls to make sure that they knew we were positioned by the bunker. After a while, the NVA would call back to us: "Hey, Marine, tonight you die!" or "You die, you die, Mr. Custer, you die!" or "Give up, Marine, or you all die tonight!" Once, Welchel yelled back, "It may be plastic, but it will kick your ass!" A reference to our M-16s.

We did this two or three more times, and then Alderete and I decided that that was enough use of his machine-gun ammo because he had used up about one-third of his can. Alderete also suggested doing the decoy tactic without his machine gun because crawling back quickly was difficult with his M-60. I crawled over and asked Welchel and O'Connor how their side of the hill was doing. They said okay, so I decided to position Alderete's machine gun on the opposite side, on our left hand, at the southwest trenchline's barricade, with an extra man and rifle to guard it. I gave directions not to fire unless there were specific targets. The machine gun now had about two-thirds of its ammo remaining, which I told them to use in short bursts and make it count.

In a separate incident concluding at 0625, Private First Class Welchel stopped an enemy squad advancing down our east-side trenchline by himself after the other Marines with him were killed or wounded too seriously to continue fighting. This was the final NVA charge against our east-side barricade.

Alderete and I continued to crawl up to the decoy bunker every ten minutes or so, in between illumination, and fired at the NVA in the north-end trenches. We didn't use any more grenades. We brought just one rifle and one magazine each. After a while, when we stopped throwing grenades and stopped using the machine gun, the NVA got bolder, no longer ducked their heads, and tried shooting it out with us. Sometimes we appeared around the sides of the bunker so they would not know where to expect us. However, that dangerously exposed our flanks and Alderete said he thought he was taking sniper fire from across the hill, from the northwest trenchline. He suggested that we take a break because his rifle barrel had been hit by gunfire. But we were still successfully drawing the NVA grenades onto the decoy bunker, so I told Alderete to take a break and had someone switch places with him.

The NVA must have wasted over 200 grenades on our decoy bunker. I am sure we saved many casualties and lives by deceiving the enemy into thinking our lines were farther forward than they really were and our surviving troop strength was greater than it actually was. If anything, this one tactic focused the enemy's attention away from our southern trenches and toward the northern hilltop interior, where we had no men except when we crawled up to the bunker. After the NVAs' second major attack down the trenchline failed and during my continuing decoy tactics, their momentum was nearing its demise.

The NVA rushed our trenchline only one more time. They tried all out to take the southwest barricade. Fortunately for us, that was about five or ten minutes after I set up the machine gun there. The machine gun stopped the charge. I heard it firing away, a volley of enemy grenades going off, then M-16 rifle fire, some feeble AK-47 reply bursts, screaming, then two or three of our own grenades going off, and then silence. My Marines had stopped the charge, but we had taken one killed and three more good Marines wounded.

That was the last enemy charge down our trenchlines. The enemy was now almost exclusively pinned down in our north-end trenchline, along with many others on the north slope. I kept up my decoy tactic, using rocks to rout them from our north trenches onto the slopes so that their own men on the slopes threw more grenades onto the north end, once again killing and wounding their own. After a while, though, they caught on to my rock tactic. But throughout the morning, at least until dawn, they never seemed to perceive that we actually had no men permanently positioned at the decoy bunker. They always tossed some grenades after I pulled back, but the number of grenades steadily declined until they were only throwing six or seven and then, finally, only two or three at a time. By dawn's first light, I think they began to realize that it was a decoy, but by then their numbers were thinned out and they must have been low on grenades and ammo, because their return fire steadily diminished each time. By daylight, 0715, it was too late for them to take our hill. I still kept up the decoy tactic, figuring that, as long as they had grenades to throw and bullets to shoot, it was better to get them to hit our decoy bunker than have them charging the barricades or throwing the grenades onto our outpost's southern end.

At about 0715, our company commander radioed that reinforcements would move out after some Vietnamese Air Force propeller-driven fighter-bombers bombed and strafed the surrounding area. I kept engaging the enemy at the decoy bunker so they couldn't pull back, keeping them thinking that someone was always at the bunker. However, the NVA set up a sniper on the west side. The last time I had someone with me, it was light enough to see, and when I pulled back, I realized I was alone. The sniper had shot the Marine who had gone along with me. He had killed him with a single shot in the temple.

I went out alone to get the sniper. I spotted him, pinned him down about three-fourths of the way up the northwest trench, and shot it out with him. We ducked down, but I didn't pull back. I changed magazines, and he must have done the same. We looked up and began shooting at each other again. We were both adjusting our bursts, which kicked up dust around the sandbags protecting us. I adjusted my last burst a split second faster than he did. His bullets hit the sandbag in front of me, about two inches too low. I stepped aside so when he adjusted and raised, he was just off to my left. He hardly grazed my elbow. I elevated my barrel and saw the last of my rounds walking right up from the dirt and sandbags into his chest, and he was flung back. One of his bullets, or a fragment of some sort, had grazed me through my shirt sleeve, but it had not drawn blood.[1]

Private First Class Seavy-Cioffi never received official recognition for his leadership of the outpost's defenses, but he was recently recommended by Wayne Welchel and Edward O'Connor for the Medal of Honor. A decision is still pending.

LtCol JOHN MITCHELL
1/9 Commanding Officer

At 0730, a relief platoon led by the Alpha Company commander, Capt Henry Radcliffe, made its way to the beleaguered platoon, and by 0900 had assaulted the eastern slope of the hill and established contact with the remnants of the trapped platoon. The southern position of the 1/9 sector, with its high ground and cleared fields of fire, lent itself well for supporting fires to Captain Radcliffe's assault. Delta and Bravo companies, supported by one section of tanks, delivered murderous fires to the flanks and front of Alpha Company, blunting enemy attempts at reinforcement. Captain Radcliffe led his combined Marines on a frontal assault across the tiny hill, and within fifteen minutes the Alpha Company outpost had been completely cleared of the enemy and positions [had been] reestablished. The grim policing of the battleground was then begun; many NVA dead and equipment littered the tiny hill outpost.[2]

1/9 Command Chronology

> At 0825, the relief column reached the crest of the hill. Fighting continued until approximately 1100, when the outpost was retaken. At the same time, Delta Company observed a large number of enemy withdrawing from the Alpha-1 outpost. Delta Company opened fire with all available arms.
>
> The results after the day's fight were 24 friendly KIA, 29 friendly WIA, and over 150 enemy bodies found by Alpha and Delta companies.

PART FOUR

THE SIEGE
February 8–March 31, 1968

Chapter 17

HILL 881S

Capt BILL DABNEY
India Company, 3/26 _____

Hill 881S was the only outlying Khe Sanh Combat Base position not assaulted by infantry on the night of January 20–21. . . . Hill 861 got hit, the Khe Sanh ville got hit. Everything I heard about around there got hit that night, except 881S, and we were the most exposed. I was convinced . . . that we were not assaulted only because we'd been patrolling aggressively for a month out to the limit of our prudence and had developed our own intelligence as a result of those patrols and had acted on it within the limits of our capabilities. I believe that the India Company recon-in-force to 881N on January 20 ran into the NVA battalion that was designated to attack us that night. We could not destroy it, but we found and fixed it in the subsequent fire fight and hit it with supporting arms. Although it may not have decimated the battalion, it probably discouraged it. Thereafter, although I was prohibited from patrolling off the hill—and could not have done so had I been permitted, because I didn't have sufficient force to both extricate a patrol in trouble and hold the hill, and reinforcement from Khe Sanh was not possible—we used what we had learned from that point forward. We intimately knew the ground around us. I mean that seriously. We knew every valley, every fold in the ground. Every trooper on that hill had made patrols around that hill several times out to about four kilometers. One platoon was out almost every day. And often a squad or so down on the other side at the same time. . . .

We found that the NVA moved in close to Hill 881S at night to avoid the B-52's, artillery, etc., so we had a regular hose-down program of our own involving indirect-fire weapons only, including 60mm mortars, and fougasse. . . . Occasionally, on signal, the hose-down involved the simultaneous throwing of a grenade by every man on the lines, which was about 300 men. Sometimes, if something was going on around us, every man would pick a grenade up, pull the pin, and throw the damn thing as far as he could at the same time. That kept them off. We had plenty of grenades by that time. Easy to deliver. Every man had a case of them. We reacted to every movement, we reacted to every noise, even every smell, with massive volumes of indirect fire. Always, and unless we had immediate and fleeting targets of opportunity, we used exclusively non-organic supporting arms. We had enough problems with resupply as it was. We didn't use anything of our own if we didn't have to.

In the daytime on 881S, unless we had reduced visibility, we had about two guys per platoon on watch plus our observation posts. Everybody else slept. There were three reasons. One, daytime is when we got indirect fire and snipers, and people who were up took hits. We reduced casualties that way. Two, we didn't have much water, and if we worked the men in the daytime, we used a lot of water because it was hot. Two canteens per man per day took a whole helicopter for 400 men, and we didn't want to call any more helicopters up there than we had to because those guys in the birds were taking hits. Third, there wasn't any reason for more men to be up. The NVA didn't attack in the daytime. They came at night if they were coming at all.[1]

LCpl WALT WHITESIDES
Tactical Air Control Party

Early in February, the new 3/26 communications officer sent a radio up to Hill 881S for us to use for calling in fixed-wing air strikes. Khe Sanh was getting beautiful fixed-wing support— sorties every five to ten minutes during daylight hours were normally controlled by an aerial observer against known targets. If we had a target of opportunity, we could divert a strike by getting on the net and talking to the aerial observer. I never heard of a tactical-air-control operator's being turned down on a target of opportunity. The four of us on Hill 881S probably ran over 300 air strikes among us.

HM3 DAVID STEINBERG
India Company, 3/26

The jets were constantly bombing around Hill 881S, working the hills around us with 500-pound bombs. One day it was green, and the next it was blown away. The hill was so high that, often, the jets were working below us.

LCpl WALT WHITESIDES
Tactical Air Control Party

One morning, LCpl Toby Jackson and I were staring through a spotting scope toward Hill 881N. Toby noticed a glint on the forward slope of a little hill between 881S and 881N, and closer examination revealed that it was an NVA soldier, probably the forward observer we had been hunting for. I quickly contacted Captain Dabney, and he arranged for the 60mm mortars to mark the position with white-phosphorus rounds while Toby was arranging for an air strike. Within minutes we were ready, and the mortars dropped a white-phosphorus round within 50 meters of the NVA soldier's position. The poor guy evidently wasn't too well set in because he immediately set to with his entrenching tool to deepen his hole. The two jets swooped in and he quickened his digging. On the second pass, one of the jets dropped two 250-pound bombs almost on top of him. I could see the guy rise with the bomb cloud. We gave the pilots "One confirmed," and the grunts around us cheered.

Capt BILL DABNEY
India Company, 3/26

What was the importance of 881S? What advantage would it have given to the North Vietnamese?

Any good artillery piece—antiaircraft artillery, 37mm, or

even a 100mm gun—could have posed serious problems for any takeoffs coming west out of Khe Sanh, especially the C-130s making their paradrops off the west end of the runway. . . . Looking out the east side of 881S, you looked virtually down the runway, just a few degrees off it, about seven or seven and a half kilometers away.

Other than giving Khe Sanh its best forward observation post, I'm not sure that there accrued any significant advantage for us to hold it, but it was, I think, damned sure useful to keep *them* from holding it, because, with decent antiaircraft capabilities, and they had those, they could have done some serious damage to Khe Sanh because they'd have had no real problem looking right into the nose of the airplane coming off that runway or making . . . drops to the west end. Also, from 881S, we gave their rocket sites, all within two kilometers of us, a lot of trouble. We used to hose them down with M-60 machine guns and 106mm recoilless rifles.[2]

MEDEVAC AND RESUPPLY

LCpl WALT WHITESIDES
Tactical Air Control Party

Hill 881S was attacked for the first time with mortars on the afternoon of January 22. The initial fire was fairly accurate, and one H-34 helicopter was shot down in the landing zone. The India Company senior corpsman, HM3 Robert Wickliffe, a Naval Reservist from Louisiana, was killed in the landing zone while helping to evacuate a casualty. Also, one of the members of the helicopter support team was critically wounded in the landing zone. It became apparent that the landing zone on the top of the hill was a registered target and that alternate landing zones would have to be established.

Eventually, we located two alternate landing zones. One was outside the wire on the Khe Sanh (east) side of the hill, and the other was in the saddle between the India and Mike company positions. Soon, Captain Dabney assigned the tactical-air-control radio operators with bodyguards for whenever we went into one of the landing zones. These individuals were to lie on top of us in the event the landing zone received incoming. We eventually had holes dug in the landing zones so the radio operators could jump in the hole and wait out the incoming. Landing helicopters became one of the most dangerous jobs on Hill 881S. LCpl Toby Jackson and I were the only two out of seven air-control and helicopter-support Marines who were not killed or wounded during the siege.

The routine for landing a helicopter went something like this: We would get word that a helo was coming in and what the cargo was. If it was an external load, it would usually be dumped on the main landing zone on top of the hill. Internal cargo, such as troops, would require the helo to land. Medevacs and troops going out would also require a landing. The birds would usually stick around for medevacs if the zone was well organized and if they didn't have to wait too long. They had about thirty seconds on the ground before incoming started landing in the zone. They could gain three to five more seconds if the mortar tubes were not registered right on the zone we selected.

The tactical-air-control operators decided which zone was to be used. Medevacs and troops would assemble in the trenchline near the zone. The operators would then occupy both zones, and when the helicopter was making a final approach, the lucky one would pop a colored-smoke grenade to indicate the selected zone. Up until that time, both zones would receive some enemy .51-caliber fire, which was not meant to hit the tactical-air operator but just get zeroed in so it could hit the helo. When the helo landed, the grunts would fire their weapons in the general direction of Hill 881N, where the NVA had an artillery forward observer.

When the helo landed, the tactical-air operator would direct the outgoing Marines onto the helo and steer the arriving replacements in the general direction of the trenchline. The helo would take off and the tactical-air operator would jump into his hole and wait for the incoming to stop.

This procedure worked fairly well unless the helo went into the wrong zone or if the troops got lost or delayed getting on or off the bird, or if the bird stayed too long. I believe that three helicopters were shot down during my stay on the hill, from January 20 until February 9.

The thing that bothered people the most, I think, was the fact that if you were wounded, you had no assurance that you would be evacuated rapidly. There were several reasons for this. First, the weather often prevented helicopters from landing. Second, even if the birds got in, they sometimes left prior to getting all the casualties aboard.

Pfc MICHAEL LEE
Helicopter Support Team

I had been in Khe Sanh about three to four days when the Helicopter Support Team (HST) guy on 881S started calling down for relief. I talked it over with my commanding officer [of Alpha Company, 3rd Shore Party Battalion], and volunteered to go up to Hill 881S.

As I waited on the landing zone for the CH-46 to pick me up, I was sitting facing the control-tower bunker. All of a sudden, a couple of guys were waving their arms and yelling at me. I looked over my left shoulder and saw a 122mm rocket coming right at me. I thought, "Oh shit! This is it!" The rocket landed about ten feet behind me. The concussion lifted me up and really rattled my brain. Some people came running over. They thought I got hit. For some reason, not one piece of shrapnel touched me. About five minutes later, my bird came in. I got on it and was on my way to 881S, to replace the HST guy up there. The ride was really beautiful!

As we came up to the hill, it really looked small! As the aircraft was coming in for a landing, the whole hill erupted in gunfire. I learned that was to keep the NVA down. The crew chief let the ramp down before we were down. As he did that, my pucker factor went sky-high. I went running down the ramp and I passed the guy I was replacing. The one thing that sticks in my mind was how scared he was. The aircraft was up and going before a couple of mortar rounds hit near the landing zone. There was only one landing zone on the hill for passengers. After I got in the trench, I was taken up to the command bunker to meet Captain Dabney.

After I was shown the three landing zones on the hill (the east end, the top, and the saddle), I was assigned to a bunker on the north side, in approximately the middle of the hill. There were two grunts there with a .50-caliber machine gun. We were facing 881N. They told me about the sniper over there called "Luke the Gook." Shit, he was everywhere.

My job was to direct the resupply and medevac birds to their respective landing zones. I would have to stand out in the open to direct the aircraft. During resupply, the whole hill would fire downslope to keep the NVA from firing at the resupply birds.

The medevacs were the worst! Captain Dabney had a policy of having the least wounded men carry the front of a stretcher on the bird. That's if there were two men wounded. When someone got hit, I would get the word from the corpsman as to the priority— routine, priority, or emergency. The routines [mostly KIAs] would generally have to wait until resupply came in. Priority—if there were aircraft in the area, they had the choice of coming in or not. Emergency—everyone dropped what they were doing, be it any type of helicopter. The worst were the emergencies. When I called down to Khe Sanh with an emergency medevac, aircraft would be given my call sign and contact me. We generally had fixed-wing aircraft and gunships on station for fire suppression.

I would direct the bird in and the casualty would be carried on. Then the bird would get out of there ASAP. We always took incoming mortars when this happened. You could see the strain in the faces of everyone. It got so you didn't pay any attention to it. Every time I would hear "Corpsman!" I would think "Shit!" because it meant another medevac.

HM3 DAVID STEINBERG
India Company, 3/26

Replacements would jump off the helos, and supplies would just fall off. A couple times we even got the gunners off the helicopters because the crew chiefs would get so panicked they just shoved everyone off. We welcomed the gunners to the hill; we gave them shovels and put them to work.

Anytime we got resupplied was the time for a corpsman to worry. We got three or four mortar rounds in every time a chopper came in. Almost every time, we had casualties. Most of them were new guys who were getting off the chopper. They didn't know where the hell they were or what to do. They'd just stand there. Unless they got down, they were sure to get hit by the mortars or the .51-caliber rounds from the guns that had us zeroed in.

One time, I heard "Corpsman, up!" and I went over the top of the hill to the landing zone. I was treating one guy after the next.

They were green, they'd just gotten off, and the chopper was leaving. It was sheer frustration, trying to get to their chest wounds. Their canvas backpacks had real thick straps on them, and I was spending too much time laying on my belly or back, trying to cut the packs off them so I could work, just so I could start to treat them. When I finished and went back to the trenchline, my platoon commander came up and said, "My God, Doc! You're hit!" I was just covered with blood, but none of it was my own.

On two occasions I was treating someone when the Marine next to me, the guy helping me, got hit. I figured if I was going to go, it would be while I was doing my job, but I never thought too much, other than doing what I had to do. How do you let down your buddies?

Pfc MICHAEL LEE
Helicopter Support Team

About the worst time I had was an afternoon I was bringing in a resupply at the saddle. I had two CH-46s, with gunships escorting. As I was directing the first CH-46 in, I noticed a winking light in the valley to the south. It was a heavy machine gun firing at the bird. The prick almost got me! I couldn't move until the bird dropped his net, as he was on his final approach. I told the pilot he was taking incoming, and he replied "Affirmative," that he could see tracers going by me. At that point, I almost pissed my pants. As soon as the bird dropped his net, I dived for the trench. I called the command post and told them I had a machine-gun position sighted. The gunships wanted the target marked, so I shot a magazine of tracers at it. They couldn't see them, so the 81mm mortars put some white-phosphorus rounds in the general area. From there, I directed the gunships on it.

Cpl TERRY STEWART
Mike Company, 3/26

The few times that our resupply was lost at the bottom of the hill was a real heartbreaker to us. We just sat there and watched as our mail was blown to hell by friendly bombers. But we all knew that there were some things that would surely survive. And obviously some did. It wasn't uncommon for Charlie, who frequently communicated to us via some kind of speaker system or bullhorn, to mention names of the guys on the hill, and sometimes the names of their family or friends. This was naturally to demoralize us, but Charlie could never know what assholes Americans can be. None of their unsavory remarks ever bothered anyone, and I cannot recall anyone ever being brought down by this tactic. Most of us would laugh or toss off insults at the antagonizers.

One net drop did not land on top of the hill or go over the side. The heavy net landed on top of one of our positions and crushed two Marines. It was gruesome.

SUPER GAGGLE

Col FRANK WILSON
Marine Air Group 36

It was the consensus of the helicopter group commander and his pilots that the resupply of the vital hill outposts would not long survive under the increasing enemy antiaircraft fire and the resulting rapid rise in the attrition of the helicopters. The UH-1E Huey gunships, though doing a valiant job, did not possess the heavy volume of fire required to keep the helicopter lanes open.

The solution was basically [that] all helicopter flights to the hill outposts would be escorted by strike aircraft in order to provide suppressive fires. Under the direction of the Commanding General, 1st Marine Aircraft Wing, Marine Air Group 12, and Marine Air Group 36 coordinated an effort which came to be known as the Super Gaggle.

In this classic example of helicopter escort operations, involving split-second timing, and coordinated by an airborne tactical air coordinator, six to eight CH-46s of Marine Medium Helicopter Squadron 364 would depart Dong Ha carrying external sling loads of cargo, proceed "in the soup" to an orbit point southeast of Khe Sanh, and await the arrival of the strike jets of Marine Air Group 12. On signal from the airborne tactical air coordinator, the CH-46s would start an approach to Khe Sanh, preceded by the Marine Air Group 12 Skyhawks, which would commence devastating attacks around the hill objectives and, at the same time, smoke the surrounding ridgelines. As the

CH-46s drove toward the hill outposts, they were joined by Huey gunships of Marine Observation Squadron 6, which would make continuous strafing attacks on the terrain within the helicopter lanes. These low-level attacks not only gave the helicopters a fighting chance to reach the objective hilltops and drop their external loads, it gave them some measure of protection during those critical moments when they were most vulnerable, i.e., when they hovered over the outposts or landed momentarily to pick up casualties or discharge reinforcements. During this phase of the mission, the jets usually laid a smoke screen, making long, shallow passes as they sprayed the North Vietnamese emplacements with clouds of teargas and chemical smoke. After their crop-dusting runs, the Skyhawks covered the withdrawal of the helicopters with more high explosives. Such tactics not only reduced the number of American casualties, they took a heavy toll of enemy gunners.[3]

Maj JIM STANTON
26th Marines Fire Support Coordination Center _____

The Super Gaggle was designed to flood the air with CH-46s bringing supplies to the hill outposts. They came in from all points of the compass at once, a sort of airborne time-on-target mission. They landed, discharged their cargoes and passengers, and got the hell out. We covered it with fire, coordinated to hit every intelligence target we knew about with air and artillery. The NVA never figured out how to counteract the Super Gaggle. There were too many targets at once, and too much going on.

HM3 DAVID STEINBERG
India Company, 3/26 _____

You'd look up in the sky and see around a dozen CH-46s out in the distance, in a circle, chasing tails. Then, all of a sudden, fighter-bombers came in to strafe and bomb the hills below us. After they were done dropping their bombs and strafing the hills, we would line up and shoot into the valley—firing full M-16 clips and throwing hand grenades. All of a sudden, we would hear the *whup-whup-whup-whup* of the choppers. One chopper would land in the saddle. Then, as soon as we heard the *boomp* of the incoming mortar, it would lift off and fly to one of the other landing zones and all the other choppers would come in at the various zones.

Capt BILL DABNEY
India Company, 3/26 ⎯⎯⎯⎯⎯⎯⎯⎯⎯⎯⎯⎯⎯⎯⎯⎯⎯⎯

For just about one minute, you could get in with external loads coming in echelons of four or five birds at once. We could get in ten helicopter loads on the hill in one minute and get the birds the hell out of there and into smoke where the NVA couldn't see to shoot.[4]

EVERYDAY LIFE

LCpl WALT WHITESIDES
Tactical Air Control Party ⎯⎯⎯⎯⎯⎯⎯⎯⎯⎯⎯⎯⎯⎯⎯⎯

By the first week of February, life on the hill had become a dreary, fearful routine. We were still constantly on alert for an attack, and we were usually short of consumables, mostly water. We had a fair supply of C-rations, and plenty of ammunition. One had the feeling that he was living in a bull's-eye, and that his time was numbered. The lines were probed at night, but there was no serious attempt to breach them. During the day, Captain Dabney put out listening posts on the southern and eastern approaches to the hill.

Capt BILL DABNEY
India Company, 3/26 ⎯⎯⎯⎯⎯⎯⎯⎯⎯⎯⎯⎯⎯⎯⎯⎯

After you've had enough of that stuff shot at you—rockets, artillery, it doesn't really make a hell of a lot of difference, with the exception of mortars—a man who's been around awhile and has been lucky can tell you where the round is going to hit when it goes off, when he hears the tube pop. Most of us who were on 881S got to the point where we could hear the damned round, either rocket fire, the rocket motor, or the artillery-tube pop. We knew whether the round was going to land near us or not. You get so you can tell within a few hundred meters where it's going to land, by the sound of the tube pop. There is a certain specific, unique sound to it, if the tube is oriented directly on you.[5]

Pfc JIM PAYNE
Charlie Battery, 1/13 _____

I perceived incoming on that hill as a single, dreaded being that I desperately tried to avoid. Incoming was a hooded gray ghost in a long, flowing robe. Incoming was a slow-moving shadow that drifted hauntingly over the 881S hilltop, ever-searching. Incoming was faceless, but I could almost hear it whisper, "Where are you, Marines? Where are you?" Incoming was piss-taste-in-the-mouth fear. If it found you, incoming was indiscriminate, unnegotiable death.

Capt BILL DABNEY
India Company, 3/26 _____

We got a message once—relayed to us by Battalion, ostensibly from Regiment—which specifically said, "Hey, we want you to overhead everything, every fighting hole up there, to withstand 82mm mortars." Great idea, I guess. I sent a message back down saying, "One, we have no capability up here, no timbers, no engineer support, no nothing—we've got only barbed-wire stakes. Two, nobody is shooting at us with 82mm mortars. They're shooting 120mm mortars at us, and I don't have capabilities to stop that with overhead without something like concrete or heavy timber." Nothing we could do to stop that. We got a lot of delay-fuse 120mm. They'd go three or four feet into the deck before they would detonate. And what little we had—logs and things—we had to use for our ammo bunkers. God! We had 1,500 rounds of 105, 2,000 to 3,000 rounds of 81, perhaps 1,000 rounds of 106 and 3.5-inch rockets, plus grenades and demolitions. They'd have blown the top off the hill if they had hit into one of those bunkers. The hill was only 75 by 150 meters on top![6]

HM3 DAVID STEINBERG
India Company, 3/26 _____

Our C-rat meal was supposed to be one-third of our daily requirement. We usually got one C-rat per *day*, but sometimes one C-rat had to last three days. If you got lucky and saved a can of peaches until you came up with a piece of pound cake, you could probably trade it for twelve cans of boned chicken.

Cpl TERRY STEWART
Mike Company, 3/26 _____

We had a code of honor on the hill—you NEVER touched another man's food or water. The code was violated once. The culprit, a lance corporal, helped himself to his partner's C-rats. It wasn't much—a can or two of something—but the thief was awarded an Article 15 punishment, and for many months after we were off the hill, the men of the platoon did not forget what he had done, or ever forgive him. It was serious.

If food was a major concern, water was doubly so. Here is where we were most careful and protective. It wasn't really critical, at least to the point that we ever really went without, but what we had was just enough, and if we were unable to get more, we would surely have been in serious trouble. There were times, quite often, that we rationed both food and water: one C-ration per day and two B-1 cans of water.

Water was delivered in the most unusual manner. Birds could not land on the hill, so it was necessary to literally drop supplies in large cargo nets suspended from the bellies of the birds. In this way, the birds could fly over the hill and simply release the net full of supplies so that it would land on top of the hill. There were times when a pilot's timing and aim were not so hot, when all our chow, water, ammo, and, most important, our mail, sailed by over our heads and tumbled down the slope into injun country. When this happened, jets were immediately called in to drop napalm and bombs on the precious cargo to ensure that the enemy did not benefit from the mishap. Even when the supplies landed on the hill, the jarring impact precluded any sensible means of delivering water. The C-rats were in cases and cans that were quite tough and able to survive the fall very well. Ammo came in cans and boxes that were designed to sustain heavy abuse. But water cans just couldn't take the drop. The problem of how to get us water was solved by partially filling plastic bags, like those used in cafeteria milk machines, with water and then stuffing the bags into artillery powder shipping canisters. This worked exceedingly well and there were side benefits. The canisters, once emptied of their precious cargo, could be used as piss tubes and crap tubes.

Cpl TERRY STEWART
Mike Company, 3/26

Stop and consider over 400 men stranded on a wasted hilltop and forced to live in the narrow, restricted confines of a simple trench system. Where do you construct heads? How do you construct them, camouflage them, and fortify them so that they can be safely used? It would have been a real mess if we'd just used catholes in the trenches. The trench would have filled up eventually, and the almost-daily rains would have had the place a real joy to live in—for a bunch of hogs.

For crappers and piss tubes, we buried the artillery powder canisters in which our water arrived—just deep enough to hold them. When they were full, we put the locking tops back on. The full canisters were kept in a shell crater on the very top of the hill at first, but soon there were too many there. One night, an 82mm mortar round found its way into the stack and it rained a most foul and disagreeable barrage down upon us. It was decided that the system must change.

Someone got the bright idea to just roll them over the edge of the hill. He explained, after nearly everyone stated that it was a bad idea because Charlie would get them, that it was okay for Charlie to have them. "Picture it," he told us. "Here comes Charlie, crawling several hundred meters from his protective cave to the bottom of our hill. He's braved mortars, artillery, and the most fearsome bombing in the history of warfare to get close to us, probe us, and pick up anything that he could find along the way. Now, near the bottom of the hill, these poor bastards find a gold mine. These tubes represent so many possibilities: live artillery shells, perhaps food, maybe they know about how our water's delivered, or maybe the tubes can be filled with earth and used to reinforce their bunkers. The Charlies risk life and limb to drag as many canisters back to their cave as possible, and when they arrive there, they very proudly present them to their first sergeant. He's a real hard-dick, but this time he is pleased with his two shitbirds and praises them for their find. After having the canisters dragged to his own tiny room in the back of the cave, the first sergeant opens one."

LCpl WALT WHITESIDES
Tactical Air Control Party _____

After a while, LCpl Terry Smith and I moved to a separate bunker on the northeast corner of the landing zone. The bunker was on the edge of what had evidently once been a gun pit. We had our communications gear and everything in there, and it was pretty comfortable. However, Captain Dabney had the idea that the gun pit would be a pretty good place to put a water trailer, which would greatly alleviate the water shortage on the hill. The pit was below the skyline and on the reverse slope from an enemy 120mm mortar. It was well protected from incoming rounds, as most of them either landed on top of the hill, on the forward slope, or in the landing zones. Since this seemed to be a reasonable request, and since Captain Dabney was a captain and I was a lance corporal, I agreed that if he could get the water trailer to the hill, I would get it off the helo and into the gun pit.

Everything was working pretty well in the planning stage until a CH-53 showed up—unannounced—with the water trailer externally loaded.

The pilot flew around while we tried to identify the zone for him without marking it. This gave the NVA mortar crew plenty of time to prepare, and they took full advantage of it. Next, after identifying the zone, the pilot announced that he couldn't drop the water trailer there because of the ground effect. I thought he was just being uncooperative. We argued for a while, and finally he said he was going to set the water trailer down on the landing zone. He also wanted us to unhook it because he wanted his slings back. I guess they were running low on nets and slings because we were then returning them at our leisure. We were not mentally prepared to unhook the slings in the landing zone, but one of the HST men said he would do it. Naturally, the slings did not unhook easily, and the HST man was wounded in the attempt, so we had to call in another helo to evacuate him. The same round that punctured the HST man also punctured the water trailer, and most of the water ran out before it could be saved. We continued to get our water in external loads of five-gallon cans and in bags loaded into 105mm shell canisters.

HM3 DAVID STEINBERG
India Company, 3/26

We got water sometimes by laying out plastic tarps during the night and licking them off in the morning.

Chapter 18

Cpl DENNIS SMITH
Bravo Company, 1/26

February 8, 1968

Dear Mother,

Two years ago today I went to boot camp. If I hadn't re-enlisted upon completion, I would be home today. It hurts.

I'm sending you my income tax thing because I don't know what to do with it.

It's been a while since we've received any mail. Ammo and food have priority on the planes that resupply us. There are about 200 people waiting at Phu Bai for transportation to Khe Sanh.

Remember the shooting galleries at the fair? I feel like one of those little ducks that move back and forth and get shot at. I ride in a jeep all day, all over the base, picking up gear and delivering it to our three platoons. Bravo Company is spread out around the perimeter. We never know when to expect incoming (except when a plane lands; we always catch it then), or where the rounds will land. Too many times they have landed too close.

Sgt FRANK JONES
26th Marines Scout-Sniper Platoon _____

On February 8, I was over by the helo pad with some buddies, drinking whiskey with dehydrated orange juice. I wrote a letter to my wife and went outside to put it in a mail bag. I was outside by the sandbag wall when three Marines carrying C-rations on their shoulders walked by. I didn't hear the rocket come in, but the next thing I knew, it seemed like everything had shifted down to slow motion, and it got real hot. I had a pain and pressure in my head I had never felt before, and it seemed like my body was jelly. I didn't even hear the explosion. The rocket hit about thirty feet from us. Those three guys in front of me absorbed most of the shrapnel. I came to on the ground. The concussion had knocked me out, and I had blood on my leg. My helmet had a big dent in it. I crawled over to this guy who was lying there on his back. His helmet chinstrap was buttoned and the helmet was filled up with this thick purple liquid. He was dead, and so were the other two guys. I got taken over to Charlie-Med and had the wound on my leg cleaned up and dressed. Then I returned to duty.

FEBRUARY 9

LCpl DAN ANSLINGER
3rd Marine Division Air Section _____

Because of the Lang Vei attack and problems evacuating survivors, one of the division air officers had to fly to Khe Sanh to help sort things out, and he took me with him. It was different there than it had been during my last visit, the first few days of the siege. The place was like a junkyard, and everything standing looked like it was falling apart as a result of the shelling. Some of the confidence and cockiness I had noticed a few weeks before seemed to be gone, and everyone was pretty grim, apparently wondering who would be next after Lang Vei.

I didn't have any bowel movements at all during the few days we were there because there was no way I was going outside to the shitter. I was within a few weeks of rotating home.

Cpl DENNIS MANNION
Charlie Battery, 1/13 (Hill 861) _____

February 9, 1968

Dear Joe,

    This day just ain't a good one for me. This morning a guy I became pretty good friends with took an 82mm mortar round right in his foxhole. Just blew him away. Not too pretty. But if you're gonna go, that's the best way. Quick.

PAY RUN

LCpl PHIL MINEER
Bravo Battery, 1/13 _____

What the hell we needed money for up there was beyond me, but Lieutenant McGrath got picked to make the pay run down to Danang. I went as his shotgun, his bodyguard. We went to take a C-123 out.

When we got near the runway, we did what everyone called "the Khe Sanh shuffle." You looked the way you were going, and you never went more than fifty meters in one shot. It was a half-slouch combined with the opposite of being cross-eyed: One eye always looked where you were going and the other always looked at an alternate route, where you would go if the rounds came in. When we got to the runway, we found a little trench and hid out there. The C-123 came in, made its swing, and kept moving. There were about a dozen body bags laid out that had to go on the plane, so they got the plane to slow down. When they got all the bodies on the plane, everyone who was waiting in the trench jumped on.

1stLt FRED McGRATH
Bravo Battery, 1/13 _____

The plane was loaded with montagnards from Lang Vei. They seemed in good spirits and were happy to be flying out. The pilot wasted no time in getting off the ground, but he had a full load and he could not climb as rapidly as he would have liked.

LCpl PHIL MINEER
Bravo Battery, 1/13

It was eerie as hell going down the runway, hearing the engines race in the C-123's effort to get off the ground. It was very slow. I looked at the lieutenant and saw that he had that thousand-mile Khe Sanh stare. He was looking at me, but he was looking beyond me. I felt the plane lift off, so I put my thumb up—"We're off the runway and we're almost out of here." But the lieutenant held up his finger—"No, wait. We're not out yet." And then here comes Luke the Gook. I could hear the *dat-dat-dat-dat* of the gun and *shwee-shwee-shwee-shwee* as the rounds went through the fuselage.

1stLt FRED McGRATH
Bravo Battery, 1/13

Bullets began striking the plane everywhere. Riding where we were—sitting on the deck on pallets and seabags—we could feel the bullets impact.

LCpl PHIL MINEER
Bravo Battery, 1/13

They hit near the rear ramp and blew out a hose filled with pink hydraulic fluid. This created some concern among the crewmen, who didn't know if they could get the landing gear down. I didn't give a shit. I really didn't. If the C-123 had to come in on its belly, at least it would come in at Danang, and not Khe Sanh.

1stLt FRED McGRATH
Bravo Battery, 1/13

But we gained altitude, gained the cloud cover, and got out of range. Just when the flight became routine, those montagnards caused a mild sensation. One asked me for a match. I gave him a book of C-ration matches, thinking he knew what he was doing. He struck one, but for some reason the whole book ignited. So we had this small ball of flame flying around the inside of the plane. The crew chief rushed over and stomped it out. That's all he needed!

LCpl PHIL MINEER
Bravo Battery, I/I3 _____

When we finally did come into Danang, they had foam on the runway, a dozen fire trucks, and hundreds of Air Force guys watching. The Air Force guys had Bermuda shorts on and Coke bottles in their hands. The crew chief lowered the landing gear manually with a crank and we got down okay, but they made a big deal out of it.

IstLt FRED McGRATH
Bravo Battery, I/I3 _____

When we arrived in Danang, we had to exit from the side hatch. The bullets had severed the hydraulic line that controlled the rear ramp. The pilot walked around his aircraft and counted seventeen holes. I am certain he considered himself lucky. So did I.

LCpl PHIL MINEER
Bravo Battery, I/I3 _____

I was wearing all my gear—flak jacket, diaper, pistol, field transport pack, and my M-16. One guy said to me, "Jesus Christ! You're *pink*!" That was the red Khe Sanh mud that had dried on me. "Where you been," he went on, "in a *war*?" It was a different world in Danang.

Those Air Force guys treated me good that night. I had a *rack*— a *real* rack—and a *real* mattress on a spring frame. And *real* sheets! They got me hot chow.

IstLt FRED McGRATH
Bravo Battery, I/I3 _____

The war had a different face in Danang. Since we had landed near the Air Force terminal, I decided to grab chow at the Air Force compound adjacent to the terminal. I approached the gate guard, not expecting any problem, even though I was pretty scruffy-looking. He noticed the .45 strapped to my leg and halted me. "No weapons inside the compound, sir." Surely you jest! Same war, right? Wrong! Since there was no way I was going unarmed anywhere, I asked directions to the nearest Marine Corps installation.

LCpl PHIL MINEER
Bravo Battery, 1/13 _____

During our three-day stopover in Danang, the lieutenant and I bought a duck and started fattening him up with C-ration crackers so we could cook him on Easter. Also, before we left Khe Sanh, I had been authorized to purchase some beer if I could. I got the beer, but by the time the lieutenant and I were ready to go back to Khe Sanh, the only way in was by chopper, and even then they were reluctant.

I talked an Air Force pilot into taking us and the duck and our pallet of beer back to Khe Sanh on his CH-53 helicopter. This guy had never flown combat before, just transport in and out of Danang. As we were coming in, I tried to tell the crew chief to tell the pilot to get down to treetop level, but they stayed up high. I kept trying to explain to the crew chief that the higher you fly, the better the bead they can get on you. Well, sure as shit, we took ground fire. A round going through the side of the CH-53 is like punching your finger through a piece of aluminum foil. But we made it in, the beer made it in, the duck made it in, and the payroll money made it in.

The payroll was all in military payment certificates, which looked like Monopoly money. That led to some heavy card games for the next few days. We built the duck his own bunker, but he got blown up just before Easter. That pissed a lot of guys off. There were feathers everywhere, but *no meat*!

FEBRUARY 10

Pfc LIONEL TRUFANT
106mm Platoon, 3/26 _____

Five of us, all new 106mm gunners, were in the transit hut in Phu Bai when a Marine who had just rotated from Hill 861 came through. The guy was shattered. He looked like a shattered person. His nerve was gone. He was smoking a cigarette, shaking. He told us about what was happening up there. He mentioned how Hill 861 was almost overrun, how they were getting hit with artillery, how the NVA were probing their lines. He mentioned how his company had lost so much manpower. And he told us it was a hell of a trip just getting out of there. That really shocked us.

We worked in supply for a few days, until they found an airplane that could take us to Khe Sanh. We went down to the airstrip, but we couldn't get out because the airstrip was getting hit too hard. The second day, we got on the aircraft, a C-130. We were standing facing the rear. Behind us was an internal load on a pallet on rollers. We were in full gear—helmet, willy-peter bag, rifle, pack. There were mostly Marines, but also a few Navy, a few Army, and a few Air Force. We took off and flew over Khe Sanh, but we couldn't land. The airstrip was getting hit too hard, so we flew back to Phu Bai.

We had to go out the next day, February 11. That morning, we went back out. While we were waiting at the airstrip, we heard a shot. A guy had shot his finger off. We knew he wasn't going to Khe Sanh. They loaded us on the plane and we flew out. It was the same situation as the day before. We were packed in the front of the plane, all dressed in full gear, and we had an internal load in front of us as we faced the rear.

I was close to a window. When we flew over Khe Sanh, it looked like a giant anthill to me. I could see all the trenches. It looked *dirty*.

The crew chief gave us instructions. He said, "This is how we're going to land. When the aircraft lands, we're going to open up the back and release the internal load. When I give the signal, all of you roll out. You jump out and run."

The word came down from the pilot that we were going to land but that the airstrip was under attack. I could envision in my mind a machine-gun nest firing at the aircraft, shooting at us when we got off the plane.

When the plane landed and the back door opened up, I came to realize how the airstrip was getting hit. I saw two well-placed artillery rounds hitting the runway. Next thing I knew, the internal load was released. But nobody waited for the crew chief to give us the word to jump out. Everybody just went hauling out of the back. It was just like jumping off the back of a pickup. The plane was still moving. I jumped off and hit the ground flat. My rifle went one way, the magazines went another way, and my willy-peter bag went a third way. My helmet was still on my head because I had it strapped on.

I picked up my rifle, I picked up my willy-peter bag, and I

grabbed about two magazines. All I could see was people running to the side. Some guy was hollering, "Come on! Come on!" So I just started hauling ass—ran and ran until I found a hole. I jumped in, but I must have tripped over someone, because I went flying into the hole. I was scared as hell.

The incoming kept coming in. Then, all of a sudden, everything stopped. Some guy came down, looked in the hole, and said, "All right, you guys, get outta there." So we got out. When I came out of that hole, everything was in a normal state. I saw a guy driving a jeep and other people jogging from place to place.

On our way to check in, another Marine and I had this great debate about the incoming sound and the outgoing sound. He said it sounded the same way it had sounded at Phu Bai, and I said it sounded different. Soon we had an answer. More incoming started. I told the other guy, "Get your ass down," and we jumped into the nearest hole.

We reported in to the 106mm Platoon commander at the 3rd Battalion headquarters, and they sent us out to Lima Company, which was holding the western end of the perimeter. There were three Marines manning the gun, and two more of us made a five-man crew.

To our left were the Special Forces and Vietnamese strike troopers. Ahead of us to the right was 1/9, on a hill outside the perimeter. To our right rear was the drop zone. The main reason our 106 was there was to protect the road leading from 1/9 to the Special Forces area. To the left of our position was a Marine-manned .50-caliber machine gun, and just to our rear was an Ontos position. The Ontos had six 106s on it. To our right was a hole manned by two M-79 grenadiers, and the hole to the right of that had an M-60. We were in a reinforced strongpoint, guarding the road. Just in our hole itself, the five of us had the 106mm recoilless rifle, an M-60 machine gun, our five personal M-16 rifles, and one .45-caliber pistol.

When I got to the gun, our living bunker was sitting on top of the ground. It had three layers of sandbags and pallets on top and three layers of sandbags all the way around. There was only one small trench, which had the 106 in it. Starting right away, we dug deeper trenches, dug the living area into the ground, and put in a separate bunker for the M-60 machine gun.

Cpl WILLIAM ROBERTSON
Logistics Support Unit _____

On February 10, a Marine Corps KC-130 fueler was coming in. We heard it and saw it circling around. Then we heard the antiaircraft fire. The KC-130 came around and touched down on the runway, and probably made it a hundred feet when the tires on the right side of the plane blew out. The pilot held it on the runway a long time—I don't know how he managed to do it, but he kept it straight for, it looked like, almost all the way. We thought he was going to make it, but finally the front end got away from him.

1stLt NICK ROMANETZ
Charlie Company, 1/26 _____

Suddenly it veered off to the right and burst into flames. The whole airplane was not initially engulfed.

Cpl WILLIAM ROBERTSON
Logistics Support Unit _____

The plane went off the runway and broke in half. It was carrying six rubber fuel bladders of helicopter fuel.

1stLt NICK ROMANETZ
Charlie Company, 1/26 _____

I sat and watched people start coming out of the hatches over the flight deck. Crash vehicles arrived and started foaming the plane down, but it kept burning more and more.

Cpl WILLIAM ROBERTSON
Logistics Support Unit _____

In no time flat, that plane looked just like molten liquid. There was molten aluminum running down the ditch beside the runway. This was right next to the concrete bunker I lived in.

1stLt NICK ROMANETZ
Charlie Company, 1/26 _____

As soon as it started burning, it drew a crowd. Boy, did it draw a crowd. My concern was that the enemy was going to pop a few mortar rounds in on us. Apparently they had a few 60mm mortars dug into the ground in front of my position, and it would have been very easy for them to cause casualties. Fortunately, we didn't take any incoming.

The KC-130 was apparently hit by machine-gun rounds and set afire before it touched down on the runway. The pilot and copilot escaped, but six crewmen and passengers were incinerated.

FEBRUARY 11

Sgt FRANK JONES
26th Marines Scout-Sniper Platoon _____

I was going back to the Blue Sector the night of February 11 and I found one of my buddies, Cpl Dennis Keefe, sitting out on a water can in front of his bunker, polishing his boots. I asked him what he was doing and he told me he was getting ready to go home on a thirty-day leave because he had just extended his tour six months. We laughed about it, that it would probably be over by the time he got back. I told him, "Take it easy and have one for me." As I turned to walk away, I heard a round coming in. When it went off, I fell and a lot of debris and dirt came down on top of me. I turned to check on Keefe, but he was gone. The rocket had hit right where he was sitting. We never found a part of him. No boots, no body parts—nothing.

FEBRUARY 12

Cpl WILLIAM HUBBARD
Echo Company, 2/26 _____

My buddy, Corporal Houska, and I went down through the trenches every day to try to get a helo out of there, so we could go home. Our time was up. But the only thing going out was wounded; they had priority. It took twenty-three tries. Finally, on the twenty-third day, February 12, we made it down to the end of the runway. I had my seabag with me. Until I started trying to get out of Khe Sanh, I hadn't seen it in the thirteen months and twenty days I'd been in-country. I didn't even remember what was in it, but it was my only connection with The World. Houska had his, too. When we got to the end of the runway, there was a little Army helicopter hovering there. The pilot was looking out the other side, so me and Houska started waving and yelling. He looked down and shook his head; he couldn't take us. But we had his attention, so we threw our seabags down. We even dropped our rifles. Less weight, less room. He set the helicopter down as close to us as he could, and we jumped in. As he went up as high as he could go, right over Khe Sanh, Houska and I ripped off our flak jackets and sat on them. We didn't want to catch a live one in the nut sack that late in the game. We rode on out of there, straight to Dong Ha, stayed the night, got as drunk as we could get, and went to Phu Bai the next day. Then we went to Danang, waited at the airport, got on the biggest plane I had ever seen in my life, and flew home. It took us twenty-five hours.

HM3 BILL GESSNER
Delta Company, I/9

12 February

Dear Dad:

Enclosed is my W-2 form. I would like you to square my income tax away, if you would.

I have a project for you and I wish you would get it accomplished as soon as possible. Our captain is leaving the company soon and we want to give him a plaque. I'll describe it and then draw it. We would like a metal heart (a large one) on shellacked wood. In the center of the heart, a Marine Corps emblem (anchor and globe) in the center (engraved) above the emblem: "CAPT SHAFER CO OF DEATH DEFYING DELTA." Beneath the emblem put: "THE HEART OF ONE-NINE." At the base of the heart put "67–68". And on a piece of metal on the back put "From the Docs of D 1/9." I would like you to get this done and send it to me as quickly as possible. We have a $50 reserve, which is the most we can spend. Do the best you can, please. Take what it costs out of my money and I'll replace it next month.

FEBRUARY 13

Capt KEN PIPES
Bravo Company, 1/26 _____

The troopers of the 37th ARVN Ranger Battalion had not been paid for several months, and, most important, the Tet Offensive was centered around the towns, villages, and hamlets from which most of the troopers had been recruited. They did not know the effect that the NVA Tet Offensive had on their families and loved ones.

On numerous occasions, we assisted each other by fire and collective action. Marines and corpsmen made voluntary nightly trips to the ARVN lines to carry wounded ARVN Rangers to the Regimental Aid Station.

Sgt FRANK JONES
26th Marines Scout-Sniper Platoon _____

We were taking fire from an NVA recoilless rifle until finally Colonel Lownds told the ARVNs to put a stop to it.

26th Marines Command Chronology _____

At 1300, a six-man patrol from the 37th ARVN Ranger Battalion ambushed a five-man recoilless-rifle site. Results of the contact: 2 NVA KIA (confirmed), 1 57mm recoilless rifle captured.

Capt KEN PIPES
Bravo Company, 1/26 _____

The ARVN lieutenant leading the patrol was severely wounded and isolated from the other ARVNs. When his troopers took casualties trying to get to him, he killed himself with his pistol so they would stop trying. That's unbelievable leadership.

Cpl DENNIS MANNION
Charlie Battery, 1/13 (Hill 861) _____

February 13, 1968

Dear Joe—

Gooks have slacked off the last couple of days. We (861) have taken no, zip, none, zero rounds in over three days. Quite a switch! It almost scares you worse than when they throw 'em in. You wonder what those sneaky fucks are doing.

FEBRUARY 14

Pfc JIM PAYNE
Charlie Battery, 1/13 (Hill 881S) _____

I was assigned to an India Company squad that was preparing to fire suppression for an incoming chopper operation. The squad occupied a stretch of trenchline on the south side of 881S, facing the hostile 689 ridgeline, a thousand yards distant. Minutes after we arrived, we could hear the choppers approaching the hill from the north and east. About that time, the squad opened up with heavy rifle fire on the distant ridgeline to the south.

While we were putting out rounds, I could hear loud chopper noises above and behind us in the direction of the landing zone. These sounds were followed by rotor noises rising up and moving away, indicating that the choppers had had a successful trip and getaway. At that point, the lieutenant leading the squad ordered us to cease fire. While the squad was still standing in the trenchline, I heard the *ka-rumph, ka-rumph* of incoming mortar rounds impacting behind us, up the hill. Someone shouted, "Innn-coming!"

As the squad scattered, the incoming rounds blew a heavy wooden cargo skid into the air, and it came down with tremendous force on my helmet, knocking me senseless and center-punching me straight down onto the trench floor.

I ended up on my back with the cargo skid across my face. I couldn't hear, I couldn't move, I was just laying there, staring up at the bright yellow sun through a narrow crack in the skid. I thought I was dead. It was sort of like the last moments of a living brain inside a dead body, taking turns watching the sun and a brilliant white ball ricocheting around inside my skull. Death was saying, "See, I'm not so bad. Just lay back and let me take you away." Life was saying, "Oh . . . fuck!"

After about thirty seconds, I started to hear noises and see shadows. Two Marines were stooping over me, and one of them lifted the wooden skid off my face and said, "You all right, Marine? You all right?" After I regained full consciousness and stood up on shaky legs, one of the Marines handed me my rifle and patted me on the back. The thought of rejoining the living world was momentarily exhilarating.

FEBRUARY 15
HURRIED DEPARTURES

Pfc MICHAEL LEE
Helicopter Support Team (Hill 881S) _____

The landing support company sent me up a teammate to hook nets and help with medevacs. We would alternate directing in the the aircraft. On February 15, we both got hit as we were bringing in a resupply on the eastern landing zone. Apparently the NVA sent rounds on all three zones at the same time. My teammate and I were standing in a shallow crater after the aircraft dropped the net and left. A 120mm mortar round hit a few feet to my right. I saw a big burst of dirt and felt a bang like a baseball bat had hit me in the right arm and went through my flak jacket. My teammate was hit in the stomach. I called for the corpsman and we dragged him to the trench. His intestines and all were bulging out. The corpsman tucked it all inside again and put a big compress on his stomach. They looked me over and put a couple of compresses on. No big deal.

I got on the radio and called my own medevac in. My teamee was a priority and I was a routine. The aircraft that had just left called back and said he would come and get us. I went back to our bunker to get our personal gear. Someone had already stolen both of our cameras and wallets.

The CH-46 came back and I took the front of the stretcher. As I went up the ramp of the 46, an updraft caught the aircraft and took it up about ten feet. The guy on the back let go, and so did I. The stretcher went up and my teamee hit the ground. I could see that it hurt. After another try, we got on the aircraft and were on our way to Khe Sanh. We landed and I walked off. From there, I was medevacked to Dong Ha. After I recovered in March, I was sent back to Khe Sanh.

Cpl WILLIAM ROBERTSON
Logistics Support Unit _____

I was supposed to have left Khe Sanh on January 22. I had my seabag packed and I was ready to leave for the rear, Phu Bai. But, since the ammo dump blew on January 21, I had to stay. My relief had arrived two or three days before the dump blew, but he was killed by an artillery shell on January 24.

A CH-53 helicopter came in on February 15. We were unloading loose 155mm white-phosphorus rounds off the back of it. We were just rolling them off when three mortar or rocket rounds came in. Next thing I knew, Corporal Baker and I were airborne. Our rifles were sitting up against a stack of ammo next to the runway, and we were gone. The next place the helo set down was Dong Ha. There was nothing else going back to Khe Sanh that afternoon, so Baker and I spent the night at the ammo dump at Dong Ha with some of our friends. In a way, this was a relief. Water had been rationed at Khe Sanh, and the only thing we used it for was to drink and maybe to shave with. I had not had a bath since January 21. Both of us got everything clean except our boots and our covers. Everything else we got from friends and put on clean. That's the only time in my life I ever wore someone else's underwear. We threw our other clothes away and stayed in the shower a long time. We even ate at the messhall!

The next morning, we were unable to get back because fog had Khe Sanh closed in. That afternoon, we were fixing to get on a helicopter to go back when the base colonel came through. He almost had a kitten because neither Baker nor I had a weapon. I think he was ready to court-martial us until he found out how we got there. Then he held the helicopter up and sent his driver over to the armory. He got two shotguns and two boxes of ammo for us. The colonel told us to turn it all over to Colonel Lownds as soon as we got back. He wished us good luck.

Until we got back, we had been unable to tell anyone at Khe Sanh where we were. All they found when they went looking for us were our rifles. They had a pretty good idea we had left on the

CH-53, but they had no idea why or where—if we had decided we had had enough and just gotten on the helicopter and left or what. I can imagine the expressions on their faces when they came up looking for us and only found our rifles.

1stLt JOHN KAHENY
1/26 Combat Operations Center

My father was very ill, and I had a suspicion that he would not live six months until the end of my Vietnam tour, so I had to get home to see him. For whatever reason, there was a delay in my orders, but on February 15 we got a message through to Division Headquarters, and they replied, saying that my orders were at Phu Bai and that I had to pick them up within two days or they would be canceled. I went over to the battalion command post to see Lieutenant Colonel Wilkinson, our battalion commander. As I walked in the door, he turned to me and said that something tragic had just happened. SgtMaj James Gaynor, the battalion sergeant major, and Capt David Ernst, the Charlie Company commander, had both been seriously wounded by a rocket that had hit the Charlie Company command post. He said, "You're the next-senior lieutenant. Do you want to take Charlie Company?" I told him then that my orders had been approved and were down at Phu Bai, and that if I didn't act I would not be able to get my 30-day leave. He was aware of my father's illness and patted me on the back and said, "Why don't you go on home." He indicated to me that I would probably be able to get another rifle company sometime after my return to the battalion. With that, I went back to my bunker, packed my gear, said a few quick good-byes, and went down to the airstrip.

At that time, the only way to get out was to hop one of the medevac choppers and help tend the wounded. Most of the helicopters went to the Delta-Med aid station at Dong Ha. So I went down to Charlie-Med, which was right next to the airstrip, and waited for a helicopter to arrive. During the wait, I heard that Captain Ernst was going to lose his arm and the sergeant major was in very serious condition.

The basic scenario was that the choppers would send word

that they were on the way in. Four or so Marines, acting as stretcher bearers, would take each wounded man and race out across the airfield to the helicopters, which would not necessarily stop because of the mortar and recoilless-rifle fire. They only stopped at that point when the stretcher bearers were getting the wounded aboard.

I waited for quite a long time. I went up to the helicopter pad to run an errand and there met Lieutenant King, who had come off Hill 881S. He was on his way to Graves Registration with the remains of a Marine from India Company, 3/26. All he had was a small willy-peter bag because the Marine had been hit directly by an enemy mortar. As I started talking to Lieutenant King, both of us were called back down to Charlie-Med because the helicopter was on its way. I was assigned to help with Sergeant Major Gaynor.

The sergeant major and I had lived together in the battalion alternate command post for the previous month or so, and I had gotten to know him fairly well. He evidently had been in the Air Wing most of his time in the Marine Corps, and this was going to be his twilight cruise before his retirement. He had made a request to be able to serve his last tour with the grunts because he had never served with the infantry and felt that one could not be a retired sergeant major of Marines without having so served. He was injured doing what he did best, which was visiting the troops on the line. I thought highly of the man, and it was very difficult for me to go down there and see him as badly wounded as he was. But I took one end of the stretcher and we raced out to a CH-53 that was coming in and got him aboard.

It was quite dark by then. We barely got out of Khe Sanh while there was enough light.

Captain Ernst was next to me. I lit a cigarette for him. I had in my hand the IV bottle for the sergeant major, who was resting on my lap. It was kind of eerie because, as we got closer to Dong Ha, he became grayer and grayer. I think that he passed away sometime on the way into Dong Ha, but I'm not sure; the corpsman still wanted to work on him.

When we hit the ground at Dong Ha—which was still in the throes of the Tet Offensive—artillery rounds were coming in. Lieutenant King and I, and the other people aboard the chopper, ran down the runway with the stretchers and met up with some ambulances. Since we had to spend the night there, we were all told to go help out at Delta-Med. Everyone there pitched in without distinction of rank. I worked in the triage center until late that evening, mopping and sweeping all the blood and gore and debris and bandages.

It wasn't until years later that I learned that Sergeant Major Gaynor had indeed passed away that evening.

Chapter 19

RESUPPLY

There would have been no Khe Sanh Combat Base—no "set-piece" strategy—without one of the biggest aerial resupply efforts in history. The effort was enormous. While it strained and stressed the capacity of air-cargo units throughout the western Pacific and Vietnam, the massive airlift barely made good the daily use of supplies by the troops and the daily loss of supplies to enemy fire. The effort is more remarkable in that it took place entirely within the period of the Tet Offensive, when U.S. military units throughout Vietnam were under unremitting pressure. Throughout February, most aerial resupply missions were flown through dense fog or enemy fire—or both.

Maj TOM COOK
26th Marines Assistant Logistics Officer _____

I was assigned as assistant logistics officer. My duties consisted of the ordering and allocation of materials required for construction and fortification and the ordering and allocation of munitions. That took up most of my time, particularly the ordering of the munitions. Every day, around 1800, I called Dong Ha on the land line and reported a long, long list of numbers, each corresponding to a particular item. I reported quantities on position, the quantities in the dumps, and the quantities that I thought were required. It took a tremendous amount of time to gather all this information every day. Probably I worked twelve hours a day on that aspect of my job. In addition, I had other little duties. From what I understand, when that report was received at Dong Ha, it was immediately forwarded to Saigon, to MACV Headquarters. From there, it was dispatched directly to the White House so that President Johnson and his staff could look at it, to make sure that Khe Sanh was not going to fall.

LtCol DICK ROMINE
Marine Medium Helicopter Squadron 165

If we stayed high and made a steep approach to Khe Sanh we were not vulnerable to the surrounding enemy antiaircraft guns (mostly 12.7mm), which were predominantly to the west. I made most of my approaches from the east of the plateau, which was at about 1,500 feet. It took only one time to realize when you'd made a bad approach and flown over the wrong positions. The clatter of rounds got your attention. The guns were impossible to spot from the air. I later observed why. Those ingenious little bastards had most of their antiaircraft guns mounted on dollies or wheels at the entrances of small caves high on the hillsides. They probably tunneled through from the other side of the hills. They stuck the noses of the guns outside just long enough to take potshots at us and then pulled them back into concealment before we could see where this fire was coming from.

LtCol JOHNNY GREGERSON
Marine Air Support Squadron 3

The majority of the cargo was lifted to the outlying outposts from a staging area at Dong Ha. It was difficult enough to sustain supply support at Khe Sanh itself without adding an additional problem of staging supplies and massing the helicopters necessary to resupply the outposts.[1]

1stLt FRED McGRATH
Bravo Battery, 1/13

I watched a CH-53 attempt a takeoff. The pilot got it about fifteen or twenty feet off the deck, then it slammed down hard and burst into flames. The pilots and crew chief escaped, but that 53 was a pile of melted metal within ten minutes. No happy hour for them that night.

IstLt NICK ROMANETZ
Charlie Company, 1/26 ——————————————————————————

On February 5, a camouflaged Air Force C-130 landed from west to east, taxied to the turnaround ramp, which was outside the perimeter, shut down his engines, and sat there. It had apparently taken some fire coming in, and the pilot apparently was unsure of the worthiness of the aircraft. I have to hand it to the pilot; he just parked it out there instead of taxiing it inside the base. Standing there watching, we couldn't figure out why he did that. I kept thinking, Hey, pal, get your ass out of there. He was easily within range of bad guys who could come up the trenches and fire RPGs or 60mm mortars at him. No crewmen came out of the aircraft. We thought those guys were really going to get it. He must have sat there for about forty-five minutes before he cranked up the engines. It turned out that the reason he didn't bring the aircraft into the perimeter was that it was loaded with ammunition. I guess the pilot was worried that there would be a big explosion inside the base.

Maj JIM STANTON
26th Marines Fire Support Coordination Center ———————————

The NVA infiltrated in a man who sat about two hundred meters off the end of the runway. He was in a little vertical hole, three feet across, just big enough for him to stand in and with a round column of dirt in the middle to support a .51-caliber machine gun. All the planes taking off and landing had to survive a burst from that gunner. We couldn't hit somebody in a hole that small.

LCpl PHIL MINEER
Bravo Battery, 1/13 ——————————————————————————

There was an NVA we called Luke the Gook. He had a .51-caliber machine gun. I could almost see his position on a big hill across from my gun, to the right. Luke took a shot at every C-130 that came into Khe Sanh. Sometimes he'd get a hit, and sometimes he missed. We knew exactly where Luke was, so we shot at him with artillery pieces—pounded the area all around him. We *had* to have hit him, but they kept sending guys to replace him. Once we called in a Phantom. It hit him with rockets, it hit him with machine guns, it hit him with bombs. But Luke got the Phantom. The jet started smoking and the pilot ejected. In fact, his canopy came down right in our gun section and the pilot came down right outside the wire. He was picked up by some guys from 1/26. The plane went right into the side of the hill; I think the pilot aimed it right at Luke the Gook. Not long after that—*dit-dit-dit-dit-dit*—the .51 was back again. We gave Luke a standing ovation and never bothered with him again.

Sgt DAVID MACH, USAF
29th Tactical Airlift Squadron

I was a loadmaster with the 29th Tactical Airlift Squadron when we flew out of Clark Air Force Base, in the Philippines, and staged through Tan Son Nhut for fifteen days at a time.

On the first mission we brought in five pallets of ammunition. I'll always remember them telling us we had five minutes total on the ground. We landed, combat-offloaded the five pallets, taxied ahead, stopped to pick up ten wounded Marines, taxied to the runway, and took off just as the mortars started to hit the base.

My second mission was a couple of days later. Same as before—five pallets of supplies—but this time we had to be gone in three minutes. We combat-offloaded the pallets and stopped to pick up fifteen KIAs. I was trying to close the ramp as we were taxiing off, as the mortars were coming in. On the way back to Danang, I was sitting on the floor with those bodies around me. I was afraid to look at the toe tags because I might have known one of them. The smell was nauseating, as always.

Within days of the total loss of the Marine KC-130 fueler on February 10,
the Khe Sanh runway was closed to all C-130 traffic.

Col GEORGE KINNEY, USAF
834th Air Division Vice Commander _____

The C-123 pilots continued to land throughout the entire operation, although only when absolutely necessary. The [C-123s],
needing only 1,400 feet of roll-out to slow sufficiently, were able
to make the 90-degree turnoff to the offload ramp. But the
C-130s had to go to the end of the runway to turn around,
presenting inviting targets for enemy gunners.[2]

Maj TOM COOK
26th Marines Assistant Logistics Officer _____

Air drops became our main means of getting supplies. We were
totally dependent on them. There was no way that the planes
could land in sufficient numbers because of the mortar fire,
rockets, and artillery that rained in if they tried to sit there long
enough to unload anything. On the whole, the air drops were
quite successful. We depended on them for artillery ammunition,
small-arms ammunition, food—everything that had to come in
there. The only thing we didn't depend on them for was water. (I
have no idea why the water point was never contaminated by the
NVA. It could have been, very easily. If it had been, we would
have been out of business.)

Maj MYLES ROHRLICK, USAF
834th Air Division _____

The drop zone was extremely small, only 300 yards square, and
located outside the Marine defense perimeter. There was no
room for it inside the camp. So we dropped only during daylight.
At night the Marines withdrew to the camp proper and, essentially, gave up the drop zone to the enemy.

In the morning they would sweep it for mines and secure it
for the day's use. And the equipment to recover the dropped
supplies was limited. Routh-terrain forklifts and trucks were used
to get the supplies to camp. The Marines and our combat
controllers were always under enemy fire in the drop zone.[3]

LCpl ARMANDO GONZALES
Bravo Company, 1/9 _____

The supplies that were dropped fell between the Rock Quarry and the combat base, so 1/9 was responsible for sweeping the drop zone every morning for any type of booby traps or ambushes. We rotated platoons and companies every morning. We found booby traps a few times, and we lost a few guys in the process.

Maj TOM COOK
26th Marines Assistant Logistics Officer _____

We went out there every morning and waited for the air drop. We had a terrible time during the month of February because it was foggy nearly every day. We could hear the planes, but we couldn't see the parachutes until they broke out of the clouds, which was at about a hundred feet. At first, our security at the drop zone, which was a different platoon every day, was never properly instructed about what to do if they saw a pallet falling toward them. When they saw the parachutes, they would take off running. Since they usually ran with the wind, the parachutes would follow them. After a few days of that, we finally got the problem corrected by telling them each day to run into the wind.

LCpl ARMANDO GONZALES
Bravo Company, 1/9 _____

Once in a while, the resupply aircraft overshot the zone and we literally had to blow up our own supplies with artillery. In a few cases, jets came in to blow it up to keep the NVA from getting it.

Through the latter half of February, most of the parachute drops were made through patches of dense fog. Often the crews of the cargo aircraft never saw the ground. The extreme visibility problem, combined with the need for pinpoint accuracy—the drop zone was extremely small—required sophisticated technical innovation. The result was the IMC—Instrument Meteorological Condition—technique.

Maj HENRY VAN GIELSON, USAF
834th Air Division _____

There was ground radar close to the drop zone, so we combined two existing systems to develop [IMC]. Marine [ground controllers] positioned the aircraft over the threshold of [the] runway. . . . Then by using the Doppler [radar] to keep on course, and calculating the exact time it took (twenty to twenty-six seconds, depending on winds) to fly to the computed air-release point we were able to put bundles on the [drop zone].[4]

LtCol FRANK HAMMOCK, USAF
21st Tactical Airlift Squadron _____

The weather had turned to instrument conditions over Khe Sanh. Cloud tops were from 4,000 to 10,000 feet and Khe Sanh was reporting cloud bases from "on the ground to indefinite."

We took on our load at Danang—32,000 pounds of artillery shells and a pallet of toilet paper. We got airborne and headed for Hue to set up holding patterns and wait our turn to start our run. As each airplane departed the drop zone, it would report being clear, and then the next airplane on the bottom of the holding stack would start its run. Taking a westerly heading from Hue and starting the letdown through heavy clouds, we headed toward a gap in the mountains that lined up with the drop zone. Charlie and the NVA owned the land on both sides of the gap for several miles. When at the planned altitude to pass through the gap, the airplane would be below the tops of the mountains around the approach path. As we reached the minimum altitude through the pass, we could hear the small-arms fire going through the skin of the airplane.

After I reached drop altitude and slowed the airplane to 130 knots, the navigator made Doppler contact and passed information to me. At that low altitude and low airspeed, the *thump-thump* of the artillery could be heard above the whine of the engines. The loadmaster finished his load check and was standing by the emergency load release—just in case. The countdown was in progress when, suddenly, the command "Green light" arrived. The load was released. I could hear the rumbling sound of the pallets as they started rolling toward the open tailgate of the airplane. I could also hear the impact of small-arms fire as it pinged through the skin of the airplane.

Things began happening very fast. I could feel the weight of the load on the controls shifting toward the tail, so I applied forward pressure on the wheel. The nose started to rise rapidly due to the shifting load, so I ran in all the forward trim available and applied power. I was no longer simply applying pressure to the wheel, I was manually pushing the wheel against the stop, but the nose was still rising. I had full throttle. The nose could not go up much more or the airplane would stall. At that altitude and airspeed, that could ruin my whole weekend. There was nothing more I could do except hold on, keep the pressure on the wheel, and hope the load cleared the tailgate.

Then the rumbling stopped and the nose pitched downward fast enough to lift me against my seat belt. I had to get the wheel back to neutral and the trim back to normal. I could still hear the ping of small-arms rounds hitting us as the airplane made it back to straight and level flight. The throttles were well forward to get all the airspeed that Hercules could handle. We started our climb-out in a wide turn to the left. I had not seen the ground through the fog yet, but our load was on the way to the drop zone. I waited for the Airlift Control Element to tell us about our drop. The call told us that we were only ten yards off the mark.

As I continued my climb-out, the copilot called to tell me that we were clear of the drop zone. I could hear the next airplane's call that it was starting its run. Meanwhile, my crew went through the usual post-drop checks. They found several holes from the ground fire, but no big deal.

When all the exacting work was finished, the inevitable joking started. The loadmaster was saying, "Man, did you see that second pallet start wobbling as it was rolling aft? I sure thought it would jam!" The laughter went through every crewmember in turn. No one cared if it wasn't funny. As we were flying back, I thought of that load having toilet paper. I knew toilet paper was needed, but I wondered if we should have been endangering an airplane and crew to drop it.

A few days later, all air drops were stopped. We had dropped all the cargo chutes into Khe Sanh, and we had none to use. To get our chutes out of surrounded Khe Sanh, several fighter strikes were coordinated with a fast run-in by an Air Force helicopter to pick up the chutes and return them to Danang.

Maj TOM COOK
26th Marines Assistant Logistics Officer _____

They decided to try the Low Altitude Parachute Extraction System—LAPES. The load would be palletized on rollers. The plane would come along the runway at about twenty feet and the crew would pop a parachute, which would drag the load right out of the rear of the aircraft. At the same time the load was coming out, the aircraft would climb out. It seemed like a neat system, but it required too much coordination between the crew chief and the pilot.

A total of fifty-two LAPES and similar GPES (Ground Proximity Extraction System) missions were run in order to deliver outsized loads—mainly construction material—that could not be dropped safely into the tiny drop zone outside the combat base perimeter wire.

Sgt DAVID MACH, USAF
29th Tactical Airlift Squadron _____

On my fourth and final mission to Khe Sanh, the day started with us and four other C-130Bs going to Danang, where each picked up a single LAPES platform of supplies weighing about 25,000 pounds. The day was rainy and foggy, and it wasn't going to get any better. The five aircraft took off five minutes apart, but when we arrived we had to hold because of the weather. It was sunny and cool above the gray clouds.

There was a combat control team on the ground that talked us down. When it was our turn, we already had the ramp and door open for the drop. As we entered the cloud, it was dark gray behind the aircraft. At about a minute out, over the noise of the our engines, we could hear the sound of the North Vietnamese shooting at us with antiaircraft guns. I asked the pilot if he could hear it on the flight deck, and he said he could. They tried but never hit us.

We broke out of the cloud at about one hundred feet and in line with the runway. The aircraft descended with landing gear down, similar to a landing approach. At three to five feet altitude over the drop zone, and on command from the navigator, the copilot started the process. I saw the green light as the copilot released the extraction parachute, which in turn extracted the supply load from the aircraft. In a second, the load was gone. When it left the aircraft, the load was traveling in excess of 100 miles per hour. Ideally, it landed rear end first, settled to the front, and slid on the ground. The last I saw of it, it was sliding down the runway, and then it was gone. Ideally, the extraction chute and the friction of the ground stopped the load within 200 yards. By then we were back in the clouds. I felt proud that we had sort of sneaked in, made our drop, and made it out without getting hit. However, I still carry a hollow feeling because I later learned that one of the LAPES loads dropped that day hit a bunker and killed at least one Marine in it.

1stLt NICK ROMANETZ
Charlie Company, 1/26 _____

One day, in the fog, I heard a C-130 making approaches and pulling out because he wasn't on line. Finally, listening to the pitch of the engines, I figured he was going to land. I thought it was still too foggy for him to try to land, but then I thought he must have been on a radar approach and in control. I was standing in my bunker with a Marine, in the trenchline not more than fifty or seventy-five feet away from the edge of the runway. We were watching Bunker 21, which was right on the edge of the runway. We knew from the pitch of the engines that the pilot was not right over the runway. Lo and behold, an Air Force C-130 came out of the fog, heading right for Bunker 21. He was off to the side of the runway by fifty or sixty feet. The pilot saw that he was heading into the bunker, which was a concrete two-story job with a .50-caliber machine gun in the second story. The pilot throttled up and tried to pull up, but his tail ramp was down because he was trying to make a skid drop. The tail ramp hit the top of the bunker just as he released his cargo, which was a load of airfield matting. It went tumbling down just to the right of the runway. The tail ramp collapsed a good part of Bunker 21, and a Marine manning the bunker was crushed. The tail ramp broke off from the C-130 and started tumbling right down toward my bunker. It landed in a hole about twenty-five feet away from us. It all took a matter of seconds, but it looked like it was in slow motion.

1stLt PAUL ELKAN
Bravo Battery, 1/13 _____

A lot of ammo we got that way seemed to get banged up. The brass got dented.

Cpl DENNIS SMITH
Bravo Company, 1/26 _____

One of the guys in my supply section was LCpl Virgil Crunk, from Ohio. All he wanted to do when he got out was drive a truck and listen to country music. He had an uncanny way of finding anything he needed on that base. If he couldn't make a trade or a deal for something, he stole it. I never asked where things came from. He ordered his parts for his jeep direct from Motor Transport and used their tools to maintain it. He was the fastest jeep at Khe Sanh, proven over and over on the airstrip against other drivers.

Virgil really proved his stuff during the worst of the shelling, when the resupply planes couldn't even land. He would be hanging around the airstrip, waiting for some supplies to be skid-dropped, knowing that everyone else would have their heads down because any aircraft *always* drew incoming rockets. In fact, we called the planes "mortar magnets." Great sport for the NVA gunners. The planes would skim down the runway with their rear doors open and pop a parachute to pull their supply skids out on the run. Our job was to recover the skids when they stopped sliding down the runway.

As soon as the cargo skid was pulled from a plane, Virgil was out on the runway, throwing anything and everything into his jeep trailer. Then he was out of there in the fastest jeep at Khe Sanh. Once, as rockets were slamming into the base, I watched him take a curve into our area so fast that the trailer flipped over. He dragged it in upside down and jumped into the hooch— laughing. Virgil was kind of hard on jeep trailers.

Pfc LIONEL TRUFANT
106mm Platoon, 3/26 _____

The only chance we had to improve on our situation came from the kamikaze truck drivers on the road from the drop zone, which ran in back of our position. Guys driving the trucks couldn't hear the incoming, so they would just *drive*—take a chance. They couldn't hear so they would drive so fast that, a lot of times, extra pallets would fall off the trucks, break, and leave C-rats all over the deck. Hell, those guys weren't going to come back and get it, so we ran out, picked them up, and brought them back to our hooch.

Chapter 20

MID-FEBRUARY
SENSORS

Maj ALEX LEE
Marine Corps Development Center (Quantico, Virginia) _____

There were photos in the press of Marines and corpsmen listening to long steel stakes driven into the ground with the purported (by the press, who put the troops up to that silly activity) purpose of listening to the tunneling by the NVA who were "expected" to blow up the combat base à la Petersburg.

Those photos and the resultant clamor from the ignorant resulted in some real scrambling on the part of the McNamara folks involved in sensors—the Defense Communications Planning Group, which was headquartered at the Naval Observatory. They were asked if their super-sophisticated sensors could detect tunneling. They ran some quick and dirty test and determined that the sensors could not, but that the AN/PSR-1 Seismic Intrusion Detector—one of my projects—could do a fair job. The device was not field-ready, but we had some in the shop at Quantico that I was testing.

I took part in the tests at Eglin Air Force Base, made my report, and, that weekend, went to get my car painted. On return to the house in early afternoon, my wife reported that I was

273

"leaving again"—something I did regularly as I tested many items in Vietnam to work out bugs.

The Defense Communications Planning Group sent three Army officers. They were full-time participants in the sensor business and were prepared to talk to all the specialists in Vietnam and to help the Target Information Officer at Khe Sanh—Capt Harry Baig—integrate information being received (and improperly understood) from the large sensor-evaluation unit in Thailand [to which it was beamed directly from the sensors seeded around Khe Sanh]. I was sent along with my Seismic Intrusion devices to hunt tunnels and—most probably—to "speak Marine" to the officers and men of Colonel Lownds's 26th Marines.

We flew nonstop to Saigon, where the chairborne commandos were universally disparaging of the conduct of the Marines at the combat base—even though none of them had been there. After this nasty reception, we were given a VIP aircraft to the north, and went immediately to Khe Sanh in a CH-53. On about February 12, we flew into the combat base with General Tompkins and had his blessing to find the tunnels. We arrived amid a spate of incoming, and the accompanying Army officers were suitably impressed. This was their first taste of shellfire.

The sensor drops had taken place prior to our arrival, however, the entire effort was coordinated from Nakhon Phanom, in Thailand, and the Marines on site—Maj Jerry Hudson, the 26th Marines intelligence officer, and Capt Harry Baig, the regimental target information officer—were not fully able to utilize the reports. In fact, the reports, known as "Spotlights," were often confused with those we knew as "Usually Reliable Source," a cute way of saying that radio battalion monitor teams heard the bad guys announcing some move or other on their communications nets. Hudson and Baig just didn't understand what they had in the way of intelligence from the sensors.

At the combat base, we were greeted with open minds and very positive interest. Captain Baig was quick to understand the fantastic value of the sensor evaluation reports from Thailand. He was, at that time, using five-inch-by-eight-inch cards to plot intelligence info on every grid square he could reach with any of his supporting arms.

I was given free run of the combat base and permitted to search anywhere and everywhere for proof of tunneling. I began doing some careful research. To make a long story short, I found that even if you went to bedrock below the base, there was only the seismic energy of falling shells, distant bombs, artillery firing, and mortars firing. The NVA were prodigious diggers, completing in one night 1,700 feet of stand-up trenches outside the base, but we found *no* signs of the tunneling that was suspected.

Since we were without specified responsibilities, two of the Army officers and I went throughout the base and discussed with the people in the fighting holes the use of the new small radars and night-observation devices (NODs), both of which had just arrived, as integrated methods of fire control. With the radar to detect movement, the NODs could find the enemy. If used at dispersed sites, you could cross lines on a map and get precise locations for time-on-target shoots with artillery and mortars on site in the combat base.

Pfc JOHN KONKO
Bravo Battery, 1/13 (Hill 558)

A major came up to me and handed me a radar receiver in a black box along with a map and coordinates of sensors that had been dropped from planes out in front of the hill I was on, Hill 558. This was because I was a radio operator forward observer. The major taught me the use of the receiver and told me it was a secret device. Then he gave me an incendiary device. In case we were overrun, I was to destroy the black box and the map.

A sequence of numbers would light up on the black box. These were the numbers on the map. By watching the box for a length of time I could figure out where the enemy was and what route he was taking past our sensors. According to what set of numbers we had, there would be a B-52 strike.

Maj ALEX LEE
Marine Corps Development Center (Quantico, Virginia)

Capt Harry Baig and I happened to collaborate on one small use of the sensors one night. We found a seismic-energy signal of the enemy digging in along Route 9. The next day, our air reported only holes. The next night, there was more seismic data. Harry intuited antiaircraft. The next morning, the first air strike went in and found and destroyed several 37mm antiaircraft guns sited to fire zero-deflection shots down the long axis of the runway. Harry could see in his mind the thought processes of the enemy commander, and, so doing, he divined that cutting our air link was uppermost. Thus, from a bunch of semi-garbled messages from Thailand on seismic-energy bursts, Harry solved the equation and kept the air link open another day.

Capt HARRY BAIG
26th Marines Target Information Officer _____

Sensors were extremely useful intelligence indicators, but they were not good for targeting purposes. As we learned to employ them and to interpret the Spotlight reports [from Thailand] against the meaning of other intelligence, we found that their value increased. Two nights of heavy activity along infiltration routes often signified a probable attack on the third night, and appropriate area clearance fire would be discharged into the assembly and attack positions to break up the enemy formations. On one occasion, enemy digging in the vicinity of the sensors gave us the location of six 37mm antiaircraft guns. Truck convoys, moving toward known supply dumps, enabled us to estimate the rate of replenishment and dump status of enemy logistic agencies. The general locations of self-propelled guns were often betrayed by the sensors. Finally, and most important, sensors clearly showed the route pattern and density of traffic along major infiltration routes on a daily and nightly basis.[1]

Maj ALEX LEE
Marine Corps Development Center (Quantico, Virginia) _____

What was important about our team going to Khe Sanh was the introduction for the first time of *real-time* sensor readouts. Army Maj Hy Stevens, who was with me, had some readout receivers. We put Baig into *real time* vis-à-vis the sensor data and helped him and, eventually, Colonel Lownds understand what the sensors meant and what the evaluation from Thailand was telling them regarding movement, targeting, etc.

1stLt NICK ROMANETZ
Charlie Company, 1/26 _____

We were worried about night probes. After a while, we had NODs and sniper scopes delivered. They worked pretty good, but we never saw any bad guys. We rotated them around the base; never got to keep them very long.

SSgt HARVE SAAL, USA
FOB-3

It was common for us to monitor the team radios and listen in on all the current events of the day. I could listen to a large selection of active radio channels. It was just like listening to a war program on NBC, except *we* were the war.

One day in mid-February, we overheard an American reconnaissance aircraft analyzing a newly discovered convoy of NVA vehicles. The way they normally reported convoys was to say something like, "I'll count off in tens." However, this day, something big was obviously happening. The pilot said something like, "Convoy spotted. I'll count off in . . . like hell I will! Convoy vehicles too numerous to count. I'm pulling out now!"

With that report, and through our intelligence sources, we learned that the NVA were using abandoned buildings in Khe Sanh ville to stockpile their munitions and repair parts. The Vietnamese high command in Saigon refused our request to destroy the enormous store of war materials in Khe Sanh ville. They said that the town was very important to the Vietnamese people and must not be disturbed by us. Actually, the town was in extreme disrepair, and very few Vietnamese people lived anywhere in the near vicinity— only about fifteen, and that was before the siege began. They *all* deserted the area posthaste on January 21. The buildings that still stood were very old and ready to topple over. We felt that the only reason the NVA used these buildings was because of sanctuary offered by the high command in Saigon.

DUEL

1stLt PAUL ELKAN
Bravo Battery, 1/13

We got hit bad one night in mid-February. We had H&I targets to shoot, but there was no comm to the guns because the lines had been cut. It was raining like hell: thunder, mud, dark, flashes, lightning, and explosions from incoming.

LCpl RAY NICOL
Bravo Battery, 1/13 ⎯⎯⎯⎯⎯⎯⎯⎯⎯⎯⎯⎯⎯⎯⎯⎯⎯⎯⎯⎯⎯⎯⎯

Sergeant Arona, Private Smart, and Private Aguilar had just gone on duty to fire their shift when two big mortar rounds landed in the gun pit, one on each side of the gun. They blew out both tires and destroyed the sight. Arona and Aguilar were not too badly hurt—Arona was hit in both legs and Aguilar was hit in the legs and arms—but Smart had been hit in the face and the upper body. He was bleeding badly, and, because of the incoming, I couldn't get a corpsman out right away. Pfc Bill Chapman and I patched Smart as well as we could and waited for the corpsman.

1stLt PAUL ELKAN
Bravo Battery, 1/13 ⎯⎯⎯⎯⎯⎯⎯⎯⎯⎯⎯⎯⎯⎯⎯⎯⎯⎯⎯⎯⎯⎯⎯

We medevacked Private Smart in a jeep. His back looked like he had been whipped with a cat-o'-nine-tails. It was shredded. He was shaking so hard from shock and the cold that the jeep shook.

LCpl RAY NICOL
Bravo Battery, 1/13 ⎯⎯⎯⎯⎯⎯⎯⎯⎯⎯⎯⎯⎯⎯⎯⎯⎯⎯⎯⎯⎯⎯⎯

After Smart was taken to Charlie-Med, I was ordered to try to find another gunsight and tires at the 155mm battery, which was at the other end of the base. I dodged incoming trying to see in the dark and managed to scrounge a sight, but not tires.

1stLt PAUL ELKAN
Bravo Battery, 1/13 ⎯⎯⎯⎯⎯⎯⎯⎯⎯⎯⎯⎯⎯⎯⎯⎯⎯⎯⎯⎯⎯⎯⎯

The section chief on that gun, Sergeant Arona, fired all night with just one other man. His ears were bleeding from concussion, the gun's tires were flat, they had no gunsight, and the section was down from five men to just three. I put him in for a Bronze Star.

Pfc LIONEL TRUFANT
106mm Platoon, 3/26 _____

We didn't stay in our holes all day. The junior troops had work details. We had to dig trenches—sometimes our own trenches—and we had to constantly work on our own bunkers. Someone had to go get the mail, someone had to go get the food, we had to re-lay comm lines whenever they were destroyed, and we had to take care of basic necessities like going to the shitter, or burning the shitter.

When we had to get the mail, we could take either of two routes. We could go through the trenches, the long way, or we could take the adventurous route, straight across the open ground. Since I and one of my buddies were the lowest-ranking personnel, we had that job a lot. We made a game of it. Sometimes we went individually and sometimes we went together. It was a game of dodging the incoming. After a while, it became part of our everyday existence.

I have never been in jail, but I can understand how a person in jail can become used to being there. Once you're there, once you get over your initial shock, you get to feel that you're not going to let it get you down. That's the way it was at Khe Sanh. There wasn't enough water, so we could not get clean. About all we could do was wash vital parts and brush our teeth. Taking a shit meant going out in the open and sitting on an open shitter. If we had built an outhouse, it would have been a target. To blend in better, we just sat on a one-holer in the open. Food was just basic C-rations.

Cpl WALT WHITESIDES
3/26 Tactical Air Control Party _____

I was reassigned to the battalion command post from Hill 881S on February 9 and was meritoriously promoted to the rank of corporal soon after that.

At first, during the day, I was put on radio watch in the battalion command post, on the tactical-air-control net. This was really cushy duty as there was absolutely nothing for the radio operator to do there except monitor the net. At the time, we had no active role. At night, the operations chief would let me sleep, or we played cards. This lasted only a short while, until the communications officer figured out that we had no real role to play.

Suddenly, the communications platoon was required to man a section of the line behind the grunts. We had to connect our bunkers with a trenchline. I was put in charge of one section of the line. I also was put in charge of getting some covered trenches dug near the base helo pad, for troops who were waiting to leave or arriving on the birds.

I arranged for some grunts from Lima Company to do most of the digging.

Pfc LIONEL TRUFANT
106mm Platoon, 3/26

On work details, we took turns listening for the incoming while the other people dug holes or trenches. One day, while we were digging a trench for H&S Company, I was listening when I heard the incoming. I told everybody to get down. The last person I saw before I went down was a private from Lima Company. The rounds hit as soon as I got down in the hole, and then I heard moaning. Someone was hit. My first thought was that it was the private I had seen in the open. I thought, Damn, I have to go out and get him. I stuck my head out of the hole and saw that it wasn't that Marine. Another Marine off to my side had gotten hit in the lower leg and knee. I went over to him, took his bandage off his helmet, opened it, and started wrapping it around the leg. While I was doing it, I had lots of things going through my mind: I had to listen for incoming, I had to stop the wounded man's blood, I had to watch him to make sure he didn't go out on me, and I had to figure out what to do if more incoming came in: Should I stay where I was, or pull the wounded man into the hole? Luckily, there was no incoming that minute. I called for a corpsman, and Doc came up and took him away. We got back to digging, more artillery came in, and I sounded off again, and everybody jumped back in the hole. It went on and on like that until we finished.

Cpl WALT WHITESIDES
3/26 Tactical Air Control Party

We got the trenchline done in a few days. The only problem was that the communications officer and I had an argument over

which way the firing ports were to face. He had the strange notion
that the ports should face the runway, *away* from the lines, as he
thought the NVA would penetrate the lines a mile or so away and
run across the runway to be stopped by troops fortunate enough
to be in the two trenches with the firing ports facing inward. We
had to take the roofs off the bunkers and redo the tops when he
discovered that I had faced the ports 180 degrees from where he
wanted them. I diplomatically solved the problem by putting
firing ports on both sides, since the trenches were 100 to 150
yards inside the main line.

1stLt NICK ROMANETZ
Charlie Company, 1/26

We had homemade fougasse devices outside our wire. They were
55-gallon drums cut in half with napalm and thermite grenades
or tripflares in them. The idea was that they would explode and
create an additional obstacle for the enemy. I don't know if they
would have burned a lot of people, but they probably would have
added a lot to the confusion.

SSgt HARVE SAAL, USA
FOB-3

I thought it appropriate to warn the elite NVA regiment in front
of FOB-3, should they find themselves inside the FOB defenses.
So I hand-printed a sign:

SIR CHARLES

IF YOU CAN READ THIS SIGN

YOU'RE ON THE WRONG SIDE OF THE WIRE!

LCpl ARMANDO GONZALES
Bravo Company, 1/9

Helicopter resupply runs always drew enemy incoming. They
usually came in with slingloads of supplies, which they dropped
off. Sometimes, for some reason, a helo would drop its sling and
then climb without leaving, hovering right over our positions.

That gave the NVA forward observers more to shoot at. The helos raised big dust clouds, and they made a lot of noise. The NVA could sight in on the clouds, the noise, and the helos themselves.

One time I saw a crewman in one of the hovering helicopters leaning out to take pictures. A young Marine in my squad we had nicknamed Baby was killed by the incoming drawn by that chopper. I *know* he would have heard the incoming if the noise from the chopper's rotors hadn't drowned it out. When I saw Baby get blown away, the pilot and crew of the helicopter were as much my enemies as the NVA around us. I took a couple of potshots at the chopper. My only regret then—and now—is that those sons of bitches didn't pay for their ignorance the way Baby and other guys did.

Sgt FRANK JONES
26th Marines Scout-Sniper Platoon

There was an NVA sniper outside the wire, at the east end of the base, who kept shooting at our guys. They couldn't find him. One evening, about dusk, when I was a little drunk, I told them I'd show them how to do it. I jumped up on the parapet of the trenchline and lit up a cigarette. A green tracer went whizzing by my face and I fell into the trenchline. They had told me he was about two hundred yards away, but I knew that he was seventy-five to one hundred yards away. We pulled a 106mm recoilless rifle around and ended that sniper's shooting at us anymore.

LCpl CHARLIE THORNTON
Lima Company, 3/26

After Lang Vei fell, I was trained to operate against tanks we expected to attack us. Although we never saw tanks at Khe Sanh, the flamethrower was used once for a rather bizarre purpose.

Capt DICK CAMP
3/26 Assistant Operations Officer _____

I overheard a Red Sector listening post call in to say they heard some movement in front of Lima Company and to ask for permission to open fire. The listening post was asked if they knew what the noise was coming from, but they said no. Permission to fire was granted. Of course the listening post knew what the target was. They just didn't want to tell anyone, in case permission to open fire was withheld.

Pfc LIONEL TRUFANT
106mm Platoon, 3/26 _____

We got attacked by a mad elephant. This big elephant came running toward the line, so everybody opened up on it. I think we all thought it was packed with explosives. Eventually we killed it, but then we had this problem with the carcass sitting out in front of our lines.

LCpl CHARLIE THORNTON
Lima Company, 3/26 _____

As the elephant lay there, the NVA discovered how to use the carcass as a shield and snipe at us during the day. We finally were sent out with the flamethrower and attempted to burn the elephant to eliminate the NVA snipers' shelter. All we succeeded in doing was singeing the hair on the elephant. I was extremely glad that an NVA tank was not our first target. We later exploded the elephant with C4 plastic explosives.

Cpl BERT MULLINS
Bravo Company, 1/9 _____

I had taken no extra clothes when we left Camp Evans for Khe Sanh on January 22 because we had been told we were going for only three days. When we finally received new clothes, I was able to get a new T-shirt. When I took the old T-shirt off, it was rotten. The collar stayed around my neck when it ripped free of the rest of the rotten fabric, which came to pieces.

LCpl CHARLIE THORNTON
Lima Company, 3/26 _____

The Marine Corps is not known for its high-tech weapons and supplies. Once we received a shipment of socks (a rare commodity) that were stamped on the heel U.S. ARMY REJECTS.

1stLt Joe Abodeely, of Delta Company, 1/7th Cavalry,
the first Air Cav officer to walk into the Khe Sanh
Combat Base.

(Compliments of Joseph Abodeely)

Capt Earle Breeding, the Echo Company, 2/26, commander.

(Compliments of Earle Breeding)

Bob Brewer, the Quang Tri Province Senior Adviser.

(Compliments of Robert Brewer)

HM3 Bill Gessner, of Delta Company, 1/9
(Compliments of William Gessner

Sgt Frank Jones, of the 26th Marine
Sniper Platoon.

(Compliments of Franklin Jones)

1stLt John Kaheny, of the 1/26 staff.

(Compliments of John Kaheny)

Pfc Jim Payne, of Charlie Battery, 1/13, in the Hill 881S trenchline.

(Compliments of James Payne)

Col Bruce Meyers, the 26th Marines commander from early April.

(Compliments of Bruce Meyers)

Capt Ken Pipes, the Bravo Company, 1/26, commander.

(Compliments of Kenneth Pipes)

Cpl William Robertson, of the Logistics Support Unit, outside the Ammunition Supply Point office in early January.

(Compliments of William Robertson)

HM3 Mike Ray, of India Company, 3/26, in the Hill 881S trenchline in early January. *(Compliments of Michael Ray)*

1stLt Nick Romanetz, of Charlie Company, 1/26.

(Compliments of Nicholas Romanetz)

SSgt Harve Saal, of FOB-3, with a Bru scout.

(Compliments of Harvey Saal)

Above, right

Pfc Lawrence Seavy-Cioffi, forward observer with 1/9. (Compliments of Lawrence Seavy-Cioffi)

Right

Sgt Mike Stahl, the 4.2-inch mortar platoon sergeant, with the AK-47 he captured and used in his Navy Cross action on Hill 861 on January 21.

(Compliments of Mykle Stahl)

Cpl Allan Stahl, of the Logistics Support Unit.

(Compliments of G. Allan Stahl)

HM3 Dave Steinberg, of India Company, 3/26, in the Hill 881S trenchline.

(Compliments of David Steinberg)

Maj Jim Stanton, of the 26th Marines Fire Support Coordination Center.

(Compliments of James Stanton)

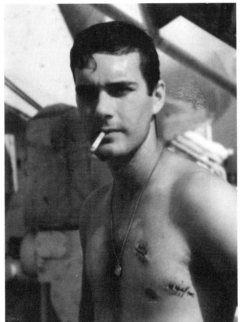

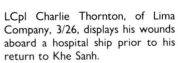

LCpl Charlie Thornton, of Lima Company, 3/26, displays his wounds aboard a hospital ship prior to his return to Khe Sanh.

(Compliments of Charles Thornton)

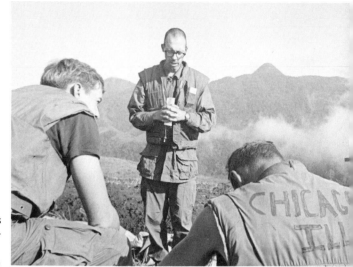

Chaplain Ray Stubbe conducts prayers at a hilltop position before the siege.

(Official U.S. Marine Corps photo)

MGen Tommy Tompkins, (left) the 3rd Marines Division commander, and Col Dave Lownds, the 26th Marines commander.

(Official U.S. Marine Corps photo)

Pfc Lionel Trufant, of the 3/26 Recoilless Rifle Platoon.

(Compliments of Lionel Trufant)

Cpl Walt Whitesides, of the 3/26
Tactical Air Control Party.

(Compliments of Walter Whitesides)

LtCol Jim Wilkinson, the 1/26 commander.

(Compliments of James Wilkinson)

Chapter 21

FEBRUARY 20

1stLt NICK ROMANETZ
Charlie Company, 1/26

We had double rows of concertina with a minefield in between. We mapped out and marked a path through the minefield for the listening posts. On the morning of February 20, we couldn't bring in the listening post at first light because it was too foggy. After a while, the Marines in the listening post called and asked if they could send a man back for some chow. I said okay, and he came back. Then another guy called and asked if he could come back and take a crap. I said okay, and *he* came back. Then the third guy called and asked if he could refill the canteens. I said okay, and *he* came back. On the way, the third guy tripped a mine. As it turned out, the lance corporal in charge of the listening post never took his guys through the second wire. Instead of being 600 meters in front of our lines, they were maybe fifty meters out. The guys who had been coming in had been walking back and forth through the minefield, but it wasn't until the third guy came back that they found out. That Marine had his foot blown off.

285

SSgt HARVE SAAL, USA
FOB-3

It became obvious to us that the Communist artillery gunners had a sense of humor. We were under an artillery and rocket barrage that climbed to about 400 rounds. It lasted about an hour. I looked up periodically from out of the trench to keep abreast of the damage being caused by the incoming and, during the course of my surveys, I started to have some strange feelings—as though something that had been there wasn't there. Then the answer became obvious.

There was some yelling from the place where the Seabees had built three new aboveground latrines just before the siege began. Only there weren't any latrines anymore. The latrines had been the targets of the entire barrage!

The yelling was asking for help. I quickly moved to where the nearest latrine had been, and found a wounded Vietnamese interpreter. He was all scrunched down in a half-barrel of dung. He was bleeding from a wound in one leg. I got him into the trench and started cleaning the wound. *Yech!* Then I heard laughter. My Special Forces brothers in the trench next to me were laughing uncontrollably over the spectacle.

Cpl TERRY SMITH
3/26 Tactical Air Control Party (Hill 881S)

[SILVER STAR CITATION] Cpl Terry Smith observed a Marine helicopter in a zone on which he knew North Vietnamese Army gunners had registered heavy mortars. He realized that the aircraft would almost certainly be destroyed if it remained in the landing zone, and attempted unsuccessfully to contact the pilot by radio. Aware that enemy rounds were probably already on the way, he restrained a Marine junior to him from going out onto the zone and, leaving the safety of his bunker, ran across the open ground, signalling manually to the helicopter crew to take off immediately. As the helicopter took off, and before Corporal Smith could reach cover, he was . . . wounded by mortar fragments. . . .

Cpl WALT WHITESIDES
3/26 Tactical Air Control Party _____

I was getting a haircut from the communications platoon barber when I heard that my best friend, Cpl Terry Smith, had been wounded while guiding a helo on Hill 881S. I remember saying, "Good," when I realized that he would be getting home because this would give him his third Purple Heart. I regret ever saying that. Terry died of his wounds.

FEBRUARY 21

Cpl DENNIS MANNION
Charlie Battery, 1/13 (Hill 861) _____

February 21, 1968

Hey Man—

War still goes its shitty way. *Still* waiting for the big gook attempt. My guess is they're building up to a strength to carry on a big fight. (Their resupply has got to be a bitch no matter how you look at it.) But we're getting better, too. I'll go so far as to say we're 100 percent better than we were a month and one day ago—and that's a lot.

Spent last three days building a new bunker—me and three other guys. It's boss. About 10 feet "down in" with a big fucking roof. Should take just about anything. I hope it never comes to that. Boing!

FEBRUARY 22

Cpl DENNIS SMITH
Bravo Company, 1/26 _____

February 22, 1968

Dear Dad,

Our little slant-eyed sniper took a few shots at me with his .51 this afternoon as I was driving around the strip to deliver water to a platoon from Alpha Company that is attached to us.

I'm about to write everything that happens here, but if I filled my letters with such stories (as I easily could) it would serve no purpose except to increase the worrying at home. I just marvel each night over the preceding day's near misses and the fact that I am still able to mark off, with shaking hand, one more day in my little calendar.

We're down to two meals of C-rations plus one canteen of water per man per day, but I'd go without a day's rations for each letter from home.

26th Marines Command Chronology

Khe Sanh Combat Base and its outposts received a heavy volume of enemy mortar, rocket, and artillery fire. Approximate incoming total: 270 rounds. Approximately 250 rounds of this fire came between 1200 and 1700. Casualties from incoming: 7 friendly KIA, 24 friendly WIA (medevacked), and seven friendly WIA (minor).

Lt RAY STUBBE
1/26 Battalion Chaplain

[DIARY ENTRY] Casualties started pouring in from 2/26. There were seven KIA, one of whom was the 2/26 chaplain, Lt Robert Brett. One of the corpsmen asked me to remove the boots from an injured man lying on a stretcher moaning, blood all over. The boots were caked with mud and blood, and my hands were red from both. The mixture began to dry, causing the skin to feel like it was shrinking, so I went to my hooch to wash my hands. All of a sudden, there was a large blast. A large piece of metal and other debris flew up in the air. A CH-53 helicopter had been hit.

LCpl RAY NICOL
Bravo Battery, 1/13

A big helicopter loaded with medevacs was about fifty feet in the air, taking off, when a recoilless rifle round hit it. The helo bounced a lot when it hit the ground, but it didn't explode. The helo went down right behind my platoon area. When it hit, the big floppy rotor blades, which were still going, got caught on the ground and big pieces of them broke off and went whipping around. I heard that one of the blades sliced off the top of the cockpit. I do know that the pilot and copilot had their heads and upper parts of their bodies severed by something. The Marines in the back—the rest of the crew and the wounded—all got out more or less okay. The Graves Registration people eventually came by and took the bodies away.

Lt RAY STUBBE
1/26 Battalion Chaplain

[DIARY ENTRY] The pilot and copilot were killed—Capt William "Rex" Riley and 1stLt Carey Smith. Father Brett's clerk, Pfc Alexander Chin, was also killed. He had been wounded twice before.

1stLt NICK ROMANETZ
Charlie Company, 1/26

Next day, a foggy, chilly morning, my platoon radioman went out to take a leak in the weeds. When he came back he told me he had found an arm. I went out there with him and, sure enough, there was a left arm, severed at the shoulder. It had a wedding band on the ring finger. I sent it to Graves Registration in a mail sack.

Cpl ALLAN STAHL
Logistics Support Unit

I was with Force Logistics Support Group Alpha, at Phu Bai, all ready to go home, when I decided to extend my tour of duty. I wanted to get in a little excitement before I went home. They sent me to Danang to pick up my orders, and they in turn sent me to Khe Sanh on a courier run. I was to stay at Khe Sanh to replace a communicator who had rotated.

I got back to Phu Bai that morning, but it was the afternoon before I eventually managed to get aboard a CH-53 that was making a late run to Khe Sanh via Dong Ha to pick up and deliver some essential artillery part. The part wasn't ready, so we sat at

Dong Ha for hours, waiting. Then, just before dusk, they decided to go ahead and make the run into Khe Sanh.

We were way up high, and then the CH-53 began to spiral down. All of a sudden, I saw this landscape. We had been flying in over dense vegetation, and suddenly we came over a red plain. It was late afternoon, very sinister, and very dark. It was also very quiet; we didn't take a single round. There were large holes in the ground, and no one was moving about. It was forbidding. The crew expected to get shot at. The gunners were looking out over their guns. The helicopter was spiraling in; I could hear it whistling down through the air.

I had been briefed: when they opened the door I had to get the hell out. I jumped out, but I had no idea where to go. Two seconds later, the chopper took off. I couldn't find a hole to jump into. All I could see was the air terminal. It was aboveground, all sandbagged. It was stone silent. It was eerie.

I had been a sort of professional courier for Force Logistics Support Group Alpha for six months. I had been hopping in and out of places worse than this appeared. But this was so much bigger, and *quiet*. I was the only man I could see. I worried that I was facing a bunch of trigger-happy nuts.

As I began to walk, a couple of guys popped out of the ground. I asked where the Logistics Support Unit was, but they said they didn't know and then went on their own way. It was getting quite dark. Everything had wire around it. Only the roads were clear. I couldn't walk in a straight line because of the wire; I had to stick to the roads. There were little units here and there, hooches piled over with rubble, all kinds of crap. So there I was, walking along through my conception of hell. I began to realize that there were people around, but I couldn't really see any. It was like being alone, way out in the country, except there were no crickets chirping. I could hear my own feet pounding on the roadway.

I happened to be walking south or southeast when I saw boxes stacked up near a big hexagonal concrete bunker. I was looking for a supply unit, so I headed for the boxes. A couple of guys were near the boxes, so I asked them where the Logistics Support Unit was. They motioned me toward the concrete bunker.

The next shocker for me was when I threw back the poncho

on the bunker door and broke through all the silence and eeriness outside. The lights were on, music was playing, there was a guy running the switchboard, and a few guys were sleeping in their racks. It was a whole different world inside there.

FEBRUARY 23

WATER DETAIL

Pfc ROBERT HARRISON
Alpha Company, 1/26 (Hill 950) _____

By February 22, our platoon outpost had been unable to get resupplied for over a week, and our water supply was nearly exhausted. I do not recall anyone being overly concerned, because of the large amount of C-rations we had on hand. Without water we could not shave and we could not have coffee. I do not consider this life threatening, and that is the way I felt at the time.

Our platoon commander, 1stLt Maxie Williams, radioed for and received permission from Battalion to send a detail out for water. Lieutenant Williams ordered Sergeant Zeiss to select a fire team from each squad, plus an M-60 machine-gun team, for the water detail. This meant that there would be about fifteen men for the detail. There was a feeling of apprehension mixed with excitement. No one questioned the order, but we did discuss it among ourselves. We came to the conclusion that the chances of making it down the hill undetected were not very good. If we were cut off from the hilltop position, rescue would be out of the question due to the fog and the lack of any sizable force close by.

I awoke in my bunker the morning of February 23 and got ready for the patrol—checked my rifle, magazine, ammo, etc. I stepped out of the bunker and noticed that the weather was still miserable, cold, and foggy. Visibility was about five meters.

Everyone on the detail wore a pack filled with empty canteens. We started to file out of the barbed-wire perimeter, trying to be as quiet as we could, but that was asking the impossible. Everyone kept catching clothes and equipment on the barbed wire, creating a lot of noise.

I watched as the point element moved out and disappeared into the jungle. The hill was covered by triple-canopy rain forest, so we were in dense foliage as soon as we cleared the perimeter. It was very muddy, and guys kept falling down, making a lot of noise. I kept thinking to myself, I hope the gooks aren't watching this trail. If they are, we've had it. One thing in our favor was the fog; it helped conceal our movement. It finally came my turn to move through the wire. I was the last man in the column, "tail-end Charlie." Sergeant Zeiss and the machine-gun team were toward the middle of the column and Cpl Thomas Birch's fire team was walking point.

The footing was difficult due to the muddy conditions. Guys kept falling down and making noise. Pfc Tony Weaver was in front of me. He turned around, looked at me, then rolled his eyes. I smiled and shrugged my shoulders. We continued to move down the trail. I turned around occasionally to check the rear of the column. Walking "tail-end Charlie" made me kind of nervous as to what was behind me, but it was not as bad as walking point. One thing that surprised me about the jungle was that it was quiet. There were no real animal sounds like you hear in movies. I guess the bombing and other activity around Khe Sanh scared off most of the wildlife.

I think we had gone about 200 meters when the pointman heard someone cough. He looked over to where the sound had come from and there stood close to a dozen NVA in a circle, shooting the breeze. As soon as he saw them, he opened fire with his M-16 and dropped a few of them. The rest of the NVA took cover and started to return fire. Corporal Birch was hit during the first moments of the fire fight. As soon as the firing broke out, the guys in front of me started to run down the trail. I followed as quickly as I could. Sergeant Zeiss was yelling to form on line. Everyone was in the prone position when Zeiss ordered, "Right front. Fire." Visibility was not too good due to the jungle growth and fog. I pointed my rifle in the general direction and began firing. I think the firing lasted three or four minutes. We finally gained fire superiority and were able to kill the rest of the NVA. The return fire slacked off and finally ended. Sergeant Zeiss ordered cease-fire.

Someone yelled, "Corpsman, up," but it was already too late for Corporal Birch. He had died in the first moments of the fire fight. Sergeant Zeiss ordered Corporal Brockway to send one of his men to help with Birch's body. I volunteered to go. I moved down the hill toward the point element. When I got there, I gave my rifle to the corpsman, Doc Richards, an ex-hippie from San Francisco. There were four of us to carry Birch's body. By the time I got there, Sergeant Zeiss had decided to try to get back within the perimeter as soon as possible. All thought of obtaining water was abandoned.

Sergeant Zeiss was on the radio to the platoon command post. He informed them of the contact and that we were returning to the hilltop position. The squad formed up on the trail and began to move out. We didn't mess with the NVA bodies by looking for souvenirs. That should tell how much of a hurry we were in. We started back up the trail we had come down. Some more firing broke out behind us, but it soon stopped. I don't know what that was all about.

Going back up the hill was worse than going down. We kept dropping the body due to the muddy conditions. I was carrying Birch by the arms and shoulder. Once I lost my grip and his head hit a large rock. I thought to myself, "That must have really hurt." Then I realized how dumb that was.

I kept thinking that we would be mortared, but it never happened. I was totally exhausted by the time we made the perimeter. Some guys came down from the trenchline and carried Birch the rest of the way in. We got through the barbed wire and into the trenchline with the rest of the platoon. Everyone was soaked and covered with mud. We took off our packs with the empty canteens in them. I got a surprise when I took mine off; there was a bullet hole through it—in one side of the pack and out the other. I hadn't even felt it.

We wrapped Corporal Birch's body in a poncho and put it in the ammo bunker. Lieutenant Williams seemed pleased with the kill ratio, but I considered the patrol a near disaster, and I think some of the other guys did, too. We did not really discuss the patrol among ourselves other than to say that we were lucky to make it back. I believe we did not want to make it seem like Corporal Birch had died for nothing, even though we failed to collect the water. The weather cleared three or four days after the patrol, making it possible for us to be resupplied. One thing is certain: no one died from thirst.

RECORD INCOMING

1stLt FRED McGRATH
Bravo Battery, 1/13 ⎯⎯⎯⎯⎯⎯⎯⎯⎯⎯⎯⎯⎯⎯⎯⎯⎯⎯

The sound of incoming is like no other in the world. We had ample opportunities to hear it, learn it, adjust to it, and finally to live with it. From descriptions of battles from World War II and Korea, we at Khe Sanh got an inkling of what our fathers experienced. It was a constant reminder that even though we were in a very picturesque mountain valley, somebody did not want us there. There were a lot of men who had fears of dying. And there were plenty of chances. Like the day and night the base took over 1,300 rounds of incoming.

HN ROD DeMOSS
26th Marines Regimental Aid Station ⎯⎯⎯⎯⎯⎯⎯⎯⎯⎯⎯⎯⎯⎯

Another corpsman and I were topside at the entrance to our bunker, talking with a couple of guys across the road, when we heard *boomp*. We went below and soon we heard the round hit close. The two guys we had been talking to took a direct hit. All that was left was pieces of two bodies.

Cpl DENNIS SMITH
Bravo Company, 1/26 ⎯⎯⎯⎯⎯⎯⎯⎯⎯⎯⎯⎯⎯⎯⎯⎯⎯⎯⎯

First Lieutenant Kim Johnson was our 1st Battalion supply officer. He was handsome, even with glasses, tall, articulate, a practicing Mormon married to a former Miss Arizona who was going to school in Hawaii while she awaited his return. He had the option of running the supply end of things at Phu Bai—the battalion rear—but he sent his gunnery sergeant there instead so he could remain with his men. The guys at battalion supply noticed the funny underwear he wore—lower-body armor. He referred to it as "anti-mortar and -rocket skivvies." He would have quiet religious discussions with his men from time to time. They loved him.

The last week of February was the peak of the siege. On February 23 we absorbed the record for the whole siege—[1,307] rockets and artillery rounds in a 24-hour period. That afternoon, during the scariest barrage of rockets imaginable, LCpl James

Jesse and I were in our house, hugging the sandbags, quietly acknowledging the absolute fear in each other's eyes. The explosions were constant as they mounted to a crescendo of head-splitting, knee-knocking sound. I can't adequately describe the terror I felt that afternoon. We should have been used to this, right?

Lieutenant Johnson was in his bunker, not far from mine, along with the battalion motor-transport officer. An explosion that knocked Jesse and me off our butts was a direct hit on the lieutenants' hooch. I looked out and saw the battalion supplymen scrambling out of their holes, so, over Jesse's protests, I ran across the road to help. The supplymen all yelled at me, "Get back. We'll handle it. Go on!" There were four or five guys there already, throwing boards and sandbags aside like madmen, machines, so I went back. During the next lull, one of the supplymen came over to our hooch. He was the picture of dejection and despair. He told us that Lieutenant Johnson was dead from a broken back. There were no other visible wounds. The motor-transport officer had been carried to the aid station; his legs looked so bad that everyone thought he'd lose them.

When the supplyman left, I just sat there staring. Something inside me had snapped. Jesse said, "Smitty, you're pale and you're shaking. Have a Salem." Right there, I started up a four-pack-a-day habit. The incoming did not stop, but it became a little more irregular. I was still sitting and staring when my eyes went to a little leatherbound Bible I kept on a shelf. On an impulse, I flipped it open with my right index finger. I was numbly looking at the 91st Psalm, verse five. Then verses six and seven. I was not feeling any comfort. All I could think was, Why the lieutenant? Why *him*?

They had told us in boot camp not to make friends with anyone we went into combat with because if he was wasted you ran the risk of coming unglued and losing your battle effectiveness. Good advice, but impossible to follow. We depended on each other too much not to become friends.

Maj TOM COOK

26th Marines Assistant Logistics Officer _____

One of the incoming rounds hit the ammo dump and created a low-order explosion that set the dump on fire. The fire kept getting hotter and hotter, and finally the dump blew. I saw all that stuff going up in the air. It was one of the most amazing sights I had seen in my life, all those mortar rounds, hand grenades—you name it—just going up into the sky. I stood there and watched, totally amazed. Then it suddenly occurred to me that all that stuff was going to come back down. As a matter of fact, it had already started back down. I was about twenty or thirty yards from a bunker. I took off running and just barely got in there when I started hearing all that stuff hitting the ground. It blew mortar rounds a mile from the dump. A helicopter pilot who happened to be flying near Hill 881S at the time told me that he thought it was an atomic blast because there was a 1,400-foot fireball.

26th Marines Command Chronology _____

Enemy incoming caused a fire in ASP-1. Fire equipment responded, but at 1705, the ammo began to cook off. The fire destroyed 1,000 rounds of 90mm high explosive, 500 rounds of 106mm Beehive, and 120 rounds of 90mm canister ammunition.

Maj TOM COOK
26th Marines Assistant Logistics Officer _____

We had to have EOD people come up from Danang and clean the whole thing up. It was a mess. It made my job a little tougher, too, because I had to get all that stuff inventoried and reordered.

Pfc LIONEL TRUFANT
106mm Platoon, 3/26 _____

The rounds just kept coming in, kept coming in. There was such a concentration of artillery hitting us! Usually, when artillery came in, we just sat in our living bunker and played cards. We just played chicken with the regular incoming, sitting in the living bunker. When it got real heavy, we would usually jump into the trenchline, which was a smaller target. But that particular day, it was coming in so heavy that three of us hid out in the machine-gun bunker, which was tiny. We were just hugging the ground, afraid. I had never smoked in my life, but that day I did. I did a lot of praying, too.

Every once in a while, one of us had to stand up and look out to make sure Charlie wasn't coming. We *knew* this was Dienbienphu. This was the day. One time, when I was looking out of the hole, a round came in real close. Dirt and rocks and stuff pounded me right in the face. I thought I was hit. I felt my face and thought aloud, "Oh God, I'm hit." One of my buddies thought it was comical. "Damn," he said, "you ain't hit."

HN ROD DeMOSS
26th Marines Regimental Aid Station _____

Two Marines escorted a gunnery sergeant into the regimental aid station. He came in shaking, wouldn't talk, had both hands holding his helmet down on his head, and every time a round hit he would shake. He was, of course, suffering from shell shock, but it surprised me because here was this tough Marine gunnery sergeant—been through all kinds of shit—and this makes him crack. I realized then that shell shock can happen to anybody.

Lt RAY STUBBE
1/26 Battalion Chaplain _____

[DIARY ENTRY] Went by the new operating-room bunker, visiting all the wounded who kept coming in during the afternoon. One had a blast wound on his foot. He was in bad pain, even with morphine. Another said his legs hurt no matter where he put them. He was also in intense pain and was given an injection of morphine, but it still hurt him. The doctor said it was broken and would continue to hurt.

More and more incoming.

The 106mm recoilless rifle bunker near us, where I had slept on February 7, took a direct hit, and the trench adjacent to it, injuring one and killing four. I ran down there, through the internal barbed wire, with the Catholic chaplain. There were pieces of arms and bodies. One had no head; we couldn't find it. There were small pieces of flesh all over the place. I knew them all intimately. . . . I took this very hard, but couldn't cry. Parts of one man's body hung out as I held him in my arms, carrying him into the ambulance. A hand, an arm, a stringy piece of flesh intertwined with cloth and caked with mud. The 106mm recoilless rifle was completely untouched.

Returned to my bunker. The west wall, by my rack, was protruding in like it would collapse on my rack. Things inside had shifted.

We had taken in the following incoming today: 476 rounds of artillery, 42 rounds of 60mm, 372 rounds of 82mm, four rounds of 120mm, 437 rounds of 122mm, and five rounds of recoilless rifle. Total, 1,313. But Lieutenant Colonel Wilkinson reported (from the regimental briefing) a total of 1,407 rounds. Major Smith, CO of FOB-3, told me we had received 1,700 rounds of incoming, counting those that landed in his area.

1stLt FRED McGRATH
Bravo Battery, 1/13

It was fortunate that the NVA gunners were short of fuses, because many rounds would have done considerably more damage if they had exploded. The rounds that were not fused were particularly eerie. They whistled. We knew they would not explode, but when they hit, they were like wrecking balls. No shrapnel damage, but what a hole! As it was, they dug up a lot of dirt and nothing more. When EOD dug them up, they found the lift lugs still in the rounds.

Bravo Battery pumped out over 1,250 rounds in reply. Bravo was really a battery and a half. That is, we controlled six 105mm howitzers of our own and three from Charlie Battery. So we combined our assets and created a nine-gun battery. During that very busy day and night, I had, at various times, five separate and distinct fire missions going simultaneously. To the everlasting credit of the Marine gunners on the line, they never missed a command or fired the wrong missions. In fact, Colonel Lownds personally came to our position the next day and thanked every Marine in the position for the superb fire support his regiment had received.

HN ROD DeMOSS
26th Marines Regimental Aid Station

One of my more gruesome duties was identifying and tagging bodies to be sent back home. I kept thinking to myself, This could be me. I was thankful it wasn't, but I felt bad because I knew this was someone who had a family or friend who would grieve over him, someone who had a girlfriend or wife back home. All I could do, though, was zip up the bag and try to make it through without ending up like that.

FEBRUARY 24

Capt EARLE BREEDING
Echo Company, 2/26 (Hill 861A) ——————————————————————————

They never stopped pecking away at us. It seemed like someone got hurt every time a round landed. On February 24, a Marine was out working on the wire when a mortar round came in and got him. LCpl Max Nelson, one of my radio operators, went out with the corpsman to pull the guy out of the wire. The next round got them. Then my exec, 2ndLt Ferdinando DiStefano, went out to pull Max out of the wire. The third round got him. The NVA always fired in threes. They should have known better. The first Marine died and Nelson and DiStefano were killed instantly, though there wasn't a mark on Max. The corpsman was badly wounded, but he survived. Another Marine was killed in another incident later that day. That's four KIAs just in one day.

Chapter 22

FEBRUARY 25
AMBUSH

2ndLt SKIP WELLS
Charlie Company, 1/26

At first, we patrolled daily to keep the NVA from getting right on top of us and to cover the completion of the defensive wire and minefields. I can still recall putting up the last (outside) row of tanglefoot and double apron one afternoon under artillery and mortar fire.

We, and every other unit, took casualties during these daily patrols, and they were cause for a lot of soul-searching every third night before our patrol. But they did do what they were supposed to do. The NVA were not able to establish any real close-in positions.

Then in early February, the company commander told us that we would not run any more patrols, "on orders from Saigon." It was explained that the casualties were wearing us down and that the supporting arms were going to cover us. Even as a boot second lieutenant, I knew that was bullshit and that we would pay for it later.

300

MGen TOMMY TOMPKINS
3rd Marine Division Commanding General _____

General Westmoreland has been criticized for tying the Marines at Khe Sanh to their perimeters. It wasn't Westmoreland, it was me. I told them that 500 meters was the absolute max. Five hundred meters, and no more. My whole plan for the defense of Khe Sanh was to make the enemy come to us.[1]

LtCol JIM WILKINSON
1/26 Commanding Officer _____

We never really stopped patrolling. We only curtailed the distance of the patrols. They had to be in visual contact with the perimeter line.

2ndLt SKIP WELLS
Charlie Company, 1/26 _____

The new Charlie Company commander called me to the command-post bunker about 1800, February 24, and gave me the order for a patrol we were to take out the next day in coordination with one from Bravo Company on the south side of the perimeter. The order was specific: only two squads with one machine-gun team. Bravo was to go at 0900 and we were to go at 1100. They would go south, then west, while we would go east of the east end of the airstrip and then south. The reason for the patrol was obvious. The NVA had closed in and constructed their own trenchlines, especially to the south and east. The position appeared to be the classic assault position.

We didn't have much time to get ready for that patrol. I picked the two squads and a machine-gun team based on who I felt was the best. I knew it would be a bad one and wrote a letter to my wife—in case. I tried to hide my feelings about the patrol, but I think they all knew it could be bad.

Capt KEN PIPES
Bravo Company, 1/26 _____

The NVA had several 60mm mortars fairly close to our lines that were dropping heavy on us. We figured the mortars were out along the access road that ran south and southeast in front of part of our company position on its way to the old garbage dump. We kept sending platoon patrols out to look for the mortars, but nothing turned up. We had to send patrols because the ground out there was rolling, undulating, and there was still plenty of high elephant grass. The B-52 strikes had burned off the grass and brush farther out, but we had a dead zone several hundred meters wide, beginning right outside our wire. We couldn't observe the mortars from our lines; we had to send people out to look for them. Second Lieutenant John Dillon led Bravo Company's 2nd Platoon out to look on February 23, but no contact was made and nothing unusual was observed.

Two heavily reinforced squads of Bravo Company's 3rd Platoon, about forty-three Marines commanded by 2ndLt Don Jacques, were assigned to go back out on February 25 to try to find the mortars. When I briefed Don on the evening of February 24, I identified three checkpoints at which he was to call in to report. Most of his route would keep him under observation from the combat base, but he was sure to get out of sight a few times in that undulating ground. The idea was to make a quick sweep to find the NVA 60mm mortars and get right back into the perimeter near the FOB-3 sector. The patrol route was to be from the southeast corner of the base westward to the southwest sector, right in front of the Gray Sector.

LtCol JIM WILKINSON
1/26 Commanding Officer

All our patrols were carefully plotted in as to route and everything was approved by Regiment, including our fire-support plan in case the patrol ran into anything. The Bravo Company patrol was to follow a diamond-shaped route—Point A to Point B to Point C and then back in.

Cpl GILBERT WALL
81mm Mortar Platoon, 1/26

The day started with me at Bravo Company's 2nd Platoon area. The 2nd Platoon commander, Lieutenant Dillon, told me to go to the 3rd Platoon command post, that I would be going out on patrol.

When I arrived, Lieutenant Jacques came out of his bunker and invited me in for breakfast and some coffee. Lieutenant Jacques and I had been to many patrols together and knew each other pretty well. He introduced me to the new platoon sergeant, a staff sergeant who asked me to call him Mac. I thanked them and started making jokes about them having such a late breakfast, because I had eaten hours ago. I started talking to some of the Marines on the line. Some I knew, but many were new.

Everybody was in a surprisingly good mood. They all were happy, loose, and relaxed. It was a nice day, and just to move out of base for a while gave me a good feeling.

I checked my gear. I had twenty-five M-16 magazines and nine hand grenades. Then I looked over my map and, following that, had my radioman get a radio check. Then I looked out at the area we would be patrolling. I knew the area very well because we had run many patrols there before.

Capt JIM LESLIE
26th Marines Assistant Communicator

Bravo Company had a platoon ready to sweep the perimeter as daylight was breaking. Our bunker was 20 meters inside the barbed concertina wire and I was going through my morning routine of washing my face and brushing my teeth on the pile of sandbags outside. I had a radio there so I could listen in on routine conversation. I switched the channel to Captain Pipes's frequency so I could monitor the station for any communication problems. The morning air was extremely heavy with fog, and I could barely see past our perimeter wire, which was only 20 meters away. I heard Captain Pipes request a delay in kicking off the sweep as the ground fog had not lifted. However, his battalion commander told him he had to get moving because they had coordinated artillery fire. Captain Pipes again requested a delay, but it was denied.

As the wind blew the fog around, I was able to catch glimpses of Marines as they slowly moved across the side of the hill between the Frenchman's plantation and our perimeter.

Cpl GILBERT WALL
81mm Mortar Platoon, 1/26

We went out the south gate by the trash dump and moved down along the NVA trenches. Although I knew the NVA were watching us, I was still very relaxed. While we were walking along the trenches, I pinpointed them on my map for future use.

We followed the trench until it came to an end, then headed south away from the base. It was open—no cover at all—but the NVA never fired any mortars or sniped at us. We moved hundreds of meters away from the base.

I was a few meters behind the platoon radioman as we got closer to the treeline at the top of the hill. As the point and his backup moved for the treeline, two NVA jumped up and started running down the road. The Marines on the front were talking fast and loud; they looked confused.

Capt KEN PIPES
Bravo Company, 1/26

I heard Don Jacques report that he had spotted two or three NVA and that he wanted to try to capture them. I wasn't sure at the time, but I had the impression that, by then, the patrol was quite far from its assigned route. If that was the case, I realized, then chasing the three NVA would take it even farther beyond supporting range, maybe as far as 700 meters from our wire.

Cpl GILBERT WALL
81mm Mortar Platoon, 1/26

Lieutenant Jacques ended the confusion by shouting, "Let's go get them!" His pistol was in the air and his hand fell forward to signal "Charge!" Then he turned and looked at me and we both smiled at the same time. It was as if the same thought went through our minds: This is what we want.

We started moving after the two NVA, and the firing began. The Marines who went to the woods first were with the platoon sergeant. The NVA put some heavy fire on them.

Capt JIM LESLIE
26th Marines Assistant Communicator _____

All of a sudden, all hell broke loose with small-arms fire. My radio was buzzing with conversation. Someone reported, "We are taking heavy casualties."

Capt KEN PIPES
Bravo Company, 1/26 _____

They were ambushed. They walked into it, and it built quite suddenly.

1stLt ERNIE SPENCER
1/26 Intelligence Officer _____

I heard the whole thing on the radio. After Bravo took four casualties, I recommended that they get their dead and get out. They tried to fight. Attack.[2]

Cpl GILBERT WALL
81mm Mortar Platoon, 1/26 _____

Lieutenant Jacques and I went with a squad to the left of a little road that came out of the treeline. Marines were getting hit or taking cover as we moved between the trees.

I moved ahead of Lieutenant Jacques and to the left of the squad. Some Marines were moving on my left when the NVA opened up on us. We were right in front of the NVA trenches and bunkers. The air was filled with screaming, shouting, gunfire, and blood.

I hit the ground, looked at the NVA trenches, and started to return fire. Then I ran toward a large tree to my left. They were very close—close enough that I could see their faces clearly.

We were putting some heavy fire out. I took out my map to call a fire mission with the 81s. I wanted to call the mission in front of the squad that had gotten hit first. The visibility was bad because of the weather, but that was not my problem. The trees that were between us and the squad, which was on my right, directly in front of their trenches, were the real problem. I was confused; I didn't know where all the Marines were. I wanted to call the mission, but I was afraid of hitting my own people. I didn't want to get careless.

When my first round landed, I could not see it, but I heard it. Between ducking and returning fire with my M-16, I couldn't place exactly where my round hit. I checked the map and found grids I wanted; I was going to go with white phosphorus, but I changed my mind. I ordered a repeat. Then I couldn't even move because I was under too much fire; I was pinned behind the tree.

Suddenly a Marine was telling me to pull back. He opened fire along with the Marine to my left, and that took the fire off me. I moved back and to the right.

Marines were wounded and screaming for help everywhere. My second round had landed, I guess, in front of the Marines but behind the NVA trenches. I couldn't see it. I made a correction to move the 81s in front of us. Then the fight to my right stopped. I looked up. All the Marines were dead.

Capt KEN PIPES
Bravo Company, 1/26 _____

Don Jacques had joined the company in December and had done very well in his first action, when his platoon had ambushed an NVA recon unit. He was learning how to lead troops, and his patrol included the company's most experienced platoon sergeant, SSgt George McClelland, and the most experienced squad leader, Cpl Kenneth Claire. From what we pieced together later, Corporal Claire immediately led his squad in an attempt to envelop the NVA ambush. However, as soon as the squad moved, it ran into even heavier fire coming from behind it. Corporal Claire and most of his men were killed. I told Don to disengage and get back to the perimeter the best way he could.

The minute the ambush closed, I requested permission from Battalion to send 2ndLt Peter Weise's 1st Platoon as a reaction force. Pete moved toward the wire between FOB-3 and the western edge of the Bravo Company sector. However, just as the 1st Platoon reached the Route 9 access road, it was subjected to extremely heavy small-arms, RPG, mortar, and machine-gun fire. Pete couldn't advance, but he was able to maintain his position about 50 meters outside the wire. From my observation post I could see that the NVA had preplanned—but had not fired

in—60mm and 82mm mortar concentrations in the general area
of the 1st Platoon's position. Several barrages from at least six
mortars fell on the 1st Platoon position, but the platoon was able
to maintain its position and provide covering fire for the proposed
withdrawal of the 3rd Platoon patrol.

1stLt ERNIE SPENCER
1/26 Intelligence Officer

Bravo sent out another platoon to assist. It got chewed up by
concentrated mortar fire from [the NVA]. Marines died trying to
save dying Marines. That is our way. It separates us from
everyone else. A Marine likes to know that someone will try to get
to him, if he's down and can't get himself out. That's what Bravo
Company tried. . . .[3]

Capt JIM LESLIE
26th Marines Assistant Communicator

I could see Marines running and falling, and corpsmen running,
and stretchers flying. Men were screaming with pain. I didn't
know what to do. I could not help as the area between our wire
and the Marines fifty yards away was heavily mined. As some of
the Marines crawled toward the fence, others were helping. I
followed their path and helped some back to safety. I couldn't
believe I was witnessing this massacre that close to our lines.

Capt KEN PIPES
Bravo Company, 1/26

I requested assistance from our tanks and Ontos, and permission
was granted. They provided excellent firepower, but their visibility was limited by the rolling terrain. I then asked that another
company move out to break up the NVA ambush and blocking
positions as well as to recover our WIAs and KIAs. This request
was denied. I was extremely bitter at the time the denial came, but
later reflection convinced me that it was a wise decision.

LtCol JIM WILKINSON
1/26 Commanding Officer

Had I based a decision to relieve them purely on emotion, pride,
and guilt, I would not only have sent a unit out, I would have *led*

it. I thought about grabbing some people, racing out there, and saving those Marines. But I decided, based on radio reports, that the heaviest casualties had already been inflicted and that, from a military commander's point of view, my mission was to protect Khe Sanh Combat Base. I was well aware of many episodes in Vietnam where commanders had sent a squad out to save a fire team, then a platoon to save the squad, then a company to save the platoon, and finally a whole battalion to save the company—all at enormous expense in killed and wounded Marines. It was a tough decision, not based on emotion. It was a hard decision.

Capt KEN PIPES
Bravo Company, 1/26

My company artillery forward observer, 1stLt Hank Norman, and the artillery aerial observer overhead worked hard to get suppressive fire on the ambush site and suspected NVA mortar positions, and the 81mm forward observer with Don Jacques, Cpl Gilbert Wall, also called in fire missions. These fires, along with our own .50-caliber machine guns, 106mm recoilless rifles, and 60mm mortars undoubtedly inflicted friendly casualties, but I feel it enabled the 3rd Platoon patrol to break contact and return toward our wire. In addition, the aerial observer controlled air strikes consisting of napalm and rockets.

1stLt ERNIE SPENCER
1/26 Intelligence Officer

After hearing the radio reports from the patrol and the backup platoon, we know only that we have taken a big hit and that we are still taking. Charlie is now sending mortar fire inside the wire. It is as though we are walking through a tunnel. J.B. [LtCol Jim Wilkinson] and I are out in the open, jumping over the trenchlines, but the doom that hangs around us forms a tunnel that encloses and guides us to the spectacle of the slaughter still going on.[4]

Cpl GILBERT WALL
81mm Mortar Platoon, 1/26

I couldn't believe how many NVA were there. I threw a grenade in their trench and killed three, but they filled the spot in no time. The more we killed and got killed, the more they came.

The screaming and shouting was so loud I couldn't hear my own voice. I was terrified. I could see clearly the deep trouble we were in. We just didn't have enough men to match their firepower.

My third round landed. I didn't see it, but I heard it very close and knew it had to be behind the NVA trenches, so I decided to move it closer to us.

The Marine to my right got hit. My radioman, who was behind a tree a few meters to my rear, put out a whole magazine as I went for the wounded Marine. I bandaged the wounded Marine and then moved back to the tree up front on the left.

I was pinned. They were chewing the bark and I could hear the bullets cracking the tree. I put my rifle around the tree and kept firing blindly. My rifle jammed, so I took the round out of the chamber. It fired three times and jammed again.

Some Marines moved to my left and took the fire off me. I looked around the tree. An NVA was looking at me. I shot him in the face. Then I turned left and noticed the Marine next to me had his ass in the air and his face in the ground. I reached over and pulled him. He was shot in the face. They had blown out the back of his head. I took his rifle and threw mine away. I was running out of ammo. A Marine moved up by the mound and asked me for some grenades. I gave him three.

I was told by Lieutenant Jacques to go back down a little hill. I jumped up and ran to him while the Marine was throwing the grenades. I told Lieutenant Jacques that I wanted to move the fire mission to their trench. The response I got was to pull back, get out of here, take the wounded, and leave the dead ones! "Chief," he told me, "get out of here. Every man for himself." Then Lieutenant Jacques started running up by the other Marines while he was shooting an M-79 at bunkers.

As another Marine and I fired, Lieutenant Jacques and the others ran out of the treeline. Then the other Marine took off, hollering, "Come on, let's get out of here." I started running to the left, through the trees, until I hit the road we had come in from originally. The NVA were firing at me constantly, but a little too high, which saved me.

I picked up two boxes of M-60 ammo when I started going down the little road. I was the last Marine to come out of the treeline. I could see the other Marines running down the hill. Some were helping the wounded and others were on their own.

As I moved out in the open area and started going down the

hill, I heard a Marine calling me. He sounded very scared. He was lying by a tree. I guess he thought all the Marines were gone and he was left there all alone. He could see all the Marines running down the hill, and when he saw me running too, he got terrified and started screaming, "Marine, Marine, help me!"

I turned around and ran back for him. Just seeing me coming toward him brought a look of relief to his face. He was hurt badly, shot in three places, so I picked him up and started running down the hill. I was carrying the wounded Marine with one hand and firing blindly at the NVA bunkers with the other hand. In no time at all, the magazine was finished. I was out of ammo. Two Marines came running back to help us. They gave me some ammo and the wounded Marine's rifle, and took him with them.

For a while I was walking backwards and firing both rifles at the same time—until the magazines were finished. I returned one of the rifles to one of the Marines, reloaded the other one, and kept shooting while we moved slowly down the hill. I believe that my radioman and I, the two other Marines, and the wounded Marine were the last ones headed for the base.

By the time we got to the rice paddy at the bottom of the hill, some other Marines were halfway up the other side and some were still trying to move the wounded over the rice paddy. We waited for them to pass by and then got moving again.

Although we were not under fire at this time, the loud noise of continuous shooting never stopped. That was because the 1st Platoon was trying to come out and help us, but had walked into an ambush on the top of the hill by the base.

We were feeling a little relief because we were getting closer to the base when the Marines behind us ran into another ambush as they entered another treeline. We were all under their fire again.

Right in the middle of all the banana trees and high grass, there was this circular open area in which we were trapped. Bullets were flying all over the place. The cracking sound of AK-47s and M-16s was all I could hear. Wounded Marines were all I could see. The odor of blood and fresh grass was all I could smell.

I thought of calling a fire mission, so I lay down on my stomach to get the map out and realized that I had lost it. The fire mission was out of the question. The bullets were cutting the big leaves above my head to pieces. Everyone was lying there, dead or wounded. There was no time to be afraid of death.

I was still on the ground when I noticed a Marine who was shot in the chest, wounded real bad. He was moaning and obviously in deep pain. I reached him and put a bandage on his chest, but he was bleeding too much and the bandage didn't do much. I knew there was not much more I could do for him. He was dying.

I saw Lieutenant Jacques, shot in the groin, lying on the ground. I reached over and started putting a bandage on his wide-open wound. All the blood went through the bandage and ran down my fingers. He was hurt very bad and I couldn't do anything more to stop the bleeding. He was trying to talk to me, but I couldn't understand him. That was when a couple of bullets hit my flak jacket on the shoulder and knocked me on my ass. Another bullet went between my arm and my ribs and left a hole in my sleeve.

Capt KEN PIPES
Bravo Company, 1/26

Though I ordered the patrol to break contact and provided what assistance I could, they could not move. As the action continued to build, it became apparent that the survivors would have to return singly or in pairs. As they left, Don Jacques was hit in both femoral arteries. Don called me on the radio to ask, "Why in the hell aren't you doing something to help us? Why are you leaving us out here to die?"

Cpl GILBERT WALL
81mm Mortar Platoon, 1/26

I started moving Lieutenant Jacques to a safer place, where there were not that many bullets flying in the air. I moved him behind a small mound of dirt. Uselessly, I tried once again to stop the bleeding, but soon I noticed a change in the color of his face. It was turning white. His head fell back, his eyes rolled back, and he died.

By this time, 1st Platoon had broken the NVA line and was in our area. The shooting had stopped and the fight was over. Marines came and took Lieutenant Jacques and the other wounded and dead bodies back to the base.

2ndLt SKIP WELLS
Charlie Company, 1/26 _____

We heard the fight start over the Bravo tactical net, which we monitored so we would have an idea what was going on. From the talk on the net, I knew they were in deep trouble. I didn't hear Lieutenant Jacques on the net, so I figured he had been hurt.

We moved through the trenchlines to just south of the airstrip, to where we were to move through the wire to the east. By 1100, when we started out from the airstrip, the Bravo patrol was already in very bad trouble. We had to use fire-and-movement tactics just to get through the gate in the wire. We had to leapfrog squads, then fire teams, to get outside the wire, and I had to call back for more machine-gun ammo before we even got out. Just as we were about to move farther east, I got the word on the radio to "get back inside the wire." As we were just about stopped anyway, it took a while to get enough fire out to move back. But, as we never got closer than about fifty yards to the first NVA trench or positions, we were able to get back. Also, we were still practically tied in to the perimeter, so our rear and right flank were secure. It took us until about dark to get back in.

Capt KEN PIPES
Bravo Company, 1/26 _____

The survivors, most of them wounded, continued to come in for quite a while. In at least one case, 2ndLt Pete Weise, the 1st Platoon commander, went out in front of his platoon position to pull in a wounded machine gunner who couldn't get all the way in by himself.

Cpl GILBERT WALL
81mm Mortar Platoon, 1/26 _____

I was very tired and weak. My jacket and trousers were covered with blood. Flies were all over me. A Marine who was obviously a new boot kept hitting them. He looked like he felt sorry for me and was trying to help. I sat there for a while, thinking about all the Marines we had lost in that fire fight. Then I called Captain Pipes and asked him what he wanted me to do. He asked me to go back to the command post.

Capt JIM LESLIE
26th Marines Assistant Communicator _____

Our portion of the base was in chaos for a couple of hours, with wounded Marines and stretchers everywhere.

HN ROD DeMOSS
26th Marines Regimental Aid Station _____

[The Bravo Company patrol] got led into a trap and was chewed up and spit out by the NVA. We had heavy casualties that day, but what was so bad about it was that a lot of wounded men couldn't make it back on their own. I recall one Marine we were trying to patch up. He kept drawing maps of where some of these wounded were. He couldn't talk because the flesh under his chin was blown away and I think that his tongue was gone, too. This guy had to be in a lot of pain, but his main concern was for the guys who had been left behind. He was one of the heroes. Later that night, we could hear the cries of the ones who couldn't make it back.

Lt RAY STUBBE
1/26 Battalion Chaplain _____

[DIARY ENTRY] The casualties started coming in in pretty bad shape from Bravo Company. A man from 1/26 came to the [Charlie-Med] operating-room bunker with a list of twenty-six MIAs. He was checking to see if any had come to our triage, but there were none. Killed (missing): 27 Marines, including Cpl Kenneth Claire, the man who always used to yell like Tarzan on the hills, who had taken a whole loaf of bread and begun gnawing it like an animal, a man who enjoyed life and made us all happy.

1stLt ERNIE SPENCER
1/26 Intelligence Officer _____

Bravo's command bunker overlooks the entire scene. It is barren, desolate terrain—red dirt with mortars hitting. Marines carrying others, dragging, crawling. This is a live show. This is no fucking Hollywood epic. This is the real thing. Those are Marines getting hit. . . .

As Ken looks back at J.B. and me, his face seems like a mask that is melting. The sorrow flows from his eyes in dry tears that seem to pass out and over his cheeks and chin like wax running down a candle. We stand together beside his bunker as the wounded stream in.

J.B. is crushed. Like a coach who knows the game's over. His Marines acted like Marines, but they lost one. Big.

J.B. says to me, "Well, Ernie, let's go see the Old Man." We walk out in the open, striding. Oblivious to possible incoming. In the dark, together and alone.

Regimental CO is where he always seems to be. In his bunker. It is the old French bunker. Khe Sanh has a lot of tradition. As superstitious as this guy is, I can just imagine the fucking tripping out he does on that.

J.B. runs down the facts for the CO. . . . Most of one platoon is left out there, status unknown. Relatives of the missing will be told in twenty-four hours. In twenty-four hours the world will know—there are news photographers at the trenchline.

J.B. asks to go out to get his men. Regimental CO tells J.B. that the battalion is needed to defend the airstrip. He is right.[5]

Cpl GILBERT WALL
81mm Mortar Platoon, 1/26

When I got back to the command post, Captain Pipes said that he wanted me to go back on patrol to get our wounded and dead people back to the base. I waited about an hour for them to clear the patrol, but the regimental commander canceled it.

Capt JIM LESLIE
26th Marines Assistant Communicator

Later that day, I went over to Captain Pipes's bunker to see how I could help. Pipes was sitting on an ammo box with fresh wrapping on his wounds, his head in both of his hands, tears running down his sleeves. He said, "Why couldn't they wait till the fog lifted? My men. I've lost most of my men."

Colonel Lownds came in, put his arms around Ken, and said, "It's not your fault, son. You did all you could do. There were just too many NVA out there. I didn't realize how many there were, or how close."

I've wondered in retrospect if the NVA might have been monitoring all of our radio conversation and knew exactly when and where and what the Marines were doing every minute while we were there.

2ndLt SKIP WELLS
Charlie Company, 1/26

When I heard about the Bravo patrol, I felt betrayed. It was my first experience of being expendable. The only difference between Jacques's patrol and mine was that he went first.

1stLt JOHN KAHENY
1/26 Combat Operations Center

First Lieutenant Walt Chapman, the Commandant's son, who was serving as the Delta Company exec, later told me that orders to leave the bodies out there came from as high as the White House.

Cpl GILBERT WALL
81mm Mortar Platoon, 1/26

The next day, Lieutenant Spencer, the battalion intelligence officer, talked to me. They wanted to know if I knew for sure who got killed. My answer was, "I saw many Marines get killed, but I don't know their names." Lieutenant Colonel Wilkinson asked me, "What happened out there? Did we have a leadership breakdown?" I answered, "I don't think so."

I don't think there is a unit in the world that could have walked into that ambush and done better. We fought good and hard, but we just ran out of men.

Of the forty-three Marines who made up the Jacques patrol, and several dozen in Lieutenant Weise's 1st Platoon who were subjected to intense small-arms and mortar fire, the official tally lists forty-seven casualties: 1 KIA (Lieutenant Jacques), 13 WIA (medevacked), 8 WIA (minor), and 25 MIA.

SIEGEWORKS

26th Marines Command Chronology ————————————————

On February 25, the first sighting of NVA trench systems being dug in toward KSCB was made. As weather cleared, aerial observers were able to pinpoint several more trenches extending to within 100, 50, and 30 meters of the combat base perimeter. The trench systems came generally from the south and southeast. Immediate steps were taken to destroy them with supporting arms.

Capt KEN PIPES

Bravo Company, 1/26 ——————————————————————

A Bravo Company patrol on February 23 had turned up no evidence of the NVA presence on precisely the same ground as Don Jacques's patrol traversed on February 25, but Don's patrol uncovered numerous trenches, from which the ambush was sprung. Some of the trenches crossed the access road and were about a hundred yards from my lines and those of the 37th ARVN Rangers.

Capt HARRY BAIG

26th Marines Target Information Officer ——————————————

Intelligence conceived that the NVA would conduct a formal siege in the best traditions of the eighteenth century. They had learned these tactics at Dienbienphu. At Con Thien, they had learned something else; namely, that we never conducted B-52 strikes at ranges less than 3,000 meters, rarely made [radar-controlled bombing] runs at less than 2,000 meters, and hardly ever fired unobserved, unadjusted artillery missions less than 1,000 meters from friendly positions. We knew these things, too. It was obvious, therefore, that General Giap would attempt to tuck himself as closely about us as possible for safety's sake (and to facilitate his construction program). A siege campaign involves three distinct phases: arrival on the scene and investment of the fortress; construction of siegeworks and preparation of supporting facilities; "T-ing" the sapheads and the final assault.

The Intelligence Section, through intelligence channels, used every discovery system to develop a picture of enemy activities.

(Ground and aerial observers, aerial photography, infrared imagery, target lists of higher headquarters, crater analysis, and shell/flash reports, Spotlight reports [from Thailand], and signal-intelligence and accurate agent reports—all these were used to give us an understanding of the enemy situation.) When compared against the target map and reasoned against known enemy doctrine in like cases, the Khe Sanh intelligence community was able to estimate to a high degree of accuracy the intentions of the enemy on a day-to-day basis. Colonel Lownds's intimate knowledge of the terrain around Khe Sanh put a final fillip to the dish that was served to him daily. Except for the attack on Hill 861A, the enemy never surprised us—and he should not have done so then.[6]

Chapter 23

FEBRUARY 25

Lt RAY STUBBE
1/26 Battalion Chaplain

[DIARY ENTRY] Walked along the Charlie Company lines. A sniper was firing at me while I was in the trenches. Then the soft sound of the "bass drum" began again—rockets were being fired—and I fell into the trench as shrapnel was flying all over the place above the trench where I was, making odd zinging sounds. Eight pallets of land mines at the Shore Party [dump] near me had taken a direct hit and exploded with such force that the shitter at the 1/26 Battalion Aid Station was almost demolished by the blast. I felt the fear! I trembled uncontrollably, close to the earth—something I hadn't experienced up to this point.

There were 1,200 enemy rounds today.

Cpl DENNIS MANNION
Charlie Battery, 1/13 (Hill 861)

A guy in one of the Kilo Company rifle platoons, LCpl William Huff, made corporal and had to go to Okinawa for Noncommissioned Officers' School. He left the hill and went into Khe Sanh. As luck would have it, Huff got hit by a rocket while he was running off the chopper that took him down to the combat base.

Lt RAY STUBBE
1/26 Battalion Chaplain

[DIARY ENTRY] Returned to Charlie-Med. There were two patients from Echo Company, 2/26, on Hill 861A. One had a head wound, the other will lose his right arm and right leg and possibly will be blind. It was a very ghastly sight—black, charred flesh hanging down from a ripped-open area of the leg, to the bone. The hand was off; the arm was a stump. One corpsman walked to where I was: "I don't want to look at that, but I have to," he said resignedly, and walked back to aid the patient. Bloody clothes, poncho, and bamboo poles that had served as a stretcher were all over the deck.

Walked over to Graves Registration and said prayers over the bodies of Pfc Billy Dale Livingston, from Combined Action Company Oscar, who died while getting out of his bunker to watch rockets being fired from a Huey; he was killed by the shrapnel. And Pvt Ransom Lee Stuck, a man who had seen me before. He was due to be "out" this month, but, owing to "bad time," had to continue to serve here. He had two scholarships.

Capt BILL DABNEY
India Company, 3/26 (Hill 881S)

For the first two or three weeks, as they fired artillery at us, we didn't get any aerial observation out to the west because they didn't seem to believe us at Khe Sanh. Finally we asked for, and up on a helicopter came, pedestal-mounted binoculars. That gave us significantly improved capability for scoping because, first, it was solidly, rigidly mounted, and second, it was a 20-power system with a good, long-range focus capability—the kind you find on a ship's bridge.

We had on the hill a lance corporal by the name of Molikau Niuatoa, an American Samoan who had come to my attention because he fired, with the M-16, a qualifying score of 241 in boot camp. That's a pretty hellacious score for a brand-new recruit. And if it told us nothing else, it told us he had pretty good eyes. He was also a bull of a man, and an extremely patient fellow. He had the patience of Job, so we assigned him to look to the west through those 20-power binoculars and see if he could figure out where the devil the artillery was coming from. "Do it any way you can!" So, the way he came up with doing it was to pick a spot that looked like it had possibilities of being an artillery position and freeze his eyes on the spot and watch it until the artillery fired. If he did not detect anything in that little area he was looking at when the artillery fired, he'd reject that and move the glass a little bit and watch someplace else until the artillery fired again. And he kept, by that sort of a process of elimination, trying to figure out where the damned stuff was.

That sounds fairly simple, but you're talking about a guy standing with his eyes glued to a naval telescope for ten to fourteen hours a day, depending on what kind of visibility we had, and watching that one spot for that length of time, looking out twelve to fifteen kilometers. Sometimes, for a whole day, the artillery wouldn't fire and he'd just stand there. You had to remember to go up there and give him chow or give him a break so he could take a leak, whatever, because he was just that kind of Marine; he'd just stand there and freeze on that damned thing and watch a spot until something happened or until he rejected it.

On February 26, I got word—I was off in the other end of the trench someplace—that Niuatoa thought he had found something, some artillery had just gone by. I walked over to him and asked him, "What have you got?" And he said, "I think maybe the two things are related." He said, "Every time I'm looking out there and I see a little kind of pinpoint of light and then, fifteen, twenty seconds later, I hear the pop. A few seconds later after that I hear this sound like a squirrel running through dry leaves as the round goes by." And he said, "It only happens when I see the flash and hear the pop, so there must be some relation between the two." I said, "Well, you got a good sight?" And he said, "Yes, sir." I said, "Well, don't lose it, just hang in there." I got on the radio and called down to Khe Sanh and told them we thought we'd found the artillery piece.

They sent up a fellow named O'Toole, who was at the time the artillery observer—the back seat of a spotter plane. "Southern Oscar" was his radio call sign. "Southern" was the call sign for the artillery regiment, "Oscar" was the first initial of the last name of the aerial observer. We had had, throughout the Khe Sanh siege, two of them, a fellow named Happy and a fellow named O'Toole.

At any rate, O'Toole came buzzing up there with his pilot in the spotter plane, asking us if we could give him some idea where the stuff was. We gave him the general azimuth and suggested to him that we fire at mid-range, and at max range, one round each from the [two Charlie Battery] 105s we had on the hill, with white phosphorus, so he could get a line, at least for orientation. It was obvious that the 105mm phosphorus round wasn't going to reach this point Niuatoa was looking at. We did so. He found the first 105 round but couldn't find the second round. And there was a lot of danger for the gun crews in standing on that damned hill for any length of time, in the artillery revetments firing the damned stuff casually, because we tended to get 120mm mortars in every time we did that sort of thing. You're liable to lose a gun crew. We'd lost a couple. So we secured that because the aerial observer couldn't find the rounds.

"Look," O'Toole finally said, "somebody believes that we found something, and I've got four flights of A-4s over me. They're going to go bingo fuel in a little while, so we've got to get on with it." And he said, "How about I just take a flight of A-4s and pickle a stick of bombs on the highest ridgeline?"—more or less where we'd been talking to him about. We could see the bombs hit, but we hadn't been able to see his marking rockets or anything. Too far out. Hell, we couldn't even see the airplane! We're talking fifteen kilometers or so out west from us, in Laos. And I'll never forget the first adjustment Niuatoa gave me—he was still on the glasses—he said, "Left one kilometer, add two ridgelines!" Major adjustment, but that's the kind of frame of reference we were working with. So we passed that on to O'Toole, he dropped a second string of bombs—more or less the same thing. Niuatoa could see them and he said, "Okay," he said, "drop about halfway down the ridgeline and come left 500 meters." Another fairly major adjustment. We pickled the third string of bombs, and Niuatoa is saying to me in his broken English, "Right below where that last string of bombs dropped, there is a vee of trees, it looks like it is running up a gully." He said, "If they find that vee out there—it is on the east face of the same ridge the bombs just hit—follow it down until the point of the vee. We may have something because that's where I've been seeing this stuff." Well, they did that as best they could, and, apparently, success-fully. I couldn't see a damned thing—8-power binoculars wouldn't help a bit. Niuatoa said, "Yes, you got them right where I want them." And about five seconds after that, Southern Oscar was on the phone saying, "Hey, we got something out here!" I asked, "What have you got?" After the last bomb string dropped, a big square hole had opened in the deck. It was a big bamboo mat that had fallen off to the side from this string of bombs when the overpressure blew stuff around. And sticking out of this hole was a muzzle of what he thought was a 130mm gun. Apparently what they were doing was rolling the gun out, firing a round or two, and then rolling it back in, putting this cover back on top and being relatively impervious to aerial observation, which was the only kind of observation we could get at that distance. This is out in Laos; this is probably seven or eight kilometers beyond the Vietnamese border.

Over the course of the next few days, not under our control, O'Toole and the other aerial observers worked their way forward and back along the Khe Sanh gun-target line from that gun and found four or five more, as best they could tell. The way O'Toole described it led me to believe that because there were so many B-52 strikes and that sort of thing, the North Vietnamese had probably emplaced those guns not in a battery position, but in single-gun positions on the gun-target line, so that in order to hit Khe Sanh they only had to adjust for range, not for deflection. And once they cranked in that range adjustment for each gun, which adjustment would remain more or less constant since Khe Sanh wasn't going to move, they could fire in battery fire, even when the guns were not emplaced in a battery position. It sounded like they had emplaced the guns at about 500-meter intervals, with the rear guns probably pretty close to max range, which is 27,000 meters for that 130mm field gun—and then forward from there. I had suspected they emplaced them that way, because although we'd always hear only one tube pop, or several pops almost simultaneously, the sounds, as the rounds came over the hill, were always separated, as if the guns were firing together, but from different ranges. As O'Toole described it, they'd probably gotten four or five. That was not the only artillery out there.

It could have not been done without Niuatoa and his incredible patience. He'd been standing there on the skyline for a couple of weeks, twelve to fourteen hours a day, under constant mortar fire, with a few sniper rounds thrown in. He was fearless. A round—120mm—would land nearby, and he wouldn't even flinch. Oblivious to danger may be a better description.[1]

FEBRUARY 27

Lt RAY STUBBE
1/26 Battalion Chaplain

[DIARY ENTRY] At the morning briefing, the adjutant announced that 1/26 had suffered the following casualties: 23 KIA, 47 WIA serious, 27 MIA, 247 WIA non-serious, 92 evacuated. Total casualties: 320.

LCpl MIKE GUESS
Charlie Company, 1/9

I was just standing there in the trenchline when a mortar round came in. By then, I was so accustomed to them that I didn't duck as low as I should have. I took three pieces of shrapnel in the back of the head, right between the edge of my helmet and the collar of my flak jacket. There was blood all over the flak jacket, but the wounds weren't serious. I went down to Dong Ha to have them fixed up. They put a few stitches in and kept me overnight.

Next morning, flying back on a chopper, I realized that, of all the guys going to Khe Sanh, only me and one or two others had been there before. Everybody else was new. There had to be twenty or twenty-five brand-new guys. I had been sitting up on our trenchline for weeks, watching the airfield get hit constantly— all day—so I knew that we were going to get rounds as soon as the chopper came in. So, there I was, the eighteen-year-old kid, giving everybody orders. All I said was, "When this chopper lands and that back door drops, just pick up your ass and get *moving*! Run to the sides. Just get going, 'cause the rounds are going to come in."

I guess by then the battle for Khe Sanh had had a lot of publicity back in the United States. Some of the guys had been hearing about it, and they were—wow!—*happy* to be going there.

That surprised me. Sure as heck, when the back door of the chopper went down, these guys *trotted* out there and just looked around like, "Hey, this is it; we're at Khe Sanh." I was in the middle of the pack, but I went storming out, knocking these guys out of the way. I just kept cruising. Sure as shit, *ten* of these new guys never even got off the chopper pad. They got killed right there.

FEBRUARY 28

Lt RAY STUBBE
1/26 Battalion Chaplain

[Diary Entry] Transferred from Khe Sanh. Landed at Quang Tri. I had quite a growth of beard and my clothing was absolutely scroungy—mud, blood, sweat. I had not been out of my clothing in weeks. A Marine took a picture of me as some sort of odd figure from another world. Several enlisted men invited me in for a beer as I walked along the road. One pilot looked up at me and said, "It must have been Khe Sanh."

Although Chaplain Stubbe was officially transferred from 1/26 to the 3rd Marine Division chaplain's office, he continued to make his way back to Khe Sanh for flying visits as he roved through the division's area of responsibility.

LCpl PHIL MINEER
Bravo Battery, 1/13

While accompanying Lieutenant McGrath to pick up the battery payroll at Danang in late February, I flew up to the 1/13 battalion rear area at Dong Ha. While I was there, I ran into an old buddy.

Cpl Ronnie Dempsey was one of the original Bravo Battery Marines. He had shipped out of the States with the battery when it first went overseas. He was one of a few original members of the unit who had extended for another tour when everyone else finished their time and went home. That got him a thirty-day extra leave that he could take anytime he wanted during the second tour. He went home right before he went up to Khe Sanh—thirty days, plus ten days for travel time. I happened to be at Dong Ha when he got back, so we hung out together. He wanted to get back to the battery, but I told him that no one was pushing him, that he ought to hang back in the rear until someone asked for him. But he wanted to go, so I drove him to the chopper pad and he flew out. Five or six hours later, somebody came to the battery area and told me that the chopper had taken ground fire getting to Khe Sanh and that Dempsey had taken a .51-caliber round under the chin that went through the top of his head. I claimed his body at Graves Registration that night.

FEBRUARY 29

ASSAULT

Capt HARRY BAIG
26th Marines Target Information Officer _____

Sensors clearly foretold the attack on Khe Sanh Combat Base during the night of February 29–March 1, and gave us time to divert two Arclights, one of which struck the best part of two battalions moving up to support and reinforce the assault battalion.

Defensive fire plans were not used to prevent an enemy assault force from closing onto the perimeter wire. They were designed to prevent him from escaping and being reinforced. Their purpose was to isolate the battlefield and to defeat the enemy in detail by fragmenting his forces and separating his elements. The fires took the following form: A three-sided box, open at the friendly side, was emplaced about the location or suspected location of the assault unit. Three batteries executed this mission. A fourth battery then closed the remaining open side of the box and rolled forward into the box in the manner of a piston within its cylinder. Having reached the far side of the box, it proceeded to roll back. And so on. The enemy force inside the box could not escape out of it and could not avoid the roller or piston effect of the rolling barrage. The use of firecracker, [COFRAM] ammunition vastly magnified the effect of this battery. This box was known as the "primary box." At the same time this was going on, the Fire Support Coordination Center put into effect a "secondary box." The latter was fired outside the former. The 175mm guns of the U.S. Army delivered fire missions in long lines about 500 meters away from the primary box, each gun zoning and shifting when required. Generally, the guns took two sides of the secondary box. On order, their fires rolled in toward the center and out again. The third side of the secondary box was closed by aircraft under the control of AN/TPQ-10 radar. Where possible, and only when we were convinced that an attack was imminent, an Arclight strike, diverted three hours earlier, would deposit its bombs across or along the main avenue of approach into the battle area.

The Fire Support Coordination Center responded to the enemy's assault by employing the pattern of [the] defensive fire [plan] described above. Primary box with a modified rolling barrage (piston effect) within it; secondary box, using 175mm guns and [radar-guided] aircraft; and two Arclights, diverted three hours before.[2]

Cpl WILLIAM ROBERTSON
Logistics Support Unit

The NVA charged the line, coming right up on the end near the ammo dump, where 105mm battery was. They were coming right up a bow in the land. I guess there were 300 or 400 of them. They were charging the line across a broad, open field. They were banging the devil out of us with mortars, right there at the artillery battery and along the edge of the ammo dump. They were going for the artillery battery more than they were going for us. There was very heavy overcast; I guess the ceiling was maybe 100 feet at the most. They charged the line three times, but the closest they got was about 100 feet from the perimeter wire. The artillery battery was unable to fire at them; the gunners had to get 81mm mortars and 105s from the other end of the perimeter to get to them because they had revetments built all around the 105s so they could shoot and not have to worry about getting hit by anything. The revetments prevented the battery near us from lowering their barrels enough to shoot directly at the NVA who were attacking. We were cutting them down pretty good with M-16s—I had an M-14—and machine guns. I saw a mess of them fall, but it looked like, each time they charged, there was just as many of them as there had been the first time. I saw them fall, but the grass was high enough that, once they fell, I couldn't see them again. I don't know if they crawled out of there, or what. Finally, jets were called in. They came in and first strafed the area—which they couldn't see—and then they dropped some bombs. One of the bombs fell into one of our bunkers and killed two ARVN Rangers. The jets didn't drop any more bombs, but the NVA never charged us again up through that area. At the last minute, they just turned back. I heard later that the 105s on the other side of the base were dropping their rounds on the other side of the NVA who were doing the charging. Instead of taking care of the ones doing the charges, they were preventing the ones coming up to reinforce from getting through. That was probably the reason they backed off.

Capt HARRY BAIG
26th Marines Target Information Officer

This attack reinforced our belief concerning the enemy's mental rigidity and inflexibility of mind.[3]

LtCol JIM WILKINSON
1/26 Commanding Officer

I visited the 37th ARVN Ranger Battalion command post on the morning of March 1. The Rangers were examining equipment and material taken from dead NVA or left behind by retreating NVA. Included were a large number of enemy devices to be used to breach the wire of KSCB. These crude but workable devices were constructed of bamboo strips laced around blocks of TNT. The enemy planned to use these as bangalore torpedoes, but they never had the opportunity.[4]

LATE FEBRUARY

Capt HARRY BAIG
26th Marines Target Information Officer

In late February, Maj Robert Coolidge and Maj Jerry Hudson [intelligence officers] discovered the exact locations . . . of twelve artillery positions and two major ammunitions dumps (not to be confused with battery dumps or ready-service dumps). These were concentrated in two general areas to the south. Two Arclight strikes, already airborne, were diverted to these two target areas. After the bombers had departed, the ground erupted for some forty minutes on account of the secondary explosions, observable from KSCB.[5]

Maj ALEX LEE
Seismic Sensor Consultant _____

One young Marine was a cook pressed into service in a line company, but he had such rotten vision that he could do no good in a fighting hole. I found him cooking in a cul-de-sac in the trenchline. He was using cans found in the blown-up dumps, and he would serve anyone who stopped by. He had rules: wash your own tin plate, no more than four guys at one time, and officers *last* in the chow line. He seemed to work twenty-four hours a day. When I suggested to his battalion CO that he be decorated for such far-reaching personal effect, I was told that I was stupid, that he was just trying to get out of line duty. Since I ate every meal there for several days, and since the activity took place in the front-line communications trench, I hardly think the Marine was a slacker.

I cannot be so thoroughly complimentary of my brother officers. Many were "bunker rats," and others failed to enforce sanitation—thereby creating the presence of more real rats in the underground command posts. Sadly, some senior officers were most guilty, throwing half-filled cans on the deck and leaving partially eaten food in the sleeping area of the CP bunker.

LCpl TIM SNELL
Hotel Company, 2/26 _____

I was the company driver. One day I received word that the supplies were ready for pickup at the supply bunker. I was driving a truck, due to the amount of supplies I was required to pick up. I arrived at the supply bunker and loaded the truck without incident. While driving to the helo pad, I was thinking about how quiet it was, and how I had not heard or seen any incoming yet. The chopper was just coming into view as I was approaching the pad. I pulled up to it so that we didn't have to carry the supplies very far to load them. As we started unloading the truck, we noticed a plane coming in to drop supplies. Just as the plane was coming in, the NVA started sending in mortar and artillery rounds to try to take it out. The first rounds weren't close enough to make us run for the nearest trench, but we kept an eye on what was going on.

We were about half unloaded when, all at once, there was a tremendous explosion right behind the truck. There were two Marines back there, an enlisted man and a lieutenant. I was standing by the truck door, on the driver's side, when the round hit. It threw me over the door. I woke up on the ground and just started running for the nearest trench. Things were happening really fast, and I didn't see the two men behind the truck. As the rounds kept coming in, I looked out to see the condition of the truck. As I started to look, we heard some yelling; someone wanted to know who the driver of the truck was. I yelled that I was, and the lieutenant yelled that he had a wounded man and wanted me to drive him and the wounded man to the battalion aid station for medical assistance.

I ran to the truck and, when I got to the back of it, where the officer was, I could see the wound in the back of the enlisted man's head. At first the wound did not look serious. The officer and I picked the man up by his shoulders and feet. I was at the head, and this is when I got a good look at the wound. The man was bleeding quite freely. With my time in-country, I had seen plenty of wounds, and I knew he was in serious trouble. The wound appeared to be at least the size of a half-dollar, and it was at the base of the skull.

The officer jumped in the back of the truck and said he would hold the man's head in his lap and help me get him into the battalion aid station when we got there. I jumped into the front seat and headed straight for the aid station. All I could do was get as low as I could in the truck and pray.

We started across the runway, and the rounds started to get even closer. Some rounds hit close enough to kick up the dirt in front of us. Having been around awhile, I knew they were just getting the range so they could drop one right in my lap. That's when I decided to duck a little lower and begin to zigzag across the airstrip. We drove from the east side to the west side of the strip without getting ourselves or the vehicle hit.

Upon arriving at the aid station, the lieutenant and I jumped out and grabbed the wounded Marine. I think that we both knew by then that the man didn't have much of a chance, but we still had to try. When we carried him to the operating table, we could see that his eyes were rolled back and there were no apparent signs of breathing. We both expected this, but it still didn't make it easier to lose another Marine.

LCpl ARMANDO GONZALES
Bravo Company, 1/9 _____

The NVA were very good at giving us just enough rope, enough confidence, to hang ourselves. While water was rationed, we sometimes went out to collect some at a little stream that ran between the Rock Quarry and the combat base. One day, as my squad was going out, one of the pointmen had set off a booby trap. As everyone dived for cover, we set off a chain reaction of more booby traps. Several Marines were killed or wounded, and it took the help of another squad from our platoon to get everyone back inside our wire.

Pfc LIONEL TRUFANT
106mm Platoon, 3/26 _____

Some nights, when I was alone on watch, it was so foggy that I thought I was the only person on Earth. I couldn't hear anything and could barely see anything in the fog. I had to be alert for the enemy—we had all seen movies where the sentry got his throat slit at night—and also for the officer or the staff noncommissioned officer who checked the lines at night. Night watch gave me lots of time to think—of things like Dienbienphu, of home, of what the hell was going to happen at Khe Sanh, about what else the NVA might throw at us.

Cpl ALLAN STAHL
Logistics Support Unit _____

I was standing sentry duty one night when the whole ridgeline outside the base lit up like when everybody in a football stadium lights a lighter. The whole hillside was speckled with lights, hundreds of them. We assumed they must be coming to get us. It went like that for three nights in a row, but nothing happened.

GySgt MAX FRIEDLANDER
17th Interrogation-Translation Team _____

One day, I stood up on top of my bunker and looked around at the countryside, which had been totally magnificent, beautiful country. When I noticed what was left of that beautiful country-side, it was a real jolt. I could see the devastation taking place on an hourly basis. Bombs from our aircraft, the strafing, the napalm, the artillery—it seemed like there were constant explosions going on. It was hard to believe so much devastation could take place in any twenty-four-hour period in that one relatively small area. The smell of cordite was always there.

As time went on, as the North Vietnamese built their trenches closer to our lines, our aircraft kept getting closer and closer to the perimeter. The accuracy of the fighters and bombers was beyond belief. On those few occasions when there were no bombs or artillery shells going off, one could stand in the open anywhere in the combat base and just get the feeling of death in the air. The silence was eerie, as if a material thing was present.

LCpl RAY NICOL
Bravo Battery, 1/13 _____

After the napalm and bombs burned off the elephant grass and cover outside the wire, we could see that trenches were being dug up to within 50 meters of the wire in some places. Napalm was dropped unignited and left to run into the trenches. Then the fighters came in and set the napalm off with rockets. After the grass burned off, we could see rats feeding on the enemy dead. Whenever the wind came up from that direction, it was difficult to eat aboveground.

Cpl DENNIS SMITH
Bravo Company, 1/26 _____

One day toward the end of February lots of rockets were coming in. James Jesse, Virgil Crunk, Jerry Dorn, and I had taken refuge in my hooch when Dorn said he had to take a dump. I told him, "Not in my house. I don't care if all the incoming in the world is hammering us; nobody takes a shit in my house."

Dorn, who was always a gentleman—he should have been an officer—says, "I'll wait until the next lull and then I'm taking off."

I picked up my watch and told him, "I'll time you." The nearest shitter was forty or fifty yards away.

We waited until it got quiet. Dorn took off. He was back through the hatch fourteen seconds later. "I did it," he said as soon as he was inside.

We all said, "Bullshit! No way!"

"I did it."

We had to ask him how.

He said he already had the shitpaper in his left hand and he unbuckled his belt as he ran. He hit the door full speed, dropped his drawers, hit the seat, let fly with everything he had, wiped on the upstroke, and was out the door running again.

Cpl BERT MULLINS
Bravo Company, 1/9

Radio operators invented simplified codes for everything we could—certain type units or certain numbers, for example. One day, one of our radio operators got confused. He was trying to tell us by means of code that he had seen one NVA, but he used the code to indicate that he had been a *platoon* of NVA. Before we could get the matter straightened out, we had an air strike coming in. The powers that be decided that we were not going to explain what happened or call off the air strike. So we let the strike come in.

The A-4s dropped their bombs where that one NVA had been, and shrapnel from one of the bombs traveled all the way over the top of the hill. I was crouching in a trenchline next to one of our bunkers. That chunk of shrapnel, which was as big as the palm of my hand and a half-inch thick, embedded itself in the wall of the trench not six inches from my head.

Capt KEN PIPES
Bravo Company, 1/26

The big stuff is what bothers most people the most when it's going on. After a while, you get immune to the smaller stuff when you're also getting hit with the real heavy artillery and rockets.

The NVA had a 57mm recoilless rifle out in front of the

ARVN Ranger position that sniped at anything that moved. Whenever I went back to battalion briefings, I usually accompanied Capt Walt Gunn, the Army adviser to the ARVN Rangers. Realizing that the 57 would snipe at us, we often ran short sprints in the open outside the trenchline—just for something unusual to do. We always made it back into the trench before they fired. We'd laugh, go down the trenchline a little farther, and do it again.

LtCol JIM WILKINSON
1/26 Commanding Officer

The NVA took advantage of periods of limited visibility to dig the trenches closer to KSCB. Marines of 1/26 used periods of good visibility to register M-79 rounds on the close-in NVA trenches. At night, during periods of invisibility, M-79s would fire a version of H&I fires into the trenches. This was an effective method of countering the trenching activity close to the perimeter.[6]

Pfc MIKE DeLANEY
Echo Company, 2/26 (Hill 861A)

We hooked a transistor radio up to a long piece of electrical wire wrapped around some old radio batteries. It was a good enough antenna to bring in Hanoi Hannah. One day she dedicated a song to Echo Company, 2/26, at Khe Sanh. It was Martha and the Vandellas singing, "No Place to Run, No Place to Hide." Talk about giving goosebumps! We sat around looking at each other like, "I don't believe this!"

Chapter 24

MARCH 2

HM3 BILL GESSNER
Delta Company, 1/9

We had harassing mortar fire, but no ground attacks as we dug, emplaced wire, and emplaced a minefield. We ran patrols out toward Khe Sanh Village. We ran two wire-sweeping patrols every day. We put out a squad-size ambush every night. Then a platoon from the 26th Marines got its ass handed to them and our patrolling was reduced to sweeping the wire twice a day. The main threat to us was the indirect fire and a guy who was sniping at us with a .51-caliber machine gun. He had our latrine zeroed in, and it was a bad idea to take a crap during daylight.

The enemy dug trenches toward our lines. We could hear them at night, but we never really did much to stop them. Mortars weren't fired because they might learn where the tubes were. Claymores were stolen. Ambushes were not permitted. So they dug. One morning the fog lifted at dawn and we caught four or five NVA trying to get away. M-79 grenadiers cornered them on a knoll, and we got permission to get them. We later found three bodies and a blood trail.

As the patrol returned, they were fired at by an NVA recoilless rifle as the lead fire team was passing through our wire and mines. The lead men were able to get to our lines, but everyone else was trapped in the lane or outside the wire. The recoilless rifle fired four or five times, then HN Tim Wethington and I went out to bandage the wounded men.

The recoilless rifle fired a few more times, hitting in the lane about twenty meters away and scaring the hell out of us. We scrambled about looking for cover and sat out the attack. During a lull, the lightly wounded men helped carry the seriously wounded men up the ridge and into the company perimeter. After we gained the safety of the trenchline, the recoilless rifle fired again. Tactical air was requested to knock out the recoilless rifle, but it stopped shooting while the air cover was around.

When the airplanes left, Tim Wethington was standing in the 1st Platoon trenchline. The recoilless rifle fired and the round hit him in the chest. The man was literally blown to pieces.

MARCH 6

Sgt FRANK JONES
26th Marines Scout-Sniper Platoon

I flew down to Danang to drop off a wounded buddy's personal gear so he would have it with him when he went back to the States. I caught a flight out under some mortar fire, but I got to Danang okay and left the gear with my buddy. But I couldn't get back to Khe Sanh. Newspeople who were trying to get in there kept asking why I was trying so hard to get back. I told them that my platoon was up there, that's what I had been trained to do, not stay down there. A *Time* magazine writer took it all down and wrote an article about the crazy Marine who wanted to get back into the siege. I finally got a seat back on an airplane. The next airplane after mine got hit and everybody aboard it got burned up.

Maj TOM COOK
26th Marines Assistant Logistics Officer

While the C-123 was on its final approach, a single-engine Air America plane swooped in and landed right in front of him. The C-123 aborted his landing and went back around. By the time he set up his second approach, the NVA knew which way he was coming and where he was going. They had him zeroed in and shot him down.

There were no survivors. The official death count was 43 Marines, four Air Force, and one Navy killed. The lone sailor was a corpsman from Lima Company, 26th Marines, who was coming back from R&R leave. Robert Ellison, a Newsweek *photographer, on his second trip to Khe Sanh, was not in the official tally.*

MARCH 7

THE BRU

26th Marines After Action Report _____

During early March, NVA propaganda teams entered [nearby Bru-occupied] villages, advising the Bru to relocate to southern Huong Hoa District, where they would be cared for. They were told the major offensive against KSCB was about to begin and that U.S. forces would strike the villages in retaliation. Many groups started south. However, the first groups found that there was no food available there, so the migration to KSCB and across country to Cam Lo began.

The Bru began arriving at the base on March 7 and continued to filter in through the remainder of the month. As many as 661 were evacuated in one day, with as high as 440 being kept overnight in the FOB-3 compound. The total evacuated through KSCB during the month was 1,428. Countless others migrated across country to eastern Quang Tri.

LCpl PHIL MINEER
Bravo Battery, 1/13 _____

On March 7, hundreds and hundreds of refugees started coming into the base. For a while, it was what the Marine Corps calls "asshole to bellybutton"—really tight living conditions on the base. But, slowly, they got them all flown out.

26th Marines After Action Report _____

Many Bru attempted to migrate to Cam Lo (in eastern Quang Tri Province); however, they were intercepted by the NVA and forced to resettle in the villages of Lang Con, Lang Bu, and Lang Vei. Some migrated into Laos. These areas were designated "no fire areas" for friendly forces.

BOB BREWER
Quang Tri Province Senior Adviser _____

The Bru, about 10,000 strong, were the montagnard people of Huong Hoa District, of which the Khe Sanh Combat Base was a small outpost. The Bru were a noble, peaceful, hard-working people. Nobody understood them better than the missionary John Miller and his family. John spent six years with them. His kids were born there. He and his wife learned the Bru language and transliterated it into the Vietnamese script, then they translated the whole Bible into Bru. By the time I ordered John Miller and his family out of Huong Hoa in mid-January 1968, Bru children were reading their own language in the perfectly logical Vietnamese script.

I said these people were peaceful. They were, more so in my opinion than any of the other montagnard tribesmen of Indochina. But they had a messiah who led fantastic patrols through and around the NVA positions. He provided intelligence of the most valuable kind. He was adored by all the Bru people, and as long as he lived, they would go anywhere and do anything if he said it was okay. Needless to say, he fell during the siege, and Huong Hoa began to unravel.

After the Huong Hoa District Headquarters was abandoned on January 22, all 10,000 Bru were brought to the lowlands of Quang Tri Province. The Communists did nothing to impede the exodus. We brought the Bru down to our major refugee community near Cam Lo District Headquarters. Soon it became apparent that the Bru tribesmen were withering away. Sickness and disease and a strange ennui were claiming them. John Clary, the chief USAID adviser in the district, said that it was the low altitude and lack of flowing water. So we found a new, wild, high country just southeast of Camp Carroll. The second move was made, and to this day I can still see the Bru children splashing and laughing in the free-flowing streams where we resettled them.

26th Marines After Action Report _____

The Bru provided valuable information on [enemy] troop dispositions and attitudes. Numerous secondary explosions [resulted from] strikes against targets plotted from their information. Those who arrived early in the month were of the impression that attack was imminent while those who arrived later indicated the NVA propaganda theme had changed to one of Ho Chi Minh would be unhappy if they [the NVA] wasted their time on only 6,000 Marines at Khe Sanh. Interesting along this line is the fact that the same general theme was echoed by Radio Hanoi's English-language announcer, Hanoi Hannah, a few days later.

MARCH 8

Cpl GILBERT WALL
81mm Mortar Platoon, 1/26 _____

This was the second day that I tried to get a plane out of Khe Sanh. In the morning, we went to the headquarters to get rifles and other weapons to carry out of Khe Sanh, which was almost guaranteed a trip on the plane.

After waiting all morning, a Marine and I got fifteen .45-caliber pistols in an artillery ammo box to take out. When we got to the area by the airstrip, the Marine who took the names of the people getting on the plane told us that whoever carried a dead body to the plane would get to go first. I volunteered to take one. We put our seabags and the box with the fifteen .45s in it alongside the dead body on a stretcher. It was almost certain that we could get to the plane—but out of Khe Sanh? Who knew?

The plane taxied down the runway, made a turn, and started dropping its load without ever stopping. When it was through unloading, they told us to go, so we started running after the moving plane. The load was so heavy that the stretcher looked like it would break any moment. We tried to keep everything on it as we were running. Twelve running Marines along with six dead bodies we were carrying were getting closer when they let all the other waiting Marines start running for the plane. In no time, they passed us and jumped on the plane. They were all standing along with the plane crew, shouting, "Run faster, run faster!" and screaming that the incoming was starting up.

I was in the back of our stretcher, trying to keep it balanced and move faster at the same time. I was scared even though I didn't see or hear any incoming.

Finally we got there and started climbing on the plane before it made for the runway. The plane moved down the runway and took off. I could hear the incoming.

The dead bodies were on the floor, so we just laid on them. I could feel the softness of the dead body and feel the fear of death itself. Nobody moved or made any noise. Everybody was terrified. I could smell the rubber of the body bag.

It was easy to guess what was going on outside the plane. I had spent many days watching the NVA shooting at the planes; I knew where the .51-cals were coming from and when they would be shooting at us from the north side or the southeast side of the base. I had seen a big plane, a chopper, or a fighter-bomber getting shot out of the air so many times that I could picture the heavy fire they were putting on us very clearly.

The plane went straight up and everybody remained very quiet. It wasn't until we went higher and farther from Khe Sanh that one of the crew members said, "All clear." After a second of doubt, we all started hugging, shouting, and congratulating each other. Some of the Marines applauded, but some got their anger and frustration out by shouting, "Fuck you, Khe Sanh." Some got emotional and started crying. We were all happy. We knew we had made it.

Pvt JONATHAN SPICER
Charlie-Med

[NAVY CROSS CITATION] For extraordinary heroism while serving with Company C, Third Medical Battalion, Third Marine Division, in the Republic of Vietnam on 8 March 1968. During an intense enemy rocket, mortar, and artillery attack against the Khe Sanh Combat Base, Private Spicer unhesitatingly volunteered to serve as a stretcher bearer and assisted in embarking the numerous casualties aboard transport helicopters for evacuation. Completely disregarding his own safety, he continued to expedite the loading of the wounded aboard the aircraft, despite the increasing intensity of the attack, and was the last man to seek shelter in a bunker at the edge of the airstrip. Observing a mortar round exploding near an evacuation helicopter loaded with casualties, he unhesitatingly left his position of relative safety to assist the wounded who were unable to move from their exposed position. Moments later, another round exploded within a few feet of Private Spicer, seriously wounding him, as he shielded a Marine from the blast with his own body. Unable to walk, he warned his comrades to remain in their protective positions while he attempted to crawl from the hazardous area to safety by himself. His selfless actions undoubtedly prevented serious injury or possible death to his fellow Marines and were an inspiration to all who observed him. By his dauntless courage, unfaltering determination, and selfless devotion to duty at great risk, Private Spicer upheld the highest traditions of the Marine Corps and the United States Naval Service.

EARLY MARCH

OUTGOING

LCpl RAY NICOL
Bravo Battery, 1/13 _____

The fog in the morning was so thick we couldn't see ten meters. A recoilless rifle started firing at us from the ridgeline to our south. It would fire two or three rounds starting at daybreak, when the fog was really thick. All we could see when it fired was a big orange flash in the fog, but we couldn't tell where the round was going to hit. Then it was too late. It hit our comm bunker one morning, and I spent an hour helping dig everyone out. Fortunately, no one was hurt. We just couldn't spot the recoilless rifle because it never fired after the fog lifted.

Maj TOM COOK
26th Marines Assistant Logistics Officer _____

Almost every morning, at approximately 0700, we had a wake-up call from a recoilless rifle. Every morning, from one position or another, the NVA would hit us with that single recoilless rifle round, right in downtown Khe Sanh, which comprised the Combat Operations Center and all the staff bunkers. We never knew where it might hit. There was a small aperture in the bunker that housed our generator. I'll be darned if he didn't put a round right through that aperture. He never knew what he hit, of course, but he destroyed our generator. Quite a shock.

1stLt FRED McGRATH
Bravo Battery, 1/13 _____

We had been taking some sporadic incoming from what appeared to be a 57mm recoilless rifle. The man was a poor shot. One day the NVA gunners became bolder than usual. They placed the gun in an unprotected position and began to fire at our position. Not having a similar weapon to engage him, one of the battery officers, adept at computation, took a Graphic Firing Table and went to a howitzer that had a direct line-of-sight to the enemy position. After three attempts, the gun crew scored a direct hit on the 57mm recoilless rifle. The crew felt it had earned the bragging rights as "Best Dingers" in the battery. They got no argument.

LCpl RAY NICOL
Bravo Battery, 1/13 _____

We also blew up the Frenchman's plantation house, south of our position, using the only concrete-piercing round I ever saw used in Vietnam. The house was being used by the NVA as a head-quarters and for cover for their snipers.

1stLt FRED McGRATH
Bravo Battery, 1/13 _____

Not all the rounds we fired hit the intended target. In fact, one round we fired never hit anything, literally. When you prepare a round for firing a 105mm howitzer, you have a projectile with fuse, powder bags, and a canister. The number of powder bags used is determined by the charge required. We had a fire mission going that had a fairly high quadrant (elevation), so the tube was facing skyward. The powderman was new, this being the first unit he was in. The charge called was four. That meant bags one, two, three, and four. I guess he was a little nervous. He only put in the number-four bag! The round never left the tube, although the propellant ignited. The projectile lodged about eight inches from the muzzle. Since there was a VT fuse on the round, we could not dislodge it by using a bell rammer. Too dangerous. We had no choice but to call EOD. They took the tube off the howitzer and blew the whole tube up! Again, the priority of Khe Sanh worked. The howitzer had a new tube two days later.

INCOMING

Cpl ALLAN STAHL
Logistics Support Unit _____

The NVA was always shooting at our supply and ammo dumps, and they always eventually hit something and started a fire. We were the guys who always got to put the fires out. They were our dumps. We didn't have any fire hoses, of course, so we had to shovel dirt on the fires to put them out. We had to let certain things burn because there was no way to put them out, or, in the case of ammo, it was too dangerous to fight the fires.

One time, after we had already put a few big fires out, we got down to ASP-1 and started giggling and acting silly. It wasn't a very serious fire, so eventually, we started pissing on burning boxes to put the fires out. I was standing there taking a piss when something went *bloomp*. It didn't hit me hard, but it did hit me, and I got all scratched up. It was a very sobering experience. That ended the joke. I picked up my radio and went on home. The party was over.

Another time, they hit the CS gas. We had a new kid, and he and I were sent to the ammo dump. We ran right into the cloud of CS. I was breathing deeply from running, and it got me. It really hurt. I panicked. I had my gas mask with me, but I really panicked. It hurt! I tried to run, but I couldn't get away from it. Finally I got hold of myself and got my gas mask on. As I got my breath back, it dawned on me that I had lost track of the new kid. I thought, if *I* panicked, there was no telling what the new kid had done. I found him lying in a ditch. He had done it by the book. He smelled the gas, put his gas mask on, cleared it, and lay down. His eyes were as big as silver dollars behind the gas-mask lenses, but he was okay. The only thing wrong with him was that he had just seen the old pro go nuts.

We had a night fire at ASP-1. I grabbed my radio and Private First Class Rodriguez followed me out of the bunker. We were running down the road when all hell started breaking loose and all kinds of stuff started falling around us. There was a ditch, but it offered no protection at all. We were in the ditch, listening to our home base call us on the radio, trying to find out where we were and how we were doing. I tried to call back, but they kept asking the same questions, so I knew they couldn't hear me. All that shit was still falling out of the sky as Rodriguez and I were lying in the ditch facing one another. Suddenly, a 60mm mortar round goes *thud* right between our faces. It was smoking! We vacated the ditch and headed back home. On the way, we passed another radio team they had sent out to find us. I was ashamed to be heading home past them, but I had had enough for one night. As the other radioman passed, he said, "I know you fuckers did something with your radio, and I'm going to find out what." I appreciated his emotion; I'd have felt the same way, but I was unnerved. Next morning, he stripped my radio down and found a damaged crystal.

LCpl ARMANDO GONZALES
Bravo Company, 1/9 _____

We got some sort of incoming every day—maybe only a round or two of heavy artillery or a few recoilless-rifle or mortar rounds, but something every day.

One day, as my fire team and two or three other guys sat around in my bunker—I was reading a book, a few of the guys were playing cards, the others were writing letters—we started getting hit by incoming. Suddenly there was a big *THUMP* and the whole bunker shook. We ran out to see what was what. We found a dud 82mm mortar round with its fins sticking right out of the roof of the bunker. It was a direct hit.

The nearest toilet to my bunker was an ammo box set over a hole in the ground and surrounded by a five-foot-high triple wall of sandbags. I was out there sitting on it one day when the other side of the Rock Quarry started taking incoming. I tried to finish up as fast as I could, but one of the first rounds to land on our side of the hill landed right behind me. It blew away the first sandbag wall, shredded the second layer, and moved the inner layer toward me. When I felt a big thump on my back, I upped and ran into the trenchline with my pants halfway up. As soon as the incoming lightened up and we all got up, one of the fellows milling around behind me said, "Oh my God! Gonzales, take off your flak jacket! Look!" I took it off and found a big chunk of shrapnel, about half the size of my fist, lodged in the back of my flak jacket.

Another time, I was standing around staring out of the

trenchline toward the Laotian border when, for no reason at all, I moved a few feet around a sharp corner. Seconds later, a round landed right in the trenchline. It killed a few Marines and blew out the corner in which I had been standing moments earlier.

Cpl DENNIS SMITH
Bravo Company, 1/26

This thing about women waiting back in The World was serious business. Showing your pictures—wives, girlfriends, kids—was a sort of sacred ritual. One soul brother from some bad-news Philly neighborhood was showing me an R-rated picture of his lady. I didn't want to comment on her looks, so I asked, "Who took the picture?" He got a funny look on his face.

Pfc LIONEL TRUFANT
106mm Platoon, 3/26

I remembered seeing the documentaries on Dienbienphu on television when I was a kid, so it naturally occurred to me that we were in a situation similar to the one the French had been in. Every day, in my mind, when the incoming got hot or when they probed our lines, I just *knew* it was going to be another Dien-bienphu. It was always in the back of my mind. We all envisioned that if they did hit us, they would send tanks down, probably at night. We heard they had rangefinders with which they could lock in on us when we fired a round, so we envisioned that our 106 would be useless after we got off only a very few rounds. Since the secondary line was in back of us, we wouldn't have anywhere to go if we did get hit. Getting back depended on our being able to talk to the people behind us on the land line we had to the rear, but the incoming often broke the communications wire. About all we figured we could do if we were attacked was fire as many rounds as possible, stick a thermite grenade in the breech, stick another thermite grenade in the ammunition, head for the trenches, and hope for the best.

LCpl PHIL MINEER
Bravo Battery, 1/13 _____

So many guys were getting wounded or blown up at Khe Sanh, and it got so hard to find replacements, that they cut a deal with the guys in the brig at Danang. They offered to commute their sentences if they did the rest of their time at Khe Sanh. Real encouraging.

BOB BREWER
Quang Tri Province Senior Adviser _____

The "military mind" tended to give low priority to the local people and their social, economic, and political needs. The brass tried, but most of the time their efforts fell just a tad short of the mark. For example, KSCB in late February or early March had information that an important NVA headquarters was operating in a village not far from the abandoned Huong Hoa District Headquarters town of Khe Sanh. Somehow this village had not been utterly destroyed yet, and some elderly civilians were still living there. I was asked my opinion as to what should be done. I suggested that a surgical combat-team heliborne operation be sent in under cover of CS or CN gas to capture as much of the NVA brass and documents as possible *and* remove any civilians who wanted out. KSCB used gas, all right. They used time-delay-fused gas rounds to force everybody out into the open, then followed with high-explosive rounds to obliterate them.

LCpl KEVIN MACAULEY
Bravo Company, 3rd Recon Battalion _____

We steadily improved our bunkers and company area. We dug a trenchline between all the bunkers so that we were below the ground most of the time we were in the company area. Our captain decided we might have to use the trenches to fight from, so he ordered us to dig roll-outs on the trench floor. We cut into the wall of the trench at the floor line and dug a hollow out of the wall that we could roll into if the NVA grenaded the trench. We now had positions two and a half feet to four feet below the trench floor for added protection from shrapnel from grenades, mortars, or rockets. However, our captain stated that they weren't deep enough; he wanted them so deep that we could stand in them and have the floor of the trench at chest level. The trench became six feet deep and the roll-outs were five feet deeper than that. Anyone sitting on the floor of a roll-out was now ten feet below ground level. What we were going to do from this position to fight the NVA was beyond the comprehension of many of us in Recon.

As the weather began to clear up for longer periods each day, the sun beat down on the base and baked the ground cement-hard. The constant shelling and rumbling of the trucks, jeeps, tanks, and other vehicles caused cracks to appear along the lip of our trench. One day, two Marines from my platoon were sitting in their roll-out, scooping the dirt that had fallen into the floor. I was about twenty feet away from them when I heard a muffled *thump*. I didn't know what it was. The captain happened to be walking by when a young corporal from Hawaii started yelling at him— yelling that it was his fault they were dead. I still didn't realize what was going on, but then it dawned on me. The earth was so dried out that about ten feet of the trench wall had collapsed down on the roll-out. Two Marines were buried under all that dirt and no one was doing anything.

I jumped into the middle of the pile of dirt and started digging for all I was worth. Someone handed me an entrenching tool, and I used that. Our company exec chased everyone from the immediate area, fearing further cave-ins. Pfc Daigle helped me with the digging; as I grew winded, he took over. As he tired, I went back to work. We estimated where the two Marines were and used the entrenching tool in the area between them. As the minutes passed away, I began to wonder whether our efforts were going to be futile. After what seemed like an eternity—ten or twelve minutes—I uncovered one Marine's head. It was bent forward and his face was in a little pocket formed between his updrawn knees. As I pulled his head free, he began to cough and cry. He was alive! He strangled and screamed until we freed his arms. We soon found the other Marine, but he was unconscious.

His face was looking upward as the dirt fell on him, and his mouth was full of the red dirt. The corpsmen started working on him even before we freed him. Someone started to force air into the second Marine's lungs. He did not respond, and he was still unconscious when they carried him to Charlie-Med. I still don't know whether he lived or died. The first Marine, Pfc Ed Stevens, was also carried to Charlie-Med for medical attention. He seemed to be in shock.

I slumped down in the trench; I was exhausted, both physically and emotionally. Guys from the company kept coming over, congratulating me for the job I had done. I felt drained. Later, that evening, I experienced my most rewarding moment in Vietnam. As I sat in my bunker, Stevens came back in, sat down next to me, and threw his arms around me. I held him as we both cried for a while. My tears were tears of joy as I realized I had saved another human being's life. His tears were tears of thanks. I told him I was only doing my job and that I was sure he would have done the same for me. He left the bunker. I don't remember seeing him anymore. I think he was medevacked from Khe Sanh soon after the incident. Being buried alive for as long as he was would have affected me, too. I went to sleep that night with the glow of self-satisfaction about me. I had made a difference.

1stLt FRED McGRATH
Bravo Battery, 1/13

Mail service was sporadic. But when it did arrive, you could almost feel the difference—and certainly taste the difference. The men would receive some of the oddest foodstuffs, like goose-liver paté! It made for a good laugh, but its rib-sticking properties were suspect! Jelly beans and peanut butter were my gifts from The World. As far as I can recall, no Marine in Bravo Battery received a Dear John letter, which, given the circumstances, could have had a disastrous effect. News from The World was always welcome. The *Pacific Stars and Stripes* was a particular favorite. Each copy was completely dog-eared by the time the next one arrived. And, although we began to think women really did fold in the middle, *Playboy* magazine was a cheered event.

I SCREAM, YOU SCREAM . . .

LCpl PHIL MINEER
Bravo Battery, 1/13 _____

For about a twenty-day period we were cut down to a quart of water. We had a water trailer, but it kept getting shrapnel through the side, so we kept losing all our water. We also got one box of C-rations per day during that time. There wasn't even enough for the rats to eat.

Cpl ALLAN STAHL
Logistics Support Unit _____

They dropped in a palletload of ice cream one day, and one of our forklift operators drove it back to the supply dump. What a terrible thing to do to us! We couldn't figure out how to disperse it without risking someone's life. We couldn't call all the troops in, and we couldn't get it out to them. It was getting dark. What an absurdity!

So, in walks the major in charge of the Air Force radar units. He knew there was ice cream on the base, and he told our skipper, also a major, that he wanted it for his troops. Our CO was sweating bullets over the dilemma the ice cream caused; he was genuinely trying to get the ice cream to the troops. He didn't need this Air Force guy, who, incidentally, rotated through the combat base with all the other Air Force guys for only a week at a time. The CO said, "I'll get you your ice cream when everybody else gets theirs. But you get fed last. I feed Marines first." The Air Force guy proceeded to get on the CO: "I want my ice cream!" They were nose to nose, arguing like two little kids. The Air Force major said his people were sharing the same risks as the Marines, and our major said that the Marines had been there for two months without rotating out like the Air Force guys.

LCpl CHARLIE THORNTON
Lima Company, 3/26 _____

We were rationing water when we learned that a resupply aircraft had dropped hundreds of gallons of ice cream at the airstrip.

What a laugh. We are rationing water and the Marine Corps sends in ice cream! We never saw any evidence of ice cream. It probably melted on the runway.

Cpl ALLAN STAHL
Logistics Support Unit

The ice cream melted on the pallets. There was no way to distribute it.

▣

Sgt MIKE STAHL
4.2-inch Mortar Battery, 1/13 (Hill 861)

Sometime in early March, we began hearing the engine noises of one armored vehicle of some sort as it moved around the base of the hill at night. The noises went on for a while. We had been able to see Lang Vei the night it was overrun, and we had seen the PT-76s firing that night. We knew what the PT-76s could do.

There had been Ontos on Hill 861 at various times before the siege, and there was a nice little tank trail from the bottom to the top of the hill. We had nothing with which to block the trail against an attack by a tank.

Finally, after about three days, I decided to go down and take a look. I had thoughts of getting a Medal of Honor. I thought I'd go down there, knock off that one tank, and come back. How hard could it be? I didn't know enough to realize that wherever there's a tank there's infantry, too.

I took a LAAW and extended it before I left the perimeter. I also had a .45-caliber pistol. I left early in the morning, after daylight, and descended through thick jungle paralleling the tank trail to the bottom of the hill. I got down to a point where I could see it, but all I could see through the bushes was where the turret met the hull. That's what I aimed for.

As I started to aim in on it, I began to hear voices. Vietnamese voices. They were to my left, they were to my right, they were behind me. Somehow I had gotten into their position. I figured I was screwed, that I might as well take my shot. The pucker factor was maximum, or I'm sure I wouldn't have missed. But, sure as hell, I squeezed off the LAAW and missed by a mile.

Immediately, AKs started to pop and I heard the *whir* of the motors as the PT-76's main gun was brought to bear on my position. I stood up and ran like a bat out of hell, straight up the hill, straight up the tank trail to the top. They were popping rounds in from everywhere, but they never hit me.

Chapter 25

MARCH 10

MEDEVAC

LCpl CHARLIE THORNTON
Lima Company, 3/26 _____

On March 10, during a routine incoming barrage, an artillery round hit the treeline just above my bunker and exploded in the air. The blast knocked me ten feet across the bunker floor into a dirt wall at the other end. I awoke dazed, my ears ringing, and I felt as if a mule had kicked me in the chest. As I began to check myself for injuries, I found shrapnel wounds in my right leg and left hand. While examining myself further, I had a sensation of something warm running down my shirt. In the dim light of the bunker I could see that the left side of my shirt was soaked in blood that was running into my trousers. There was a hole in my chest the size of a half-dollar. Shrapnel had entered the left side of my chest at a downward angle, exited under my armpit, and creased my bicep. After being stabilized by a corpsman, I was taken to the airstrip for evacuation.

Pfc LIONEL TRUFANT
106mm Platoon, 3/26 _____

I hated it when I was sent down to be part of the medevac detail at Charlie-Med. Number one, Charlie-Med was near the airstrip,

351

which was hit the most with the heaviest incoming. Number two, I saw suffering every day at Khe Sanh—we were always seeing someone getting it or who had been hit—but Charlie-Med had worse suffering than anywhere.

We sat there, waiting in trenches and behind bunkers. When the helicopters came in, we had to run out and put the stretchers aboard. It was timed to the second. The helicopters had to judge when to come in because they were going to draw incoming, and we had to judge when to bring the wounded out to put them on the helicopters. When the signal was given, two guys would grab hold of each stretcher, haul ass, and stick them on the helicopters.

LCpl CHARLIE THORNTON
Lima Company, 3/26

The evacuation process at Khe Sanh may have been one of the worst fates that a Marine could encounter. Helicopters would land on the runway to pick up the dead and wounded. Each time they landed, the NVA gunners would pound the airstrip with incoming rounds. Charlie-Med had a deep bunker next to the airstrip where the wounded would be placed on stretchers to be taken to the helicopters as they arrived. As I lay there in the bunker on the stretcher, I heard the incoming rounds begin to impact the airstrip, so I knew the helicopters were approaching. It was a truly helpless feeling as two Marines picked up the stretcher and began running toward the helicopters. I could see the impact of the rounds "walking" down the runway as the NVA gunners zeroed in on the helicopters. The helicopters used to evacuate the wounded were mostly H-34s, which were widely used in Korea for medevacs. Once we were loaded into the helicopter, it seemed like an eternity before we left the ground. The helicopter had so many wounded Marines aboard that it actually had to get a running start to get off the ground.

I can remember vividly looking out the helicopter door as we circled Khe Sanh and seeing the trenchlines and bomb-scarred terrain become smaller as the helicopter flew higher. I thanked God for allowing me to be wounded in order to escape that hellhole.

Maj TOM COOK
26th Marines Assistant Logistics Officer

Once I saw several Marines loading stretchers on a CH-46 when mortar rounds started coming in. The helicopter took off while two Marines who weren't flying out were still on the rear ramp, standing on the cargo rollers. All of a sudden, here come these two bodies, off the ramp from about fifty feet in the air. One, who was due to be rotated the next day, wound up with a broken leg, and both were shaken up, but they both survived.

Another time, a CH-46 which was coming in hovered and fooled around back and forth—obviously he wanted to land but didn't know where to set down. But the NVA knew exactly where he would land if he ever figured it out, and they were ready for him. Finally, after about ten minutes, he settled down onto the pad. He was down only fifteen seconds when a recoilless rifle round hit right in the center of the aircraft. The pilot immediately took off. He got 600 or 700 feet down the runway and then crashed.

MARCH 11

LCpl MIKE GUESS
Charlie Company, 1/9

After I got back from my one-day medevac to Dong Ha, I went back to my unit and started right in re-digging my new bunker in the exact spot that the round that had gotten me had hit. I was sure it was like lightning, that two rounds wouldn't hit in the same place. This was the Taj Mahal of bunkers. It was off the trench-line, then into the trenchline, then down about four feet, then in again. If the NVA wanted to get me, they'd have to come in there and get me. I was ready for them as much as I could be.

As I was digging my new bunker, I noticed some replacements moving up the hill toward Bravo Company. There he was—Danny Meysembourg, a guy who lived in my neighborhood back in Madison, Wisconsin. I couldn't believe it! It was like I was dreaming, like a mirage. After that, I walked up the trenchline every chance I got to visit Danny. We shared our letters from home or just talked. One day we got just about a direct hit on his bunker that buried us. After other Marines dug us out, we found that all we had gotten was a little shaken up; nothing hurt except our pride.

I should have qualified for my second Purple Heart, but the CO wouldn't give it to me because I wasn't supposed to be up at Bravo Company when I had my bell rung. I was disappointed because it took three Purple Hearts to get out of country. I didn't want to get killed and I originally didn't want any Purple Hearts, but after I got the first one, I started thinking about getting the other two I needed. I wanted to get out of there.

Danny Meysembourg lasted fourteen or fifteen days. On March 11, a direct hit got Danny. He didn't even know what hit him.

MARCH 15

HM3 BILL GESSNER
Delta Company, 1/9

15 March

Dear Family:
How are you all on this overcast day? I am pretty good. A little head cold, that's all.

Three water buffalo presented themselves near our wire today. Since they could have set off mines, we got permission to shoot them. Three of us went after them. I had the one on the right who refused to show me anything but his south end. The others had good shoulder shots. Sergeant Grubbs opened up on his and dropped him where he stood. The other guy, Staff Sergeant Duden, got a body hit. Me—I think I hit his tail.

Needless to say, I was upset that mine got away clean, but it was a diversion from the daily routine anyway. We got credit for one "KIA" and two "WIAs." The 3rd Platoon didn't get a significant wound two days ago when they spotted one, and the whole platoon opened up on him, too. So I don't feel too bad. What a title for a book—"Water Buffalo Hunting in Vietnam—A Dual Danger."

All has been quiet here for some time. Well, at least no one wounded seriously. My house took a direct hit yesterday. Thank God I built it strong. The only things I sweat are delayed fuses. So far, the gooks have shot only two in our area of the hill. So I guess they save them for Khe Sanh itself.

Well, I must close. Much love to you all.

P.S. I have a gray-black Vandyke at the present.

Pfc LIONEL TRUFANT
106mm Platoon, 3/26

One day, two water buffalo came in toward our line. We didn't know what the hell they were, but they gave us the opportunity to get some frustration off. We opened fire on them. I'm sure we didn't kill them outright, but an M-79 round hit one on the butt.

MARCH 18

PAYBACK

LCpl PHIL MINEER
Bravo Battery, 1/13

All the movies I watched as a kid—the John Wayne movies—all that bullshit went out the window at Khe Sanh. Nineteen-year-olds are supermen, immortal? Most of us were sure we were going to get blown the hell away. Every day we saw somebody getting hit— a guy losing an arm, a leg, getting blown all to shit.

When I was in Khe Sanh, I wore what everybody called a diaper—lower-body armor. I always kept my flak jacket buttoned, and I always wore my helmet. Stuff was always going through the air. You never knew.

Cpl Lou Goi was older. He was twenty-two, and going bald. His hole was right across from mine. We always used to get in Lou's shit about buttoning up his flak jacket. One day he got tired of being in his hole—being *driven* in that damn hole—and he went outside. He was going to eat his chow sitting on the side of the parapet. One of the guys said something about his flak jacket, and Lou said, "Fuck it."

By that time, the NVA had been trenching in. They had trenches right out in front of the wire, maybe eight hundred or a thousand meters. We could see them with the naked eye when they came up to relieve themselves. They had a 57mm recoilless rifle on sticks. A couple guys would lift it up, lay it on ground level, and take a shot into the combat base. A round from the recoilless rifle hit to Lou's left. The full effect got him in the chest and the head.

1stLt PAUL ELKAN
Bravo Battery, 1/13 _____

I heard this call for a corpsman over the phone from Gun-4. It was my practice to go out to wherever anybody was wounded and try to help. Two people were wounded out there. One of them had a chunk of shrapnel near his heart; we got him to the aid station. I couldn't tell who the other one was. The entire top of his body had been blown off from the left shoulder to the right side. There was no chest and no head. I had the troops cover him with a blanket and get him out of there; I didn't want people getting too shook up, looking at what was left of the body. As I was walking back to the executive officer's pit, I asked somebody who the dead man was. "He was Corporal Goi, sir."

I got back to the exec pit and broke down. That was the only one that got right next to me. I had known Louis Goi a long time. I got him a job and tried to keep him in the battalion fire-direction center so he wouldn't get hurt. I promoted him to corporal just a few days before he got killed. I never let anyone get close to me after that. It was too hard.

LCpl PHIL MINEER
Bravo Battery, 1/13 _____

That day, after Lou was killed, I was in the exec pit with the skipper, Capt James Uecker, talking to Regiment, telling them that this mission or that mission was shot, and also recording everything that was going on. As we were firing, the NVA got lucky with a recoilless rifle round. It came in the entrance to the exec pit. I got a little concussion when I was knocked back against the wall. I seriously thought the skipper got it. The exec, Lieutenant Elkan, was sleeping in the back of the pit, but he sure woke up when the round came in! It threw up a bunch of red dirt that all fell on the lieutenant. When he got up, he looked like a red Stepin Fetchit.

By the time I left the exec pit after firing the Mini-Arclight, I was pissed. I hooked up with a kid named Smith, who was a forward observer with 2/26. I said, "We gotta get them bastards. They got Lou." Smith had field glasses, so we stood out there for hours, waiting for someone to come up out of the NVA trench. Meantime, we were hooked up with my gun, Gun-3. We leveled the tube for direct fire and I calculated for an airburst with a VT fuse. The only problem was that the fuse was armed by means of centrifugal force only after it had flown a certain distance. Eight hundred meters was a little short, so I had to cheat a little. As a result, the first fuse started smoking and we had to get it off the gun real quick and throw it. But we finally worked it out. After a long wait, a lot of NVA got brave and came up. We took the shot, and it went off about twenty-five feet over their heads. That was the first time I realized I was a little sick. When I saw those body parts going through the air, I was glad. I was really glad. That one was for Lou Goi.

MID-MARCH

Cpl ALLAN STAHL
Logistics Support Unit _____

Everybody had bad days or pet bitches, but I never saw any bad morale. I never saw a minute of bad morale. Certainly, there were none of the morale problems depicted in the newspapers. My attitude—the attitude of the average Marine there—was that this was our moment in history. There was no doubt that they were coming through the wire. That was accepted fact. But there was no doubt that we were going to deal with them. There was no lack of confidence. Each individual had to live with the fact that he was going to be one of the survivors, but that there weren't going to be very many. We all looked at ourselves as future survivors of Khe Sanh.

Pfc LIONEL TRUFANT
106mm Platoon, 3/26 _____

We heard a rumor that the NVA were going to attack us in biplanes. We didn't know what to expect.

Cpl ALLAN STAHL
Logistics Support Unit _____

My CO called me in late one day and said, "Stahl, do you know anybody over at Regimental Communications?" I told him that I knew a fellow communicator over there, so he said, "Get your ass over there. I just spoke with someone who told me there are MiGs heading south toward us. Find out if it's true." The skipper was really nervous, so I hightailed it over to the regimental communications center. It was pandemonium there, sheer panic. There was obviously something going on. I found my friend and asked what was going on. "They picked up planes on the radar. They're coming in from the west. They're over Laos and headed this way, and the Navy can't get them."

I had seen the effects of bombing every day I had been at Khe Sanh. I knew what an air strike could do. This was serious. I ran out of the comm center to report. The whole base went on Red Alert and everybody went underground.

Thirty minutes later we started asking ourselves, "Where are the MiGs?" There were certainly no airplanes above us. Soon, word came out that there were no MiGs. The Red Alert was relaxed, and that was the end of that. But we had to know what had caused the flap, so the skipper sent me back to the comm center to find out. The enlisted pipeline gave as absolute gospel that a bunch of planters from Cambodia were flying up in biplanes to get a firsthand look at the war. They were intercepted by the Navy and turned back. Unbelievable! I have no idea if that's what really happened.

LCpl ARMANDO GONZALES
Bravo Company, 1/9 _____

We had a thing we called "doing the job." It meant intentionally acquiring a wound, usually a self-inflicted wound. One day, during incoming, one of the fellows raised his hand above the trench, hoping to get it nicked. The shrapnel took off the whole hand. He got more than he bargained for, but he got out of Khe Sanh alive.

Capt JIM LESLIE
26th Marines Assistant Communicator _____

In mid-March, water was at an all-time low. By then, it was used only for drinking, for coffee, or for brushing teeth. It was not for washing one's face, showering, or washing clothes. This was not a big problem, as most Marines by this time had reverted to their basic animal needs—living in a hole, eating one C-ration a day, and existing from one day to the next. The mind was in neutral gear, no longer creative, intuitive, or willing to learn. The mind was just idling. The "real world" was a million miles away, something we would probably never see again.

First Lieutenant Jack Blyze and I were ambling up the road inside the perimeter along the airstrip. I don't recall where we were going. As we approached the old Staff-and-Officers' Club, Jack remarked about how the club used to be a nice place to go after work, before the offensive began.

"Let's go check it out," he said. I recall orders being passed that no one was to go near the old club, as it had been targeted by the NVA gunners. Each day it was the first place to receive incoming artillery in hopes of catching some of the leaders there as they had done in early January. No one went near the club, partly because it was off limits and partly because of the beating it took daily from the NVA artillery, rockets, and mortars. At about 1400, we decided that the NVA artillerymen were probably asleep, so we proceeded over to the club.

The club was mostly underground, with only the roof above-ground. The tin roof had a few sandbags on top to keep the tin from blowing off during windstorms. It also had large, gaping holes from many rounds of artillery and mortar shrapnel.

We walked down eight steps to the plywood door, which was secured with a hasp and lock. Jack solved that problem with a strong kick with the sole of his boot. The door swung open. It was surprisingly light inside because of the holes in the roof. The red plastic bar tables and chairs were upside down, scattered over the floor. It was apparent that no one had been inside the club for months. We righted a table and two chairs as we surveyed the situation.

We found the greatest treat of all lying behind the bar—a full rack of red pistachio nuts. This was a find too good to be true! Salty nuts, untouched by the mice or rats. I brought the whole rack of nuts over to our table and we sat down, took out our canteens of precious water, and set them on the table. What a find we had!

We began to eat the nuts and drink our canteens of water just like we were in a real bar with real beer. Just having something a little more than the next Marine made us feel superior. We talked about unimportant things as we broke open the red-shelled pistachio nuts and sipped on our canteens of lukewarm water.

"I wonder what's behind that door," Jack said. Simultaneously, we both got up and walked over to the plywood door in the corner. Without command, the sole of each of our boots struck the door at the same time. The door swung inward and—would you believe!—we found a room full of Budweiser beer. Cans and cans of beer! The room must have been ten feet square, and it was *full* of beer. Cases of beer! More than we could ever drink. We each grabbed a case, carried it over to our table, and popped a top. We were in heaven. We toasted the Marines, our boss—Maj John Shepard—the Commandant, President Johnson, and the war protesters. We each drank a can, then a second, then a third. Then we slowed down. We propped our feet up on a couple of extra chairs, broke open pistachio nuts, and drank beer. We were in seventh heaven.

Two hours and almost two cases of beer later, a shadow swept across the hatch. Then the shadow returned. We heard footsteps coming down the steps. Our boss, Major Shepard, had tracked us down. He stood in the doorway, hands on his hips, and shouted, "What in the hell are you two doing? I've been looking everywhere for you. I thought you were in trouble, and here you are drinking beer." Then, after a slight pause, "Hey, where'd you find that beer?"

We told our story as we cracked open a beer for the major. By a few beers and a few bags of nuts later, Major Shepard was one of the boys. He helped us to demolish the rest of the second case of beer.

"We must make this beer available to the rest of the Marines," Major Shepard said at length. So we stumbled back to our bunker two hours later and announced our find over the radio to our friends in other companies. At dusk, we loaded cases of beer on jeep trailers and passed the treasure out to lines of open-armed Marines who lined up to get their rations of gold. Of course, we took several cases back to our bunker for storage. We had a great day; we had found a fortune and shared our wealth with our friends.

SSgt HARVE SAAL, USA
FOB-3

One day, just after the end of a barrage, a newly arrived Special Forces radio operator was told to run a new field-phone wire system from the main bunker to the front gate. The "newbee" was gone for what seemed to be a long time, so someone went looking for him. The young radioman was found sitting down in the bunker at the front gate. He was completely out of breath; he looked like he had just finished running a marathon. When asked if he had run the field-phone line to the bunker, the young man said he had. The guy who found him picked up the field phone and tried to call the main bunker, but there was no answer. Asked why the field phone wasn't working yet, the radioman pointed down to the *full* roll of wire on which he was seated. "You mean I ran this heavy roll of wire all the way out here and now it don't work?"

1stLt FRED McGRATH
Bravo Battery, 1/13

Life at Khe Sanh was somewhat different from other areas in I Corps. You developed a bunker mentality at Khe Sanh. When I was at Phu Bai or Dong Ha, we had sandbagged holes to jump in, but we slept and moved aboveground. Not so at Khe Sanh.

The situation at Khe Sanh tended to isolate one unit from another. I cannot remember having any contact with any other unit, except by radio or telephone. It was as if we had our own little war going on, and, although we knew the 26th Marines were out there, we were alone. At night, we would recieve H&I fires from a U.S. Army 175mm gun unit at the Rock Pile. They would shoot at prearranged targets just outside our perimeter. Fortunately, they were good shots. But radio and wire were our only physical contact with the rest of the base. It is easy, now, to understand why that had to be. But there were times when we wondered if the grunts really were up in those hills.

1stLt NICK ROMANETZ
Charlie Company, 1/26

Some of the reasons Charlie Company didn't do much real patrolling was because of the terrain in our sector and the fact that Lang Vei had been overrun, because we knew there were snipers out, and most of all because there was the threat of a large-scale attack. And, of course, the loss of the Jacques platoon had an impact. However, somewhere into March, we were finally allowed to do some patrolling. I got the green light to take my platoon out to the Finger, about 800 meters in front of us. I was very cautious and concerned that we might get ambushed or come upon something like snipers in spiderholes who would shoot us after we walked by. Since the elephant grass was still pretty high in front of our position, we would have to stick pretty much to the trails. I took the platoon out and conducted a sweep from the left flank through the whole sector north of the combat base, where 1/26 had responsibility.

The battalion intelligence officer sent out an intelligence scout with us, to help us look for information or signs of enemy activity. When we came to a fork in the trail, I split the platoon and sent half up one trail and led the other half up the other trail. I wanted to at least stay in radio contact with the other half of the platoon. My gang stayed out for about another hour, sweeping along the Finger. We never found any enemy, and we could never make any radio contact with the other guys. They later swore they were up on the net, but the best I can figure, the sergeant I put in charge of the reinforced squad got a little uptight, shut his radio off, and headed right back into the combat base, as soon as we split up. The thing that really bugged me was that the intelligence scout went back and reported that we didn't find anything because we got lost.

Maj TOM COOK
26th Marines Assistant Logistics Officer

I don't know whose idea it was—it might have been mine—but at one time it was suggested that when the rear-area supply people didn't have a full aircraft they might put some fresh fruit aboard for us. Everybody thought that was a great idea, and the first morning we got a pallet of apples we thought it was great. We brought the pallet back and allocated apples out through the organization, trying to make sure nobody got cheated. From then on, we kept getting apples. Sometimes we got four or five pallets of them in one day. It just went on and on until we had pallets of apples sitting all over the combat base. But the people had had their fill of apples, so they just sat there—all over the place—rotting. Finally, during one of my nightly calls to Dong Ha, I asked them what the hell was going on: "I need artillery ammo in case we get attacked. What do you want us to do, throw apples at them?"

Cpl ALLAN STAHL
Logistics Support Unit _____

One day a guy we called Corporal Red herded a Marine grunt into our command post and told the major he had found the guy stealing food from one of our supply dumps. The major never batted an eye and said, "Corporal, I told you to just shoot the next son of a bitch you caught stealing food."

Of course, the major never actually had said that, but Red picked right up on it. "Yes, sir, you did. But I thought maybe you'd want to do it."

"No," the major picked up, "I don't *want* to do it. But I think we have to set an example around here."

The captive was shaking in his shoes when the major spoke directly to him for the first time in a real soft, easy manner. "Marine, you see how it is, don't you?" And the kid actually nodded his head. "Sure, you do. See, you probably think we get more to eat than anyone because we're the supply unit and all that stuff they fly in goes through here. You probably think it's okay to get a little for you and your buddies, huh?" The kid just kept nodding his head. "Well, son, take a look around here. You see any fat Marines in this bunker?" The kid looked around at us with big, wide eyes, then shook his head. "That's because we only take our share. In fact, we get fed last. Do you think you deserve more than any other Marine on the base?" The kid shook his head. "I told the corporal to shoot you, but I think he didn't because he feels we're all in this together. Do *you* feel we're all in this together?" The Marine nodded his head. "Maybe I ought to let the corporal take you out back, where you can settle it. Then one of you can have the ration." The Marine shook his head. "Well, are you going to do this anymore?" The Marine shook his head. "Look, you can't do this anymore. Pass the word around your unit that we're not keeping anything back from anyone." The kid walked out of there, all put back together. What psychology!

Capt EARLE BREEDING
Echo Company, 2/26 (Hill 861A)

I was relieved as Echo Company commander on March 8 and ordered to the battalion staff to take over as logistics officer. However, I kept hanging around on the hill until Battalion told me I absolutely had to turn Echo Company over to my relief. That was around a week after I was supposed to take off.

The first chopper I could get off 861A was a medevac, which took me straight to Dong Ha, where the 3rd Marine Division forward command post was set up. I got off the chopper looking like I'd just been through a battle. Almost right away, the division sergeant major came running out to tell me that the division chief of staff was upset because my uniform wasn't neat. The sergeant major took me down to the supply hooch, but the supply sergeant didn't want to give me fresh utilities because I wasn't a member of his battalion. The sergeant major told him he would if he wanted to live. Then, a short time later, I went into the Officers' Club for a drink. Naturally, I kept my helmet on. Some staff captain started going on about how, since I had not uncovered, I would have to buy everyone a round. Then they wanted to take my pistol away. Next, I went up to the showers. Some lieutenant colonel I met there began telling me how tough they had it at Dong Ha. He even showed me a little bitty shrapnel hole in the corner of the plywood shower hooch. I agreed with him that he was really seeing the war.

Chapter 26

LCpl PHIL TORRES
India Company, 3/26

I landed at the Khe Sanh airstrip on February 14 and was immediately sent to help man the perimeter lines with Lima Company, 3/26. There was very little movement on the lines; everybody had to stay under cover, everybody had to wear flak jackets and helmets. Heaven help anyone caught without his flak jacket and helmet on. This was the first time since I had arrived in Vietnam, a few days earlier, that I worked with a loaded weapon. Occasionally I heard a spurt of small-arms fire or a barrage of "freight trains" coming in overhead, with explosions nearby. I kept thinking, What the heck have I gotten myself into? It was never-ending. A tent would get hit, some stored ammunition would go off, a Marine would be hit by shrapnel, rockets would hit the base.

On my second day at Khe Sanh, February 15, all the new guys were told to test-fire their weapons, to make sure they were okay. Then some of us were assigned to India Company, which was on Hill 881S. Others were assigned to Mike Company, also on Hill 881S, and Kilo Company, which was on Hill 861. As we boarded the CH-46 helicopters, there was a lot of talk about 881S. Even before I had left the States, people who were coming back from Nam were talking about 881S—about blood and guts, and all the glory. Fear started creeping in as we were told that helos were being blasted right out of the air as they tried to land on the hill. They told us that our chopper would take all kinds of fire when it tried to land—mortars, machine guns, and small arms. They told us we would *not* be getting 122mm rockets because of their trajectory. We heard about .51-caliber machine guns ripping through the helos, cutting Marines in half. The likelihood of becoming a casualty at this early stage was very high.

There was a lot of noise, a lot of commotion, as we arrived to land on the hill. I understand that there was a .51-caliber trying to cut the chopper down, that we came very near to losing the chopper and all the troops in it.

As soon as the chopper hit the ground on the hill, we had to move about a hundred meters, run from the saddle between India and Mike companies to the top of the hill, which was India Company's area. That had to be the roughest hundred meters I ever crossed. I was scared, there was a lot of noise, a lot of gunfire, I didn't know which way it was going, or who was firing what. I was told that the enemy was going to wipe us out. I believed everything I heard. Machine guns were shooting at us, and there were snipers in the treeline on the next hill over who were shooting at us, trying to pick off the people trying to get off the helicopter.

I met my new company commander, Capt Bill Dabney, just as I finished crossing the hundred-meter open space. He was a big Marine—a giant Marine—who didn't seem scared of anything. This guy looked like he could eat rocks. He wasn't getting down, he wasn't doing anything. He was just out there, making sure we were getting to the top of the hill all right and putting us into the trenches. He was not standing in the trench, he was standing outside, pushing us in.

Cpl TERRY STEWART
Mike Company, 3/26

The day-to-day life on Hill 881S was a combination of many things, the most notable of which were the frustrations of being confined in a static position and unable to carry the fight to the enemy, the loneliness, the dreary, sometimes ugly weather, and the feeling of uselessness. The morale, however, was very high in spite of the many negative factors that could have—should have—dominated our spirits.

For the most part, we spent our days talking of home, girls, cars, girls, food, girls, sports, girls, and, most important, girls. Quite often the talk was serious—of family and loves won and lost. The war and the home front's attitudes were also heavy topics. I can honestly say that every man I'd spoken to felt "right" about being in Nam.

There was maintenance to perform, as well. This was basically tending to our weapons and equipment, and the constant work we performed on our fortifications and trenches.

We had a couple of small, Japanese-type transistor radios in the group, but batteries were always a big problem. We managed to rig a squad-radio battery and some comm wire to run the radios. The scratchy music was like a live concert to us. Mostly we listened to Hanoi Hannah.

We nearly always had some kind of a battle with the rock apes. These feisty primates would sneak up on us and frighten the living shit right out of us. I know of one case where one literally did just that. The damn thing got up on a moonless night and grabbed hold of the muzzle of a man's rifle. When he did, he screamed like a woman being raped and jumped up and down. The Marine, frightened beyond description, screamed, let go of his bowels, and then pulled the trigger. The two of them screaming and the rifle going off on a long blast alerted everyone on the line. Instantly, men were up and firing, believing that somewhere in the pitch blackness we were being attacked by the whole North Vietnamese Army. It was frightening, but funny as hell when it was over.

We had a bit of a ritual with the flag ceremony each day. This we shared with India Company, too. In the saddle between our two ends of the hill there was a place we called No-Man's-Land. Set out there was a radio antenna that we rigged as a flagpole. It wasn't very high. The NVA had No-Man's-Land zeroed in with their 82mm mortars real good. They could hit anywhere in the saddle that they wanted to. Each day, two Marines would crouch in the trench just before 0800 and then dash out to raise the flag. As soon as they cleared the trench, we could hear the enemy mortars fire. The two men had exactly twenty-two seconds to get out there, raise the colors, salute, and get back before the rounds impacted. This same ritual was performed at night. The NVA rarely fired more than just two rounds, and not once did anyone ever get hurt during Colors. There were some close calls, but not hits.

LCpl PHIL TORRES
India Company, 3/26

We lived like moles, never leaving the trenches or bunkers. We were constantly digging—it never stopped—day and night, filling sandbags, digging trenches, carrying food. We were always laying German Tape concertina wire, which was very dangerous to work with because it was covered with razor blades. At least six separate strands surrounded the entire hill. There was about a hundred meters of clearance between the concertina and the trenches. We built homemade bombs from 106mm recoilless-rifle shell canisters filled with C4 plastic explosive, machine-gun links, expended M-16 cartridges, anything we could find. We put the bombs down by the concertina wire and ran a Claymore mine detonator line back to the trench.

We normally slept by day because the enemy could see us if we went into the trenches during the day. If they did see anyone, all hell would break loose. One person stepping out into the trenchline could bring in a whole barrage of mortars. Every morning the hill would be above what seemed to be a cloud. That was nice because the enemy was not able to see us and we would be able to come out of the trenches, see what needed fixing, and fix things up a little. As the sun heated up the air, the fog went away, the enemy was able to see us, and we had to stay in the trenches or bunkers. So we did most of the work by night. It was strange, living that way. It was difficult to sleep during the day, so we listened to the radio, to Hanoi Hannah. The 122mm rockets could not hit the hill because of their trajectory, but everything else could—mortars, artillery, machine guns, small arms.

I received a lot of mail, more than the average trooper. I would write a letter to my mother, and she would dramatize my letter—adding words here and taking them away there—and take it down to the Spanish newspaper in New York City, and they would print the letter with my address. I had all kinds of people—young females—writing to me. At times, I got as many as fifty or more letters from various states and even some from outside the United States. Most of them were Hispanic women who were proud to have one of their own fighting for the United States. They sent me pictures and body measurements and cute little lines asking me to look them up when I got back. That definitely picked up my morale, got me through some of the rough times.

Capt BILL DABNEY
India Company, 3/26 _____

We had a probe one night. We had several minor probes, but this, as best we could tell, was about a platoon-size probe, and the only thing we got out of it was the fact that the average Marine can throw a Mark-26 hand grenade downhill a hell of a lot better than the average NVA can throw a Chicom grenade uphill. It was a pretty one-sided sort of thing. I don't think we had two or three guys hurt. That was a pretty steep hill.[1]

LCpl PHIL TORRES
India Company, 3/26 _____

Because of the heavy concentration of enemy in the area, we were not able to send out patrols, but one of the things we constantly had to do on 881S was go out to man the listening posts. We went 200 or 250 meters outside the perimeter, about a quarter the way down the hill. The first time I went out, my third night on the hill, I almost didn't make it back. Sometime during the night, either us or some enemy snipers or an enemy patrol made some movement in the area near us. The people on our own lines, up the hill, decided to throw a couple of hand grenades in the direction of the movement. The grenades landed pretty near us. Luckily, we had a mortar crater that the three of us managed to squeeze into. Normally, a mortar crater wouldn't hold one person, but we managed to find room for three. Some of the grenades were landing a couple of meters away.

Cpl TERRY STEWART
Mike Company, 3/26 _____

We sometimes played games with the NVA. One game was
"Maggie's Drawers." Maggie's Drawers is what Marines call the
red flag that is waved across the face of a target at the rifle range
when the shooter completely misses the target. Well, we made a
large bull's-eye target from a sleeve that went over a case of
C-rations. One side was split, and the cardboard was folded out
so that it was quite large. We propped this up just above our
trench, in a place not too near any of the bunkers. We put it up
just for the hell of it, with the hope that one night when the NVA
hit us, we would catch a stray round. The target sat there for a
few days without anything touching it. Soon we all forgot about
it. Then, one afternoon, we received a single sniper round. That
wasn't unusual, so we all just sort of ignored it. The first round
was followed by another and, a few minutes later, another.
Again, not too unusual, except that the rounds were all hitting in
the same place. Someone yelled that they were shooting at our
target, and everyone made a dash to get close enough to see. It
was foolish. If one mortar round had hit in the trench on either
side of that stupid target, it would have wiped out half of the
platoon. But we all wanted to see the sniper try to hit our target.
One of the guys slid into position under the target. He hastily
fashioned a sort of Maggie's Drawers from a rag and a piece of
stick. After the sniper fired again, the Marine waved the flag to
indicate a miss. Actually, the sniper had hit the lower edge of the
target with his last round. I guess that this really pissed off the
sniper and one of his friends. The sniper sent us three or four
quick rounds with his SKS, and then his pal cut into us with a
quick burst of .51-cal fire. Those .51s are huge rounds and no
joy to be anywhere near when they were fired in your direction.
The bunch of us scattered like bugs in the kitchen when the
lights come on.

A few days later, after talking about our little game and
having a laugh, one of the men was moving down the trench to
return to his bunker and, for no apparent reason, jumped onto
the berm and began waving his arms and yelling, "Get me, you
motherfuckers." He had no sooner gotten the words out of his
mouth than the big machine gun barked and a round nearly took

the guy's head off. The platoon corpsman kept him alive for two whole days. He died just as a medevac was coming in.

RESUPPLY

LCpl PHIL TORRES
India Company, 3/26

A lot of chopper pilots got scared when they caught a lot of fire. They often released their external loads a little too soon or a little too late, and a lot of the food landed outside the India Company perimeter, in enemy territory. We had to send out patrols at night, secure the area, and get our food. Sometimes we had to fight for our food because the enemy wanted it, too. Many times, we had no food or water. Sometimes, days passed with no resupply whatsoever, and all the food would run out. When that happened, we scrounged through packs and bunkers to see what kind of food we hadn't wanted earlier. When we ran out of that, we went through the trash pit to get the little cans of jelly, peanut butter, and cheese most guys threw away. We had fights over those little cans. Marines offered fifty dollars, a hundred dollars for a can of food scrounged from the trash pit. Usually, the Marine with the food laughed and said something like, "What am I going to do with money? I don't need money; I need food." I know people who ate C-rat cigarettes, just to get something on their stomachs. At the time, none of us knew that Captain Dabney had quite a bit of food stored underneath his bunker. It was there for a *real* emergency. He would have taken care of us.

Capt BILL DABNEY
India Company, 3/26

At the beginning of the monsoon season, about the end of October 1967, we were issued rainsuits, sized a certain mix of small, medium, and large. About the middle of February, it was cold up there at night in those hills, foggy. I sent down a request for some more rainsuits. "Don't have them, not available," was the reply. Actually, I had to put an order out to the company, directing that anything they ordered through Sears or Mom had to be olive drab, because mothers were sending them air-sea-rescue-orange things.

I brought this up to the supply officer, a major or lieutenant colonel down at the 3rd Marine Division Command Post, and he said, "Well, when a guy rotates, take the rainsuit from him and give it to his replacement." Now, does this tell you something about the supply system? I didn't have anybody rotating. They all went out on stretchers or in body bags. And I have yet to discover a way, when a round goes through a man, to keep the son of a bitch from going through his rainsuit first! But the supply system didn't think that way.

Socks. Goddamn, I hate to think of how many messages were sent, asking for socks. "Hey, you guys got socks in your basic issue." No. "Give us some socks, I want two pair of socks per week per man." "Wash the ones you have." "With what?" Two helos a day to bring water to wash eighty-nine-cent socks! In *that* antiaircraft environment! But they never took it that far in the supply system. The supply system was just a supply system. Nobody programmed socks. They figured everybody over there for just a year and the number of pairs of socks that was issued out to be able to do it. No shit. But here we're sitting on this damn hill with no water and with troops standing in those lines night after night. We had trenchfoot, infection, jungle rot, all that stuff. Couldn't get any socks, never did get any socks. Maybe it was just my battalion, I don't know. Get some more water? Well, it took a helicopter for two canteens of water per man. And that wouldn't have been enough to wash one pair of socks. Ask a helicopter pilot whether he would rather haul up fifteen pounds of socks or 5,000 pounds of water! That kind of thing. I still haven't gotten over that.

Stretchers. Same thing. They couldn't seem to understand that the operational requirement for the guy that was hit was all that mattered in the end. For example, dustoff birds—medevac—carried spare stretchers. But we didn't evac with dustoff birds up on the landing zone. For one thing, when we got hit by NVA, we got hit hard. Too many medevacs for a regular medevac bird. For another, we usually needed an emergency resupply of ammo after the first-round bell, and had it planned and staged. So we put our wounded on the logistics bird, a CH-46 usually diverted from another mission. But they didn't carry spare stretchers. What now? We couldn't just dump the poor guy on the floor of the bird just so we could keep our stretchers! So, a dozen or so hit, and our company had no stretchers. Ever tried carrying a 200-pounder with a sucking chest wound in a poncho under fire? It takes four men—men needed up front! Two can do it with a stretcher. We sent messages asking that spare stretchers be carried aboard CH-46s for one-on-one trade during medevacs. They don't weigh that much and don't take up much space, broken down. Nothing ever came of it, though.

I never had a supply officer visit us. You know, they stay in warehouses. The stuff is all on the shelves real nice, but it doesn't help people! We put a requisition in for 60mm firing pins because they were wearing out and we were shooting mortars, 200 to 300 rounds a day. Couldn't get the goddamned things. Sent a gutsy, thieving PfC down to Danang with a bottle of Scotch that he'd scrounged up from someplace. He went to the Naval Support Activity, Danang, and found a chief petty officer who would machine those damn 60mm mortar firing pins on a lathe in return for the Scotch. Because the supply system said there weren't any in the system. Shit, make them! That's a pretty bottom-line sort of thing! Our flak jackets were falling apart—rotting. Sent down for forty or fifty replacements. Got a message back saying, "Send down the unserviceable ones and we'll survey them!" Yeah!

Slings and nets for helo external loads: Once we realized what the NVA could do to us, and that didn't take long, all supplies came in external. After two or three resupplies, five or ten birds each, we had a bunch of nets and slings on the hill. We'd get a message to stage them for pickups and reuse. We'd send back that it was too risky. We'd get a message back to have them ready for pickup or they couldn't resupply us anymore. So we complied. We lost three helo support teams doing that, two or three men each, and one bird, a CH-46. You see, the bird had to come in and hover exactly over the load, in the wind blowing across the crest, under .51-caliber and AK-47 fire, while the poor bastard from the helo support team stood, outlined against the skyline, on top of the pile, and married the sling to the cargo hook. If he didn't get hit by them firing at the bird, he'd marry, jump off, and run like hell for the nearest hole as the bird beat it out of there. They—the helo support and helo folks—both knew that the 120mm mortars were already on the way. We didn't always make it. One bird took a few rounds of .51 through the Plexiglas between the front seats just as the Marine was marrying the sling-loop to the hook. Well, the bird launched as if it had been shot from a slingshot, sling engaged, with the HST man still standing on the load. He tried to jump off, but his foot got caught in a net, and he rode down to Khe Sanh hanging upside down by one foot under the load, while his buddy with the radio, now deep in a hole, tried to tell the pilot what had happened! I guess the guy made it, but he never came back up the hill. I'm not sure I blame him! Now I don't know what nets and slings cost, but it was damned sure less than the cost of six Marines and a CH-46! And while we didn't have enough nets and slings in the Air Wing to avoid those risks, the fat cats were still driving Cadillacs at Miami Beach and the civilians at the supply depots were still beating the 1600 whistle out the gate. But I guess that'll never change.

Body bags. Couldn't get them. Ever watch rats crawling in and out of ponchos holding what's left of two men hit by a 152? The troops did! They were up there five days. Weather socked in. Ripe. We were told we couldn't bury them. We did anyway. Had to. Also told we couldn't send the bodies out external. Too risky to bring a bird down and load them. Too many men in one place. Took too long. So we buried them under piles of nets and slings and sent them out anyway. We did that several times. We'd tell the pilot after he'd lifted off. Those guys understood. The rear didn't.[2]

LCpl PHIL TORRES
India Company, 3/26

We lived like animals. We couldn't take any baths, we rarely shaved, we never had haircuts, we rarely changed clothes. We lived like moles: in by day, out by night. The only morale booster we had was mail. Sometimes they brought us hot beer, but any consumable item raised the morale, even hot beer. In our imaginations, it was ice cold. We craved for sweets, for anything that was different than the C-rats.

HM3 DAVID STEINBERG
India Company, 3/26

There was some obscure rule that if you're not paid within ninety days, you can leave combat. So they dropped us our pay.

HILL 861

Pfc ELWIN BACON
Kilo Company, 3/26 _____

The days following the January 21 attack on Hill 861 turned into weeks and months of a complete fortification program. Tunnels were built, and sandbags completely surrounded the hill. Days were filled with sandbag details or other working parties. We dug a system of tunnels that would have allowed the enemy to completely overrun our hill without their seeing one Marine. Supplies could be brought from the landing zone to the command post totally underground. We gradually built up one hell of a wire system and placed mines with 55-gallon drums of chopper fuel over them, to be set off by command from our bunkers if needed.

Hill 861 became a turkey shoot for snipers on both sides. We had to stand watches on a point looking north. If we saw any rockets being launched from the DMZ, we had a direct line with the main base at Khe Sanh. All we had to say was "Incoming," and the sound of sirens bellowed out from the valley to the south. Boredom became a daily thing, except for the nearly hourly mortar attacks that we began to tell the time of day by.

One day I was looking out toward the northern ridge of the hill next to us and saw someone watching us. I knew he was well out of distance to shoot him, and besides, we had orders not to fire unless we got permission from the command post. (Fire control, right?) Anyway, I knew he saw me, and the only thing I could think of was to wave to him. He disappeared immediately, but looked up once more before departing completely.

Another time I was on early-morning watch and was eating breakfast when I spotted a head directly across from mine. The NVA had a radio on his back and was watching our hill very closely. I got down off the top of my bunker very casual-like and went to my lieutenant's hut. I took his glasses and set them on my helmet. The lieutenant looked through and identified my find. He sent me down the trenches and up the back side of the hill to the 106mm recoilless-rifle position and had them site in on the dude. They were about to fire on the target when a 3.5-inch rocket tube went off. It turned out that the lieutenant had had them try to get the dude with it, but they missed. Anyway, the 106 fired on the same position and had a direct hit, but I never knew if we got the guy or not—thanks to the lieutenant.

Hill 861 became an island that was surrounded by a bunch of bees that were just waiting to get their stingers into us. Supplies were very hard to get in to us. Enemy fire took down some of the choppers, and I just knew those bastards were eating my cake from home and reading my mail. We were down to half a canteen of water a day and one box of C-rations each. It got to the point that Marines were sneaking out in front to search for food in the old crater we used as a garbage dump. It would drive us crazy at night because the rats would make so much noise in the garbage dump. We were never quite sure what kinds of rats were out there.

During the day we had a bird's-eye view of everything that took place in Khe Sanh, to our south, on Hill 861A, directly to our east, and up to the DMZ, to our north. Between the daily rocket attacks on Khe Sanh and the ever-increasing jet attacks on positions in every direction, we grew to be very nonchalant about the whole thing. Many times we took our chances by fixing the wire and mines out in front of our positions.

Many a night we stayed awake watching the B-52s working away around us, and that old standby, Puff the Magic Dragon, burning up the midnight oil and a lot of ammo. Puff was one of the principal deterrents of enemy buildup in that area. The short-timers were reluctant to leave the hill because of the chopper problem and the constant shit that was hitting Khe Sanh. At least we were only getting hit with mostly mortars and, once in a while, an RPG.

I began to get very disturbed over our lack of actually doing anything about the situation. We were not trained to just sit and take that kind of shit, day after day, with no way to get back at those bastards. The guys were doing anything to break the monotony. We played football in the open landing zone until someone would holler "Incoming." Then everyone would hit the trenches. Some guys would run around the hill naked in the heavy rain, singing songs. I spent some time making toy rockets out of the pop-up illumination canisters and loose increments from mortars, and sent them across to the next ridge. To the NVA we must have seemed crazy, and I think they were right. Stir-crazy.

From time to time, in the evening, we would hear the NVA

hollering at us from a distance. We had a Marine who spoke Vietnamese, and he would holler back at them. I never understood the conversation, but we all got a chuckle out of it.

There was a guy who flew overhead in a spotter plane and dropped some cartons of cigarettes down to us. I think his son was on the hill with us. We all appreciated the efforts that were made to get us some kind of supplies.

Sgt MIKE STAHL
4.2-inch Mortar Battery, 1/13 (Hill 861) _____

Water was a very big problem. When they couldn't get it in to us by helicopter, and we ran out, we had to send a heavily armed water detail to a stream at the bottom of the hill to fill canteens. That was always good for a few casualties.

There were always a few fresh NVA bodies in our wire. When the food situation got really bad a few times, some of us crawled out to retrieve the rice bags all of them carried. It was that grim.

Chapter 27

SSgt HARVE SAAL, USA
FOB-3

Early on the morning of March 20, about 0200, my recon team departed the FOB using a starless sky to cover our movement. The mission was a basic area recon. We moved several kilometers from camp and awaited first light. With the first hint of dawn, we began moving. At full light we entered a large defoliated mass of hilltops. We felt that we had NVA trackers on our trail.

All of a sudden, all hell broke loose. *Thump! Whoosh! Blam!* We were under NVA mortar fire. We were forced to move toward a hill without vegetation. Then, *Bam! Bam!*—the launching of two 122mm rockets. *Boom! Boom!*—they impacted in our area. Geez, I thought, they're shooting *rockets* at a small recon team; they must have millions of them! *Thump! Whoosh! Blam!* More mortar shrapnel whistled through the air.

I called in to a prearranged frequency and call sign which had been coordinated between myself and the Marine operations and artillery planner. I needed help to get that mortar fire stopped, even just a delay of a few minutes—anything! I had one wounded Bru, and I knew we would take more casualties if we didn't get some help soon. I made the recon team start moving

378

through an opening and up to the edge of a defoliated hill. I tried the radio again.

I finally got through to a Marine artillery officer, told him where the NVA mortar was located, and that we needed artillery fire placed on that location. He said, "Mission cannot be fired." I frantically asked, "Why can't you fire?" He said, "There's friendlies in the area!" It took me only a split second to realize what he had said and another second to notify him that those friendlies were us.

The Marines never did honor my request for artillery support that day. One Bru gave his life that day for the defense and security of that Marine officer, who was safe to hide inside a bunker and drink his hot cocoa and make life-or-death decisions.

Cpl DENNIS MANNION
Charlie Battery, 1/13 (Hill 861)

March 20, 1968

Hey Man—

No incoming in 48 hours. We've been getting fucking A-number-one air support the last few days (mainly because of clear weather) and that's the stuff to keep the mothers down.

NBC was here yesterday, spent the night, and left this morning. Three guys, very Hollywood. Loud talk, many discussions about this or that shot or background, lights, action, camera, Act III, Scene 201. Bullshit. Made me sick. Supposed to be doing a special on the hill. They did cover the hill pretty well.

One incident. Funnier than hell. The 106mm recoilless rifle is a mother (bigger than the 105mm cannon I shoot). It's recoilless—all the blast comes out of the breech and can kill or maim you if you're standing 100 feet behind it. The tube is nine feet long, weighs 215 pounds. On top is a single-shot .50-cal. You fire the .50-cal, watch the tracer hit—adjust the .50-cal onto the target—and the 106 will hit the same hole. Okay, the photogs want a live shot of the 106—to catch the backblast. They're in a line. A tall, loudmouthed, skinny asshole has the camera on his shoulder, eye glued to the sight. "Okay, shoot," he says. Our 106-man fires the .50-cal. *Bang!* One correction to the left. (They're shooting at a possible bunker.) Another .50-cal. *Bang!* A last correction. *Bang!* At this moment, as our 106 man's hand is closing the distance between the top of his finger and the firing button, the asshole cameraman yells out, "What the fuck! I ain't seeing any smoke at all. Is it broke?" *Wham!* I laughed till I couldn't, then laughed some more. When the dust, dirt, pebbles, and debris settled, there's our friend, flat on his fucking ass, camera about ten feet away. By that time, I'm laughing so hard I fall into my bunker, weeping with hysteria. Oh, God—only two or three times in my life have I laughed so hard. I laughed till I was sick. So beautiful.

One thing they did get was some fantastic flicks of Phantom jets dropping the heavies in close. Keep a lookout for the special. I don't know if I'm in it or not. The only time they were close to my hooch, I was in the middle of a fire mission—25 NVA in the open. We knocked down thirteen or so.

MARCH 21

Capt HARRY BAIG
26th Marines Target Information Officer _____

[Bravo Company, 1/26] was directed to dispatch a platoon patrol into the trench system, south of Gray Sector, at dawn, to determine what had happened to the enemy. The Fire Support Coordination Center developed a fire plan to protect the patrol. In essence, this plan was an offensive version of the defensive boxes. Nine batteries of artillery participated. Marine artillery formed the primary box and the rolling barrage. The Army's 175s and [radar-guided] air formed the sides of the secondary box, which fell on those pieces of ground that overlooked or could influence the patrol area. The patrol moved out seventy-five meters behind the rolling barrage into the sides of the box. Then, as the patrol continued to advance, the entire primary box also advanced, with the patrol inside it and the rolling barrage also inside it and in front of the patrol. Outside the primary box, as usual, the secondary box's sides opened and closed over the terrain like an accordion.

During the ninety minutes of the patrol [0630 to 0800], over

1,300 rounds—shell mixed and fuse mixed—were fired. Whether or not this was too much support for too small a force may be debatable. A measure of its success lies in the fact that, though the enemy made an attempt to retaliate (two volleys of mortars, which were quickly stopped), not a man was injured as a result of direct enemy action.[1]

26th Marines Command Chronology _____

> Several enemy explosive devices were found and blown in place. During the patrol, 14 rounds of incoming 82mm mortar fire caused three friendly WIA (evacuated) and six friendly WIA (not evacuated).

MARCH 22

Capt JIM LESLIE
26th Marines Assistant Communicator _____

We decided that one of the communications teams needed a new bunker as theirs had taken a direct hit which injured a few Marines. Our project was to build them a new bunker between artillery barrages.

Material to build a sturdy bunker was not available, so we utilized the "field expedient," which is anything that is available. We had plenty of empty 55-gallon fuel drums, sandbags, and red dirt, but the thing we needed most was wood for frame construction. The best material on hand was the runway matting or eight-foot-by-eight-foot aluminum pallets used by helos to deliver our C-rations. We decided to steal some of the aluminum pallets from the airstrip. However, they were so much in demand that the military police had stationed a man near the pallets to keep other Marines from stealing them.

My well-thought-out scheme was, as the guards changed each day about 1800 in the evening, at about dusk, I would take a jeep, trailer, and three young Marines and drive down the runway, throw twelve aluminum pallets on the trailer, drive up the runway about fifty meters, and get away through the barbed-wire fence.

Just at 1800, the guard left for chow, as we anticipated. We casually drove the jeep and trailer along the side of the runway, pulled up beside the stack of pallets, and loaded on twelve— valued at $5,000 each. A young private who jumped in the driver's seat as the other three of us jumped on top of the pallets cautiously started to drive down the runway. Simultaneously, as the guard yelled for us to stop and fired a couple of warning rounds into the air, the NVA started dropping in mortar rounds about twenty yards behind us. The young private at the wheel had never driven a stick shift before; he didn't know how to go faster. As the next mortar round landed a little too close behind us, I leaped from the trailer to the backseat of the jeep and pushed the private over to the passenger side. At the same time, the other two Marines on the trailer jumped into the backseat of the jeep.

I pushed the pedal to the metal and jammed the transmission into second gear. At that point, all of the pallets went flying across the runway behind us like a loose deck of cards. We escaped without injury and went back the next night to grab the pallets.

The Seabees dug a large fifteen-foot-by-twenty-foot hole in the ground with a bulldozer and we built our $60,000 mansion in the ground. We used ten of the twelve pallets below ground level and built a second roof by placing dirt-filled 55-gallon drums on the first roof and covering them with the two remaining pallets. Concealed by sandbags, this second roof created a false ceiling or dead space. If an artillery round hit, it would explode between the first and second roofs and only give the Marines inside a headache. This bunker took at least three direct hits during my tenure, and no one was ever injured.

1stLt NICK ROMANETZ
Charlie Company, 1/26

Our company gunny, GySgt John Grohman, was living in my bunker with me because they didn't want the company commander, exec, and gunny in one place in case it got hit by incoming. On March 22 we got the word that we could expect an incoming artillery barrage that night and a possible ground assault on the combat base. When we were put on Red Alert for the evening, Gunny Grohman told me he thought it would be best if he went up to the command post. The command post was brand-new because the old one had been blown up about a month earlier. It was strong; its roof had an initial row of runway matting, then two or three rows of sandbags, then 55-gallon drums filled with dirt, and then another row of runway matting with more sandbags on top. The idea was that a round with a delay fuse would go through the top row of matting and sandbags and detonate prior to reaching the bunker. It also had good beams inside; it was real sturdy.

26th Marines Command Chronology _____

At 1830, the KSCB came under heavy fire.

1stLt **NICK ROMANETZ**
Charlie Company, 1/26 _____

Capt Walter Egger, Gunny Grohman, 2ndLt Paul Bush [company exec], and the company radio personnel were in the bunker by then. The command post took a direct hit. Captain Egger, Lieutenant Bush, and Gunnery Sergeant Grohman were all killed.

Also that night, one of my platoon's bunkers took a direct hit, probably from a 122mm rocket. There were three Marines inside the bunker. Two were killed, but, strangely, the third one came out without a scratch.

We were on Red Alert when the rocket hit. Everyone was supposed to be in their fighting positions, with their helmets and flak jackets on, and weapons at the ready. Yet, when we excavated the bunker the next day, the two dead men were found in an upright position, sitting there with no shirts, no helmets, and no flak jackets on. I found this to be very unusual because the two dead Marines were "salts"—old-timers—each with about two months in-country.

Eventually I heard through scuttlebutt that the two salts had been sitting up smoking dope. The new guy had his helmet and flak jacket on and he was lying down flat in the bunker when the stuff was coming in. Lucky guy. He was too green to break the rules.

LCpl PHIL MINEER
Bravo Battery, 1/13 _____

On March 15, the scuttlebutt going around had said that our intelligence people thought the major NVA units around Khe Sanh were withdrawing. That lightened things up a little. The only reason we believed it was because we went about three days and only received about twenty rounds. Just little harassment stuff; a pop here and pop there. But on March 22—just like on February 23—over a thousand rounds came in. We answered it. It never let up, and we never quit firing back.

We called the Charlie Battery executive officer, Lieutenant Eberhardt, "Mister E." He was a good guy. The best. We'd have done anything for him. He wasn't even from my battery, but he'd come down to the gun, break out rounds with us, and work just like the regular sweathogs. He was a gymnast, on rings. He had the biggest forearms I ever saw. He'd move his fingers and all the muscles in his arm would ripple. He was a gym teacher and a guidance counselor, too. He kept my head right a few times. Mister E and Sergeant Whiteknight, also from Charlie Battery, were right there when the ammo dump blew. We were firing the battery and they were hauling stuff out of there. I saw White-knight with smoking rounds in his arms. They threw that stuff on a truck and Whiteknight drove it out of the area. It could have blown up anytime.

Soon we had to stop firing and lay low in the bunkers. The rounds in the dump were cooking and popping. We heard them going off. The worst part was feeling the concussion, when it compressed my chest and I could feel my diaphragm move. The bunker walls were thick, and we were all taking it pretty well. Some of the teargas had gone up, and we were all sitting there and the gas was getting us. Of course, we had all left our gas masks in our sleeping bunkers. We had a 5-gallon water can and dunked pieces of parachute to hold over our mouths and noses. It worked pretty good—if you stayed calm. But one of the new guys snapped out. Just like in the movies, he stood up and started screaming hysterically, "I'm gettin' outta here!" I just looked at him and said, "Whatta ya doin'?" There was terror in his eyes, and tears rolling down his cheeks. I said, "Where the fuck are you gonna go? You gonna go outside the bunker and catch a taxicab? Come on!" LCpl Thom Keaton, our section chief, and I held him.

Every time the rounds hit, he shivered. It reminded me of the first time I had been rocketed at Con Thien. After that, the kid didn't have a whole lot of fear.

Soon after the ammo dump went, one of the guns took one right in the center. The rounds on the parapet went, and they set the gun on fire. The guys in the crew were hurt pretty bad. It was raining, the gun was on fire—we were trying to get foam on it—rounds were coming in, and we were trying to get the crew evacuated to Charlie-Med. One guy had a real bad abdominal wound; we were holding his intestines in and had a poncho wrapped around his chest. It was too far to Charlie-Med to hump him on a litter, so we got a Mighty Mite and loaded him on. But there was too much mud. We were trying to hold him on the Mighty Mite, but it kept sliding from side to side and we kept slipping. The rain mixed with the kid's blood, and it was all over the place. In the end, we finally got him to Charlie-Med. Later they told us he made it, he survived.

26th Marines Command Chronology _____

> Damage assessments for the 1,049 rounds of incoming received revealed two 105mm howitzers damaged and temporarily out of action and one 105mm howitzer destroyed. Approximate ammunition losses were 300 rounds of 81mm mortar, 2,163 rounds of 3.5-inch rockets, 700 M-72 LAAWs, 800 rounds of 105mm white phosphorus, 100 rounds of 105mm "firecracker," 28 boxes of VT fuses, 10 boxes of point-detonation fuses, and an undetermined amount of Class II ammunition and pyrotechnics.

MARCH 23

Cpl ALLAN STAHL
Logistics Support Unit _____

It was the worst day of the siege for me. We heard that an NVA trench under the base had caved in, that an attack was imminent, that the NVA were coming. There would have to be a posted walking guard in each company area at all times, twenty-four hours a day. The Logistics Support Unit had to post a noncommissioned officer and another Marine to walk the area on two-hour watches.

Our area included the supply dump, which was piled high with boxes. They were piled up like skyscrapers. At night, that was a *spooky* place. I have never been more frightened in my life than when I was walking patrol in the middle of the night in the supply dump.

I had a shotgun and I was with another communicator. It was obvious to me that we were sacrificial lambs. Our duty was to fire a round to alert everyone else as we died. I had the equal horror that everyone in the combat base was armed and looking to shoot at moving shadows—*any* moving shadows, like us.

It was eerily silent except for occasional artillery fire. As I walked, I expected someone to jump out of literally every corner. There was no relaxation at all. Finally, I had enough. I couldn't do it anymore. I was in charge, so I took charge. We got down in a corner, where we had protection, and sat there and breathed to muster every bit of courage we could put together. Then we took another walk, and then we stopped to pull ourselves together. The guy with me kept raising his weapon to shoot at shadows, but he never fired. Finally, after four or five times, we stopped walking altogether.

When I got back, they told me to unload the shotgun so I could turn it over to the next man. I tried, but I didn't know how to work the pump on the thing. I realized that I couldn't have fired the shotgun.

LCpl PHIL MINEER
Bravo Battery, 1/13 _____

They came down with a Red Alert. That meant "Everybody awake for as long as the alert lasts." They took guys from the artillery and put them on line with the grunts. We were all assigned a field of fire. That evening I heard that an NVA sniper got hung up in the wire. A lot of tripflares went up, and they shot him. He was hanging on the wire in the morning. We were waiting to hear the bugle and watch the 304th NVA Division come swooping in on us. We were ready for them, but the attack never materialized.

Next morning, when I got relieved from my position out on the perimeter, I went back to my bunker, sat down, and wrote four letters. After I wrote them, I put them in the bottom of my seabag and instructed my buddies to make sure the seabag got home if anything happened to me. One letter was to an old girlfriend—my first love—one was to my mother and father, one was to my aunt, and the last was to my brothers and sister. I just said the things a guy would say when he's ready to die.

MARCH 24

1/9 Command Chronology

> At 1130, a platoon patrol from Alpha Company dispatched a squad to the northwest to reconnoiter the area. Contact was made resulting in two friendly KIAs from heavy small-arms fire from an estimated fourteen NVA in well-constructed bunkers and fighting holes. A second squad was sent to reinforce this squad. In the resulting fire fight, three more friendly KIAs were sustained, and four WIAs. The enemy strength increased to an estimated thirty NVA, and twenty more were spotted moving down the ridgeline.

Pfc LAWRENCE SEAVY-CIOFFI
Bravo Company, 1/9

After recuperating from the wounds I suffered defending the Alpha-1 outpost on February 8, I returned to 1/9 in mid-March and was reassigned as an artillery forward observer scout with Bravo Company, 1/9.

I was manning an observation post outside the northwestern perimeter line of the Rock Quarry when the patrol was ambushed. I was watching as Huey helicopters came in. One of them was shot down about 300 yards west of the observation post. It didn't quite crash; it hovered down slowly. One guy jumped before it hit the ground. He was lucky the helicopter didn't topple over on him. Other helicopters had to come in and rescue the crew.

1/9 Command Chronology

> Friendly tanks, artillery, mortars, and Huey gunships were used in support and, coupled with fire from the two squads, resulted in 31 NVA KIAs (confirmed), four bunkers, and two 60mm mortar positions destroyed.

MARCH 25

LCpl RAY NICOL
Bravo Battery, 1/13

On March 25, I was repairing one of the three howitzers in the battery that had been damaged on March 22. The recoil mechanism was acting up, and I was the only one left in the battery who knew how to repair it. The gun was nearly repaired when I got shot through the right elbow. I remember seeing a red tracer after the bullet left my arm. I ran into the next gun pit, which was below the ground, to avoid being hit again. At first, I didn't know I had been shot. There was no pain right away, and very little blood.

I was taken to Charlie-Med for treatment and to await a medevac to Dong Ha. By nightfall I was in tremendous pain as the shock wore off. I had to have a shot of painkiller.

Late the next day, during a lull in the shelling, a chopper came in. I got aboard with six other Marines. I was more afraid at that moment than I had been at any time during the siege. As the chopper gained altitude, the NVA gunners started firing at us. We could see tracers going by the open door, and I could feel them impacting on the aircraft. But we managed to get away.

At Dong Ha they changed my battle dressing, gave me another shot for the pain, and then cut off all my clothes. They even cut off my new boots. Then they put me on a stretcher and covered me with a sheet. All they bothered to clean was my wounded arm. The rest of me was incredibly filthy. Red dirt was stuck to every part of my body.

Just before dark, I was flown to Phu Bai for further medical attention. They operated on my arm there and put me to sleep for a whole day. Then I was flown to Danang. They kept me in a transient ward until the next morning and sent me to Japan aboard a C-141. After being shipped around to several hospitals in Japan, I reached Great Lakes Naval Hospital on Easter weekend.

MARCH 26

Pfc LAWRENCE SEAVY-CIOFFI
Bravo Company, 1/9 _____

Each night I manned a sensor receiver, and each day I was accompanied by a fire team and a radioman to man one of two Bravo Company daytime observation posts located well outside the perimeter wire.

The northwestern Bravo Company observation post, which I manned, was within sight of the battalion main perimeter. We left the perimeter at about 0730 each morning, in the fog so we couldn't be observed, and worked our way to the top of the little hill. I spent the day moving around the top of the hill, scouting possible NVA positions with my binoculars, trying to see over and between patches of trees and elephant grass to spot enemy movement to the north. We left around 1630, as it began to get dark.

On March 26, we left at 0645 through a rolling fog and were nearing the top of the hill when the pointman, right in front of me, heard movement and saw an NVA soldier putting on his helmet.

The pointman had an M-79, which he leveled and fired at a target only fifteen or twenty feet away. The thing clicked, and the pointman cursed and opened it up. It had misfired. He put another shell in while I took a grenade out. As soon as the pointman got the M-79 reloaded, Chicoms began raining down on us.

Cpl BERT MULLINS
Bravo Company, 1/9 _____

I heard a whispered voice on the radio asking me if there was supposed to be anybody else out there on that hill. I said, "Negative." Only a few seconds passed before I heard firing in the distance. Immediately, over the radio, I heard more firing when the handset was keyed by the radioman. He was yelling that there were NVA out there.

Pfc LAWRENCE SEAVY-CIOFFI
Bravo Company, 1/9 ⎯⎯⎯⎯⎯⎯⎯⎯⎯⎯⎯⎯⎯⎯⎯⎯⎯

The bullets were kicking up all around us as we pulled back to the bottom of the hill. It was a miracle we didn't take any casualties. I figured there was a squad of NVA up there, fifteen or twenty. But there were a lot more than that.

Cpl BERT MULLINS
Bravo Company, 1/9 ⎯⎯⎯⎯⎯⎯⎯⎯⎯⎯⎯⎯⎯⎯⎯⎯⎯

I told the radioman to get out of there, immediately. This was actually beyond the realm of my authority, but it felt right at the time. They managed to get back down off the hill.

Pfc LAWRENCE SEAVY-CIOFFI
Bravo Company, 1/9 ⎯⎯⎯⎯⎯⎯⎯⎯⎯⎯⎯⎯⎯⎯⎯⎯⎯

We took cover in some brush at the foot of the hill, but more bullets starting kicking up dust on our flank. Someone looking over at the treeline to our right said he saw flashes from an automatic weapon. Apparently it was an L-shaped ambush.

We moved back farther as bullets kicked up all around us. We continued to move back, three men at a time, while the other three fired up at the hill and the automatic weapon on the right. We leapfrogged back into a ravine, but they could see us from the top of the hill. One of the grunts said that he heard movement farther down the ravine. The NVA could have been flanking us, so we again leapfrogged back toward the 1/9 perimeter. My radioman took a round in the radio, but we took no casualties. I don't understand why no one was hit.

We made it back to the 1/9 lines and explained what had happened. They had heard the fight, but no one had been able to see what was going on.

1/9 command chronology ⎯⎯⎯⎯⎯⎯⎯⎯⎯⎯⎯⎯⎯⎯⎯⎯⎯

Two squads from Bravo Company were deployed to regain the observation post.

Pfc LAWRENCE SEAVY-CIOFFI

Bravo Company, 1/9 _____

I decided to accompany the assault force back to the observation post. We had been unable to get any artillery support, so I had no reason to go out again. But I did.

We made it to the base of the hill and one squad moved up the slope. I stayed back with the other squad. I saw a head up there, had it right in my sights, but someone told me not to shoot yet. We waited and then moved up. As we did, we took Chicoms and mortar fire.

As we pulled back from the base of the hill, a Marine near me was hit by mortar shrapnel. I yelled over and over for the corpsman, but he didn't come.

Cpl BERT MULLINS

Bravo Company, 1/9 _____

All our corpsmen carried smoke grenades taped to the strap of their aid bags so they could mark a zone for medevac helicopters. The corpsman with the assault group had a green smoke grenade taped to his aid bag. When he was killed by a mortar round, the smoke grenade ignited. It was a pitiful sight; we all knew what had happened.

Pfc LAWRENCE SEAVY-CIOFFI

Bravo Company, 1/9 _____

Everyone around me was pulling back, and I was left alone with the wounded grunt. He was hit in the chest and I didn't know what to do. He said, "Don't leave me here." I asked him if he could stand, and he said he could, so I helped him up. The grunts were regrouping and I kept asking where the corpsman was. I asked the wounded Marine if he could walk, and he said he could, so I walked him back to the edge of the battalion perimeter and called for a corpsman to come down. They brought a poncho and carried him up the hill.

I had a piece of shrapnel in my arm, but I picked it out and avoided treatment. It would have made my third Purple Heart, but I couldn't turn myself in after seeing the condition of the Marine I had helped. My wound just didn't seem like much.

1/9 Command Chronology ⸻

> One reinforced squad assaulted the hill and was taken under fire by enemy small arms. The enemy strength at this position was estimated to be of company size, heavily armed, and in well-prepared positions.

Cpl BERT MULLINS
Bravo Company, 1/9 ⸻

It was an eerie sight. It was like watching a real, live war movie taking place in front of me. In the distance I could see the group of Marines form a line and work their way up the hill. All of them threw grenades when they got close to the top. I saw the grenades explode and then the men were firing their rifles as they worked their way up to the top of the hill. They eventually took the hill, but they suffered several killed and wounded in the process. It was unnerving to me.

1/9 Command Chronology ⸻

> Maximum supporting arms were utilized against the enemy while the platoon returned to the perimeter. The contact resulted in the confirmed killing of 26 NVA and the capture of one AK-47 rifle, one RPG round and launcher, and five Chicom grenades. The unit sustained three KIAs and 15 WIAs.

MARCH 27

Capt HARRY JENKINS
Mike Company, 3/26 (Hill 881S) ⸻

The first casualty Mike Company incurred after I arrived on March 22 and took command on March 24 occurred on March 27. It was a fully moonlit night, and my Marines were out working at various assigned details. Pfc Irwin Sobel was working on the north side of the perimeter, digging to try to improve his fighting hole. All of a sudden, he was engulfed in a tremendous explosion.

Cpl TERRY STEWART
Mike Company, 3/26 (Hill 881S) _____

I was returning from the platoon command post and heading down the trench to my squad area when there was a terrific explosion just behind me. There was a slight turn in the trench just behind me and that alone is the only reason I am here today. As soon as I shook off the shock of the explosion, I jumped to my feet and ran back toward the command-post pit. It was damaged, and I could hear our platoon guide moaning in pain. I called for a corpsman, and the call was passed on down the trench. At the same time, I heard a man screaming just behind me, from over the wall outside of the trench. I stood up and glanced over. There was a guy flopping around crazily in the concertina wire. I noticed that he kept falling over and flailing with his arms. What I didn't notice right away was that he had no legs; they were blown off at the hips. I jumped the trench and raced out to him. I reached the man at the same time as one of the corpsman. Snipers had already started to ding at us, but the darkness kept their shots from being accurate. We got the man back to the trenches and I turned him over to the doc. I then ran to my squad sector to prepare for who knew what. At that time, we didn't know what had caused the explosion; we thought it may have been a rocket and the beginning of another attack.

Capt HARRY JENKINS
Mike Company, 3/26 (Hill 881S) _____

We thought initially that an incoming round had landed in the hole with Private First Class Sobel, but it was really probably a dud round that had been buried there from some time in the past. Sobel's shovel or pick struck the round, and it went off.

Sobel lost both feet in the blast. A corpsman got to him very quickly and tried to arrest the bleeding. We dragged him down the hill to the landing zone, and initiated a medevac.

Night medevacs were extremely dangerous and very difficult to put together, especially as far out as we were. It took us a while to get the request back through channels, but finally word came back from the combat base that an H-34 was on the way along with a gunship escort. We put Sobel on a poncho and the corpsmen were working on him frantically, trying to keep him alive. When the helicopter got there, we put Sobel on board and the helicopter immediately took off into the night. The last I heard was that Sobel died on his way to Charlie-Med.

Chapter 28

Capt HARRY JENKINS
Mike Company, 3/26 (Hill 881S)

During the day, our 106mm gunners lay still and searched the hills opposite Hill 881S for targets. One day at the end of March, the lance corporal commanding the 106 on the south side of our hill indicated that he thought he had spotted a sniper's position but wouldn't be able to tell for sure until the sniper moved or we received another resupply mission, in which case all the snipers would become active.

The gunner waited two days, until we got the word that an aerial resupply would be coming in. He told me that he would watch the position at which he thought the sniper might be to see if there was any movement out there. As it turned out, it was a sniper's position. The gunner saw the NVA move around in what was apparently a sniper hole. As soon as the helicopters came in and began their approaches on the central landing zone, between India and Mike companies, the sniper began to shoot at them. Our gunner cranked off a 106mm round which went right into the sniper's spiderhole.

There was a huge explosion from the recoilless rifle's back-blast and a great shower of dirt on the hill. That scared the hell out of the pilots, who all waved off, thinking the landing zone was

395

under artillery attack. They came in after we assured them that it was just the 106 going off to protect their interests.

Pfc ELWIN BACON
Kilo Company, 3/26 (Hill 861) _____

During the last few weeks on Hill 861, things seemed to lighten up a bit. The enemy mortars subsided considerably, but we still were reminded on occasion that they had not left completely. We had communications with Hill 861A, and were doing daily patrols between the two points. However, I have always felt a little guilty about asking some of my squad to go down on one of the first trips between the two outposts. I had received word that someone from my hometown was down there, so I asked permission to go down and see him. I was allowed to go get our mail if I could get some guys to go with me. An Echo Company Marine was supposed to lead us through their minefield outside the wire, which he did, but one of my buddies set off a charge. It resulted in his death, and several others were seriously wounded and had to be medevacked out. To make the incident worse, my reason for going came to nothing; the friend had left a week before to go on his R&R.

Pfc JIM PAYNE
Charlie Battery, 1/13 (Hill 881S) _____

On the day I rotated off Hill 881S in late March, a bunch of us short-timers were hunkered down in the trenchline near the saddle, facing the Mike Company hill. While we were waiting, Captain Dabney walked down and joined us.

One of the Marines was muttering a prayer as fixed-wing aircraft came screaming in low and smoked up the entire area. A minute or so later, two CH-46s approached and began descending down onto the southern side of the saddle.

Captain Dabney was grimly pacing back and forth when the moment came to scramble out of that particularly deep section of trenchline and run for those waiting choppers. I leaped up to the top of the trench but lost my footing. As I was falling backwards, the captain grabbed the seat of my trousers and gave me a hell of a fling back out of the trench while shouting, "Get out of here, Marine, and don't you *ever* come back!"

Amid smoke and incoming, I ran about fifty yards across No-Man's-Land and boarded the nearest helicopter before it lifted off. The second CH-46 got hit and those poor boys went down somewhere near Hill 861. The chopper I was on took several rounds while departing, and in my last violent act as a U.S. Marine, I emptied my sixgun into Hill 881N. A few days later, I was a civilian.

Capt HARRY JENKINS
Mike Company, 3/26 (Hill 881S) _____

We got a call one day at the very end of March that three resupply helicopters bound for Hill 861 were being diverted because of bad weather and heavy incoming over 861. The understanding was that we could keep whatever the bird dropped off.

The three helicopters with external loads came winging in as part of the normal Super Gaggle air show, dropped their loads, and took off without incident. They left three pallets on the landing zone.

HM3 DAVID STEINBERG
India Company, 3/26 (Hill 881S) _____

We didn't know what the hell it was. It turned out to be filled with Foremost ice cream.

Capt HARRY JENKINS
Mike Company, 3/26 (Hill 881S) _____

It turned out that the ice cream was supposed to be dropped at Hill 861 *and* Hill 881S, but we got it all. There was almost enough ice cream to feed an entire infantry battalion.

We divided all that ice cream up between men who had been

living on one C-ration per day, many of whom had not eaten any rich foods for months.

LCpl PHIL TORRES
India Company, 3/26 (Hill 881S) _____

We got melted ice cream, but it was beautiful, it was delicious, it was the best ice cream I ever had.

HM3 DAVID STEINBERG
India Company, 3/26 (Hill 881S) _____

We ate ice cream until we all had the shits. The diarrhea was unbelievable.

1stLt FRED McGRATH
Bravo Battery, 1/13 _____

Chow was a challenge. How do you make C-rations appetizing day after day? Occasionally we would get some B-rations, but never enough to break the monotony. Besides, by the time they got around to us, usually only mayonnaise was left. I hate mayo! The C-rations in 1968 still contained white bread, so you could invent a fairly tasty sandwich with a little imagination. But I found that, after a while, one or one and a half rations per day was all I needed or wanted. Unfortunately, for one of our Marines, that was not the case.

Not all Marines were comfortable with the situation at Khe Sanh. We had a Marine who did not cope too well. To relieve the pressure, he ate. And ate. By the time we discovered the problem, he weighed so much he could not walk. His ankles would not support him. He had been eating a *case* of C-rations a day. I think each *meal* was 1,600 calories. That times twelve meals per case is just too much. Combined with little or no exercise, he just ballooned. He had to be medevacked. I ran across him at Camp Pendleton about seven months later. Even though he had lost weight by then, he still tipped the scales at 280. We discharged him. His overweight condition was a direct result of what a Navy psychiatrist had diagnosed as anxiety neurosis. The Marine was afraid of dying. But then, so was everyone else. And everyone else dealt with their fears differently.

HM3 BILL GESSNER
Delta Company, 1/9

We had an incident that punctuated my experience with drugs in Vietnam—which was none. One of our platoons received a replacement. On his first or second night, he lit a joint (marijuana) and offered it to the man he shared a foxhole with. That man excused himself and came back with a couple of other guys. They gave him a lecture about dope in the field. He told them to "mind your own business." They broke both of his arms, and we never saw him again.

HN ROD DeMOSS
1/26 Battalion Aid Station

During the siege, my papers came through for R&R in Sydney, Australia. I had been waiting seven months for this R&R, but I was almost too scared to take it. There weren't many planes landing, and what few planes did land never stopped. If you got on one, you had to run to catch it as it made its turn to take off. Also, the plane was a magnet for mortar and rocket rounds. Several times, as I waited out by the runway, I was tempted to say "Forget it." I was taking a big risk just being there, and then I was going to have to worry about coming back under the same circumstances. But I made it onto the plane, which took a few rounds just a few feet from where I was sitting. I had a hell of a time in Sydney for six days, then I was flown to Danang and tried to get a flight back to Khe Sanh. I caught three different airplanes before I could make it back. The first two planes flew all the way to Khe Sanh, but they wouldn't land due to heavy shelling. Finally the third flight landed and I had to jump off because it wouldn't stop. Most of the pilots were leery of landing because, while I was in Sydney, a C-123 was hit and crashed on the airstrip. I was a nervous wreck by the time I made it back. I was on my way from the airstrip to the 1/26 Battalion Aid Station when I heard a *zing* and saw dirt fly up on a sandbag next to me. I had almost been hit by a sniper.

Sgt DENNIS SMITH
Bravo Company, 1/26

One of the Marines from Los Angeles took his R&R in Hawaii, bought a ticket home, and spent a few days watching us on the TV news. Then he returned to Khe Sanh. We asked him, "Why didn't you stay back in The World?" He said he got to thinking about his brothers back at Khe Sanh and knew we wouldn't make it without him, so he came back.

MARCH 30

Capt KEN PIPES
Bravo Company, 1/26

We had been planning to go back out and retrieve the bodies of 2ndLt Don Jacques's patrol pretty much from the day they were ambushed, on February 25. It quickly shaped up as a company raid outside the lines—get out there, get the bodies, and get into the perimeter. It had to be Bravo Company. We wanted to do it. We *had* to do it. I don't think any of us would have settled for anything else.

The planning was ongoing, but the execution kept getting delayed. I don't know why it was delayed. There was a lot going on. The fact that we were given the go-ahead at the end of March might have had to do with intelligence information that said the NVA was pulling back.

We knew exactly where the bodies were. We had aerial photographs, and they were monitored daily by aerial observers.

It got to the point where we had rehearsed going through the trenches. We were going to be relieved on the line early in the morning by Bravo-Recon. We had our routes laid out. We had a couple of intermediate objectives. 2ndLt John Dillon's 2nd Platoon was going to move first, then 2ndLt Pete Weise's 1st Platoon. I was right behind Pete, and 3rd Platoon was behind the command group.

We were relieved, as planned, hours before dawn. It was very crowded in the trenchline as we followed the route we had rehearsed in the dark at least two or three times. The lead platoon somehow got fouled up in one of the turns in the trenchline. It took time to get that straightened out, but we got to our jump-off point inside the wire and launched the raid.

HM3 DICK BLANCHFIELD
Bravo Company, 1/26 _____

"You bloody bastards," was all I could think of when I heard the lieutenant tell us that we—Bravo Company—would be going out beyond the perimeter at 0530 in order to try to locate some dead Marines killed weeks before and pick up their remains, which were in the middle of NVA-held territory. What bullshit was this after seventy-four days of rockets, artillery bombardment, and constant mortar attacks spewed upon us?

The men of Bravo Company had been assigned a mission, and I knew, as an ex-Marine and now a Navy corpsman, they would, as ordered, follow it through to the best of their ability. The company was at least one-third below strength, maybe more. Many of the men had been wounded two or three times in the siege. Many of the men's feet were infected, many were weak from poor diet, and some were on the verge of mental breakdowns.

I kept asking myself that night, while waiting for "jump-off hour," why, after all these past days of hell and madness, should Bravo Company go out on this suicide mission, knowing that we would walk into hell with no air support and only fifteen minutes of artillery cover before battle? Why? Because some general or colonel decided to test his map-pinned, board-strategy thinking with the lives of the men of Bravo Company as his chess pieces.

HN ROD DeMOSS
1/26 Battalion Aid Station _____

On March 29 we were called together by the battalion surgeon, Dr. Harvey DeMaggd, and told of the plan for Bravo Company to go out and recover the bodies from the massacre in February. Dr. DeMaggd told us that corpsmen would be needed to set up a forward aid station just behind the firing line. He said that he was going and that he wanted volunteers. I volunteered. I had treated some of the wounded following the February ambush and I felt like I had to volunteer. That's not saying I wasn't scared as hell.

Capt HARRY BAIG
26th Marines Target Information Officer _____

Captain Pipes asked for and received [a rolling artillery box barrage]. Marine artillery formed the primary box and the rolling barrage. The Army's 175s and [radar-guided] air formed the sides of the secondary box, which fell on those pieces of ground that overlooked or could influence the [combat] area. The [company] moved out seventy-five meters behind the rolling barrage into the sides of the box. Then, as [it] continued to advance, the entire primary box, with the [company] inside it and the rolling barrage also inside and in front of the [company], also advanced. Outside the primary box was, as usual, the secondary box, whose sides opened and closed over the terrain like an accordion. Added to the support were the fires of six heavy and medium machine guns, employing overhead- and direct-fire techniques. After ten minutes of continuous fire, with Bravo Company advancing swiftly behind the rolling barrage inside the moving primary box, the diverging movement of the platoons caused the sides of the box, on order of Captain Pipes, to collapse so that he could accomplish his mission. The fires of the two boxes were shifted to other targets to prevent reinforcements from reaching the battle area and to suppress the fires of enemy mortars and artillery (the latter were very badly handled).[1]

Capt KEN PIPES
Bravo Company, 1/26 _____

Our artillery fire went off, as planned, long before we moved outside our wire. In fact, it had been going on for days so it wouldn't draw undue attention to our move. Also, the morning fog was obscuring our position.

At 0600, shortly after first light, Dillon's 2nd Platoon went out and, unopposed, seized the first intermediate objective at 0615. As Dillon moved, a CIDG unit from FOB-3 moved out deep off our right flank, down along a ridgeline southwest of their perimeter sector. Their job was to shield our flank.

As soon as Dillon reached the first objective, the rest of the company moved to the line of departure and prepared for the next phase of the assault. The main body of the company was held up at the line of departure for nearly an hour because rolling fog obscured our objectives and routes of advance. The main body jumped off at 0725 and quickly linked up with Dillon's 2nd Platoon. As we did, Dr. Harv DeMaggd and the medical folks moved up to the first objective and set up an aid station in a big bomb crater.

HN ROD DeMOSS
1/26 Battalion Aid Station

We had no sooner gotten out of the perimeter than the fight started.

Capt KEN PIPES
Bravo Company, 1/26

At 0750, I requested ten-minute prep fires on all our objectives. When the main body of Bravo Company jumped off from the first objective at 0800, there was a lot of fire and action going on to our front. Hand grenades were thrown as I moved out with the two assault platoons, 1st and 3rd. Second Platoon remained in reserve at the first objective, covering us and our withdrawal route. We followed a rolling barrage by no more than seventy meters. Flamethrowers and demolitions were used to clear NVA strongpoints.

I had set up a plan with the 106s inside the wire so that I could call and adjust preplanned fire on various targets to our front. I also had contact with the 81s. Bravo Company's 60mm mortars were on the intermediate objective, and I had my artillery forward observer, 1stLt Hank Norman, right beside me. We had plenty of on-call fire support.

We got out 500 or 600 meters, to our limit of advance, overrunning several NVA positions on the way. In the process, however, we took a lot of fire ourselves. Looking up, I could actually see their mortar rounds coming in on us. Dozens of them. Most fell in among the assault platoons.

As I was talking to someone on the radio, one of the mortar rounds hit right on top of my command group and three or four others hit around us. Everyone was hit. I was knocked down and my radio operator had his arm very badly mangled. Also, 1stLt Hank Norman, my artillery forward observer, took a lot of shrapnel from the one that landed on top of us. Hank had his flak jacket unzipped and took a large piece of shrapnel through his chest. I was dazed; it took me a few moments to realize what had happened. When I knelt down beside Hank, he was expiring. I told him to hang on, that I'd get a corpsman up, but by the time I finished speaking, he was dead. I held him for a bit, but we had to move on. I had also been hit by shrapnel down through my arm and down through my chest cavity, but my wounds felt minor, so I stayed with what was left of the command group. Everyone except myself and the forward air controller's radiomen was out of action. Several of our radios were damaged or out and we had to switch frequencies to get comm reestablished. When we did, I called my exec, 1stLt Ben Long, from the reserve—2nd—platoon area. Ben, who brought up two squads of 2nd Platoon, helped me reorganize and evacuate the wounded, and then we resumed the advance.

HM3 DICK BLANCHFIELD
Bravo Company, 1/26

Contact was made with a North Vietnamese unit to my left—I was with the 1st Platoon, on the far right—and soon afterwards my platoon was engaged full force with the North Vietnamese. Mortars and automatic fire erupted on us, and casualties were quickly sustained by the 1st Platoon. The terrain was barren due to B-52 bombings, making cover almost impossible to find, except for bomb craters. My platoon had lost contact with the 2nd and 3rd Platoons, and the fighting was man-to-man, with no quarter given.

Marines were yelling, "Corpsman, Corpsman," which meant a Marine was hit and needed me to keep him alive. I ran, ducked, dropped, and kept moving until I jumped into a bomb crater filled with two dead North Vietnamese soldiers, a wounded Marine with his brain matter dangling out of his head, another Marine with his left arm almost blown off, and six other Marines huddled together, firing. At first glimpse, I thought the Marine with the severe head wound was dead, but his eyeballs were just barely moving, so, after treating the Marine with the arm wound, I bandaged the head wound and placed him on a stretcher.

The other Marines and I knew we could not stay in the bomb crater long, so we decided to make a run for the ridge. With some luck, we would connect up with the other platoons. We placed the Marine with the head wound on the stretcher and started working our way slowly up from the crater. But by this time the enemy mortars were falling in and around us in a steady volley.

We were just about to reach the top of the crater when, all of a sudden, a mortar landed right on top of us. The blast knocked me back down into the crater with a murderous pain in my left shoulder and hand. I automatically looked up to check on the others. They were all down. Two of the Marines' heads were blown off, and the others were motionless.

I checked my left arm and hand and knew that I was badly hit and losing blood rapidly. The pain was intense. I gave myself a morphine shot in the right upper leg and realized that if I remained in the crater the North Vietnamese would soon be upon me. I decided to give it a try and started climbing out. It took me two tries to get out of that death-filled crater, and when I reached the top, I stood up and looked all around me. My only thoughts at that pain-filled moment: My God, what an absurdity, what an absurdity!

Pvt DONALD RASH
Bravo Company, 1/26 _____

[NAVY CROSS CITATION] For extraordinary heroism while serving as a rifleman with Company B, First Battalion, Twenty-sixth Marines, Third Marine Division, in connection with operations against the enemy in the Republic of Vietnam. On 30 March 1968, while conducting a reconnaissance in force near the Khe Sanh Combat Base, Company B suddenly came under a heavy volume of small-arms fire from a numerically superior North Vietnamese Army force occupying fortified positions. Although the majority of the hostile fire was directed at his squad, pinning down his companions, Private Rash disregarded his own safety as he unhesitatingly left a covered position and launched a determined assault against the enemy emplacements. Ignoring the hostile rounds impacting near him, he fearlessly advanced across the fire-swept terrain, boldly throwing hand grenades and delivering a heavy volume of rifle fire upon the enemy force. Although continuously exposed to the intense hostile fire, he resolutely continued his vicious attack until he had destroyed five enemy positions and killed numerous North Vietnamese soldiers. When his company was subsequently ordered to withdraw while under accurate enemy mortar fire, he steadfastly remained behind, and as he delivered suppressive fire to cover the evacuation of casualties he was mortally wounded. His bold initiative and resolute determination inspired all who observed him and were instrumental in his company accounting for 115 North Vietnamese soldiers confirmed killed. By his courage, intrepid fighting spirit, and selfless devotion to duty, Private Rash contributed immeasurably to the accomplishments of his unit's mission and sustained and enhanced the highest traditions of the Marine Corps and the United States Naval Service. He gallantly gave his life for his country.

Capt KEN PIPES
Bravo Company, 1/26 ⎯⎯⎯⎯⎯⎯⎯⎯⎯⎯⎯⎯⎯⎯⎯⎯

When we reached the limit of advance, I called back to report that we needed some more help, that we had not reached most of the bodies we had been sent to retrieve. I was told that there was no one else to send out. I replied that we would do the best we could, but that the fire was building up. Shortly after that, I was directed to break contact and bring back as many bodies as I could. So far, we had recovered only two of the dead, but we began breaking contact, as ordered. We also had one prisoner and some captured gear, several mortars and heavy machine guns that had been overrun. We began leapfrogging back over the ground we had just attacked through.

Capt HARRY BAIG
26th Marines Target Information Officer ⎯⎯⎯⎯⎯⎯⎯⎯⎯⎯⎯⎯

When the Marines eventually retired, after having successfully accomplished their mission, the primary and secondary [artillery] boxes closed back with them. The fires of the machine guns and four 106mm recoilless rifles contributed heavily to the overall outcome of this operation.[2]

HN ROD DeMOSS
1/26 Battalion Aid Station ⎯⎯⎯⎯⎯⎯⎯⎯⎯⎯⎯⎯⎯⎯⎯

I went to the aid of a Marine whose arm had a tourniquet applied to it. I lifted the arm up to inspect the wound, and it seemed like a gallon of blood poured from it.

The Marines who brought in the body of another Marine were beside themselves because the dead man had only a few days left in-country. Now he would be going home in a body bag.

Capt KEN PIPES
Bravo Company, 1/26 _____

The night before we went, Pfc David Anderson came up to me and said he had about ten days left in-country and that he just didn't want to go. Anderson was a good Marine, a fellow who had done everything he had been told to do. He said he had some bad premonitions. I explained that we needed everybody we could get and that he was an experienced machine gunner, that we needed him. He said, "Okay. I can understand that. I just wanted to talk to you, Skipper, and let you know what my feelings are. I'll be ready to go." Dave Anderson stayed behind to cover the final withdrawal from the reserve area with his machine gun, and he was killed.

Cpl KENNETH KORKOW
Bravo Company, 1/26 _____

[NAVY CROSS CITATION] For extraordinary heroism while serving as Mortar Section Leader of Company B, First Battalion, Twenty-sixth Marines, Third Marine Division, in the Republic of Vietnam on 30 March 1968. During a search-and-destroy operation in the vicinity of the Khe Sanh Combat Base, Company B suddenly came under intense small-arms and mortar fire from a well-entrenched North Vietnamese Army battalion. Fearlessly exposing himself to the hostile fire, Corporal Korkow quickly deployed his mortar section into firing positions and, moving about the fire-swept terrain from one squad to another, directed heavy barrages of accurate fighting against the enemy, destroying four fortified bunkers. Alertly detecting a hidden mortar site which was pinning down elements of his company, he advanced to a position dangerously open to enemy fire and, employing his own mortar, singlehandedly destroyed the hostile emplacement. As the battle intensified, Corporal Korkow repeatedly disregarded his own safety as he moved from one position to another, encouraging his men and directing their fire. Observing a Marine fall wounded by an enemy explosive device, he selflessly rushed into the hazardous area and assisted his injured comrade to an aid station established to the rear of his company. Although seriously wounded while returning to the forward area after assisting more casualties to the aid station, Corporal Korkow resolutely continued to encourage and assist his men and comfort the wounded until he was medically evacuated. His intrepid fighting spirit inspired all who observed him and contributed immeasurably to the final defeat of the numerically superior enemy force. By his uncommon valor and selfless devotion to duty in the face of extreme personal danger, Corporal Korkow reflected great credit upon himself and upheld the highest traditions of the Marine Corps and the United States Naval Service.

HN ROD DeMOSS
1/26 Battalion Aid Station _____

Finally, it was over. We were told to pull back to the combat base. It seemed like we just kind of straggled back.

I helped three Marines carry a wounded Marine back. As we got close to the perimeter, a senior corpsman came out and took my place. I walked on and caught up with Dr. DeMaggd. I heard a couple of sniper rounds zing past us, and as we got back into the base, mortar rounds hit on both sides of us. That scared me silly.

When I got back, one of the other corpsmen told me about what he had seen going on out there. He could see it from where he was, inside the base, but I was right in the middle of it and hadn't seen a damned thing.

Capt KEN PIPES
Bravo Company, 1/26 _____

When we got back in, I was still a little dazed from the mortar rounds that had hit my command group halfway through the advance. I knew I was bleeding, but there were so many others in worse shape that I didn't pay much attention to my wounds. As soon as the company got settled in, I went down to Battalion to report. When I got there and threw my helmet down, a piece of shrapnel the size of my index finger fell out from between the helmet and the liner. I hardly noticed. The gunny from the 81mm mortars asked me if I wanted some coffee, and I said okay.

Later he told me he gave me a cup with a little coffee and the rest bourbon—twice. I didn't even know it; I thought it was good coffee. He found the piece of shrapnel and asked me what it was. I said I didn't know and, for the first time, looked at the helmet. It had a big hole just above the center of the forehead.

After we debriefed, I went up to the Battalion Aid Station to have my wounds treated. Dr. DeMaggd got most of the shrapnel, but when he probed a deep one at the point of my shoulder, I got sick. He told me he couldn't get that piece out, that he would have to leave it in there. The shrapnel was about two inches from my heart.

The remaining Marines killed during the Jacques patrol of February 25 were recovered by Delta Company, 1/26, on April 6. After jumping off in much the same way as had Bravo Company on March 30, Delta Company encountered zero opposition.

1stLt JOHN KAHENY
1/26 Combat Operations Center _____

It was very difficult to get back into Khe Sanh in late March, following my special emergency leave at home. I would have thought that it would be easy, what with all the flights in to pick up the wounded, but not many airplanes were landing and it was difficult to find out where the medevac choppers were leaving from.

On March 30, I went to the battalion rear at Phu Bai because I knew that if I got the payroll from Disbursing that I would get priority seating on any aircraft. So, as the "pay officer," I got priority on a CH-53. When I got to the helo pad, I hooked up with Captain Champion, who just wanted to get in to Khe Sanh to take over Bravo Company. Nothing was going to stop him. He was a rather large man who pushed and shoved everybody out of the way to fight his way onto the helicopter leaving for Khe Sanh.

The helicopter dropped us off at the landing zone. The place had been battered by incoming during the forty-five days I had been gone. All of the buildings were flattened, so the only way I could get my sense of direction was by looking at the hills to figure out which way was east and west. I led Captain Champion to the 1/26 command post and was greeted there by the survivors. I could sure tell they had been living underground for the six weeks I had been gone.

HM3 BILL GESSNER
Delta Company, 1/9

March 30, 1968

Dear Dad:

I got some goodies for you. Delta Company caught eleven in the grass just outside the wire yesterday. We got five confirms and the jets got the other six. Clean sweep.

I got a banana clip full of the 7.62mm shorts that they use in the AK-47. That's a total of 31 that I have for you now. The slug itelf is brass-jacketed. They look very cheap. Well, anyway, I have the K-44 round, too. A Chicom grenade (disarmed) that we got yesterday, and the magazine itself. I have some war souvenirs. I'll be sending the rounds out in small groups. The Chicom and the banana clip I'll have to carry out.

Well, I'm okay and out of news so I will close.

P.S. Just got the plaque [for Captain Schafer]! It's just great. Pop, thanks a million. I'll tell you what he says after we give it to him.

MARCH 31

HM3 BILL GESSNER
Delta Company, 1/9

At 1630, I gave the skipper, Capt Fran Schafer, the going-away plaque I had ordered through my father. He was flabbergasted. All he could say was "I'll be damned!" He showed it to the company exec, who said there were newsmen there. One of them took pictures.

At 1830, some new men were getting a pep talk from Captain Schafer while Weapons Platoon was carrying ammo from the command post to their area. A mortar round wounded one of the men in Weapons Platoon. He wasn't seriously hurt, but he needed a stretcher, so I went down to the company sickbay to get one. Captain Schafer decided to come up and talk to the wounded man. After we loaded the man on a stretcher, we were mortared again. We all were okay except for the wounded man on the stretcher, who had again gotten a minor wound, and, when he rolled into the trench, his foot got stuck in the damn stretcher. Also, the Weapons Platoon commander got a small wound in his shoulder. Captain Schafer told me to stay and bandage the lieutenant, then he got four other men to load the enlisted Marine back in the stretcher and take him to the battalion aid station. They got about fifteen meters when some rounds dropped all around them. Three Marines were killed. Captain Schafer and two more Marines ran out to help them. Another mortar round killed all three of them.

We all loved the CO, and there were a lot of prayers said and tears shed for that man.

1stLt **NICK ROMANETZ**
Charlie Company, 1/26 _____

We had some NVA out in front of our lines, firing a mortar from time to time. We could never see them, but we could see a puff of smoke whenever they dropped a round into the tube. They fired on us every day, in the mid- or late afternoon. We always saw the puff of smoke and heard the tube pop, so we always had time to yell and get everyone out of the way in their holes. The 60mm mortar rounds were nothing unless they fell right in your hole with you.

Sgt Arnold Ferrari reported in to the company in mid-March. He was assigned to my platoon, and I made him my right guide. He was a junior-college student from California, a Reserve who volunteered for active duty in Vietnam. He was a football player, handsome, a good physical specimen. He had his heart set on winning himself some kind of medal. He spoke to me quite a bit about it; he wanted to know when we were going to go out and fight the enemy—hand-to-hand—and quit just sitting there and taking a pounding like we were doing.

Unfortunately, on the afternoon of March 31, the NVA mortarmen popped a round in when nobody was looking. The thing came out of nowhere and exploded in the trench. I heard a yell for a corpsman and ran down there. It had gone off knee-to-waist-high, right where Sergeant Ferrari was standing. One of his legs was blown off and the other was hanging by a thread. There was no blood; the heat of the exploding round had cauterized the wounds. When we picked him up to put him on the stretcher, the other leg fell off. The troops put both legs on the stretcher and carted him off. He was white-faced and moaning. I looked at the boy and knew he wasn't going to make it. I got a call on the land line that Sergeant Ferrari had died at the hospital. Shortly after he was taken away, we found his boot lying outside the trench. It still had his foot in it, so we buried it in front of the line.

PART SIX

BREAKOUT
April 1–18, 1968

Chapter 29

OPERATION PEGASUS

MGen JOHN TOLSON, USA

1st Cavalry Division Commanding General _____

On January 25, I was directed to prepare a contingency plan for the relief or reinforcement, or both, of the Khe Sanh base. This was the first in a chain of events that was later to emerge as Operation Pegasus.

The mission was threefold:

• Relieve the Khe Sanh Combat Base.

• Open Highway 9 from Ca Lu to Khe Sanh.

• Destroy the enemy forces within the area of operations.

This was the basic concept of operations: The 1st Marine Regiment, with two battalions, would launch a ground attack west toward Khe Sanh while 1st Cavalry [Division] would air-assault the high ground. On D-plus-1 and D-plus-2, all elements would continue the attack west toward Khe Sanh; and, on the following day, the 2nd Brigade of the 1st Cav would land three battalions southeast of Khe Sanh and attack northwest. The 26th Marine Regiment . . . would attack to secure Hill 471. The link-up was planned at the end of seven days.

It became evident during the planning that the construction of an airstrip near Ca Lu would be a key in the entire operation. This airstrip, which became known as LZ Stud, had to be ready well before D-Day.[1]

Work on LZ Stud began on March 14 and a 1,500-foot-long, 600-foot-wide airstrip and associated facilities were completed by March 26. Between March 26 and D-Day, April 1, elements of the 1st Cavalry Division thoroughly reconnoitered the route of approach—generally along Highway 9 between LZ Stud and Khe Sanh—and an integrated fire-support plan was prepared. NVA positions along the route of approach were identified and targeted for reduction or bypass. Pre-assault air and artillery preparations were intensified from March 26 onward. As overall commander of Operation Pegasus, General Tolson ordered Colonel Lownds to participate by means of breakout sweeps from the static positions at and around the combat base.

26th Marines After Action Report _____

Operation Pegasus opened with exact enemy dispositions uncertain. The 304th NVA Division remained located to the south of Khe Sanh Combat Base, and east along Highway 9, with the 325C Division remaining to the west and north of Khe Sanh Combat Base.

APRIL I

MGen JOHN TOLSON, USA
1st Cavalry Division Commanding General _____

At 0700 on April 1, 1968, the attack phase of Operation Pegasus commenced as two battalions of the 1st Marine Regiment . . . attacked west from Ca Lu along Highway 9. The 11th Marine Engineer Battalion followed right on their heels. At the same time, the 3rd Brigade of the 1st Cavalry [Division] was airlifted . . . into LZ Stud in preparation for an air assault into two objective areas farther west. Weather delayed the attack until 1300, when the 1/7th Cavalry [1st Squadron, 7th Cavalry Regiment] . . . air-assaulted into LZ Mike, located on prominent ground south of Highway 9 and well forward of the Marine attack. The 2/7th Cavalry went into the same LZ to expand and develop the position. The 5/7th Cavalry . . . air-assaulted into an area north of

Highway 9 approximately opposite LZ Mike.... Both landing zones were secured and no significant enemy resistance was encountered. A battery of 105mm howitzers was airlifted into each landing zone and [3rd Brigade headquarters was moved] into the northern landing zone, LZ Cates. . . .

The bad weather of D-Day was to haunt us throughout Operation Pegasus. Seldom were we able to get in high gear before 1300. . . .[2]

APRIL 2

MGen JOHN TOLSON, USA
1st Cavalry Division Commanding General

On D-plus-1, the 1st Marine Regiment continued its ground attack along the axis of Highway 9. Two Marine companies made limited air assaults to support the regiment's momentum. The 3rd Brigade air-assaulted the 2/7th Cavalry into a new position farther to the west while the other two battalions [1/7th Cavalry and 5/7th Cavalry] improved their positions [LZ Mike and LZ Cates]. The 2nd Brigade . . . moved into marshaling areas in preparation for air assaults the next day, if called upon.[3]

1stLt JOE ABODEELY, USA
Delta Company, 2/7th Cavalry

[Diary Entry] 0645. We air-assaulted to the top of this mountain. It's jungle and grassy. I jumped from the chopper and hurt my arm.

As we walked along, I smelled the distinctive, unforgettable, sweet odor of burned flesh. Someone nearby had gotten napalmed.

[Diary Entry] I could see bomb strikes off in the distance as the sky lit up and the ground shook.

1000. The sun is out. We're on a high mountaintop surrounded by a river on three sides. Today, Delta Company is to air-assault to a new location to set up there. We just got a [logistics] ship with food and water. It was nice sleeping last night.

1720. Delta Company led the air assault to where we are now. My platoon led the ground movement. We found a site for a .51-caliber antiaircraft gun. Also, some of my platoon found some NVA ammo and grenades. Now we're waiting to see where we'll set up. We're hot and tired.

APRIL 3

MGen JOHN TOLSON, USA
1st Cavalry Division _____

Our initial thrusts had met lighter enemy resistance than expected, so the 2nd Brigade was thrown into the attack a day earlier than the original schedule, with three battalions moving into two new areas south and west of our earlier landing zones. . . . They met enemy artillery fire during the assaults but secured their objectives without serious difficulty. We now had six air cavalry battalions in enemy territory.[4]

1stLt JOE ABODEELY, USA
Delta Company, 2/7th Cavalry _____

[DIARY ENTRY] 0953. We are sitting in the jungle right now. The 3rd Platoon hit some NVA a little while ago. They got one of their men KIA.

The 3rd Platoon had run into a light machine gun in the trees. The dead man, a sergeant, had gone to get it and they shot him. He was actually still alive when the battalion operations officer carried him back and laid him on the ground near us. I heard a gurgling sound and saw fluids dribble out of the sergeant's mouth. It was the first time I had seen anyone die like that.

[DIARY ENTRY] We're waiting for artillery to come in. There are huge bomb craters all around. I can hear helicopters circling the area now. There are trees, high grass, and ferns all around.

1808. We moved to this hill (Hill 242). NVA mortared us. We had ten or eleven WIA. NVA have surrounded us now. One platoon from another company tried to bring us food and water but got pinned down. I hope we make it through the night. We dug in and made overhead cover.

We were surrounded. No one could get in or out, so we set up a perimeter and built fortifications. We put our ponchos out to collect water and drank what we could get. Another platoon tried to come down the road using Mechanical Mules, but they got several people killed and pulled back. That night we received a lot of incoming, but there were no explosions. I heard on the radio that other parts of the battalion were experiencing the same thing—lots of incoming that wasn't detonating. We didn't know if it was gas or delayed fuse or bad fuses. We could hear things crashing in, making impact but not going off.

APRIL 4

MGen JOHN TOLSON, USA
1st Cavalry Division Commanding General _____

[The 2nd Brigade] assaulted a battalion into an old French fort south of Khe Sanh. The first contact resulted in four enemy killed. The remaining uncommitted brigade [1st Brigade] was moved into marshaling areas.[5]

1stLt JOE ABODEELY, USA
Delta Company, 2/7th Cavalry _____

[DIARY ENTRY] 1540. We are now back at [LZ Cates].

1800. I have my platoon in position on the perimeter. As we came back today, we picked up a couple of dead and wounded who tried to get supplies to us yesterday. When we got back here, we saw more dead and wounded. The 2nd Platoon leader of Charlie Company was killed. One medevac chopper was shot up. The NVA here are dangerous. I don't like this area. I hope we all get out alive. I got a card from a friend today which cheered me up. We didn't have any food or water yesterday and for most of today. Everyone is tired.

With the relief forces only days away from the combat base, the breakout phase of Operation Pegasus began on D-plus 3. 1/9 was ordered to sweep across the hills south of the combat base. Three companies of 1/9 jumped off on April 4. The first objective was Hill 471, an important terrain feature due south of the combat base and overlooking Highway 9.

HM3 BILL GESSNER
Delta Company, 1/9 _____

I felt naked when we left the holes and trenches behind and moved to the battalion's first objective.

Delta Company was in a blocking position on the west, and Alpha Company conducted the main attack. As we moved into our blocking position, we had to cross a finger on a ridge that exposed us to the artillery in Laos. The NVA took advantage of that, and pounded us. Somehow, we didn't take very many casualties.

1/9 Command Chronology _____

At approximately 1500, following an air strike, Alpha Company initiated its assault on Hill 471 across a narrow approach with Delta Company providing a heavy base of fire. Alpha Company assaulted Hill 471 with the 2nd Platoon in the lead, the 3rd Platoon in trace prepared to take the right half of 471, and with the 1st Platoon in reserve. The assaulting elements slowed down near the top of Hill 471 due to heavy enemy small-arms fire and grenades. Alpha-1 was sent to move through Alpha-2 and continue the assault. At approximately 1530, Alpha-3 secured the left half of Hill 471 and provided fire support for Alpha-1 and Alpha-2 to secure the remaining portion of Hill 471. Hill 471 was secured at approximately 1600.

Cpl BARRY THORYK
Alpha Company, 1/9 _____

[NAVY CROSS CITATION] For extraordinary heroism while serving as a Machine Gun Section Leader with Company A, First Battalion, Ninth Marines, Third Marine Division, in connection with operations against the enemy in the Republic of Vietnam. On 4 April 1968, Corporal Thoryk was participating in a company assault on Hill 471 near Khe Sanh, when his platoon came under an enemy grenade attack and intense automatic-weapons fire. Although he sustained multiple fragmentation wounds in the initial moments of the attack, Corporal Thoryk refused medical aid and singlehandedly launched an aggressive assault against an enemy machine gun position, killing three of its defenders. Having expended his ammunition, he quickly obtained an enemy weapon and delivered fire at two enemy soldiers, killing them as they ran from their position. With complete disregard for his safety, Corporal Thoryk continued to maneuver forward, retrieving enemy hand grenades and throwing them at several hostile positions as he advanced. His courageous actions and steadfast determination were instrumental in seizing the enemy-occupied hill and inspired all who observed him. By his intrepid fighting spirit, bold initiative, and selfless devotion to duty, Corporal Thoryk upheld the highest traditions of the Marine Corps and the United States Naval Service.

HM3 BILL GESSNER
Delta Company, 1/9

Alpha Company had its hands full. Battalion called for medics to go to help on the objective. I went by myself instead of sending a platoon medic. The NVA were still firing a lot of artillery as I took cover near the assault position. When I had a chance to look up, I saw dozens of khaki-green lumps at the foot of the objective, and I thought, "They must *all* be hit!" Then I realized that I was looking at their packs. They dropped them at the bottom of the hill. In the assault position, I found enough wounded men to exhaust my supplies, so I went to the Battalion Aid Station for more. The battalion surgeon told me to go back to Delta Company, so I did.

1/9 Command Chronology

On April 5, Alpha Company, 1/9, and Charlie Company, 1/9, were situated at Hill 471. H&S Company, 1/9 and Delta Company, 1/9 were on an adjacent hill.

At 0430, April 5, Charlie Company came under a heavy enemy counterattack by an estimated two NVA companies. Fighting was intense, with small arms, automatic weapons and heavy machine guns, grenades, and RPGs in their assault. The enemy was well disciplined. It was observed that the NVA were uniformly dressed in green utilities and steel helmets and well equipped. The enemy broke off their assault at approximately 0630 and retreated to a hill southeast of Hill 471. From this position, they continued sporadic small-arms, mortar, and RPG fire in Hill 471. The fire was returned by 1/9 elements who maintained fire superiority over the enemy. As a result of the attack on Charlie Company, the following enemy equipment was captured: 1 60mm mortar with ammo, 13 machine guns, 4 RPGs, 28 AK-47s, 30 AK-47 magazines, 3 SKSs, 13 drum-type magazines for automatic weapons, and other miscellaneous gear. 1/9 killed 148 NVA (confirmed) and captured 5 prisoners. By 0800, the enemy had ceased their small-arms fire on 1/9's position.

Total friendly casualties sustained by 1/9 on April 5 were 1 KIA, 21 WIA (serious), and 7 WIA (non-serious).

The abortive attack on 1/9, apparently conducted by a composite unit drawn from all three battalions of the 325C Division's 66th Regiment, was the last serious effort by the NVA to keep Marine battalions bottled up at or around the combat base. Thereafter, all contacts achieved during the breakout phase of Operation Pegasus were against NVA rearguard elements, which were usually manning static defenses at key terrain features. After Hill 471, the remaining intact elements of the 325C and 304th NVA Divisions were perceived as withdrawing from the Khe Sanh plateau.

MGen JOHN TOLSON, USA
1st Cavalry Division Commanding General _____

On D-plus-4, the 2nd Brigade continued its attack on the old French fort, meeting heavy resistance.... The ARVN 3rd Airborne Task Force was alerted to prepare to airlift one rifle company from Quang Tri to link up with the ARVN 37th Ranger Battalion at Khe Sanh. Units of the 1st Brigade ... entered the operation with the 1/8th Cavalry air-assaulting into LZ Snapper, due south of the Khe Sanh and overlooking Highway 9. The circle began to close around the enemy.[6]

1stLt JOE ABODEELY, USA
Delta Company, 2/7th Cavalry _____

[DIARY ENTRY] 1550. I got word today that our battalion may walk into Khe Sanh tomorrow. This could be disastrous. We've incurred a lot of killed and wounded since we've been here. I hope to God we make it alive. I've had a lot of close calls and I'm getting scared again. Everyone is scared of this area. The NVA are numerous and good fighters. We're digging in again for tonight.

1720. Jets keep circling this hill. There are also a lot of choppers in the air. Artillery keeps pounding the surrounding areas also. I hope the NVA move out. They ambush a lot here.

APRIL 6

26th Marines Command Chronology _____

0700: 1/26 executed a morning assault on an NVA trench and bunker complex located parallel to the access road which runs southeast from KSCB to Highway 9. Delta Company seized the objective against light resistance, policed the battlefield, and returned to KSCB at approximately 1200. The remains of 21 Marine bodies were recovered, accounting for all those declared as MIAs on February 25. Enemy casualties were 6 NVA KIA (confirmed).

MGen JOHN TOLSON, USA
1st Cavalry Division Commanding General _____

On D-plus-5, the 1st Marine Regiment continued its operations on high ground north and south of Highway 9, moving to the west toward Khe Sanh. The heaviest contact on that date was in the 3rd Brigade's area of operation as the 2/7th Cavalry . . . continued its drive west on Highway 9. Enemy forces blocking along the highway offered stubborn resistance. In a day-long battle which ended when the enemy summarily abandoned his position and fled, the battalion had accounted for 83 enemy killed, one captured, and 121 personal and ten crew-served weapons seized. The troops of the 1st Cavalry Division were airlifted to Hill 471, relieving [1/9] and permittting them to drive toward Hill 689, some 4,500 meters to the northwest. (This was the first relief of the defenders of the Khe Sanh.) Two companies of [Cavalry] troopers remained on [Hill 471] while two other companies began an attack to the south toward the Khe Sanh hamlet.

The 1st Cavalry forces on LZ Snapper were attacked by an enemy force with mortars, hand grenades, and rocket launchers. The attack was a disaster for the enemy, and twenty were killed.

At 1320, the 84th Company of the ARVN 8th Airborne Battalion was airlifted by 1st Cavalry Division aircraft into the Khe Sanh Combat Base and linked up with elements of the 37th Ranger Battalion. The lift was without incident and marked the official link-up by forces at Khe Sanh.[7]

The ceremonial ARVN link-up was barely mentioned in official Marine Corps documents relating to the siege, and all but overlooked by individual Marines at the combat base.

1stLt JOE ABODEELY, USA
Delta Company, 2/7th Cavalry

[DIARY ENTRY] 1400. Well, we tried to walk from this LZ [Snapper] to Khe Sanh, but we had to come back as the two forward companies received effective fire. Now our company is supposed to air-assault to within 500 meters east of Khe Sanh. This is a glory push to see who can be first to walk into Khe Sanh. I hope we make it. We have many reporters with us.

The reporters thought this was going to be a parade down Main Street. They were with us for a little while, but they moved on when nothing happened.

As the Cavalry sweep and Marine road-clearing operation drew closer to Khe Sanh, the battalions of the 26th Marines became more actively engaged in patrolling and preparing to mount sweeps across the northern and western ridgelines overlooking the combat base. The first order of business was to locate close-in NVA units and clear them from the immediate area. Especially active in this regard were 1/26, at the combat base, and 2/26, at Hill 558. Also, once relieved of Hill 471, 1/9 began a sweep westward along the 689 ridgeline.

APRIL 7

26th Marines Command Chronology

0800: The 37th Ranger Battalion conducted a sweep in front of their position and discovered trenches, bunkers, and a large amount of ammo and equipment. . . . The Rangers also found 70 NVA KIA (confirmed) believed to be results of supporting-arms fire directed on enemy sightings during the last two days of March.

MGen JOHN TOLSON, USA
1st Cavalry Division Commanding General _____

On April 7, the [ARVN] 3rd Airborne Task Force air-assaulted three battalions into positions north [of Highway 9] and east of Khe Sanh to block escape routes toward the Laotian border. Fighting throughout the area was sporadic as the enemy attempted to withdraw. U.S. and ARVN units began picking up significant quantities of abandoned weapons and equipment. The old French fort, the last known enemy strongpoint around Khe Sanh, was completely secured.[8]

1stLt JOE ABODEELY, USA
Delta Company, 2/7th Cavalry _____

The 2/7th Cavalry's order of march from LZ Snapper to Khe Sanh had my 2nd Platoon as the last unit of the follow-up company. However, when the lead company met opposition, it was decided to leapfrog Delta Company over the fight and on down to Khe Sanh. Since we were the last unit in the column, we were the first to be picked up. That put us at the head of the column.

Cpl TIM SNELL
Hotel Company, 2/26 _____

During the late afternoon, about an hour before dark, our rear command post got word that an Army unit had started up one of the nearby hills and had gotten caught in a vicious crossfire. We had seen the activity on the hill, but it wasn't noticeable until after dark, when the tracer rounds showed up much better. We didn't know who was on the hill, but we did know that they had their hands full. We were told that they had been allowed to advance halfway up the hill against token resistance, but once they were halfway up, the enemy, who were hiding underground, popped up in front, turned on them, and attacked. Artillery support was out of the question due to the position of our people, literally on top of the enemy in both directions. The Army unit was in a terrible spot, but it fought valiantly.

As soon as the situation was reported by their radioman, a medevac was called in. When our first sergeant said they needed volunteers to help with the medevacs, only three or four of us were willing to go because of the incoming. The word came that they wanted us at the landing strip to wait for the choppers to arrive. We all jumped into a jeep and headed down to the strip. It wasn't long before we heard the *thump-thump* of the choppers. It was starting to get dark by then, and we got the word that the pilots needed someone to help guide them in. We had had trouble earlier in the day with snipers, and that was on everyone's mind, so no one was really too anxious to jump up and stand out in the open to direct the choppers and dodge incoming rounds at the same time. Finally, I said I would guide them in. There was no argument over my decision. When the first chopper was in sight, I ran up on the landing strip and started to direct it as best I could. None of us had any formal training in landing planes, but we knew that we could do whatever it took to get them in safely.

As I stood out there all alone and wondering if I was doing a good enough job, I got a sudden surprise. The first chopper turned on its landing lights and scared the *hell* out of me. But he turned the lights off again and continued landing. Next thing I knew, he was on the ground and the wounded began to unload.

As soon as the chopper touched down, the other Marines with me were on the strip, ready to do their best to help the wounded. The thing that struck me was the total lack of concern some of the wounded had for themselves. If they could walk on their own, they told us, "I'm okay. Take care of the ones who need help." These men had holes in their shoulders, legs, and arms, but they were most concerned with their buddies' well-being instead of their own.

Another thing that struck me was the care we took to ensure that the dead were treated with dignity and respect. They were not thrown around like used baggage. Instead, we laid them on the edge of the strip until all the wounded had been cared for. I was so proud to have had a small part in bringing these brave men in safely, and to have seen the care we all shared for each other.

Every one of these medevac choppers landed and departed safely.

1stLt JOE ABODEELY, USA
Delta Company, 2/7th Cavalry _____

[DIARY ENTRY] 1045: We air-assaulted to an open area on a mountaintop and received light sniper fire. We found an NVA complex with rockets, mortars (tubes and ammo), AK-47s, and all sorts of material. I have a sharp AK-47, which I hope to keep. We are to go to Khe Sanh.

The complex was huge, bunkers everywhere. It was right on Highway 9, near the road that branched off to the Lang Vei Special Forces Camp. We found some bodies in the bunkers, and tons of equipment. One of my men found an old French bugle. He made a tassel for it out of parachute cord and gave it to me. The same trooper created a sensation that afternoon when he shot a cobra he found in the trenches with the unauthorized .38-caliber snub-nosed revolver he carried.

After we finished sending off all the captured gear we weren't going to keep, we marched down the road off the mountain toward Khe Sanh. We found other bunkers along the way, but nobody was there. We found rucksacks, medical supplies, ammunition, and a few bodies.

[DIARY ENTRY] 1700. We are at Khe Sanh, camped outside the east entrance on Highway 9.

We saw some Marines there, going to a garbage dump. They were really surprised to see us. The Marines had not been able to go down the road we were on for about two months

APRIL 8

1stLt JOE ABODEELY, USA
Delta Company, 2/7th Cavalry _____

[DIARY ENTRY] 1130. Today, Delta Company was the first to walk into Khe Sanh on Highway 9 in two months. My platoon was the first in.

There was a Marine captain standing there at the gate. I must have looked interesting to him. I had all my normal equipment on, but I also had my bugle and the AK-47 I had picked up the day before.

We were the cavalry, so, as we were walking in, my company commander asked if I could play the bugle. I told him I had played trumpet in my high school band. He asked if I could play "Charge." "Sure," I said, and I blew the cavalry charge as we walked in.

I walked up to the marine captain, saluted him, and said, "Sir, Lieutenant Abodeely reports with the 2nd Platoon, Delta Company, 2nd Squadron, 7th Cavalry, to relieve you." He gave me a disdainful look and said, "Lieutenant, your people will take this position, from here to there." No "Hi, how are you"; "Thanks"; "Welcome"; "We've been waiting for you"; "We're glad to see you." Nothing. I thought that, under the circumstances, he was being an asshole.

MGen JOHN TOLSON, USA
1st Cavalry Division Commanding General _____

At 0800 on April 8, the relief of Khe Sanh was effected and the 1st Cavalry Division became the new "landlord." The 3rd Brigade airlifted its command post into Khe Sanh and . . . the 2/7th Cavalry successfully cleared Highway 9 to the base and linked up with the 26th Marines.[9]

LCpl PHIL MINEER
Bravo Battery, 1/13 _____

We saw newspapers that said the 1st Cavalry Division opened the road and rescued us. But, by the time the Air Cav arrived, guys in the base were moving around in the open, sitting in the air, joking. It was done with by the time the Air Cav came in. They filled the sky with helicopters and a few walked in with a general and a bunch of news photographers. They were posing like, "Here we are. We saved you." That is a bunch of bullshit. One newspaper said we were so glad to see them that we were throwing C-rations to them. Absolutely! I was standing on top of my bunker with cans of ham and lima beans—what the Marines called "ham-and-mothers" because they tasted so good—and I was throwing them *at* the Army troops. I didn't want those guys anywhere near me. I could see that attitude.

1stLt ERNIE SPENCER
1/26 Intelligence Officer

Charlie must have said, "Hey, let's watch the U.S. Army embarrass those little fuckers at Khe Sanh." When the doggies get there, everyone else is pulling out. The Marines feel it is just about over.[10]

1stLt NICK ROMANETZ
Charlie Company, 1/26

When a bunch of Air Cav guys set up in front of our lines, they set their tents up above the ground. They got a couple of mortar rounds that night. I'm sure no one was hurt because there were no medevacs flying, but I bet they dug in the rest of the time they were around Khe Sanh.

Cpl ALLAN STAHL
Logistics Support Unit

The fun was over. The face of the war changed. Suddenly, all night long we were under an umbrella of flares. That offended our macho.

We had been eating one C-ration per day, and there was a time when we had had to ration water. Now the siege was lifted, and things were looking up.

An Army unit set up right down the trenchline from us. Starting right away, the Army flew in hot chow in insulated ration cans, something we hadn't seen in months. We were so hungry when we saw this that we went over and asked to get in their chow line. The sergeant in charge said, "We feed our people first. Come back later." Fair enough. We went away for a while and then returned. At that moment, the sergeant we had seen earlier had a ration can in his hands and was dumping mashed potatoes on the ground. "Hey," I called, "we'd like some of that chow." The guy got a real surly look on his face and turned his can up.

"There," he offered as the last of the potatoes fell to the ground. "Fucking Marines need to eat off the ground."

As the inevitable shouting war got louder, the guy I was with picked up some food that had been set aside and dumped *it* on the ground. "If we don't eat it, nobody eats it." With that, three Army guys came at us. The sergeant stepped up to me and I let loose on him. I'm no fighter—I had only had my first lesson a few days earlier—but he rolled. Then we took off running and giggling.

It was tense with the Army from that moment on. We were ordered to stay clear of the Army.

Capt BILL DABNEY
India Company, 3/26 (Hill 881S)

There wasn't really a hell of a lot of fighting out there when the siege was lifted as such. The Air Cav came in with all these buzzy helicopters and things. They went hill-hopping, but they didn't go down in the valleys much. But there was just not a hell of a lot of fighting. I think the North Vietnamese just melted away.[11]

MGen JOHN TOLSON, USA
1st Cavalry Division Commanding General

The 3rd Brigade elements occupied high ground to the east and northeast of the base with no enemy contact. Now it became increasingly evident, through lack of contact and the large quantities of new equipment being found abandoned on the battlefield, that the enemy had fled the area rather than face certain defeat. . . . Operations continued to the west.[12]

APRIL 9

MGen JOHN TOLSON, USA
1st Cavalry Division Commanding General

On April 9, all of the 1st Marine Regiment's objectives had been secured and Highway 9 was repaired and secured with only scattered incidents of enemy sniping. Enemy mortar, rocket, and artillery fire into Khe Sanh became increasingly sporadic.[13]

> 0720: 1/9 on Hill 689 received 18 rounds of enemy 82mm mortars resulting in 2 KIAs and 4 WIAs. An artillery mission was fired on the enemy mortar position and no further rounds were received from that location.

LCpl MIKE GUESS
Charlie Company, 1/9 _____

Each squad took turns sending a guy about twenty-five yards to the rear, right off the front lines, to guard the CO and communicators. When we took a defensive position on Hill 689 on the night of April 8, it happened to be my turn. They decided to dig into a B-52 bomb crater. The officers and communicators were toward the back of the crater, and I dug a fighting hole within the bomb crater. I got up to take a leak and had just gotten back into my hole when the first round of the morning came in. It got me; tore me up pretty good—lower legs, waist, back. The thing that scared me was the smell of the powder. I had been hit or had close calls twice before. I got sick to my stomach all three times from the powder smell. It all went so fast and the metal was so hot that I didn't feel any pain at first. Just that smell. But I was lucky. The mortar round had landed at the rear of the bomb crater and killed all the communicators back there. A corpsman got back right away and wrapped me up real good, but that was the start of a fire fight, and they couldn't get me out on a chopper right away. I don't know how long I sat out there because I kept phasing out and they kept waking me up.

I finally got on the medevac chopper, but I was the only *wounded* guy. Everybody else was in body bags, but I was wrapped up in my poncho liner up to my neck. There was a gunner shooting out the side of the chopper. He was shooting away and shooting away and shooting away until they finally got the chopper away. I was just lying there, in and out of consciousness. One time, as I came to, the gunner was leaning in the door of the chopper with his foot up, lighting a cigarette. I said, "You got another one of those?" I thought the guy was going to jump out of the chopper. I guess he thought everybody on the chopper was dead. He came over, gave me a cigarette, and shot the breeze with me.

They got me to an aid station somewhere—I don't know where—and they cut out as much shrapnel as they could. I spent the night there, the only wounded guy on the ward. I knew I was dirty—everybody around me for three months had been dirty—but I didn't realize how filthy I was until a doctor came in and made this poor Air Force medic give me a sponge bath. I felt sorry for the medic.

Cpl BERT MULLINS
Bravo Company, 1/9

Bravo Company stayed to hold the battalion perimeter at the Rock Quarry while the rest of the battalion went to Hill 471. As soon as the rest of the battalion left, we pulled into a smaller perimeter and went to work policing the whole Rock Quarry position.

The 1st Air Cav came up and relieved us at the Rock Quarry. We were all packed up and ready to go. They marched out of Khe Sanh, right up the road to us.

We had stockpiled quite a bit of canned orange juice in our position before the battalion pulled out and left us. There were cases of it because we had gotten a little tired of it after a while. The first Cav trooper to reach the juice staked a claim and started *selling* it to his buddies as they filed past the cache. Those of us who saw the incident absolutely could not believe we were seeing a guy making money off his own buddies. I was there only about another thirty minutes, but from the time he started until the time I left, he was still selling cans of orange juice.

I saw my first thirty-round M-16 magazine there, when the Cav came up. An officer had one in his M-16, which he put down next to me. If I had had about thirty seconds, I'd have been the first Marine I knew with a thirty-round magazine, and he'd have been an Army officer with a twenty-round magazine.

We cut a direct path across a low area in order to rejoin the battalion on Hill 552. As we moved, we came upon a stream, at which point it was decided that everyone should have an opportunity to take a bath. We took about an hour, and we got the entire company bathed in the stream—our first baths in over two months. After we all got through bathing, we marched upstream and found a thoroughly decomposed elephant lying right in the stream.

On the way from the bathing pool, I saw the devastation caused by the B-52 Arclights. There were massive craters and shredded trees all around. It was a sight to behold.

By the time we got to Hill 552, the other three companies had already moved to Hill 689, a higher hill. There was not enough room for the whole battalion on 689, so Bravo formed a separate perimeter on Hill 552.

1stLt JOHN KAHENY
1/26 Combat Operations Center

Pegasus was a very strange operation. The Army came in and we assumed we would be sent somewhere to be refitted. But we ended up being in the center as the 26th Marines pushed the NVA back toward Laos. The battalion did not see much action during the operation. We went out just short of Hill 881S and took some casualties, but we didn't see any NVA. They hit us with long-range recoilless-rifle fire.

On the way toward Hill 881S we had to go through what was known as Leech Valley, which the Air Force had seeded with gravel. This was supposed to expire after so many days, but they apparently gave us the wrong expiration date. That held us up.

1stLt NICK ROMANETZ
Charlie Company, 1/26

We broke out along the 784 ridgeline. The whole time we were out there—a week or ten days—I only saw a half-dozen NVA. I did see a lot of prepared positions. But I really had to wonder if the great numbers that were surrounding us were really out there. There were a lot of dead animals. We took a few enemy mortar rounds, which unfortunately killed a company radio operator. Also, someone put some bum dope on our guns, and a Marine artillery unit put some white phosphorus on a friendly unit and caused some casualties. The 1,000-pound bomb craters were impressive. We also came on an area where there were toe-poppers [gravel]—little chemical packets that went off like a big firecracker if enough pressure was applied.

Pfc ROBERT HARRISON
Alpha Company, 1/26 _____

The Air Cav relieved us from our position on Hill 950 and we rejoined Alpha Company for the purpose of conducting a combat sweep west of the main base. We were walking through abandoned NVA positions when we noticed thousands of small bags, about the size and shape of teabags, scattered on the ground. LCpl Jack Bibbs picked one up and it blew two of his fingers off. Jack was one of my best friends. He was from Texas, and was nineteen years old. He got married before he came to Vietnam. His wife delivered a baby girl while he was on Hill 950 with us. Jack had to be medevacked, and the rest of us tried to avoid stepping on the bags. This was impossible and quite a few were stepped on, but they didn't penetrate our boots. Interspersed among the small bags were chrome balls about the size of softballs. We kept moving trying to leave the area before nightfall and it became impossible to see them on the ground.

We later learned that the bags and chrome balls were dropped by our planes. They were small booby traps called "gravel" by the Air Force. The gravel was intended to hinder enemy movement, especially during the night. What is odd is that we were not told to expect this type of booby trap. It was the first time any of us had seen anything like it.

APRIL 10

MGen JOHN TOLSON, USA
1st Cavalry Division Commanding General _____

The 1/12th Cavalry . . . under the 1st Brigade, seized the Old Lang Vei Special Forces Camp . . . against light resistance.[14]

Operation Pegasus/Lam Son 207A was terminated much sooner than expected. When told on April 10 by LtGen John

Rosson [commander of the Provisional Corps, Vietnam] to initiate extraction and start planning for an immediate assault into the A Shau Valley, it all came as a complete surprise. One immediate result was that I had to cancel a large number of air assaults that were scheduled for that afternoon, which would have extended our activities a considerable distance in all directions from Khe Sanh.[15]

Pfc ROBERT HARRISON
Alpha Company, 1/26

It was near midday on April 10, and Alpha Company was moving in column through dense terrain. The pace was fast, considering the amount of equipment everyone was carrying, and some people had trouble keeping up with the column. Private First Class Pruitt was in front of me; he was one of those people having trouble. Our platoon commander, 1stLt Maxie Williams, came back from his position near the front of the 3rd Platoon to offer words of encouragement to Pruitt. Then he moved back to his original position in the column. This was the last time I saw the lieutenant alive.

The column was moving when suddenly there was an explosion. We halted, and there were cries of "Corpsman, up!" My fire team was called up to help. We moved to where the explosion had occurred and found that a booby trap had gone off. I don't know for sure what type of booby trap it was. Lieutenant Williams was killed outright and Lance Corporal Higuerra, the lieutenant's radioman, was wounded. The company commander called in a medevac. The chopper arrived and we put the lieutenant and Higuerra on it. The column re-formed and began moving again.

Cpl ALLAN STAHL
Logistics Support Unit

The sergeant in charge of the ammunition supply point had boasted days in advance that he was going to throw us a spaghetti dinner, and he came through. I have no idea where he got the spaghetti and sauce, but he did it. We got a big old cauldron going out in back of our bunker. We even had beer. It was glorious. The only thing that put a damper on it was when one of the guys who didn't drink tried to *sell* his beer for ten dollars a can.

APRIL 11

MGen JOHN TOLSON, USA
1st Cavalry Division Commanding General _____

Highway 9 into the Khe Sanh Combat Base was officially opened on April 11 after Marine engineers had worked day and night to complete their task. In eleven days they had reconstructed more than fourteen kilometers of road, repaired and replaced nine bridges, and built seventeen bypasses. Many sections of the road had to be cleared of landslides and craters.[16]

APRIL 12

CHANGE OF COMMAND

Col BRUCE MEYERS
26th Marines Commanding Officer _____

I was serving as Operations Officer of the 9th Marine Amphibious Brigade, whose actual headquarters was at Okinawa, but all of whose units were deployed in Vietnam. As the brigade operations officer, I began coming to Khe Sanh in August 1967. My last visit as brigade operations officer was in January 1968, just before the "siege." I then assumed command of the 2,200-man Special Landing Force Alpha, where I was aboard the helicopter carrier *Iwo Jima*. In that unit, I had a Marine battalion landing team and a Marine Sikorsky H-34 helicopter squadron. We were making amphibious raids along the coastline from Danang north to the Cua Viet River, on the DMZ. In that my landing force assets were 9th Brigade assets (under operational control of MGen [Tommy] Tompkins, the 3rd Marine Division commander), I was in-country daily to visit my units, and on a number of occasions I went into Khe Sanh with my H-34s, which sometimes flew resupply and medevac runs for the 26th Marines.

Dave Lownds and I had been battalion commanders together in the 2nd Marine Division, and we had known each other for years. He was my predecessor as 9th Brigade operations officer.

When the brigade commander called me by scrambler radio from Okinawa, I was in my sea cabin aboard the *Iwo Jima*, just having returned from the mouth of the Cua Viet River. The general asked, did I "want a regiment?"

As the youngest colonel in the Marine Corps, having been a grunt my entire career—twenty-six years at that point—I had obviously aspired to a regiment as the capping of infantry command. (I had commanded a platoon at the close of World War II, a rifle company in Korea, had been first commanding officer of 1st Force Reconnaissance Company as a major, and a battalion commander in the Mediterranean 6th Fleet as a lieutenant colonel.) I replied, "Hell yes, General." We arranged for me to turn over command of my landing force in the morning, and by 1100, I was dodging the 12.7mm antiaircraft in the early-morning Khe Sanh fog aboard the first chopper I could get.

Dave Lownds and I walked the perimeter that day, April 11, and his staff gave me briefings on the situation. The next morning, April 12, we had a very brief change of command about the time the usual morning fog lifted (to avoid being targets for the gunners on Co Roc Mountain). Dave took off by chopper for what later proved to be a trip to the White House to receive his Navy Cross and the 26th Marines' Presidential Unit Citation.

CHANGE OF MISSION

MGen TOMMY TOMKINS
3rd Marine Division Commanding General _____

I don't think it was General Westmoreland's decision to abandon Khe Sanh. He was out of town, in the United States. General Creighton Abrams, who had already been designated as his relief, held a meeting at Phu Bai, I believe, and announced that we were going to get out of Khe Sanh. I was charged with the phase-out of the Marines and the dismantling of the base.[17]

Col BRUCE MEYERS
26th Marines Commanding Officer _____

I was told that the future of Khe Sanh as a forward base in I Corps was under reconsideration. My mission was to roll back Khe Sanh Combat Base proper and all installations. . . . My mission was twofold: tactically to patrol actively and aggressively with the regiment with four battalions in the field—the 1st, 2nd, and 3rd Battalions of the 26th Marines, and the 1st Battalion, 9th Marines. The second portion of the mission was that of a logistic retrograde of all material located at Khe Sanh Combat Base on back to the Force Logistic Command echelons for necessary repair after the heavy artillery and mortar and rocket attack damage. The instructions were to completely demolish Khe Sanh Combat Base after taking everything usable. The mission was to be accomplished by a phased reduction in size of the operations base of the battalions in the field. Initially, the close-in battalions would draw into the base, assist in the demolition of the base, extracting all unnecessary material for the future mission of a light screening and reconnaissance base, and then eventually closing down the ring around Khe Sanh until eventually the final elements would be phased out predominantly by use of air.[18]

MGen TOMMY TOMPKINS
3rd Marine Division Commanding General _____

When General Westmoreland returned and took control again, he was quite adamant that Khe Sanh would not be abandoned until such time as General Abrams was in the chair, that he, Westmoreland, felt it was necessary to retain Khe Sanh.[19]

APRIL 13

Col BRUCE MEYERS
26th Marines Commanding Officer _____

In the early-morning hours of April 13, the 26th Marines received additional guidance indicating there would no longer be a retrograde action and that Khe Sanh Combat Base was to continue in existence with a heavy and very active patrolling, screening, and reconnaissance series of missions . . . going out from the Khe Sanh Combat Base proper.

Upon receipt of this additional guidance, our planning

continued and progressed for a battalion-by-battalion relief of the 26th Marines, including the attached 1st Battalion, 9th Marines, by other battalions of the 1st Marine Division.[20]

Maj TOM COOK
26th Marines Assistant Logistics Officer _____

I left Khe Sanh on a CH-53 with the advance party to Dong Ha. When we got there, I had a lot of troops to get fed, but no one knew we were coming, and no one knew where we could stay. It wasn't fun. As I worked, I happened to start noticing that people were looking at me funny. And then I noticed why. I was orange. My face was orange. My uniform was orange. I looked at my troops, and they were all orange. All the other people had green uniforms on. It was the funniest feeling I ever had in my life. I was an orange person and the rest of the world was green.

Chapter 30

THE EASTER OFFENSIVE

APRIL 9

On April 9, for the first time since its Christmas sweep, 3/26 was to be reconstituted in its entirety preparatory to a series of planned sweep operations centered on Hill 881S. The battalion headquarters, weapons detachments, Lima Company, and Mike Company's 3rd Platoon were to be flown to the hill from the combat base, and Kilo Company was to be flown from Hill 861.

LCpl CHARLIE THORNTON
Lima Company, 3/26

I recuperated from my wounds over a period of about thirty days, but I was released from the hospital ship about two weeks earlier than I felt I should have been. The ship was supposed to sail from Vietnam to the Philippines, so the doctors discharged all of us who were within a couple of weeks of full recovery. I was still extremely weak, and my wounds were very tender. The sutures had been removed only two days before my release from the ship. I returned to Khe Sanh by helicopter, which landed without drawing any incoming. The pace in general was much less tense than when I had been medevacked in March. Everyone greeted me enthusiastically.

Within days of my return, we saddled up, destroyed the bunkers that had been our homes for the past several months, and simply walked out of the perimeter toward Hill 881S.

Pfc LIONEL TRUFANT
106mm Platoon, 3/26 _____

The day they externally loaded our 106 out of the combat base to Hill 881S was the first time in Vietnam I put on a pack and carried heavy equipment. I had two cans of ammo for our M-60 machine gun, the tripod, plus my own personal gear, and my M-16. I had never packed a backpack before; I didn't know how to pack it. Nobody told me how to do it because Marines like boots to find out the hard way. So, I packed the machine-gun ammo down at the bottom of the backpack. We waited for the helo a long time, and the weight of the pack was just killing me.

While we were waiting for our ride, a helo from the 1st Air Cav landed and this guy without a flak jacket on got out. He walked around like he was thinking, This ain't shit. I could feel the tension and see the looks on the faces of all the Marines there. We resented it. We had been sitting up there, playing Russian roulette with the artillery for the last two months, watching our buddies get blown away, get hurt, get constantly harassed, facing psychological stress and physical stress every day. And here was this guy, walking around like it wasn't shit. For all we knew, he might have been in the thick of shit, too. I could see the resentment all the way from our staff sergeant on down.

A CH-46 landed and we loaded aboard. Then we flew to Hill 881S. My first impression of Hill 881S was that it looked like an anthill. When the helicopter started going in, we were sitting in two rows, across from one another. The gunner opened up and the word was that the landing zone was "hot." When the helicopter hit the ground, I felt like we were the wagon train, 881S was the fort, and 881N was the Indians. They were shooting at us, and our guys were shooting back at them. We started running off the helicopter, and all the weight in the bottom of my pack was just kicking my ass. The first thing I was looking for was a trench. I was running downhill toward a trench and finally got into it. The shooting kept going on. They kept shooting 82mm mortars at us, and our 81mm mortars kept shooting back. Small-arms fire was hitting everywhere.

Next we had to climb to the top of the hill. The weight in my pack was killing me. On the way, it started raining. When I got to the top of the hill and finally took my pack off, it felt like I didn't have a lower back or buttocks.

Hill 881S was very different from the combat base, where we dug into the ground and built a top over us. On the hill, the Marines were inside the ground. In most cases, living quarters were dug into the ground off to the side from the trenchline. The first living quarters they put us in were literally underneath the ground. There was barely enough space to sit up. It was dark. The setup was more of a community thing than at the combat base because the trenchline went all the way around the hill; there were more people going back and forth than in the combat base, where we were isolated in our own holes. They got hit by a lot of rockets and mortars, but not as much artillery as we had had at the combat base.

Pfc ELWIN BACON
Kilo Company, 3/26

Just prior to our leaving Hill 861 for good, we received more food and ice cream than we could ever eat. Actually, it got a lot of us sick because we had gone so long on short rations that our stomachs couldn't take it.

We received the word that we were going to push on Hill 881N the next day. The word passed down the line that we were to get our shit together and prepare for the worst. They expected heavy resistance to our advance.

We were given extra C-rations and a special package for each squad consisting of soap, cigarettes, writing paper, and that sort of thing. We knew that most of the stuff would have to be left behind, but the evening was mostly spent getting the gear together and feasting on everything we liked best out of the extra rations. Most of us made hogs of ourselves, but we thought this might be our last big meal.

In the early-morning hours, we began a systematic transfer from Hill 861 to Hill 881S, which was the jumping-off point for the operation. We were placed in teams and given instructions on when to move up to the landing zone. The anticipation that we would get mortared was correct. When the choppers came in to pick us up, we received some incoming, which put everyone more on edge. The holes around the landing zone were packed with men.

When it was my squad's time to load up, we heard the sound of incoming and ran back to the hole. Then we heard someone didn't make it. He had fallen down. A round landed between his legs and did a real number on him. They carried him to the chopper with us and set him down in front. Both of his legs were gone below the knees, and he had tourniquets made of web belts on both stumps. He was just sitting there, nonchalantly viewing his situation and shrugging his shoulders like he didn't care. Either he was in shock or he just knew his duty was over. I thought I might be in a position like that in the near future, and I wondered what my reaction would be.

We made a diversion to Khe Sanh Combat Base to unload the wounded man, and I got my first glimpse of the base since before the start of the siege. The place was completely covered with fresh dirt, and everything in sight was damaged. I felt very uneasy while the chopper was being unloaded. I just knew the rockets were on the way in, but nothing happened.

After we landed on Hill 881S, we moved to a small ridge and dug in. Our first chance to see what we were in for came while we spent a few days on the ridge. We could see up along our route of advance. It gave us a lot to think about, but it seemed to help morale.

LtCol JOHN STUDT
3/26 Commanding Officer _____

The perimeter around Hill 881S was expanded: the high ground immediately to the north, Pork Chop Hill, was occupied and close-in patrolling was initiated. An extensive complex of abandoned enemy fortifications was uncovered within 300 meters of the defensive wire. Pork Chop Hill was covered with interconnecting fortifications but was evacuated by the enemy without a fight following extensive air attacks, including CS gas.[1]

APRIL 10

Capt HARRY JENKINS
Mike Company, 3/26 _____

We got word from Battalion that the restriction on patrolling outside the wire had been lifted. The first thing we wanted to do was clear and screen the areas around the base of the hill, mainly to the north and west. To help us do this, I put together a reconnaissance patrol and requested that scout-dog teams be brought in to cover the patrol's point position. I was able to get one dog to the hill, a big, beautiful sable German shepherd named King.

I was also worried about the Marines I would be sending out on patrol. Many of them had lost their physical conditioning after being cooped up on the hill since late January, and no one had eaten properly in weeks and months. The troops were not really in condition to go out and hump those hills. So I decided to try to do as much as possible within the limits of what I thought the troops could handle. The result was a series of patrols beginning at the west-end gate on Mike Company's end of the hill.

The first mission was to scout around the entire base of the hill to determine what was there. The first patrol, with King on the point, went out on the afternoon of April 10 and quickly came upon a series of North Vietnamese positions—fighting holes, spiderholes, caves, trenches, and so on—all around the north side of Hill 881S. Fortunately, they were not occupied, but it appeared that the positions had been prepared in anticipation of an attack on 881S as well as for protection against air strikes. Marines on top of the hill didn't know there were NVA living at the base of the hill and, in some cases, beneath the hill itself.

As the patrol proceeded, King alerted his handler with increasing frequency that there was something ahead of the patrol. Finally, the handler let the dog go. King took off into the bushes and a big fracas commenced. Apparently, King jumped an NVA soldier. There was a lot of yelling and growling, and then the dog and the NVA went crashing off through the brush. When the handler called King back, he promptly returned and the patrol deployed and screened the area to the west, about three hundred meters out. They found one AK-47 on the ground, but nothing else. The patrol returned to the top of the hill that evening.

A second patrol was sent out four hours after the first patrol returned. It went off down the same trail toward the positions at the base of the hill and set up an ambush.

APRIL 11

Cpl TERRY STEWART
Mike Company, 3/26 _____

As I was on my third tour, I was elected to lead the patrol. We waited until late that evening, around midnight, and departed the wire on the western end of the hill. We went straight down off the side of the finger and moved ever so slowly and cautiously. Without telling me, my platoon commander, 2ndLt William Ammon, had dropped off two men to act as a rearguard to cover our back door. The rest of us, with me as point, continued on down. We carried only our rifles, a few extra magazines, and a couple of grenades. We wore soft covers. We were light, silent, and mobile.

As we neared the foot of the hill, we heard very faint sounds. It wasn't determined what the sounds were; they were indistinct. At the bottom of the hill we could smell the smoke from the enemy's cooking fires, and there was rustling in the bushes to our front. As there were only about eight of us and we had no idea what we were up against, we pulled back. I whispered to the lieutenant that we should pull back a hundred meters and figure out how to go on from there. It was agreed.

The usual practice would have the patrol simply invert so the tail would become the lead. If this had been done, there would not have been any problem. However, the lieutenant had me lead the way back up; we just sort of snaked around. I put the man who was behind me at point and just told him to retrace our steps back about 100 meters and then stop. Neither of us knew about the rearguard, which was expecting us to return along the same track. They did nothing as we approached, but my pointman, when he was right on top of them, noticed a boot sticking out from a bush right next to him. He was quite startled when he touched it and it moved. He opened fire with a long burst.

The remaining member of the rearguard was several feet away. When I dived off the track and sought cover, he ended up directly in front of me, not more than ten feet away. I heard the bushes rustle as he turned to see what was going on. I almost opened up on him, but something held me off; something didn't feel right. Even though all this happened so suddenly, there was still only the one M-16 that fired a burst. If we were being ambushed or had jumped the enemy, there surely would have been more firing. Anyway, in a second or so, I heard an American voice whisper, "Are you all right?" I knew then that the person in front of me was a Marine. At first I thought that somehow the patrol had gotten twisted around. Safeties were clicking and I just knew that all hell was about to break loose, so I loudly yelled to cease fire. The person just in front of me in the bushes called my name and we finally got control of the situation.

Unfortunately, Pfc Charles Finley, the poor guy whose boot was sticking out from the bush, lay very seriously wounded. We quickly got him into a makeshift stretcher that we prepared using our shirts, and started up the hill. It was rough and steep and miserable. I know it had to have been very bad on the wounded man. We all had to take turns carrying him. It was exhausting work. We were also frightened because we were making incredible noise going up; we were easy targets for any NVA that we had attracted. I fell back about twenty-five or thirty yards after my turn on the litter. I lagged the rest of the way back to cover the others. I cannot be sure if it was imagination born of fear or if we were followed, but I believed that I heard pursuers and saw fleeting, ghostlike shadows only a short way behind me. If they were real, I can't imagine why they did not try to take us.

We got Finley up the hill in a few hours. After a few more hours, it was nearly dawn and a medevac arrived. This was very dangerous for everyone. When the bird was coming in, the NVA gave us all they had. Small arms, rockets, and mortars came at us and the bird. But whoever was flying that thing had a set of nuts that were definitely fourteen-karat gold-plated lead. Knowing that he couldn't land on the saddle, the normal landing zone, because the NVA had it zeroed in, he hovered just off our positions on the north side of the hill and backed the baby right

up to us. The ramp hit the side of the hill and two men walked
Finley into the bird and then hopped off. The bird took off. We
all thought that it was a clean mission. Later we learned that the
bird had evidently sustained a serious small-arms hit and crashed
on the way out. I heard that all on board were lost.

Finley had studied in the seminary and had taken a leave to
join up and volunteer for Vietnam so that he could learn the
lessons that it would have to offer him.

Capt HARRY JENKINS
Mike Company, 3/26

Our third patrol off the hill included King, the scout dog, with the
point element. It went off on April 11, about seven hours after the
ambush patrol was aborted. The patrol was moving along without
having made contact when, for some unknown reason, our
4.2-inch mortars on Hill 861 struck in the immediate vicinity. A
white-phosphorus marking round landed upslope of the patrol,
and the second marking round landed right behind the patrol.
We sustained three relatively minor casualties from phosphorus
burns. King was also burned, more seriously than the three
Marines. Scout dogs were considered so valuable that King rated
the highest priority for medevac, and an H-34 was immediately
dispatched to get him—and the burned Marines. We received
another scout-dog team that evening.

APRIL 12

Col BRUCE MEYERS
26th Marines Commanding Officer

Major General Tompkins gave me broad guidance and directed
me to "move out from the perimeter at Khe Sanh." On April 12,
my first day as regimental commander, I visited every unit on the
surrounding hills (1/26, 2/26, 3/26, and 1/9, as well as my two
ARVN battalions). LtCol John Studt, battalion commander of
3/26—he had been a Pfc in my rifle company in Korea—requested
permission to retake Hill 881N from his battalion's position on
881S. I gave approval, and my staff worked closely with his. In
one day and one night of intense requests, we had laid on every
possible bit of air and artillery prep that we could. Lieutenant
Colonel Studt wished to avoid the mortar fire and direct

automatic-weapons fire from 881N that had previously struck his units (India and Mike companies) on 881S.

APRIL 13

LtCol JOHN STUDT
3/26 Commanding Officer

On April 13 the commanding officer, 26th Marines, ordered 3/26 to attack 881N the following day. Detailed plans had already been prepared, including an extensive fire-support plan, as a result of an earlier warning order.

It was estimated that an NVA battalion was defending the 881N complex, with numerous strongpoints on the intervening ground between 881S and 881N. In addition to organic weapons, the enemy was supported with 12.7mm antiaircraft guns, 120mm mortars, and 122mm/140mm rockets. Moreover, the entire operation was within easy reach of his 130mm and 152mm artillery in Laos. After evaluating his various capabilities, two questions were of primary concern.

Would he use his artillery/rockets against us, or would our attack progress rapidly enough to disrupt his capability to adjust fires on our maneuver elements?

Would he reinforce? After all, we were threatening his primary rocket site for attacks on the Khe Sanh Base.

3/26 possessed all its organic elements plus the normal reinforcing units: shore party, engineers, scout-snipers, and two scout-dog teams. In addition, we had six .50-caliber machine guns taken from downed helicopters. Fire support would be provided by LtCol Jack Hennelly's 1st Battalion, 13th Marines, at the Khe Sanh Combat Base; three 105mm howitzers were actually located on top of 881S, a handy but hazardous arrangement. The 175mm gun batteries at Camp Carroll would reinforce 1/13, and finally, our traditional Sunday punch would be provided by Marine fixed-wing.

Col Bruce Meyers . . . assured us of priority of fire for all supporting arms.

Drawing heavily on Captain Dabney's familiarity with the terrain and on the keen mind of my operations officer, Maj Matt Caulfield, we developed a plan involving the following key factors:

1. Maximum maneuver forces. We would attack with three full rifle companies and one rifle company minus. Hill 881S would be manned only by H&S Company and one rifle platoon. Captain Dabney, now a major selectee, had been relieved of his company a few days earlier by Capt Lawrence Luther. Captain Dabney would command 881S and control our organic fire support. If the bulk of the battalion became too heavily engaged to make it back by night, no one was better qualified to defend 881S with limited forces if it came to that. Moreover, although Captain Dabney apparently lived a charmed life, his luck had about run out. With his predilection for exposing himself at the thickest point of any fire fight, it would have been a tragic conclusion to the ten-week siege of Hill 881S to lose the man who had contributed so much to its successful defense.

2. Maximum organic fire support. All the battalion's supporting arms would be organized into a provisional weapons company:

Eight 81mm mortars, organized in two sections with separate fire-direction centers to permit firing two simultaneous missions.

Eight 106mm recoilless rifles positioned on 881S to provide direct fire against point targets to the north. They were to prove invaluable for precision destruction of enemy forward-slope bunkers during the attack.

Six .50-caliber machine guns.

Three 105mm howitzers.

Three 60mm mortar sections from Lima, Mike, and India companies. Kilo Company's mortars would support them from Pork Chop Hill.

3. Surprise. Since the slightest observable movement invariably brought mortar fire on 881S, just getting through the wire and off the exposed slopes of 881S was a problem. The obvious answer was night movement. On the night of April 11, security patrols worked their way into positions covering the entire route to each company's attack position. Remaining concealed and motionless in daylight, they would serve three functions: reconnaissance, security for the battalion's movement to attack positions on the night of April 13–14, and guides for each company's night movement. Dog teams would also move with the company points until initial contact was made.

4. Maximum stand-off destruction of the enemy prior

to infantry assault. This was key to the whole operation and required maximum use of supporting arms. Fire support was planned in great detail, by the book. Every known and suspected enemy position was pre-plotted for "on-call" fires. Lieutenant Colonel Hennelly's guns at Khe Sanh Base would be firing with the long axis perpendicular to our axis of advance, an ideal arrangement. Fixed-wing strikes could then be run on deeper targets simultaneously with artillery missions, with air attacking parallel to the artillery trajectory.

Heavy prep fires by artillery and [radar-guided] bomb runs by aircraft would commence at midnight, April 13. Each objective would be heavily prepped just in advance of attacking infantry while aircraft hit deeper targets.

Finally, company commanders would exercise extreme care to avoid getting lead elements pinned down close-in to heavily resisting enemy strongpoints. In other words, they would do everything to counter Charlie's favorite tactic of knocking down our lead elements so close to his position as to prevent our further use of supporting arms. If heavy enemy fire was still encountered following our planned preps, the attacking companies would pull back and further supporting arms would be employed prior to infantry assault. Since the ground was not to be held, the mission was to inflict maximum casualties on the enemy with minimum loss of Marines.

5. Maneuver. The battalion would attack with three companies up, moving along three roughly parallel avenues of approach to 881N. The command group, with the fourth company (minus) as battalion reserve, would move in trace of the center company. If particularly strong resistance was encountered by any assault company, an adjacent company would be maneuvered to turn the flank of the strongpoint and/or deliver supporting fire. The reserve could be employed in any direction.

6. Speed. This was important to capitalize on surprise before the enemy could react by reinforcing or adjusting his heavy mortars or artillery or the attacking battalion. 3/26 was given one day to complete the operation.[2]

Pfc LIONEL TRUFANT
106mm Platoon, 3/26

After moving our 106mm recoilless rifle around the top of Hill 881S a few times, we set into a permanent position next to the landing zone. We had eight 106s up there—the four guns that had been up there the whole time, the two we brought up from the combat base, and two more from Hill 861. At that point, they told us that we were up there to help take Hill 881N.

I could see the NVA hill. It was like we were all on one side and they were all on the other side. As soon as we got our guns set in, we started firing on their hill. It was the first time we had really had a chance to fire our gun. The 106 gunners who had been on 881S told us how to use the recoilless rifles up there. Several times we used them to blow away mortar positions, or against snipers. They had us use the .50-caliber spotting rifle attached to the 106 to fire spotting rounds so we could plot in targets.

We just knew something big was coming. There was a great sense of anticipation. We had been taking all that shit all that while, and now we felt like giving some of it back.

Cpl DENNIS MANNION
Charlie Battery, 1/13 (with Kilo, 3/26)

Kilo Company left the hill early on Saturday morning, April 13, and cautiously walked downslope using trails into the draw between Hill 881S and Hill 881N. We dug in there with Marines from other companies. Having had the experience of Hill 861, we were really fearful of getting attacked. We dug good, deep, covered foxholes and cleared fields of fire with machetes. No one I know of slept that night.

APRIL 14

Col BRUCE MEYERS
26th Marines Commanding Officer

During early-morning darkness of Easter Sunday, April 14, LtCol John Studt and the major portion of his battalion wound through the "gate" in the wire and into attack positions.

LtCol JOHN STUDT
3/26 Commanding Officer _____

Security patrols covering the approach routes to attack positions had reported no enemy contact. Artillery preps commenced at midnight and continued throughout the night, with emphasis on bunker-busting, large-caliber rounds: 155mm and 175mm. Since heavy shellings in this area were not unusual, it was not anticipated that the enemy would necessarily be alerted to our attack. Known enemy positions to the south and west were also hit to further confuse the enemy as to our intent. . . .

The approach routes had been carefully studied by key personnel the previous day. Security elements along the routes acted as guides and joined their units as they passed.[3]

Capt HARRY JENKINS
Mike Company, 3/26 _____

The night of April 13–14 was very clear, with a three-quarter moon. It was very easy to see as Mike Company left the perimeter and moved down the hill into its attack positions. Starting at midnight, we worked down off the finger, into the ravine, carefully picked our way through the NVA positions at the base of the hill, and moved into our attack positions. The scout dog with the point platoon alerted its handler a few times as the company moved through the NVA positions, but nothing happened. As the point broke out of the brush and mounted a bare knoll, the dog gave a strong alert. The pointmen saw movement and opened fire. Screams were heard and the point moved forward to clear the area. All we found were two NVA packs. We did not find the people involved, or any signs that we had inflicted casualties. Lima Company, which had moved off Hill 881S right behind us and had veered off to the west at the bottom of the hill, made no contact of any kind. Neither did Kilo Company, which followed Lima and veered off to the east.

As soon as we got into the attack positions, I told my troops to lie down in the grass and get as much rest as possible. I was still very concerned with their physical conditioning. The terrain was steep, and if it was a hot day, a tremendous amount of physical exertion would be required. I wasn't sure how they would do.

LtCol JOHN STUDT
3/26 Commanding Officer

By 0530 all companies were in position; Lima and Mike companies were putting out scout elements with dog teams toward their first objectives. Just before first light, approximately 0545, both Lima and Mike companies' scout elements had made contact with the enemy's outposts on the approaches to Objectives 2 and 3. As the familiar staccato of AK-47s and NVA machine guns suddenly erupted to the front, we all knew that the surprise was over; the battle was on and it would be a fight all the way. Thanks to early warnings by the dogs, only one scout was wounded.

Mortars were adjusted on the enemy positions, and they were quickly overrun. The battle began to unfold exactly as planned.

Artillery was adjusted on Objectives 2 and 3 while mortars covered Objective 1. By now an aerial observer was on station and directing fixed-wing air strikes on Objectives 4 and Alpha.

As Lima moved out against Objective 3, they received heavy automatic-weapons and small-arms fire. They held up while further preps were called with 81s and 106s.[4]

LCpl CHARLIE THORNTON
Lima Company, 3/26

As we moved, we suddenly came under fire from a strong force of well-entrenched NVA. They had occupied a small hill and built a very strong defensive position of bunkers. As we tried to advance up the hill, we were turned back by heavy automatic-weapons fire and other small-arms fire.

The bunkers were well-concealed and we had trouble determining from where the fire was coming. I was the gunner of a 60mm mortar, which we moved back to a hill approximately fifty yards to our rear in order to improve our line of sight. Artillery had begun to support our position, but they were unable to destroy the bunkers or even slow down the fire we were receiving. I set my mortar up without using the sight because the angle of the hill made the line of sight impossible. I aligned the gun, pointing the barrel toward the targets by using my judgment and eyesight. The distance was very short, and the gun's trajectory was almost straight up. As we began firing white-phosphorus rounds to get on target, the NVA began to concentrate their fire on our gun. We fired high-explosive rounds until our ammunition was gone. We then moved forward to join the other Marines in assaulting the hill. My gun was later credited with five kills made by direct hits on the NVA bunkers.

Pfc ELWIN BACON
Kilo Company, 3/26

We started the climb up Hill 881N by breaking the company up into platoon-size units. Although there was small-arms fire going on everywhere, we seemed to be lucking out. As the 2nd Platoon moved slowly up the hill, we heard reports of all kinds of sightings of enemy units running along the ridges in great numbers. They seemed to be avoiding us as much as possible. At least, they were trying not to get boxed in by the Marines.

As we gained ground, we found heavily used trails and bunkers throughout the area. I got the feeling that there were a hell of a lot of those dudes around there somewhere. We found all kinds of things—food, clothes, and belts. I thought of some of them running around trying to shoot at us while they were holding their trousers up.

Cpl DENNIS MANNION
Charlie Battery, 1/13 (with Kilo, 3/26)

It was a classic, company-on-line advance. As long as the terrain didn't dictate differently, we stayed on line. Artillery from the combat base was firing tremendous numbers of rounds in front of us. They fired whole grid squares at a time, using the time-on-target technique, in which all the rounds fired land and detonate at one time. More impressive and more helpful to us, however, were the 106mm recoilless rifles and .50-caliber machine guns lined up in the trench along the top of Hill 881S. They were able to fire directly over our heads, into the treeline 150 yards ahead of us, just churning the place up as we moved forward. As we advanced, they raised the elevation on those guns and kept on firing.

Capt HARRY JENKINS
Mike Company, 3/26

As Mike Company started to push up to the final part of Objective 2, the pointman from one of the lead platoons was shot in the head and fell down on top of the position. The first thing we had to do was try to regroup and drag him back off the top of the hill. As we tried to do that, the NVA started rolling grenades down the steep portion of the hill, which was right in front of us. These caused people in the 1st Platoon to veer off to the right and I had to pull my command group back somewhat. We were able to get the casualty off the top of the hill, but he was already dead.

LtCol JOHN STUDT
3/26 Commanding Officer

Mike Company . . . ran into a reverse-slope defense, the first real surprise of the day. A grenade-throwing contest developed along the crest. It began to look like a long day! Mike was ordered to pull back 300 meters to permit the use of supporting arms. This was not easily done, as they now had one KIA on the crest and several wounded. Moreover, after months of being pounded by the enemy with little opportunity for the infantry to strike back, it was difficult to hold back the troops from premature assault. These Marines wanted to settle a score—and did before the day was over.[5]

Capt HARRY JENKINS
Mike Company, 3/26

The 106s lined up along the top of Hill 881S cleaned off Objective 2, in front of Mike Company, and after a lot of noise and confusion, we went back up the hill.

LtCol JOHN STUDT
3/26 Commanding Officer

As additional preps were delivered on Objectives 2 and 3, Kilo Company moved on Objective 1 and then slightly north of Objective 1 to bring fire to bear on the reverse slope of Objective 2. Only sniper fire was encountered by Kilo Company.[6]

Cpl TERRY STEWART
Mike Company, 3/26

I was lead for the whole movement, and I had Cpl Bob Saffle, my 1st Fire Team leader and his team, on point. I was right behind them. Halfway up the naked slope, we took vicious small-arms fire from several automatics. Bob's only two men were cut down without the chance to even fire a shot. Bob was pinned behind a small bush not twenty feet up to my left. Just ahead of him, I could see the muzzles of the enemy rifles sticking out of a well-camouflaged firing port. I called to Bob, but he was in a sort of shock; he wouldn't move in any direction. After several moments, I made a dash to him and pulled him back to a crater in which we could take cover.

Bob was crying and mumbling something about losing his whole team. He wasn't really very rational. I shook the shit out of him and he snapped right out of it. Once I had his attention, we decided that we had to knock out that bunker fast; the whole unit was pinned and, if we didn't get rolling, we could get flanked and end up in serious trouble. It was decided that we would both rush and draw the shooters to separate targets. This worked, and we got to spots that we knew were in areas that would be hard for anyone in that bunker to see. We were apart by maybe twenty-five yards, lying flat. The plan was for Bob to place sustained, well-aimed rounds directly into the firing port while I rushed from the right front and planted a grenade.

It looked like it was going to work, but as soon as I started to raise up to start my rush, a half-dozen Chicom grenades fell toward me. I guess we hadn't fooled anyone. I hugged the deck so low that an ant would have had to look down at me. I buried my head in my arms and slammed my legs together. I heard several of the grenades land near me, but the explosions I heard were not that awfully close. When the shock waves settled, I looked up. There were three duds within arm's reach of me. The remaining grenades had landed far enough away that I had escaped harm.

I wasted no time. Bob was keeping his end of the bargain, so I completed mine. I hit the bunker with a home run and went right on past to set up for the first men behind us. It was all over very quickly. We captured a couple of NVA from that hole. One was a warrant officer.

On the way up the hill, some poor guy was shaken real bad when an NVA round set off a LAAW he was carrying slung across his chest. The rocket went off and blew this poor bastard for a loop. Somehow he wasn't injured, but it must have made a devout worshiper out of him.

Capt HARRY JENKINS
Mike Company, 3/26 _____

We were able to go right over the top of Objective 2, consolidate our gains, and hold for further orders.

LtCol JOHN STUDT
3/26 Commanding Officer _____

Lima Company now launched an assault on Objective 3. Approximately fifty enemy broke and ran to the northwest, where they were promptly brought under fire by artillery, then air. The rest died in their positions, some by the preps, the others by close-in fighting as Marines cleared the position bunker by bunker. In ten minutes Objective 3 was secured.

The spirit of the assault troops was typified by Lance Corporal Patterson, a cool, slow-speaking Kentuckian. As he led his squad into the enemy positions, an NVA sniper popped up ten meters distant and fired. Patterson was knocked down by a round grazing his skull. Finding himself still alive, he jumped up with his M-16. As the enemy soldier attempted to chamber another round with his bolt-action sniper rifle, Patterson cut him down with a burst of automatic fire, then continued the attack. As Lima Company moved back onto 881S that night, Patterson was sporting a bloody head bandage and a scope-mounted NVA sniper rifle. After hearing the story, I asked him if he didn't feel pretty lucky. Patterson replied in a matter-of-fact tone that it all boiled down to his having cleaned his rifle the night before; Charlie apparently had not. In examining his trophy, Patterson noted that the NVA weapon had a cartridge jammed in a dirty chamber. Patterson, who had led his squad with distinction throughout the attack, was promoted to corporal on the spot.

Now that the high ground to both flanks was occupied, the enemy on Objective 2 decided it was time to pull out as Mike Company resumed the attack. Again the fleeing NVA were well covered with supporting arms.[7]

Capt HARRY JENKINS
Mike Company, 3/26

The battalion command group came up on my position, surveyed the situation, and ordered Mike Company to continue the attack to the north. The game plan was for Kilo Company to continue on its axis toward Hill 881N itself. Mike Company was to attack straight downhill behind Objective 2 toward a large, wooded bowl in a low area between Objective 2 and Hill 881N. Lima Company was supposed to stay in its position to support Kilo or Mike if it was needed. India Company remained in the rear, as battalion reserve. We jumped off again shortly after noon.

LtCol JOHN STUDT
3/26 Commanding Officer

Now a new threat developed. Observers on 881S reported that, in addition to the enemy trying to pull out to the west, approximately one NVA company was apparently taking up supplementary positions on the southern slope of 881N (Objective A), obviously planning to hit Mike Company as they came down the reverse slope of Objective 2. This was beautiful! While Mike Company held on the forward slope, for the next hour the NVA on 881N were hit with everything: air, artillery, mortars, and, not least, Captain Dabney's 106s. It was an unparalleled employment of recoilless rifles. Clearing my observation post on Objective 2 by inches, Captain Dabney adjusted his powerful weapons directly on individual enemy positions, literally blasting the NVA out of their bunkers. With eight guns and hundreds of rounds stockpiled on 881S, the hill was a veritable land battleship. The enemy attempted to suppress this fire with 122mm rockets.[8]

Pfc LIONEL TRUFANT
106mm Platoon, 3/26

We were peppering Hill 881N. The assaulting troops called in targets, and they were relayed to the guns from the battalion fire-control center through the 106 Platoon commander and our section chief, Cpl Gary Smith. When we fired, all we could see was the round going into trees and the trees getting blown out. We kept firing and hearing that the fire was effective.

We got a call from Corporal Smith that the NVA had just fired some 122mm rockets at us. Just as he finished talking, the rockets came in. When the first explosion sounded, I looked up and saw a body being thrown in the air. I knew who it was. It was Pfc Marvin Smith, the assistant gunner on the other gun in our section. Everybody on my gun just stopped. Then another rocket came in and exploded. That really stopped us. Our land line was out, we didn't know who was hit, we didn't know what was happening. After a minute or two, though, we started firing again. But the NVA had stopped our guns for a few minutes.

We kept firing until, finally, the word came down that helicopters were coming in. We started carrying the wounded guncrew down to the landing zone. One of them was Marvin Smith. He had been hit across the face and across the midsection. Pfc Gary Smith, the section leader, had his knee messed up. Another guy had his ear blown off, and another guy had a stomach wound.

My emotions were mixed. I talked to the guy with the stomach wound while I was waiting to put him on the helicopter. I had tears coming out of my eyes, but I still did what I had to do. The one that impacted the most was Marvin Smith. He was a buddy. I hated seeing him like that. The helicopters came in, we put them on the helicopters, and then we went back to our guns and started firing again.

LtCol JOHN STUDT
3/26 Commanding Officer

Four 106 crewmen were wounded, but our counterbattery fire quickly removed this threat.[9]

Pfc LIONEL TRUFANT
106mm Platoon, 3/26

One of the guns ran out of ammunition, but they needed ammo because they had a bunch of NVA caught in the open. I was an ammo man, so I had to carry two heavy rounds on each shoulder, running through the trenches to the gun that needed them. Mortars and rockets were still coming in, but we kept going.

The good thing about the 106s is that we could keep firing even when air strikes were coming in because their trajectory was so low. The mortars had to stop firing, but the 106s didn't. That meant we were free to fire immediately whenever the grunts got resistance from bunkers that were facing us.

Col BRUCE MEYERS
26th Marines Commanding Officer

The 106s and the .50s were used in a superb manner by the gunners in close coordination with Studt's lead elements. Always cautious of treelines, I remember seeing several treelines literally blown away, just yards in front of the advancing Marines. The barrels of the 106s got so hot at one point that we took turns joining the 106 crews in cooling the barrels by relieving ourselves and pouring water from our canteens on the steaming tubes.

Cpl DENNIS MANNION
Charlie Battery, 1/13 (with Kilo, 3/26)

Kilo Company was on the extreme right of the battalion line. Because of a point in the terrain where it got real steep, part of the company moved ahead while the other part got slowed down. I became extremely concerned because I knew what the artillery were doing. I was afraid the part of Kilo Company that was moving ahead faster would be hit by our own guns in an area I knew was going to be subjected to a time-on-target bombardment. I called the base and told them they had to shift the mission by 500 yards because I felt that part of Kilo Company was already on the fringes of the target grid square. The mission was shifted.

LtCol JOHN STUDT
3/26 Commanding Officer

By now it was all but over for Charlie. An aerial observer reported more NVA breaking from positions around 881N and running into the jungles to the west. Two flights of fixed-wing reported good target coverage, although no casualty assessment could be obtained due to the vegetation.

At approximately 1400, Kilo Company attacked 881N while Lima occupied the high ground just short of Objective 4, which was now deserted of live enemy. Mike Company, changing its direction of attack to the northwest to parallel Kilo's axis of advance, continued to mop up a vast complex of bunkers, tunnels, and storage caves between Objective 2 and 881N. Numerous bodies were found, mostly killed by supporting arms, which had caved in many bunkers. Two NVA wounded were also picked up, one an officer.[10]

Capt HARRY JENKINS
Mike Company, 3/26

What we had was an entire bunker complex—freshly dug holes, spiderholes, underground bunkers, all kinds of trenches. There were enough positions in there to hold a battalion. Fortunately, there was nobody in there.

Col BRUCE MEYERS
26th Marines Commanding Officer

As the advancing elements of 3/26 approached the hated crest of 881N, some of the NVA defenders broke and ran. My air officer heard from an air spotter, who asked for the lead elements to hold up while he called an air strike in on the fleeing NVA. However, with the exhilaration of nearly regaining what had once been theirs, the lead elements fixed bayonets and broke over the crest in a bayonet charge—despite the request to hold up from Studt's operations officer, Maj Matt Caulfield. The company commander said that he "could not stop them."

Cpl DENNIS MANNION
Charlie Battery, 1/13 (with Kilo, 3/26)

There were numerous dead North Vietnamese, but not in great quantities. They were scattered here and there, in caved-in bunkers and trenchlines. I fired my M-16 at two guys I saw running diagonally from my right. They went down under a hail of fire.

When we got to the top of Hill 881N, the smell of cordite and gunpowder was in the air. The smell was just incredible, more than I ever experienced during my tour. The torn-up landscape was something else.

One of the Marines on top of the hill had a flag. Another guy and I helped him up one of the few trees still standing, and he hung the flag up there.

LtCol JOHN STUDT
3/26 Commanding Officer

At 1428, Kilo Company, meeting only light resistance, swept across the scarred slopes of 881N and raised the National Colors.[11]

Pfc ELWIN BACON
Kilo Company, 3/26

When we reached the top of Hill 881N, I was surprised that the resistance was so light. There were many wounded and some KIAs, but the NVA didn't seem interested in holding the hill.

Cpl TERRY STEWART
Mike Company, 3/26

When we got to 881N we found an incredible mess. The hill had been devastated by B-52s, air strikes, and artillery. It was cratered like the moon, and all the trees were twisted and broken. It was an awesome sight. Some of their bunkers were sitting, ready to fall, at the very edge of bomb craters. I entered a couple. They were made of trees, dirt, and banana stalks.

Col BRUCE MEYERS
26th Marines Commanding Officer

I remember my burst of pride in seeing one of the lead Marines shinny up one of the shrapnel-torn trees and take a small American flag he had obviously been carrying in his pack for just such an event and raise the Stars and Stripes. That was the signal for the completion of the retaking of 881N.

The former defenders continued to retreat north on the reverse slope, on which we called an air strike, with excellent results. The battalion had been ordered to make a limited incursion, which they had done with success. They then began the planned withdrawal, bringing two slightly wounded NVA prisoners—one was an officer—whom I took back on my chopper to Khe Sanh for medical treatment and interrogation. There were 106 NVA killed in contrast to six Marines killed and nineteen Marines wounded and medevacked. We considered our "Easter egg hunt" to be a solid success. The night approach for the dawn assault paid off.

None of the subsequent actions pushing out from our original "siege" positions in the hills surrounding Khe Sanh had the success of LtCol John Studt's raid and subsequent withdrawal.

LtCol JOHN STUDT
3/26 Commanding Officer

Colonel Meyers, who had flown in during the height of the battle in spite of rocket and mortar fire hitting 881S, sent his congratulations. Throughout the attack he had personally ensured that the battalion received maximum fire support; this support, both artillery and air, was superb and a key factor in the success of the operation.

The final tally: 106 NVA bodies, two prisoners, numerous individual and crew-served weapons captured. No count could be obtained of the fleeing enemy killed by air and artillery in the jungles and eight-foot elephant grass to the west. Colonel Meyers personally landed near 881N and picked up the prisoners in his helicopter.

The cost: six Marines killed and thirty-two wounded, nineteen of which were medevacs. The battalion closed back on 881S that evening under a dense, protective fog. It was an unforgettable sight to study the Marines of 3/26 trudging back through the wire on 881S. After months of static defense, they were near exhaustion; they were filthy, bearded (water was scarce), and ragged, in tattered remnants of uniforms; some of them wore bloody battle dressings. But they were loaded with captured NVA weapons, and they were all grinning. An old score had been settled![12]

Chapter 31

BGen JACOB GLICK
Task Force Glick

I was sent up here on verbal orders from Major General Tomp-kins, Commanding General of 3rd Marine Division. At the time I was sent up here, I was Assistant Division Commander of 3rd Marine Division. I was sent to be prepared to take command of the forces here upon termination of Operation Pegasus, which was being run by the 1st Cavalry Division.

On April 15, at 0800, the remaining forces from Pegasus passed to the operational control of the 3rd Marine Division, and, in turn, passed to my operational control.

My mission is to continue offensive operations in the . . . area, to mop up enemy forces, to locate and capture enemy material and equipment, and to continue operations with mobile and flexible forces using maximum air, artillery, and all nature of supporting fires.

There are still extensive enemy forces in this area. We estimate ten to twelve enemy battalions, and our purpose will be to search out and continue to destroy enemy forces.

My initial mission when I came was to roll back the Khe Sanh Combat Base. The forces were going to be withdrawn from here, leaving only one battalion of highly mobile forces to be primarily a reconnaissance screen. That has since been changed, and my new mission is to remain here to continue the offensive operations against the enemy, to search him out and destroy him.[1]

Col BRUCE MEYERS
26th Marines Commanding Officer

The plan of withdrawal [includes provisions that on] April 15, 1st Battalion, 9th Marines, is to stay in position. . . . 3/26 will come into the base for lift-out the next day, April 16.[2]

Cpl DENNIS MANNION
Charlie Battery, 1/13

First Lieutenant Benjamin Fordham was about the same size as me—five-eleven, about 190 pounds—and liked to play football, like me. He liked to read, like me, and liked to talk about books, like me. In fact, when one of us got a book, he would read a chapter or two, then tear out that section and pass it on to the other until the book was gone. We shared a lot of books that way. And we shared some laughs about some of the books. As the Kilo Company artillery forward observer, I wasn't responsible to anyone except the captain, so I sort of got to free-lance all over the place. That allowed me to spend many hours with Lieutenant Fordham—bitching, planning, and speculating on the war, the Marine Corps, the country, and life in general. Even though he was an officer and I was enlisted, we got pretty close.

We spent the night of April 14—following the Easter Offensive—on the saddle between Hills 881N and 881S. As we were being choppered off the saddle on the morning of April 15, Fordham's platoon had landing-zone security. Two of the rifle platoons had already been lifted out. As the company command group crawled to the edge of the zone, I happened to be stretched out in the dirt next to Lieutenant Fordham. As we watched the last two CH-46s approach, we both laughed and touched hands. We were on our way out!

Just as my chopper touched down, two good-sized rounds exploded in the scrub trees about 100 yards from us. We looked at one another and shrugged. As I ran past him, he yelled up to me to say that he would be right behind, on the last chopper. Four minutes later, I stepped off my chopper at the main base. I was greeted with the news that, as the lieutenant's men rushed for the last CH-46, two mortar rounds hit at the edge of the landing zone.

Lieutenant Benjamin Fordham was the last member of Kilo Company killed at Khe Sanh.

Capt HARRY JENKINS
Mike Company, 3/26

When we were lifted off Hill 881S to the combat base by helicopter, it appeared that Mike Company's role in the siege had ended. We landed at the edge of Red Sector, just off the airstrip, and were told that we were to be lifted out of the combat base by helicopter later that afternoon.

The only cover I was able to find for the company in this area was the old trench that followed the perimeter between Red Sector and Blue Sector. It was only three feet deep at its deepest point. I spread the company along the trench for a distance of 250 meters. Shortly thereafter, we began undergoing an ordeal the likes of which Mike Company had not experienced the entire time it was on Hill 881S.

About 1300, the 37th ARVN Ranger was moving en masse from one end of the perimeter to the other, from east to west along the airstrip. The NVA artillery forward observers in the hills picked up the movement and we began to take artillery fire from the 130mm and 152mm batteries located at Co Roc, in Laos.

The initial incoming rounds impacted about midway along the runway. As the ARVN Rangers continued to move, still somewhat en masse, the NVA forward observers continued to adjust their artillery. Gradually, over a period of forty-five minutes, the artillery was continually adjusted and moved farther west, toward Mike Company.

After about an hour of this, the ARVN Rangers were almost at the western end of the runway and into our area, where they appeared to go to ground. At that time, the NVA artillery began firing for effect—entire batteries of four or six guns opened up with one or two rounds per gun. It just happened that, as they tried to blanket the area where the ARVNs were located, their artillery fell on us.

What occurred over the next ninety minutes was what I would call a mass artillery attack. We could hear the guns going off in Laos and had to sweat it out for ten or fifteen seconds before we could hear the shriek of the rounds coming in and impacting. Initially we were not harmed, but the artillery was eventually adjusted, shifted from the ARVN Rangers to where we were. We could not move, we could not dig, there was no place to go.

Dozens of artillery rounds fell within our area. By the time it was over, the majority of the troops in Mike Company were thoroughly shaken by the experience.

Cpl TERRY STEWART
Mike Company, 3/26 _____

I was assigned as an advance man. I had lost most of my men, and the remaining few were sent to other squads. I had the mailbag and was supposed to take one of the first birds out of Khe Sanh to Quang Tri to help get ready for the rest of the company. I was sitting well away from my unit, at the edge of the airstrip, when the big guns in Co Roc cut loose. My platoon commander, 2ndLt William Ammon, and my platoon sergeant, Staff Sergeant Harriman, were tucked up beneath a tank at the edge of the strip when a single round came in and hit just under the lip of the tank. It was a million-to-one shot that propelled both men out the other end like rifle bullets. The lieutenant was killed instantly and Staff Sergeant Harriman was critically injured.

Captain Jenkins got in touch with me since I was the next-senior man in my platoon. I rushed back to Mike Company under heavy artillery. I would get only a few steps and have to dive for cover in the trenches that bordered the strip. I couldn't move through them because they were packed with men. At one point, I dived as I heard a round coming in and landed right on top of another Marine. I hit him sort of hard and knocked the wind out of him. As I was helping him, he saw "MICH" on my helmet and asked where I was from. I told him I was from Charlevoix. He said that he was from Hudsonville. I mentioned that my grandfather was from there, also. He asked his name and I told him. He nearly jumped out of the trench. We had the same grandfather! The guy I landed on was my first cousin, whom I had not seen since we were about five years old. It was a very quick reunion and I was off as soon as I heard the air was clear.

Capt HARRY JENKINS
Mike Company, 3/26 _____

The artillery attack disrupted the plans to get 3/26 out of Khe Sanh on April 15. We had to spend another night in the combat base. We dispersed into a number of abandoned bunkers and spent a quiet night.

APRIL 16

Col BRUCE MEYERS
26th Marines Commanding Officer _____

On April 16, the 3rd Battalion, 26th Marines, would fly to Quang Tri; the 1st Battalion, 26th Marines, would come on into the Khe Sanh Combat Base; and a battalion of the 1st Marines would come up and relieve 2/26 in the northern tier of hill positions.[3]

Pfc LIONEL TRUFANT
106mm Platoon, 3/26 _____

We flew back to Quang Tri on CH-53 helicopters. I felt good, but I also felt bad because we had lost a lot of people. Even though Khe Sanh was a bad place, it was like a lot of other places—once I left it, I felt like I was leaving something there.

Pfc ELWIN BACON
Kilo Company, 3/26 _____

As we lifted off the ground, I was very tight and nervous about the whole thing. And just when we started to circle until the other choppers were airborne, more rockets came in. All of a sudden a loud bang came from the bottom of our chopper. My thoughts were, Oh, shit! The pilot took the bird down sharply, probably out of instinct, but he then leveled off. As I looked out the window, I could see a flare floating down below. It seemed as though the rockets had hit a flare bunker, and one just happened to come up to meet us.

HM3 DAVID STEINBERG
India Company, 3/26

Finally, almost at dusk, they brought choppers in for India Company. One of our guys had just been hit, and I put down my pack with everything I owned in it. I lifted the wounded Marine onto my back and carried him over to Charlie-Med. When I got there, a reporter stuck a camera in my face and asked, "What you got there?" I put down the wounded Marine and said, "I got my fist." And I punched the reporter in the face. I'm not that way, but I had a lot of emotions going on. Instead of helping me carry the wounded Marine across an open field, under incoming, all he wanted to do was take a picture and do an interview. My buddy came first.

When I left Charlie-Med, I saw the open back of the chopper. Someone yelled, "Come on, Doc. It's the last chopper out. We're gettin' outta here." The back of the CH-46 was open and the rotors were going. Over to the left was my pack. I had two choices: all the material things in my life that were in the pack, or getting on the chopper. I made a right turn and got aboard the chopper, which took off right away. I never saw my pack again, but my wallet reached me about two months later.

Pfc ELWIN BACON
Kilo Company, 3/26

There was a small band and a number of people waiting there to greet us. We must have looked as bad as we smelled, and I noticed that most people kept their distance from us. The band played while we stripped naked in front of God and the world and walked through open showers, which were set up like a bunch of coatracks. As long as we were up there, I felt as though we were being treated like a bunch of hogs getting washed for slaughter.

HM3 DAVID STEINBERG
India Company, 3/26

It was dark by the time we got to Quang Tri. We had red sand instead of red clay. The people of India Company, 3/26, had made it out of Khe Sanh. It was party time! We had showers! They gave us new clothing! We shaved! They had steaks for us, and beer! We drank beer and we ate and the war was over for us. Everything was happy and gay. We slept in tents right across from the Quang Tri airstrip. We felt so secure and safe—until 0300. The eighteen survivors of the original India Company on Hill 881S became twelve. They rocketed us! Six of them were killed that night when one of the 122mm rockets hit their tent. It was like they followed us down to kill the rest of us off.

HM3 BILL GESSNER
Delta Company, 1/9

On the night of April 15, the [ARVN 3rd Airborne Task Force] moved off their ridge and attacked south. On the morning of April 16, 1/9 moved down off Hill 689 and over the ridge vacated by the ARVN. Alpha Company was leading, and Delta Company was last in the formation. Alpha Company walked into a big ambush. The battalion commander committed Bravo and Charlie companies right away to relieve the pressure on Alpha Company, but the NVA were too well positioned. Delta Company joined the fight. We assaulted the southern slope and got up to the enemy's first foxholes, then we were stopped. The battalion commander, already wounded once, was wounded again while visiting the Delta Company command post. I put a dressing on him, and he continued on his way.

Our second attack was stalled by furious small-arms fire. I was crawling toward a hole when an NVA soldier stuck his head up to see. I froze. Fortunately for me, someone else saw the man and shot him. I pulled him out of the hole and climbed in. I was joined by a couple of Marines, and we decided we couldn't go any farther. Just then, our CO crawled by and told us to get moving— so we did. I crawled another few yards and tumbled into a bomb crater. The forward air controller and another Marine joined me. Then a wounded man crawled into the bomb crater with us. I was squatting over him to bandage his wounds when the lights went out.

When I came to, I sat up and checked the wounded man. He was dead. I looked around and saw the forward air controller lying on his back. I found he had a sucking chest wound and another less serious wound. The other Marine was dead. The forward air controller asked me to help him down the hill. When I started to drag him, I found out that I'd been wounded in the left leg. I put a bandage on the leg, and we started down to the rear of the hill. Battalion had designated a casualty collection point on a piece of level ground on the east side of the hill—so helicopters could land. When I got down to the casualty collection point, it was crowded with wounded. Some had been treated and others had not. I didn't see any other corpsmen there, so I stayed and treated the Marines on the pickup zone. During the day, small-arms and incoming artillery kept medevac choppers from extracting any of the wounded. Several choppers were shot down. Finally, after dark, choppers started taking casualties out. The CH-53s couldn't land on the hill; they had to hover while casualties were loaded. I helped load several choppers before my leg gave out. I rode out to Dong Ha and the 3rd Medical Battalion.

Before my letter arrived home, the Navy casualty reporter at Quonset Naval Air Station called my father at the house. He wasn't home, but my stepmother was. She asked, "What is the call about?" The casualty reporting officer replied, "I can't tell you over the phone. When will Mr. Gessner be home?" Naturally, my stepmother assumed the worst. She told the casualty officer to come at seven that night. Then she called my dad and my fiancée. Dad tried to call the casualty officer back, but he couldn't get him.

When the casualty officer arrived, my fiancée and the whole family was there. He said, "You son was wounded in the left leg in fighting near Khe Sanh."

My dad asked, "Well, how serious is the wound?"

"I don't know. But because he's still at Dong Ha, it means it's either really bad or not too bad at all."

After I heard about that, I refused a Purple Heart for another minor wound.

The April 16 fight involving 1/9 resulted in very heavy casualties: nineteen KIAs, thirty-six serious WIAs, an unknown number of minor WIAs, and sixteen MIAs. It took 1/9 days and cost more lives to locate and recover most—not all—of the MIAs, all of whom were from Alpha Company. An unknown number of NVA solders died in the action that involved, at the most, one NVA company.

Pfc MIKE DeLANEY
Echo Company, 2/26 (Hill 861A) _____

We got word on April 14 that we were going to the combat base. Not that we were leaving Khe Sanh, but that we were leaving the hill, and we're leaving it ASAP. When they told us to start tearing down the hill, we said, "You gotta be kidding, when are we leaving?" They said, "Tomorrow morning." So, we asked, "What are we going to do tonight?" They told us to bayonet our sandbags—all of them—and pour them out into the holes, to tear up everything. We were being asked to spend the night on top of the ground, in the open. Nothing had ever slowed down; there was still shit happening all the time. That made everybody very uneasy. We had to think, Do we rejoice? We're getting off this hill, but is it any better where we're going? Nobody had the answers, just that we were leaving the hill. One minute we were very pleased, then we were scared to death. I had been fighting my ass off to stay on that hill, and now they were asking me to walk down it. They weren't going to chopper us off; we were going to walk off. I thought that was kind of neat because we were leaving by our own will.

We tore it all apart for a day and a half, and left it.

LCpl WILLIAM MAVES
Echo Company, 2/26 _____

Of the original sixteen or eighteen men in the company command group, all but me and the two corpsmen had left, one way or another. The CO and two others rotated, while the rest were either killed or wounded. We turned Hill 861A over to the Army when they were flown in, and we were to join the rest of the battalion on Hill 558. After ninety-two days without washing and wearing the same clothes, we were looking forward to bathing in the creek we knew flowed just outside the 558 perimeter. Several of us were in that creek the afternoon we got to 558, including me and my two corpsmen friends. We had just dug our hole together and had put a poncho roof on it for our last night in the Khe Sanh valley. Tomorrow, we were to fly out to Camp Carroll.

Thirteen of the two dozen or so of us bathing in the creek headed back toward the wire. I couldn't go just then. Doc wanted to, but the water was just too nice. I told him I would come back with the second group. The first group crossed the open ground in front of the wire, and Charlie dropped a salvo of three 122mm rockets. Of the thirteen Marines ready to leave, seven were dead, five were wounded, and one stood untouched except for shell shock. I sat in the creek, shaking, crying, and laughing. A second salvo of three rockets came in over our heads and into the trees, hurting nothing except the landscape. I remember a lieutenant asking me if I was all right or if I was hit. I could only stare at him and nod. Somehow, I felt all the rockets were aimed at me, that none of the originals were supposed to escape. The corpsmen were both dead, and Charlie had only one more of us to get. I sat up that night in our hole, wondering when they would come for me.

Midmorning the next day, April 17, I flew out of the Khe Sanh valley, forever. I left alone.

APRIL 17

Cpl TERRY STEWART
Mike Company, 3/26 _____

After my platoon commander was killed by the artillery attack on April 15, I was given the command of my platoon. We were all the way at the end of the trench and the last unit of 3/26 to be lifted out. At sundown, April 16, the fog started to roll in and the birds were called off. As far as I knew, there was just one pit of about thirty men left in all of Khe Sanh. Mine. I was instructed to find a secure position and hold on until daylight. I took the men to the Combat Operations Center and we set up a very tight perimeter around there. We were all on the line all night. I plotted more "on calls" than any artillery battery could possibly fire, but I was assured that guns were up and ready for us on a moment's notice. It was one restless night. We sat with rifles in our shoulders all night, ready to fight like we'd never dreamed of. After all, it was said that there were 60,000 NVA in the area during the height of the siege, and Lang Vei, down the road, had been overrun with over 500 defenders guarding it. But the night passed with nothing more than the scurrying of rats. We were used to them, so it wasn't all that traumatic.

The next morning, April 17, the birds came in and started to drop off men from another Marine regiment. I had my men broken down into helo teams long before dawn, and we wasted no time boarding the choppers as they emptied. I was the very last man. I stopped only for a brief second to look back at the base. It was a mess! Then I glanced out at 881S, way off in the distance. The fog was just lifting, and I was struck by how beautiful the hill looked from where I was standing. It was hard to imagine that it wasn't as peaceful and beautiful as it appeared just now. I watched it the whole time the bird was lifting off and flying away.

Cpl WALT WHITESIDES
3/26 Tactical Air Control Party

All were in high spirits since it was apparent that the worst of Khe Sanh was over. While it probably couldn't be called a victory, survival in itself was reason to be grateful. Several of the Marines I knew that had been on the hills for a long time were nervous about being in comparatively large spaces at Khe Sanh. One wireman, Pfc Tommy Williams, remarked to me that it was different, that he was used to listening for the pop of a mortar, not the distant boom of artillery or the sound of incoming rockets. Unfortunately, that day, Tommy was caught in an upright position and wounded by shrapnel. LCpl Toby Jackson and I tried to save him, but he was very badly wounded in the torso and abdomen. He bled to death before we could get a corpsman to the scene.

APRIL 18

Col BRUCE MEYERS
26th Marines Commanding Officer

The decision having been made to withdraw the 26th Marines as a unit from Khe Sanh, we airlifted out the few pieces of regimental equipment that were still operable. By then, Route 9 had been opened. We thus were able to use Route 9 to bring out the larger, road-bound pieces of equipment, such as Ontos, tanks, and generators. However, the vast bulk of the regiment's equipment had been severely damaged during the siege.

I sent my two ARVN battalions out a day or two ahead of the regiment and used headquarters units and adjacent Marine units to fill the gap in the perimeter where the two small ARVN battalions had been. The major airlift of the 26th Marines was on April 18.

1stLt NICK ROMANETZ
Charlie Company, 1/26 _____

Helicopters bringing in a new battalion brought us out of Khe Sanh. One of the birds landed with its ass end at the edge of a minefield, with his belly straddling the triple concertina wire. Before anyone could do anything, he dropped the ramp and Marines came running out. They took at least two casualties when they tripped our own mines.

Flying out of the base, it still looked beautiful. There were a lot of pockmarks, but it looked pretty. My parting thoughts were that I could still remember how pretty the place looked when I was coming in. It was still pretty, but it was a moonscape pretty, with a lot of the jungle all torn up and the elephant grass gone. I was glad to leave it.

My platoon had about sixty guys in it throughout the siege. We had seven guys killed—a couple by snipers and the rest by incoming.

1stLt ERNIE SPENCER
1/26 Intelligence Officer _____

I take a seat next to the door gunner on the forward jumpseat of a CH-46. Half a rifle platoon has boarded with me.

As soon as we're at cruising altitude, the pilot removes his flight helmet and places it on his lap. Looking back at me, he says, "Relax, I'm going to get you out of this." He's got a big fucking John Wayne smile on his face.

I jump to my feet and lunge at him. "Fuck you! Fuck you!" I scream.

I watch that John Wayne smile melt. I'm not sure if he can hear what I'm saying, but I know he is bothered by my snarl. I stare at him until he turns his John Wayne ass around. He puts his helmet on and does not look back.[4]

Col BRUCE MEYERS
26th Marines Commanding Officer _____

On one of the last of the choppers making the withdrawal of the 26th Marines from Khe Sanh, I asked the pilot to make a final swing—out of range of potential 12.7mm antiaircraft fire. I remember vividly commenting to my regimental operations officer, "It looks like the mountains of the moon!"—a reference to the Arclight bomb craters that virtually ringed Khe Sanh and its surrounding hill outposts. I thought to myself that the earth and jungle torn up from the numerous B-52 missions was a superb visual example of how the concentration of American firepower—combined Air Force and Navy/Marine Corps close air support, supplemented by massed artillery—was the nemesis of General Giap in his frustrated attempt to replicate his victory over the French at Dienbienphu.

The bulk of the regiment—2/26 and 3/26—was airlifted to Quang Tri while 1/26 went to Dong Ha. The troops were given hot showers and a steak through the efforts of General Tompkins. Our first task was to reassemble all of the missing field equipment—trucks, jeeps, generators, and crew-served weapons—to replace those that had been either destroyed or damaged in the siege. All units in III Marine Amphibious Force were scoured, and many people surplus to the official unit tables of organization were pulled away and given to the 26th Marines. I am sure that many of my fellow regimental commanders had few kind words to say about this temporary depletion from their units to replace our gear.

Pfc MIKE DeLANEY
Echo Company, 2/26 _____

April 18, 1968

Dear Mom and Dad,
What are you guys doing? Well, I'm not at Khe Sanh now, or on Hill 861A. We're at Camp Carroll, a Marine base by Dong Ha. I sure am glad to be off that hill and out of Khe Sanh. We lost better than 200 men there. It was just a living hell.

Cpl DENNIS MANNION
Charlie Battery, 1/13 _____

Quang Tri, April 18, 1968

Dear Joe,

I'm out! Khe Sanh has been left behind! Don't get me wrong. I'm not being cocky. Only the lucky get out of Khe Sanh alive. Being good or talented doesn't help there.

From Hill 881N, we were helilifted to Khe Sanh, where I was detached from 3/26 and sent back to Charlie Battery. Meanwhile, Kilo and the rest of 3/26 were choppered out of Khe Sanh. On the third day, they decided to cut Charlie Battery some slack and decided to send us back to the rear with 3/26. Twenty-four hours later, I'm stepping off the chopper at Quang Tri, abandoning my gear and clothes, and stepping into a hot shower.

I got new clothes, a steak dinner, root beer, and Black Label beer. So fantastic! Like being brought to a new world. Today and tomorrow we'll be sitting on our asses.

1stLt JOHN KAHENY
1/26 Combat Operations Center _____

When we went down to the airstrip for the extract from Khe Sanh, the new battalion commander, LtCol Frederick McEwan, asked me to stay with the tactical air control party that was running the helilift. I was to ensure that everyone got out okay and to check out with Regiment. There were just the four of us sitting on the airstrip.

We ran out of helicopters. We filled them all up, but the air officer, our two radio operators, and I were left. The air officer got on the radio and complained bitterly that none of us—especially me—wanted to stay another night at Khe Sanh. I had gotten there just short of a year earlier. Well, a lame CH-46 came around; it's rear ramp would not come down, but he said if we could catch him on the runway he would let us pile in.

He came down and we ran out. First we threw the radios in, then the radio operators, then the air officer. Someone gave the "up" sign to the crew chief, indicating that I was aboard. But I hadn't really gotten over the edge of the ramp yet. As they started to pull me in, the helicopter took off and banked sharply to avoid enemy fire. My cartridge belt and trousers caught on the lip of the ramp, so the harder they pulled the more my pants went down. I was finally rolled into the aircraft with my cartridge belt and trousers around my ankles.

I've always thought it was very fitting to leave the combat base that way—mooning two divisions of the North Vietnamese Army.

EPILOGUE

The Khe Sanh Combat Base was razed to the ground approximately three months after the siege was lifted. Khe Sanh's traditional screening and surveillance missions were shifted approximately twelve kilometers east, to Ca Lu, because LZ Stud—renamed LZ Vandergrift by its Marine tenants—could not be reached by North Vietnamese 130mm and 152mm artillery emplaced in Laos. Over the next seven years of war, the ruins of the old combat base and its airstrip were occupied from time to time by both sides, but not permanently.

Capt HARRY BAIG
26th Marines Target Information Officer

Throughout the siege, there were three phases of combat. The first was the face-to-face confrontations of Marines and North Vietnamese as they met at the wire or in the vicinity of the Khe Sanh Combat Base. The second was the daylight attacks by supporting arms on known targets or on targets of opportunity. Air, artillery, and mortars, during this phase, were controlled by forward observers, by aerial observers, or by forward air controllers under the overall management of the Regimental Fire Support Coordination Center. The third and, to my mind, the most important phase was the planned nightly schedule of fires of artillery, the schedule of radar-controlled aircraft and B-52 Arclight strikes, all employed together for the saturation bombardment of enemy fortifications, weapons positions, and troop concentrations, and all under the closest control of the Fire Support Coordination Center. In addition, there were many nighttime targets of opportunity.

The actual battle plan for the reduction of KSCB and its surrounding outposts was revealed by Lieutenant La Thanh Tonc on January 20, 1968. The enemy never deviated from that plan. Tonc's revelation of the concept of operations, prior and detailed knowledge of the NVA methodology, the requirements of siege warfare, and the lessons of Dienbienphu and Con Thien, gave the intelligence and target team all the information we needed to plan the nature of the supporting-arms countermeasures. Though on occasion I had cause to question the accuracy of my assumptions, nevertheless events tended to prove that we were correct. The manner in which Colonel Lownds assimilated his intelligence and welded together his fighting assets, from private to pilot, speaks volumes about the effectiveness of the Marine response to General Giap. In a sentence, Colonel Lownds employed traditional Marine tactics and doctrine of the twentieth century against an enemy who chose to put his faith and fortune in usages of the eighteenth.

Throughout the siege, our main concern was with the southeastern sector. Here, in an area some five kilometers square, the Fire Support Coordination Center coordinated a good proportion of the supporting arms; here was felt the weight of the Mini and Micro Arclights; here were fired the majority of the artillery clearance fires. Throughout this area, too, the enemy prepared his siegeworks, bunker complexes, trenches, parallels, saps, and connectors. So intensely did the NVA prepare the ground that targets ceased to be regarded individually; instead, ground, and that which lay within it, was the target. . . . From a distance of 500 to 1,500 meters outside the perimeter, the ground was subjected to saturation bombardment. The fact that the enemy never altered his intentions for this area is a further indication of his inflexibility and rigidity. . . .

There is no question that to Colonel Lownds goes the credit for the successful defense of Khe Sanh and for the destruction of two NVA divisions. To my mind, his greatest gift lay in his ability to use his staff. Recognizing that his offensive capability lay with his supporting arms, Colonel Lownds called upon the Fire Support Coordination Center for more and greater efforts. Given enough supplies, he could have held indefinitely. This was not only his view, but the opinion of everyone, too.

But some of the credit must go to General Giap and the NVA. They gave us a good fight, and in the process they destroyed themselves. A man and a force, both known as past masters of guerrilla warfare, infiltration techniques, and siege tactics, were finally revealed as stolid, rigid, inflexible, and unbelievably foolish opponents. Our experience, during those seventy-seven days, legitimately raises the question, "Who besieged whom?" For a man who in civil life was alleged to have been a teacher of mathematics, General Giap had not studied his Vauban very closely. Had he profited from the teachings of the eighteenth-century French master of siegecraft, Giap could have caught us in the "toils of Euclid"—to our possible discomfort.

Newspaper correspondents never knew of the total weight and effectiveness of our artillery. . . . Inexperienced as they were, they magnified the volume of the enemy incoming rounds and disregarded the relative ineffectiveness of the enemy artillery. Had the NVA been capable of our artillery techniques, they could and would have blown us out of Khe Sanh. The siege clearly established not only the bankruptcy of the NVA master plan, but also the ineptitude of their vaunted artillery. And the press never saw this clearly.[1]

BOB BREWER
Quang Tri Province Senior Adviser _____

What we should have done was go right back in immediately and retake Huong Hoa District Headquarters after we lost it on January 20–21. But, by then, our military leaders had embraced the idea of the set-piece battle, which they expected to win. My several meetings with Colonel Lownds, General Tompkins, and General Truong [1st ARVN Division Commander] at Khe Sanh Combat Base in late January and February revolved around this issue. Truong wanted to retake Huong Hoa. In fact, he always resented the fact that I had ordered Capt Bruce Clarke to abandon the district headquarters and fight his way to KSCB on January 21. I felt after the eventual failure of the Tet Offensive that the Communists around Khe Sanh were just playing games, and that a breakout and reestablishment of order in what was left of Huong Hoa District were of paramount importance, but the U.S. military wanted to *operate*. That mentality, in the end, broke our support at home, in Vietnam, and elsewhere. We lost the war because too much was made of military victories and too little of day-to-day civil-political losses.

Capt EARLE BREEDING
Echo Company, 2/26 _____

The NVA we killed on Hill 861A on February 5 were clean-cut, and they had good haircuts. Their gear was in immaculate condition, hardly worn at all. It was all good stuff, all new. The clothing was all good. They were young, most of them. I believe they were the last of the NVA's hard-core troops, the last of their home reserves, the last of their young generation of soldiers. I think they went for broke—and lost. They didn't launch another major offensive like Khe Sanh or Tet until they went down and took Saigon in 1975. But that was the next generation. In 1968, they lost the last of their best new troops during Tet and at Khe Sanh.

Capt HARRY JENKINS
Mike Company, 3/26 _____

The United States had men in space while we were at Khe Sanh, yet we couldn't get the basic essentials like toothbrushes and soap to the troops manning the combat outposts without a great amount of difficulty.

1stLt FRED McGRATH
Bravo Battery, 1/13 _____

There are many accounts in existence concerning the pros and cons of defending Khe Sanh. Those concerns never entered our minds on the ground. The Marines I dealt with saw Khe Sanh as a chance to grapple with Charlie in a set piece. This did not happen very often in Vietnam, so the chance to do so was exciting. As time wore on, that enthusiasm did not wane. It was always the case that "Charlie is out there. Let him come and get it!" Marines tend to be apolitical. We couldn't have cared less whether General Westmoreland had ulterior motives in assigning the defense of Khe Sanh to the Marines. We had a mission. No sweat.

Maj JIM STANTON
26th Marines Fire Support Coordination Center _____

One school of thought has it that the NVA opened the siege in order to fix a reinforced regiment of Marines in an unimportant corner of the country and oblige us to divert thousands of sorties away from the real Tet objectives, such as Hue City and Saigon. That is a legitimate observation from a strategic point of view. Another school of thought has it that we wanted to be there because Khe Sanh lay astride their major infiltration route from North Vietnam. In fact, they were going around us, but if we had been able to patrol actively out of the combat base, we would have been able to raise havoc on the infiltration routes. So this school of thought feels that the NVA pinned us inside Khe Sanh to relieve pressure on the infiltration routes.

About midway through the siege, I was privy to a heated debate between Colonel Lownds and MGen Ray Davis, a Marine who was then serving as the deputy commander of the provisional Army corps operating in I Corps. General Davis was furious with Lownds for sitting inside the base, for not aggressively attacking the NVA. I knew that Lownds wanted to be out there moving—Marines hate to be cooped up—but he was under orders from the division commander, General Tompkins, to sit and take it. So there was Lownds, defending a strategy I don't really think he believed in to a general whose views coincided with his own but who had no authority to change things. Later that year, when General Davis got command of 3rd Marine Division, Khe Sanh and a lot of other fixed bases were dismantled and the division's battalions and regiments were sent out to the field to operate.

MGen JOHN TOLSON, USA
1st Cavalry Division Commanding General _____

On my visits to Khe Sanh Combat Base during the latter part of March and the first half of April, I always felt that I had been to the most depressing and demoralizing place I had ever visited. It was a very distressing sight, completely unpoliced, strewn with rubble, duds, and damaged equipment, and with troops living a life more similar to rats than to human beings.[2]

LCpl PHIL MINEER
Bravo Battery, 1/13 _____

The news clippings we got kept referring to Dienbienphu. There we were, 5,000 Marines in this little base, surrounded by twenty times as many NVA led by General Giap. They had us written off. But it wasn't that way inside the combat base. Nobody gave up. It was shitty—really bad—but all we wanted to do was go out after them. But they wouldn't let us. We were ready. All we wanted to do was kick ass. We had had enough of it.

I got home on Mother's Day, 1968. Sometime later, I was watching the news when I heard they were folding the combat base, destroying the bunkers, and pulling out of there. It burst my bubble. It made no sense. I knew the blood that went down there. I knew what guys went through to hold on to that place. And they just folded it up. All along, everyone was saying it was so political. That confirmed it.

LCpl CHARLIE THORNTON
Lima Company, 3/26 _____

The worst part of the duty at Khe Sanh was our inability to fight back effectively. We had to sit and endure the constant shelling without a way of striking back except for the response of our own artillery shelling. There were many times when we wished for an opportunity to move outside the perimeter to seek out the NVA. We ultimately did exactly that. However, it was not until April, when the siege was ending, that we were allowed to move into the mountains surrounding the base.

This was, of course, the end of the siege. We just packed up and left like nothing had ever happened. We certainly did not think at the time that it would be an event that would gain such notoriety. We were completely unaware of the detailed news coverage that was being broadcast to the States. The shame of it all is that we lived and died through such dreadful times just to give it all back.

During Khe Sanh and the rest of my thirteen-month tour of duty, I became close to men from all walks of life and cultural backgrounds. We became comrades and brothers because of common desires—not to defeat an enemy, but to survive thirteen months and go home alive. There was very little patriotism left in anyone after a tour of duty in Vietnam. We all loved our homeland, but we knew this war only served to bolster some general's ego in Washington as he recorded the daily body counts.

LCpl ARMANDO GONZALES
Bravo Company, 1/9

No country, no government, no military has the right to do what our government, country, and military did to us. Without any intention of winning, they put us out as bait. That was totally wrong.

HN ROD DeMOSS
1st Battalion, 26th Marines

We had held Khe Sanh, which earned us a Presidential Unit Citation, but we also just abandoned Khe Sanh, which really disillusioned me. We had risked our lives to hold this place, and then we just walked off and left it.

MGen TOMMY TOMPKINS
3rd Marine Division Commanding General

What was my reaction? Nothing. Khe Sanh had served its purpose. Now they were going to do something else.[3]

1stLt JOHN KAHENY
1/26 Combat Operations Center

Being home on emergency leave during late February and all of March was an interesting experience. The press had built up the siege at Khe Sanh to the point where people I met couldn't believe that I had just been there, much less that I was going to be going back, or that it was so easy—relatively speaking—to get in and out of there. I was much distressed while watching news accounts on television when I first got home, because I was catching up on incidents that had occurred while I was still at Khe Sanh. There seemed to be a general sense in the United States of doom and gloom about the siege that I found hard to believe. I was most distressed when I picked up the March 24 issue of *Newsweek* and found that the centerpiece of the Vietnam news was devoted to showing the results of the incident in which the platoon from

Bravo Company had gotten ambushed on February 25. What disturbed me most was that the platoon commander, Don Jacques, whom I knew quite well, was shown with his groin shot out and being dragged through the wire. The editors lacked common sense and feeling toward Don's parents. There was no reason to show him the way they did. The general thrust of the article—and everything else in the press—was that the Marines were hopelessly outnumbered, that it was another Dienbienphu. We used to joke about *Hell in a Very Small Place* because we had a copy of it in our operations center, but we knew we were not in such dire straits as the French had been. As a matter of fact, the general attitude of most Marines was that they couldn't wait to get going back out there to drive the enemy away from Khe Sanh.

If President Johnson had had one-tenth the courage of the Marines at Khe Sanh, the siege wouldn't have lasted as long as it did.

2ndLt SKIP WELLS
Charlie Company, 1/26

When I got home in August 1968 and read the articles that my wife had saved, I realized that those articles were universally either untrue or completely out of line with the actual events.

I never felt any threat of a ground attack. I wanted it because I believed we would defeat it and because the *constant* artillery, mortars, rockets, and snipers were really a pain.

I still feel a certain bitterness about Khe Sanh. Not the actual fighting or being there. I'm very proud of that and of the Marines I served with there. I guess I'm still bitter about the whole Vietnam experience. It seems that it was such a waste, and to me, Khe Sanh is the classic example of that waste.

I recall talking to one of the fire-team leaders about "why we were in Vietnam." He said it was to "help the people stay free," and that he was prepared to die for that cause. Right or wrong, he was a brave and noble person, like most of them, and deserved a whole lot better than he got.

Pfc ELWIN BACON
Kilo Company, 3/26

I guess the worst part of the whole deal of being up at Khe Sanh came to me at a much later time, when I realized that Khe Sanh as well as the rest of the war was, from the beginning, a waste of blood and time. Even though we had intentions of doing the best job possible and doing it for the idea of freedom, those who were our leaders, it seemed to me, knew from the start we were not to win this one. No matter what actually was achieved through our efforts, the final reasoning and justification for Khe Sanh and the Vietnam War was not in the hands of the military, but in the politicians who ordered us there. God help them when they meet their Maker!

If nothing else was gained by the Vietnam experience, at least let it be a warning not to let it ever happen again. If this becomes a reality, then and only then Vietnam will have its value.

Pfc LIONEL TRUFANT
106mm Platoon, 3/26

I think Khe Sanh will always be part of me, but I'm not the type of person who still lives with Vietnam. It's just a memory, it's in my head sometimes, but I don't let it restrict me in my functioning as a person.

Was Khe Sanh worth it? I ponder that question every time I think about Khe Sanh. It has to be worth it to me because of my experience there, because of what I had to give up as a person—the stress, the strain, the hurt, the emotional burden—because of what I saw my fellow Marines give up—friends of mine, guys I didn't know. It had to be worth it. Militarily, I assume it was worth it because we were supposed to have pinned down two crack North Vietnamese divisions, which, through the bombing, we helped decimate. It makes me wonder when I realize that a few months later they just flattened the whole place out. It makes me wonder why they didn't do it six months sooner.

Cpl BERT MULLINS
Bravo Company, 1/9

I lost a lot of good friends at Khe Sanh. I remember all of them to this day. A lot of people died needlessly up there. At the time I did not realize I was participating in a battle of the magnitude we know today. I can discuss it somewhat dispassionately, but I think about my friends who died there, and I'm not sure it accomplished much.

Notes

CHAPTER 3

1. Col William H. Dabney, Marine Corps Historical Division [MCHD] Oral History Interview. Hereafter, *Dabney MCHD Interview.*

2. MGen Rathvon Tompkins, MCHD Interview. Hereafter, *Tompkins MCHD Interview.*

3. *Dabney MCHD Interview.*

4. Maj Mirza M. Baig, comments on Marine Corps Khe Sanh Monograph, December 23, 1968. Hereafter, *Baig Comments.*

CHAPTER 4

1. *Dabney MCHD Interview.*

2. Dabney, Col William H., "Under Siege," *The Elite,* Orbis Publications (Vol. 2, No. 13).

3. Excerpts from an endorsement for a Bronze Star award recommendation for LCpl James Schemelia, a member of the 2nd Platoon's 2nd Squad.

4. Dabney, "Under Siege."

5. Ibid.

6. Ibid.

7. *Dabney MCHD Interview.*

8. Ibid.

CHAPTER 5

1. *Baig Comments.*
2. *Dabney MCHD Interview.*

CHAPTER 6

1. LtCol James B. Wilkinson, comments on Marine Corps Khe Sanh Monograph, December 19, 1968. Hereafter, *Wilkinson Comments.*

CHAPTER 7

1. Spencer, Ernest, *Welcome to Vietnam, Macho Man* (Walnut Creek, Calif.: Corps Press, 1987).
2. *Tompkins MCHD Interview.*
3. Col John F. Mitchell, comments on Marine Corps Khe Sanh Monograph, January 31, 1969. Hereafter, *Mitchell Comments.*
4. *Dabney MCHD Interview.*
5. Ibid.

CHAPTER 8

1. Maj Jerry E. Hudson, comments on Marine Corps Khe Sanh Monograph, January 2, 1969. Hereafter, *Hudson Comments.*

CHAPTER 9

1. Maj Kenneth Pipes, comments on Marine Corps Khe Sanh Monograph, undated.
2. *Mitchell Comments.*
3. *Dabney MCHD Interview.*
4. Ibid.
5. Ibid.

CHAPTER 10

1. Spencer, *Welcome to Vietnam.*
2. Ibid.
3. Ibid.

CHAPTER 12

1. *Tompkins MCHD Interview.*
2. *Baig Comments.*
3. Spencer, *Welcome to Vietnam.*
4. *Baig Comments.*
5. Ibid.
6. Ibid.
7. Ibid.
8. Ibid.
9. LtCol Johnny O. Gregerson, comments on Marine Corps Khe Sanh Monograph, January 3, 1969. Hereafter, *Gregerson Comments.*

CHAPTER 13

1. Spencer, *Welcome to Vietnam.*
2. Ibid.

CHAPTER 14

1. Statement of MGen R. McC. Tompkins, USMC, November 13, 1970. Hereafter, *Tompkins Statement.*
2. Statement of Maj Jerry E. Hudson, USMC, date unknown, 1970. Hereafter, *Hudson Statement.*
3. *Hudson Comments.*
4. *Hudson Statement.*

5. *Tompkins Statement.*

6. *Hudson Statement.*

7. *Baig Comments.*

8. *Hudson Comments.*

9. *Baig Comments.*

10. *Hudson Comments.*

11. *Baig Comments.*

12. Ibid.

13. Ibid.

CHAPTER 15

1. *Wilkinson Comments.*

CHAPTER 16

1. Adapted from "Our Victory for Alpha One," by Lawrence J. Seavy-Cioffi. (Unpublished manuscript, used with permission.)

2. *Mitchell Comments.*

CHAPTER 17

1. *Dabney MCHD Interview.*

2. Ibid.

3. Col Frank E. Wilson, comments on Marine Corps Khe Sanh Monograph, January 6, 1969.

4. *Dabney MCHD Interview.*

   Ibid.

   Ibid.

CHAPTER 19

1. *Gregerson Comments.*
2. Kashiwahara, Capt Ken, "Lifeline to Khe Sanh," *The Airman,* July 1968.
3. Ibid.
4. Ibid.

CHAPTER 20

1. *Baig Comments.*

CHAPTER 22

1. *Tompkins MCHD Interview.*
2. Spencer, *Welcome to Vietnam.*
3. Ibid.
4. Ibid.
5. Ibid.
6. *Baig Comments.*

CHAPTER 23

1. *Dabney MCHD Interview.*
2. *Baig Comments.*
3. Ibid.
4. *Wilkinson Comments.*
5. *Baig Comments.*
6. *Wilkinson Comments.*

CHAPTER 26

1. *Dabney MCHD Interview.*
2. Ibid.

CHAPTER 27

1. *Baig Comments.*

CHAPTER 28

1. *Baig Comments.*
2. Ibid.

CHAPTER 29

1. Tolson, LtGen John J., III, "Pegasus," *Army,* December 1971.
2. Ibid.
3. Ibid.
4. Ibid.
5. Ibid.
6. Ibid.
7. Ibid.
8. Ibid.
9. Ibid.
10. Spencer, *Welcome to Vietnam.*
11. *Dabney MCHD Interview.*
12. Tolson, "Pegasus."
13. Ibid.
14. Ibid.
15. LtGen John J. Tolson, III, comments on Marine Corps Khe Sanh Monograph, January 2, 1969. Hereafter, *Tolson Comments.*
16. Tolson, "Pegasus."
17. *Tompkins MCHD Interview.*
18. Col Bruce Meyers, Oral History Interview 2777, April 15, 1968. Hereafter, *Meyers Interview.*

19. *Tompkins MCHD Interview.*

20. *Meyers Interview.*

CHAPTER 30

1. Studt, LtCol John C., "Battalion in the Attack," *Marine Corps Gazette,* July 1970.

2. Ibid.

3. Ibid.

4. Ibid.

5. Ibid.

6. Ibid.

7. Ibid.

8. Ibid.

9. Ibid.

10. Ibid.

11. Ibid.

12. Ibid.

CHAPTER 31

1. BGen Jacob Glick, Oral History Interview 2777, April 15, 1968.

2. *Meyers Interview.*

3. Ibid.

4. Spencer, *Welcome to Vietnam.*

EPILOGUE

1. *Baig Comments.*

2. *Tolson Comments.*

3. *Tompkins MCHD Interview.*

Bibliography

BOOKS

Nalty, Bernard C. *Air Power and the Fight for Khe Sanh.* Washington, D.C.: U.S. Air Force, 1973.

Pisor, Robert. *The End of the Line: The Siege of Khe Sanh.* New York: W. W. Norton & Company, Inc., 1982.

Shore, Capt Moyers S., II, USMC. *The Battle for Khe Sanh.* Washington, D.C.: U.S. Marine Corps, 1969.

Spencer, Ernest. *Welcome to Vietnam, Macho Man.* Walnut Creek, Calif.: Corps Press, 1987.

PERIODICALS

Dabney, Col William H. "Under Siege." *The Elite,* Orbis Publications (Vol. 2, No. 13).

Kashiwahara, Capt Ken, "Lifeline To Khe Sanh." *The Airman,* July 1968.

Pipes, Maj K. W. "Men to Match Their Mountains." *Marine Corps Gazette,* April 1974.

Studt, LtCol John C. "Battalion in the Attack." *Marine Corps Gazette,* July 1970.

Tolson, LtGen John J., 3rd. "Pegasus." *Army,* December 1971.

Watts, Maj Caludius E., III. "Aerial Resupply for Khe Sanh." *Military Review,* December 1972.

UNPUBLISHED MANUSCRIPTS

Camp, Richard D., Jr., with Eric Hammel. *Lima-6: A Marine Company Commander in Vietnam.*

Seavy-Cioffi, L. J. *Our Victory for Alpha One.*

OFFICIAL SOURCES

Various and voluminous official documents were used in piecing this story together. Among them were the Command Chronologies and After Action Reports submitted for the siege and breakout periods by the 26th Marine Regiment; the 1st, 2nd, and 3rd Battalions, 26th Marines; the 1st Battalion, 9th Marines; and the 1st Battalion, 13th Marines. Also, many of the letters by participants commenting on draft copies of Capt Moyers Shore's official Marine Corps Khe Sanh monograph are quoted, as cited, throughout the text. All of the documentary materials are archived at the Marine Corps Historical Center, located at the Washington Navy Yard in Washington, DC.

PRIVATE SOURCES

The bulk of this book is composed of excerpts from taped accounts and interviews and letters collected by the author from siege participants. It is safe to assume that any undocumented entry was obtained from the person cited at the head of the quote. The author has donated this collection to the Marine Corps Historical Center.

EDITORIAL NOTE

For purposes of clarity, style, and consistency, many—perhaps most—of the passages appearing in this book have been edited or corrected by the author. However, the substance of the edited quotes has not been altered except in the case of errors of fact corrected by the author.

Index